Studies in German Literature, Linguistics, and Culture:
Literary Criticism in Perspective

Studies in German Literature, Linguistics, and Culture

James Hardin & Gunther Holst
Managing Editors

Editorial Board
Literary Criticism in Perspective

James Hardin (*South Carolina*), General Editor

Eitel Timm (*Waldorf School, Vancouver*), German Literature

Benjamin Franklin V (*South Carolina*), American and English Literature

Reingard M. Nischik (*Mainz*), Comparative Literature

About *Literary Criticism in Perspective*

Books in the series *Literary Criticism in Perspective*, a subseries of *Studies in German Literature, Linguistics, and Culture,* and *Studies in English and American Literature, Linguistics, and Culture,* trace literary scholarship and criticism on major and neglected writers alike, or on a single major work, a group of writers, a literary school or movement. In so doing the authors — authorities on the topic in question who are also well-versed in the principles and history of literary criticism — address a readership consisting of scholars, students of literature at the graduate and undergraduate level, and the general reader. One of the primary purposes of the series is to illuminate the nature of literary criticism itself, to gauge the influence of social and historic currents on aesthetic judgments once thought objective and normative.

Distinguished Outsider: Robert Musil and His Critics

CHRISTIAN ROGOWSKI

Distinguished Outsider: Robert Musil and His Critics

CAMDEN HOUSE

Copyright © 1994 by
CAMDEN HOUSE, INC.

Published by Camden House, Inc.
Drawer 2025
Columbia, SC 29202 USA

Printed on acid-free paper.
Binding materials are chosen for strength and
durability.

All Rights Reserved
Printed in the United States of America
First Edition

ISBN 1-879751-52-6

Library of Congress Cataloging-in-Publication Data

Rogowski, Christian, 1956-
    Distinguished outsider : Robert Musil and his critics / Christian Rogowski.
        p. cm. -- (Studies in German literature, linguistics, and culture. Literary criticism in perspective)
    Includes bibliographical references and index.
    ISBN 1-879751-52-6 (alk. paper)
    1. Musil, Robert, 1880-1942--Criticism and interpretation.
2. Criticism--History--20th century. I. Title. II. Series.
PT2625.U8Z8724 1994
833'.912--dc20   94-4385
                                                                 CIP

Acknowledgments

In chronological order: thanks are due to Amherst College for an Amherst College Research Award in support of my research on this project in Austria and Germany. I am indebted to Prof. Josef Strutz of the Robert-Musil-Archiv at Klagenfurt (Austria) for his repeated generous hospitality. I would also like to express my gratitude to Prof. Marie-Louise Roth for the hospitality I enjoyed at the Arbeitsstelle für Robert-Musil-Forschung at the Universität des Saarlandes in Saarbrücken (Germany). She and her staff create a pleasurably unbureaucratic atmosphere that makes this a splendid place at which to work. Above all, I wish to thank Dr. Annette Daigger for her helpfulness and generosity.

I am grateful to the staff of the Amherst College Computer Center for helping me wrestle with the intricacies of computers and printers — those delightful and bestial machines — and the programs they run. Thanks are also due to the unsung heroes of academia, the Interlibrary Loan staff at Robert Frost Library, Amherst College, and their colleagues elsewhere, for silently and swiftly working bibliographic wonders.

It has been a pleasure working with the editors of *Literary Criticism in Perspective*, James Hardin and Eitel Timm.

My colleagues at Amherst College, Ute Brandes and Donald O. White, provide a supportive and generous working climate, for which I am deeply grateful.

Last but not least, thanks to Nona and Adrian for bearing with Musil and me.

Meinen Eltern. In Dankbarkeit.

Contents

Preface	1
Introduction	4
A General History of Musil Criticism	8
1: The Reception of Musil's Works During his Lifetime	8
2: The Interim Phase (1942-1952)	18
3: "Collateral Campaigns" (1952 to the Early 1970s)	22
4: Toward the Age of CD-ROM (Early 1970s to the Present Day)	37
Criticism of Individual Works	58
5: *Die Verwirrungen des Zöglings Törleß*	58
6: *Vereinigungen*	72
7: *Die Schwärmer*	89
8: *Vinzenz und die Freundin bedeutender Männer* and Drama Criticism	100
9: *Drei Frauen*	113
10: *Nachlaß zu Lebzeiten*	130
11: *Der Mann ohne Eigenschaften*	146
Concluding Unscientific Postscript	176
Bibliography	179
Index	219

Preface

THE AIM OF THIS volume in the series *Literary Criticism in Perspective* is to give an outline of the critical reception of Austrian writer Robert Musil (1880–1942). Generally regarded as one of the prime masters of modernist prose on account of his unfinished grand novel *Der Mann ohne Eigenschaften* (1930–43; translated as *The Man without Qualities*, 1953–60), Musil has received much critical attention not only in the German-speaking countries, but also abroad. With some scholars and readers, his main work is even said to have achieved the status of "a kind of secular bible" as an object of special veneration (Schönwiese 1981, 161). In academia, Musil has inspired a thriving interpretive industry in several countries. The fervent devotion of a limited number of cognoscenti is, however, all too frequently offset by the respectful indifference of the nonspecialist reader. Moreover, the general readership knows comparatively little about Musil. To this day, the contradictory situation has changed little: despite an abundance of scholarship on Musil, even large parts of the academic audience tend to avoid him as an author reputed to be difficult and overly intellectual. The vast body of exegetic literature produced during the last four decades can be said to block rather than facilitate access to Musil's works.

This survey of Musil scholarship not only seeks to trace the tendencies and transformations of Musil studies. It hopes to offer, as it were, a map that may guide scholars and general readers through the labyrinth of Musil criticism. Another, and perhaps more important, goal of this book is to encourage readers to set out to approach Musil's works for themselves. In the first part I trace the critical responses to his oeuvre in general terms. The second part offers detailed accounts of the shifting interpretations of individual works. The emphasis throughout is on the interconnection between a given critic's view and the underlying methodological and ideological assumptions that inform a specific approach. It will be seen that critical opinion is highly dependent not only upon the personal bias of the critic concerned but also upon the general social, political, and historical context from which a work of literary criticism emerges.

The reader will find that my assessment of a given contribution may on occasion dramatically differ from opinions expressed in earlier surveys of Musil criticism. All the same, I gratefully acknowledge my indebtedness to the work of those that have gone before me. Ulrich Karthaus (1965) gives a valuable overview of the first decade or so of Musil criticism. Jürgen C. Thöming's critical bibliographies (1968 and 1972) combine a masterful command of resources with a degree of panache and wit rare in German academia. Able and highly readable accounts of the state of Musil studies were later provided by Wolfgang Freese (1983) and Bettina Kümmerling (1987), with a focus primarily upon book-length studies. Robert R. Roseberry's monograph on Musil criticism (1974) is less useful, since it largely lacks a critical vantage point.

Although I have made every effort not to exclude any contributions I judge to be significant in the field, the reader should not expect a "complete" bibliography of Musil studies. Unfortunately, the field is far too diverse and growing too rapidly. For instance, there is at present no single source of bibliographical information. Helmut Arntzen's two volume *Musil-Kommentar* (1980 and 1982) contains comprehensive bibliographies for the period up to their respective dates of publication. For later years, I refer the reader to the bibliographies listed at the end of this book. The recent bibliography by Ingeborg Fiala-Fürst (1991) covers the years 1984 to 1991; a critical supplement provided by Reinhard Markner (1991/92) brings information reasonably up to date. These sources offer an impressive but — I fear — still far from complete bibliographical overview of Musil studies. Inevitable omissions and oversights concern above all scholarly activities in countries or disciplines outside the academic mainstream of criticism of German-language literature.

With few exceptions, I have excluded from this survey doctoral dissertations or master's theses that are not readily available to a general public in published form as articles or books. Such works are proliferating at breathtaking speed; few of them are documented in standard bibliographies and are therefore difficult, if not impossible, to trace. While such contributions may contain useful insights, their impact is limited because of the restricted audience they reach. More often than not, they tend to repeat rather than advance debates carried out in mainstream Musil studies. This is not to say that publication guarantees quality and acts as a safeguard against redundancy. On the contrary, as will become evident in this survey, Musil studies is a field severely clogged with "recycled" material.

Over the decades, Musil criticism has developed its own specialized jargon that tends to exclude, or perhaps alienate, the unprepared reader. For the most part, this jargon is based on concepts coined by Musil himself, whether it be key terms of his thinking such as *Essayismus, anderer Zustand, Fernliebe*, and *Utopie der induktiven Gesinnung*, or conceptual binary oppositions like *ratioïd* vs. *nicht-ratioïd, Wirklichkeitssinn* vs. *Möglichkeitssinn*, and *Leben in* vs. *Leben für*. Much of what passes for Musil criticism consists in repeated efforts to define or to elucidate the precise meaning of such Musilian terms. To facilitate analysis, critics frequently bandy about acronyms such as *aZ* (for the concept of the *anderer Zustand* or "other condition") and *MoE* (for the title *Der Mann ohne Eigenschaften*) that must appear cryptic to the uninitiated reader. For instance, few critics bother to explain the term *Kakania*, Musil's ironical name for the chaotic Austro-Hungarian Empire that he derived from the ubiquitous bureaucratic abbreviation *k. u. k.* with which the Dual Monarchy characterized itself as both *kaiserlich* (imperial) and *königlich* (royal). The reader is thus confronted with a discourse that appears to feed upon itself; by and large, the self-contained world of Musil criticism is not conducive to welcoming the interested non-specialist.

I have attempted as best I could to introduce the terms of the debates and to provide English equivalents or translations whenever specialized concepts occur. Likewise, in the interest of readability I have refrained from using the handy, if deplorable, abbreviation *MoE* for the title of Musil's novel in the main body of my text. I will restrict acronyms to bibliographical references in accordance with what has become common practice in Musil criticism. In citations in brackets, *MoE* stands for Musil's grand novel in Adolf Frisé's edition of 1978; *GW* for Musil's other works collected in the same year by Frisé in the companion volumes under the title *Gesammelte Werke*. *TB* (short for *Tagebücher*) refers to Frisé's edition of Musil's journals (1976); *Briefe* to Frisé's edition of Musil's letters (1983). In each case, a Roman numeral indicates the volume number, followed by the page number in Arabic numerals. A similar short citation format is used for references to the critical sources. In these the year of publication precedes the page number. The reader can thus refer to the bibliography at the end of this book, where contributions are arranged chronologically according to their first date of publication, with entries in each year listed alphabetically according to the respective author's last name. All translations of quotations from sources not originally written in English are my own. One last point: the term *Nachlaß* refers to Musil's literary estate, containing his unpublished manuscripts and notes (some of which are now available on CD-ROM), and should not be confused with the book Musil published in 1936 under the title *Nachlaß zu Lebzeiten* (translated in English as *Posthumous Papers of a Living Author*, 1987).

Introduction

ROBERT MUSIL IS PERHAPS as highly respected in literary circles as he is little read. Various factors have contributed to prevent Musil, his works and his ideas, from reaching a wider audience: for one thing, Musil's output was too sporadic and too seemingly inconsistent to enable a contemporary reading public to develop a coherent image of the author or to appreciate the specific nature of his concerns. What, to us, in hindsight marks a continuous evolution of Musil's voice as a writer, to a contemporary audience must have appeared mainly as the idiosyncratic intermittent utterances of an outsider. It is no surprise to see that few of the standard histories of literature published during Musil's lifetime find Musil worth mention as an important author. Those that do either restrict themselves to cursory remarks or else dismiss his texts as downright marginal and contrived. All the same, Musil twice managed to attract a select group of readers who were convinced that his work-in-progress, the vast novel *Der Mann ohne Eigenschaften*, was significant and promising enough to warrant financial support: in 1932 in Berlin and 1936 in Vienna, societies were formed to provide the struggling author with money that would enable him to continue his project (see Fürst 1960).

Musil may still be, in the words of Frank Kermode, "the least read of the great twentieth-century novelists" (1965, 7), but among those who do read him, he inspires an uncommon degree of dedication. The late Austrian chancellor Bruno Kreisky, for instance, fondly recalled that after the Nazi *Anschluß* of Austria, when he — as a young Jewish Social Democrat — was forced to leave his home country, Musil's grand novel was among the few personal belongings he was able to take along (1980, 517). The undeniable fascination exuded by *Der Mann ohne Eigenschaften* frequently leads to the assumption that Musil is essentially the author of this one book. As I hope to show, nearly all of Musil's published works are aesthetically rich and fascinating literary works in their own right that have inspired a wide variety of readings. Moreover, it should be noted that Musil, at the outset of his literary career, contemplated a whole range of artistic projects, often based on autobiographical material. Some of these, but not all, eventually found their way into his magnum opus. Christoph Hönig (1973) reminds us, for instance, that at least one large-scale project, a satirical science fiction novel under the working title "Land über dem Südpol oder Der Stern Ed" (Land above the South Pole Or Planet Ed) occupied Musil from about 1911 well into the late 1930s. One should thus, it seems to me, resist the temptation to construct from hindsight a kind of metaphysical logic that somehow predestined Musil to devote a large part of his existence to a single work.

During his exile in Switzerland and after his death, Musil was all but forgotten in the minds of critic and reader alike. From the 1950s onward, in several countries a meteoric rise to prominence set in, producing a vast amount of critical literature on Musil that attests to the fascination of his oeuvre. In this survey, I can only hope to sketch the outlines of the critical reception of Musil. Musil criticism has developed in markedly different directions in the various countries where interest in Musil's works is highest. For practical reasons, I restrict myself here largely to Musil criticism in German, in English, and to a lesser extent, in French. Musil's work has attracted a great deal of attention throughout the world, notably in Italy, France, Japan, and the former Soviet Union. These countries to a certain extent have developed their own critical traditions. For reasons of space and lack of familiarity with some of the languages, the considerable range of scholarship produced there can be considered in this survey only if contributions from critics from these cultures either were written in German or English or are available in translation. It would, I am sure, be fascinating to explore the extraordinary interest in Musil in Japan — where, for instance, two rival translations of *Der Mann ohne Eigenschaften* appeared in the same year. Unfortunately, I can assess this apparently flourishing tradition of Musil studies only in the few instances when works by Japanese scholars become accessible to me in translation.

I would like to refer the reader to the following sources for information regarding Musil reception in other countries: Elisabeth Castex-Rieger (1974) documents the early reception of Musil in French-speaking countries, where he came to be hailed as "the Austrian Proust" ("le Proust autrichien," 383). Here, Marie-Louise Roth is clearly the main advocate of Musil's cause, not only through her wide range of publications but also through her organizational work in arranging conferences and overseeing editions. Of her writings in French two publications need to be singled out as of seminal importance: a two-volume study of *Nachlaß zu Lebzeiten* (1980) and a general monograph of 1987 (incorporating contributions by Annette Daigger, Rosmarie Zeller, and Anne Longuet-Marx). The latter serves as a useful introduction to Musil and to Musil studies and includes a wealth of information on the international reception of Musil's work. The close association between the Saarbrücken Arbeitsstelle für Robert-Musil-Forschung and French-language culture is evidenced in a special supplement to *Musil-Forum* published there (1987), in which Claude Chevalier and Jacqueline Magnou give a overview and an annotated critical bibliography of Musil studies in French.

Another supplement of *Musil-Forum*, edited by Ingeborg Fiala-Fürst (1990) and focusing on Musil criticism in Eastern European countries, features a bibliography as well as essays by Egon Naganowski (on Poland), Srdan Bogosavlevic (on Yugoslavia), Alexander W. Belobratov (on the former Soviet Union), and Ludvík E. Václavek (on Czechoslovakia). Josef Strutz (1980) and, more recently, Fabrizio Iurlano and Aldo Venturelli (1991/92) have provided accounts of Musil's reception in Italy, a country where Musil, in the words of a title of a symposium and a subsequent book, edited by Paolo Chiarini (1986), is hailed as *nostro contemporaneo* — "our contemporary." Beginning with Claudio Magris's seminal study of the "Habsburg Myth" of 1963 (translated into German in 1966), in which Musil is presented as the most astute chronicler of the disintegration of the Austro-Hungarian monarchy, Italian scholars have focused above all on Musil as a critic of civilization, producing important studies on the philosophical and ideological aspects of Musil's work. Perhaps the most significant contribution here is Enrico De Angelis's monograph on Musil of 1982, which traces Musil's intellectual development through a comprehensive analysis primarily of the journals and *Der Mann ohne Eigenschaften*. Almost all of Musil's writings are easily available in Italian translations. Italy can perhaps boast the most remarkable degree of commitment to and enthusiasm for Musil outside the German-speaking world.

The English-speaking reader is privileged to have several excellent introductory monographs on Musil. While Burton Pike's book of 1961 may be somewhat outdated, it still provides stimulating reading. More recently, Hannah Hickman (1984) and Lowell A. Bangerter (1989) have provided fine and, on the whole, reliable general introductions to Musil. David S. Luft's intellectual biography of Musil (1980) assembles a vast amount of material concerning Musil's background as artist and thinker in a degree of comprehensiveness unmatched in German Musil scholarship. Compared to the sensitive and sensible work of such scholars, the book by Frederick G. Peters (1978) appears oddly biased and limited. A monograph by Philip Payne (1988) offers a detailed and insightful assessment of *Der Mann ohne Eigenschaften*. I cannot, however, recommend the same author's companion volume on Musil's early works (1987). The chapters on Musil in Thomas Harrison's study of essayism (1992) ably highlight an important aspect of Musil's work in a manner accessible to the interested layperson. These monographs are complemented by an array of essays and articles in English that address more specific aspects of Musil's literary oeuvre. An American doctoral dissertation that unfortunately has not been published also deserves mention: it is a study by Geoffrey C. Howes (1985) on the influence of Ralph Waldo Emerson on Musil, an important topic that had been insufficiently addressed by Musil criticism. As we will see, regard for the nonspecialist reader distinguishes the best of these contributions from the vast bulk of Musil criticism in German.

Musil's work, Maurice Blanchot aptly wrote in 1958, is "more commented upon than read" (301). His reputation is that of a "difficult" author, and a sizeable interpretive industry appears to confirm the notion that his works cannot, or should not, be approached without the guidance of "experts." Yet only too often it is precisely the attempts at mapping Musil's intellectual and artistic world that are apt to produce a sense of bewilderment in the reader. Musil attributed to literature the vital function of providing existential orientation in a world of confusion and turmoil. His difficulty is commensurate to the task thus outlined and is reflected in the seriousness and dedication with which he pursued what he regarded as the job of the creative writer in the modern age. It is his sense of the writer's epistemological and ethical mission that did not allow him to take things lightly. At the same time, he never set out to alienate his readers directly through provocation or gratuitous experimentation. For all his interest in literary innovation, Musil remained to a large extent aesthetically conservative; though pushing at the expressive limits of language, he never crossed the line that separates a serious effort at communication from indulgence. One sometimes wishes that the same could be said for Musil criticism.

1: The Reception of Musil's Works During his Lifetime

ROBERT MUSIL ENTERED THE literary landscape with a flash. Upon the publication of his first novel, *Die Verwirrungen des Zöglings Törleß*, in 1906 (translated as *Young Törless*, 1955), Alfred Kerr, one of the most celebrated literary and drama critics of the period, welcomed Musil's debut piece as "a book that will remain." Kerr's review covered no fewer than eight columns in the influential Berlin periodical *Der Tag* of December 21, 1906. Such extensive and enthusiastic recognition of the work of an unknown beginner was quite unheard of. Kerr, who had helped Musil revise the text and apparently also lent a hand in placing it with a publisher, hailed Musil for the intellectual brilliance and psychological sophistication of his book. He particularly praised the mature style of the young writer, which in Kerr's view lacked any of the clichéd sentimentality of most of his contemporaries. Kerr also commended Musil on the extraordinary delicacy and candor with which he treated controversial matters such as the sadistic homosexual rituals in the boarding-school atmosphere in which the novel is set. Kerr's review ensured Musil's novel a readership, among both sophisticated readers interested in a new literary voice and those who might be attracted by the potentially sensational aspects of the book. Of all of Musil's works, *Törleß* is the only one to have sold reasonably well during the author's lifetime. To this day, it is, alongside the story "Die Amsel" (The Blackbird), his most widely read text in the German-speaking countries; it is, for instance, frequently assigned as high-school reading because of its ostensible focus on the problems of adolescence.

Törleß also was frequently rejected on moral grounds for the very reasons that Kerr had commended it. Yet it gained its author a considerable degree of respect among fellow intellectuals. For instance, it won him the friendship of Franz Blei, one of the time's most agile and influential men-of-letters. In his review of the book (1907), Blei infers a certain affinity between Musil and the generation of *Young Vienna*, above all the introspective writings of Leopold von Andrian (1875–1951). Through the support of Kerr and Blei, Musil gained access to the artistic circles of Berlin, most notably the intellectual community around the art dealer Paul Cassirer. Instead of pursuing a literary career with full dedication, however, he preferred to complete his academic studies in philosophy and psychology, declining an offer from his publishing house to write a second novel. Thus Musil's second publication in book form was his doctoral dissertation on the Austrian theorist of science Ernst Mach, *Beitrag zur Beurteilung der Lehren Machs* (1908, translated as *On Mach's Theories*, 1982).

Because of his decision to defer literary activity until his academic education was completed, Musil, if not forgotten altogether, was associated in the public mind mainly with the stigma of notoriety. The few literary histories published during his lifetime that mention him at all mostly label him a writer obsessed with the "perverse" aspects of the human psyche. Some critics even went so far as to transfer their moral judgments from the text onto the person, branding the author himself altogether perverse. Significantly, scholars sometimes in fact misconstrued the title of Musil's novel as "Die Verirrungen [the aberrations]" rather than "Die Verwirrungen [the confusions] des Zöglings Törleß" (see Hall 1976). This error is perhaps a measure of the moralistic indignation of the scholars concerned. On the other hand, the uncanny frequency with which the mistake recurs offers a telling insight into the nature of a particular type of *Literaturwissenschaft*: it seems that some writers formed their "scholarly" opinion by merely copying their predecessors, without so much as looking at Musil's book.

The critics who had read *Törleß* agreed in defining its author as a primarily psychological writer. For a while, Musil actually received letters from enthusiastic readers who thought they had found in him an ally in their campaign for educational reforms. To them, Musil's novel had daringly exposed the corruption of the Austrian military boarding-school system. Musil was quite dismayed by what he considered a misunderstanding of the nature of his creative concerns, since he professed no interest in the study of *milieu* as a vehicle for a public political or educational debate.

Musil's literary output, however, was much too sporadic to alter his initial reputation. His second book, *Vereinigungen* (Unions), published in 1911, a full five years after his auspicious literary debut, in fact appeared to confirm the initial image. The two novellas that made up the volume, "Die Vollendung der Liebe" (The Perfection of Love) and "Die Versuchung der stillen Veronika" (The Temptation of Quiet Veronica), seemed to deal with similar sexually charged and ethically problematic subject matter, this time transposed onto the psyches of unstable female protagonists. Musil had invested the better part of two and a half years in the two novellas, pushing the imaginative potential of narrative prose to the limit in a daring literary experiment. This time, however, the critical response was less than enthusiastic. While *Vereinigungen* did not, as is sometimes maintained, meet with general disapproval (Corino 1974), it left bewildered even most of the readers who had been sympathetic to Musil's vision. Most major critical voices of the period, including that of his mentor Alfred Kerr, remained conspicuously silent on his second literary publication. Musil was particularly vexed by the charge leveled against him by Otto Stoessl (1912) that he had not mastered the formal problems of the novella genre (*TB*

II, 698f.). The slim volume was acclaimed most by expressionist writers such as Ernst Blass and Kurt Pinthus, who saw in Musil a forerunner of their own movement (Mae 1988). Alfred Wolfenstein's hymnic review of Musil's slight volume, for instance, culminated in the emphatic exclamation, "He who is not sympathetic towards Musil's poetic achievements does not live in the present" (1913/14, 219).

In his perceptive essay entitled "Ein Beginner," Robert Müller, an Austrian representative of anarchic expressionism and one of Musil's closest friends, argued along similar lines, hailing Musil as a bold innovator, an author who uncovers new artistic territories. Müller draws connections between modern forms of abstract painting and the manner in which Musil's narrative technique moves away from the world of concrete objects to that of psychic correlations (Müller 1920/21). Moreover, with his provocative thesis that Musil's writings should be a "treasure trove for the psychoanalyst" (862), Müller is the first to point out a strange contradiction in the response to Musil's works: Musil is generally viewed as a psychological author, yet exponents of contemporary psychological theories, especially adherents of psychoanalysis, appear to neglect or avoid Musil and his texts altogether. It seems then that Musil's professed distrust of Freudian psychoanalysis appears to have been reciprocated; it was not until the 1960s that approaches drawing from psychoanalytic theories began to be applied to readings of his oeuvre.

Despite the indifference on the part the general reading public, Musil was well respected in literary circles: in the spring of 1914, for instance, he secured a position as editor of Samuel Fischer's *Neue Rundschau*, one of the most prestigious literary periodicals of the time. While working in Berlin, Musil came into contact with some of the leading intellectual figures of the period, among them Alfred Döblin, Walter Rathenau, Rainer Maria Rilke, and Franz Kafka. Musil was in charge of reviewing newly published books, a position that could have gained him a great deal of influence in the world of letters. Yet the outbreak of the war put an abrupt end to this phase of his literary career before it really started.

The First World War and the ensuing political and social chaos severely disrupted Musil's literary career, creating a gap of ten years between the publication of Musil's second and third books. When his first drama *Die Schwärmer* (translated as *The Enthusiasts*, 1983), was finally published in 1921, it was greeted with a great deal of respect. Franz Blei (1925), for instance, enthusiastically hailed it as the harbinger of a new form of drama. Between 1913 and 1929 Blei functioned as a tireless advocate of Musil's cause, first by monitoring the progress of the dramatic project, then by helping to arrange the publication of the play in book form, and finally by assisting Musil in his efforts to see the play performed by a first-rate theater company. In a letter to Sibyllen-Verlag of Dresden, the house that published the play in 1921, Blei stressed what he considered the essentially new aspect of Musil's work: the drama rendered obsolete "Psychologismus," the traditional focus on individual character psychology (quoted in Hall 1975c, 165).

Addressing *Die Schwärmer* primarily as a printed text, most critics were impressed by the intellectual complexity of the play's poetic language, though some voiced reservations regarding its suitability for the stage. Despite the debate over whether or not the play was an unperformable *Lesedrama* (reading play), Musil was awarded the prestigious Kleist Prize for the play in 1923 upon the recommendation of novelist Alfred Döblin. Similarly, he was among the first writers to receive the newly inaugurated Kunstpreis der Stadt Wien in 1924, possibly upon the suggestion of Hugo von Hofmannsthal (Hall 1989). Awards like these enhanced Musil's literary reputation and provided welcome financial supplements to the precarious existence of "Austria's most serious writer," as Musil — without a trace of irony — once labeled himself (*Briefe* I, 650). By the mid-1920s, then, Musil appeared to have established himself finally on the German literary scene as a major author. Yet respect among the literati did not translate into financial success: as late as 1926, a full five years after the publication of the play, the first print run of *Die Schwärmer* had not been sold completely (Hall 1975c, 157). Likewise, Musil's efforts to see his play produced by a major theater company failed miserably, despite extended negotiations with the leading directors and producers of his time, including Max Reinhardt and Berthold Viertel.

Partly in an attempt to enhance his reputation as a playwright and to help his first play on the way, Musil wrote the farcical comedy *Vinzenz und die Freundin bedeutender Männer* (Vinzenz and the Lady-friend of Important Men, published in 1924). Carl Zuckmayer reports that during his stint as playreader at the Deutsches Theater in Berlin, he left the manuscript to his colleague, the young Bertolt Brecht, for evaluation. The next morning he found that Brecht had scribbled his comment across the title page — the single unflattering expletive word *Scheiße* (see Heald 1977, 244). Despite such outspoken negative criticism from this expert fellow writer, the play gained a moderate success when it was performed: it was produced in rapid succession at three different theaters (in Berlin, 1923 and in Teplitz-Schönau and Vienna, 1924). The critical consensus was that while the play was entertaining and reasonably well crafted, it was ultimately too derivative of the social comedies in the mold of Frank Wedekind, Carl Sternheim, and Georg Kaiser that dominated the German theater at the time. One of the few voices to counter this consensus was that of Alfred Döblin, who in his review of the Berlin production defended the play and its author against the charge of epigonality by stressing the exceptional intellectual quality of the play's dialogues (quoted in Stefanek 1981, 135).

Musil's only moderate success with the general public did not affect his stature among fellow writers. He was elected vice-chairman of the Austrian

Schutzverband deutscher Schriftsteller (Association for the Protection of German Writers) in 1923. Together with its chairman, Hugo von Hofmannsthal, he served this organization until 1928 (Hall 1977b). He was also invited to join *Gruppe 1925*, a loose configuration of liberal and left-wing intellectuals inaugurated in Berlin by Rudolf Leonhard. The group, amorphous and short-lived, included among its some forty members notable writers Alfred Döblin, Ernst Toller, Johannes R. Becher, and Egon Erwin Kisch; director Erwin Piscator; artist George Grosz; philosopher Ernst Bloch; and the young Bertolt Brecht (Petersen 1981). Perhaps the most significant testimony to Musil's impact upon intellectual circles during his lifetime is the essay "Grenzen" (Borderlines) by Béla Balázs, published in 1923. Like Robert Müller, Balázs dismisses traditionally psychological readings of Musil's works. In sharp contrast to Müller, however, he also rejects the notion of a parallel between Musil's artistic interests and those of Freudian psychoanalysis. With regard to the nature of the psyche in *Törleß*, for instance, Balázs writes, "This soul which resides *underneath life* is not the 'subconscious' of which Freud speaks" (1923, 346; emphasis in the original). It is interesting to note that Balázs advocates an implicitly political reading of Musil; he views Musil's oeuvre as a critique of alienation in modern society, finding in *Die Schwärmer* an expression of a sense of "outrage over the false interpersonal unions in today's society of ours" (349).

While the 1920s were a period of great productivity for Musil, they did not bring the desired recognition with the general public. It has to be noted that most of the praise for his work came from people with whom he was closely associated: among them were his literary mentors Alfred Kerr and Franz Blei; fellow writers like Alfred Döblin and Hugo von Hofmannsthal; and personal associates and friends like Béla Balázs, Robert Müller, and Oskar Maurus Fontana. Musil was a frequent contributor of essays and reviews to the leading journals of the time, yet his literary output remained sketchy. *Drei Frauen* (Three Women), his second collection of short narratives, was published in 1924. Two of the three novellas collected in this volume — "Grigia" and "Die Portugiesin" (The Lady from Portugal) — had already appeared separately to a limited audience in bibliophile editions in 1923. *Drei Frauen* was generally received with considerable respect. Most critics, however, echoed the assessment of *Vereinigungen*, noting that the three new stories were devoid of a plot in the traditional sense (see Zeller 1981b). Robert Müller was one of the few critics to express unqualified enthusiasm over them, hailing Musil as the "most erotic writer" (1924).

In 1927, after a hiatus of three years, Musil published *Rede zur Rilke-Feier* in book form, the speech he had given in Berlin in January of that year on the occasion of the death of the poet Rainer Maria Rilke. Two years later, despite Musil's public protests, *Die Schwärmer* finally received its first production in a badly mutilated version by an inexperienced fringe theater company. Understandably, the play received scathing reviews and disappeared after only ten performances (Schneider 1973). In the context of the interest in the literary movement called *Neue Sachlichkeit* (New Objectivity), which dominated the stage during the final phase of the Weimar Republic, the play appeared to be outdated. One anonymous critic of the 1929 premiere, for instance, dismissed Musil's piece as an antiquated "soul mystery in the style of Ibsen" (quoted in Hall 1975c, 171).

Later that year, however, Musil once again achieved some public recognition when he was awarded the Gerhart Hauptmann Prize. Long forced to work as drama critic and essay writer for various journals, Musil placed high hopes in the prestige associated with the award — to say nothing of the money. Because of a series of misunderstandings, however, he did not see any of the money until he appealed to Hauptmann himself, who reluctantly agreed to pay it out of his own pocket to avoid public embarrassment.

If financial success is a gauge of an author's reception, it is clear that Musil's works were not appreciated by the reading and book-buying public. Prior to *Der Mann ohne Eigenschaften*, his literary output was slight: in the twenty-five years between 1905 and 1930 he had produced only one short novel (*Törleß*), two collections of short prose (*Vereinigungen* and *Drei Frauen*), two plays (*Schwärmer* and *Vinzenz*), and three bibliophile publications (the Rilke speech and two of the *Drei Frauen* novellas), hardly the kind of oeuvre to secure a livelihood. In fact, Musil was never able to support himself through his creative writing alone. Virtually all his life he remained financially dependent on outside resources. Up to the age of thirty he received support from his parents. Later he derived his income from his wife's modest private fortune. This source of support was largely depleted during the inflation of 1923, along with Musil's own family inheritance. On several occasions Musil had to hold various administrative positions, in response to which he developed some clearly psychosomatic symptoms. For years he was forced into journalistic work he detested, eking out a meager living writing reviews and essays. During most of the 1920s and 1930s he was supported by advances from his publisher and by a variety of wealthy sponsors. Yet despite his resentment against financial dependence, Robert Musil always insisted on a modicum of bourgeois comforts. Even under the strained circumstances of exile in Switzerland, for instance, the Musils hired domestic help. For years they also paid for the upkeep of their modest apartment in Vienna, until the hope of being able to return dissolved (Corino 1987).

Difficulties like these enabled Musil to construe an image of himself as an unjustly neglected writer, a "distinguished outsider," as he put it ("nobler Außenseiter," *GW* I, 964). This self-image, it has to be noted, is not entirely free of self-pity. For instance, Musil considered it a matter of course that his publisher, Ernst Rowohlt, support him and his work-in-progress *Der Mann ohne Eigenschaften* with cash advances, although for years, for both external and personal reasons, precious little of the projected work materialized. In view of Musil's nearly pathological problems with writing and meeting deadlines, amply documented in an interesting article by Werner Fuld (1983), Rowohlt's patience, his trust, and his understandably reluctant generosity must be admired.

In the face of all kinds of adversity, Musil appears to have maintained the conviction that his projected novel would constitute a singular achievement that would bring him acclaim in the world of letters. The contradiction between Musil's artistic self-assurance and the precarious circumstances of his material existence bred in him a degree of resentment and envy with regard to fellow writers. Musil's ambivalent attitude toward Thomas Mann is well documented (Corino 1971). In many respects, Musil thought that Mann achieved the kind of commercial success that by right was due to himself. While Musil rejected Mann as a *Großschriftsteller*, a kind of figurehead of a literary cottage industry that lacked intellectual integrity, he nevertheless repeatedly appealed to Mann for help. Likewise, he displayed a certain rancor towards Viennese author Hermann Broch (1886–1951), at one time even leveling unwarranted charges of plagiarism against his young colleague (Durzak, 1968).

In December 1930, Musil was finally able to present to the reading public the first installment of his main work, comprising the first book, parts one and two, of *Der Mann ohne Eigenschaften*. People as diverse as Hermann Hesse and the Austrian socialist Ernst Fischer recognized the novel as a major contribution to modern prose. Reviewers, among them Efraim Frisch, Ludwig Marcuse, Franz Theodor Csokor, and Oskar Maurus Fontana, hailed it as one of the great novels of its time, placing it alongside the works of Marcel Proust, James Joyce, and — much to Musil's dismay — Thomas Mann. Musil kept no fewer than 150 press clippings of reviews of the work that would secure his rank in world literature. He was particularly pleased with Efraim Frisch's review in the *Frankfurter Zeitung*, noting to Ignazio Silone years later that he felt Frisch was the only one who fully understood the work (Silone 1970, 350). Even abroad, Musil's novel was greeted with admiration and respect. In France, in a comprehensive appraisal of Musil's entire career, Paul Jacob hailed him as a chronicler of a civilization in decline, "one of the great poets of our tragic era" (1932, 517). At age fifty, Musil finally seemed to have attained the public recognition for which he had been striving so desperately. Yet even at that point, his work mainly appealed to a select group of literary cognoscenti. The first part of the novel achieved eight editions during Musil's lifetime; with only a thousand copies for each print run, however, the sales could hardly procure the author an income commensurate with the time he invested in the project, some ten to twelve years by the time the first part appeared in 1930. Moreover, Musil failed to cash in on the literary reputation he was now beginning to build. Despite high hopes, it took over two years for the second installment of the novel to appear, and it comprised only thirty-eight chapters, presenting a continuation of the second part of book one. David S. Luft notes that, notwithstanding the continued respect for Musil's project, the volume disappointed critics, who had expected more than an incremental continuation (Luft 1980, 213).

After the publication of the first volume of *Der Mann ohne Eigenschaften*, Musil's ambivalent self-assessment, oscillating between self-confidence and dejection, self-aggrandizement and frustration, took some rather bizarre turns. It appears that Musil hoped he would be awarded the Nobel Prize for literature in recognition of his magnum opus. Not content with merely waiting to be nominated, he engaged the help of his friend Johannes von Allesch, who was supposed to write a monograph about him that, it was hoped, would reinforce Musil's claim to such a distinction (Dimter 1989, 980). The plan came to naught, yet shrewd strategic moves such as this belie Musil's self-styled image of a *Dichter*, a writer helplessly at odds with the mechanisms of the literary marketplace; Musil was not above aggressively promoting his own interests on occasion.

On January 30, 1933, the day Hitler assumed power in Germany, the Section for Literature at the Berlin Academy of the Arts granted Musil a small stipend to support his work. In the ensuing months the political situation rapidly changed, making it impossible for the Musils to stay in Berlin. In June, a few weeks after books of his friends and fellow authors were burned in public, Musil and his wife Martha, who was of Jewish extraction, left Berlin for Vienna. Critic Walter Benjamin — himself a man-of-letters not known to make too many concessions to his readers — wistfully commented on Musil's departure, "I bade farewell to this author by saying to myself that this writer is too smart for his own good" (quoted in Corino 1988, 398).

Initially Musil's absence from Nazi Germany did not cause his works to be completely rejected or forgotten there. In 1933 and 1935, Musil's later editor Adolf Frisé still managed to publish articles praising his literary achievement (Frisé 1987). And in November 1935, when Luigi Pirandello was awarded the Nobel Prize for literature, a journalist writing under the pseudonym Wolfgang Ystade published a list of supposedly more deserving (that is, German) authors that — surprisingly enough — included Musil's name (Schröder-Werle 1976, 193).

Pre-*Anschluß* Vienna hardly turned out to be an environment congenial to Musil's literary project. The city, shaken by political and social unrest, appeared to render Musil's painstaking analysis of the collapse of the Habsburg Empire an anachronistic undertaking. Despite occasional instances of public recognition such as the enthusiastic response to Musil's speech "Der Dichter in dieser Zeit" (The Writer in the Present Age), delivered on December 16,

1934, to mark the twentieth anniversary of the founding of Austria's Schutzverband deutscher Schriftsteller (Hall 1977b, 214), Musil's sense of isolation increased. In the summer of 1935 he participated in the first Congress for the Defense of Culture in Paris, an international convention organized by André Malraux in an effort to establish a unified strategy among European intellectuals in the fight against fascism. In the context of the endeavor to create a consensus of antifascist forces, Musil's pronouncedly apolitical speech apparently alienated virtually all participants, causing a considerable degree of outrage (Schiller 1988, see also Frisé's comment in *TB* II, 744). To Musil, fascism was not so much a threat to European culture, as it was the logical catastrophic outcome of the contradictory structure of this fundamentally problematic civilization. Thus, he contended, it was more appropriate to reexamine ostensibly timeless humanistic values rather than uncritically to call for their defense. His insistence on the freedom of the creative individual as the only remaining value provoked a venomous joint attack from Bernd Uhse and Musil's former colleague and friend Egon Erwin Kisch, who pointed to the reality of torture and persecution that, they argued, rendered Musil's individualist scruples obscene. With his uncompromising rhetoric of Nietzschean cultural skepticism, Musil unwittingly maneuvered himself, as Bernd Hüppauf phrased it, into the position of an "outsider among the outsiders" (1991, 57).

Financial difficulties and a fear of being entirely forgotten moved Musil to publish a selection of prose pieces and narratives in a volume bearing the bitterly ironic title *Nachlaß zu Lebzeiten* (dated 1936, translated as *Posthumous Papers of a Living Author*, 1987). Musil placed the book with a Swiss publishing house, most likely a move, as Beda Allemann (1983) suggests, in preparation of a projected exile in Switzerland. Over the years, Musil had already published most of these prose pieces in various newspapers and literary journals, skillfully using them as a precarious but steady source of income. The book, however, had hardly any impact; it neither reestablished Musil as a major author, nor yielded him any significant monetary gain.

In March 1937, Musil gave a speech in Vienna entitled *Über die Dummheit* (On Stupidity), which was to become his final publication in book form during his lifetime. In December of the same year he gave a public reading from his works. This reading, attended by some four hundred people, was his last major public appearance. His friend the sculptor Fritz Wotruba reports that the event had the atmosphere of a swan song about it: the audience largely consisted of intellectuals and upper Middle-class Jewish businesspeople, all of whom had gathered for what was to be the last time (1960, 401). Following the Nazi *Anschluß* of Austria only a few months later, Musil, like the majority of his audience, was forced to go into exile. He was permitted to reside in Switzerland on condition of not accepting any employment or publishing in that country (Kieser 1984). Because of peculiarities of the laws governing aliens in Switzerland, Musil was careful not to present himself as a political refugee, although he was regarded an undesirable writer in Germany and Austria; nor did he claim for his wife Martha the status of a racially persecuted person, although she was of Jewish extraction. The precarious political situation, Musil's ill health and his constant bureaucratic and financial difficulties, combined to intensify his pathological writing problems: he spent virtually the entire last four years of his life continually revising a handful of chapters that were to continue, but not yet conclude, his grand novel.

In October 1938, *Der Mann ohne Eigenschaften* was banned in Germany and Austria, and in 1941 the ban was extended to all of Musil's writings. With his readership dispersed and his writings banned, Musil sank into almost complete oblivion. One of the few people who attempted to keep his memory alive in exile was Franz Blei, his longtime mentor and friend, who included a sympathetic biographical sketch of Musil in his *Zeitgenössische Bildnisse* (Contemporary Portraits), published in 1940 in Amsterdam, in which he defended Musil against the charges of being too intellectual and too contemplative (227). Much of Musil's energy was absorbed by efforts to secure visas for himself and his wife to go to Great Britain or the United States. He depended upon the charity of a handful of friends and supporters, notably Swiss pastor Robert Lejeune and American philanthropists Barbara and Henry Hall Church. Musil died in Geneva on April 15, 1942; his funeral two days later was attended by eight people.

Not surprisingly, the world took little notice of Musil's death. Halfway around the globe, in his own exile in Mexico, Egon Erwin Kisch wrote a moving obituary for his former superior in the Austrian army. Kisch put aside his objections over Musil's appearance at the 1935 antifascist congress in Paris mentioned above, now praising Musil's speech there as "nobly thought through and unequivocal"; what mattered now was not Musil's supposed political stance but his "incomparable sense of responsibility towards the German language" (Kisch 1942, 29). Robert Lejeune, who conducted the funeral services, decided to publish an expanded version of his funeral oration in the same year, first in a journal, then as a separate booklet (a revised version of Lejeune's eulogy is reprinted in Dinklage 1960). It is a bitter irony that Lejeune's booklet, containing an appreciation of Musil the person and the artist by someone deeply impressed by the writer's true stature, was to be in effect the first independent publication on Robert Musil.

2: The Interim Phase (1942–1952)

AFTER MUSIL DIED IN 1942, his widow Martha devoted herself almost exclusively to preserving his work. Under difficult financial circumstances she assembled a series of chapters and drafts from the projected continuation of her husband's unfinished novel and had these published privately under subscription by a small printing press, the Imprimerie Centrale in Lausanne, Switzerland. This third installment of *Der Mann ohne Eigenschaften* appeared in 1943 and contains twenty-four chapters in reasonably finished form as well as sixteen selections from Musil's *Nachlaß* in various stages of completeness but without any attempt at a particular order that would suggest the definitive conclusion the novel was supposed to take. In 1944 Martha unsuccessfully negotiated with Gregor Müller, the head of the newly founded publishing house Pegasus in Zurich, for an edition of Musil's collected works. The only result of the planned cooperation was a republication of Musil's three novellas *Drei Frauen*, which appeared in the fall of 1944.

Throughout the 1940s some short texts of Musil, such as selections from *Nachlaß zu Lebzeiten* and from *Der Mann ohne Eigenschaften*, appeared in various journals in Switzerland and France and later in Austria and Germany. Martha and a limited number of people, most of whom had known Musil during his lifetime, did what they could to keep Musil's memory alive. Strictly speaking, then, it is mistaken to think that he was completely forgotten in the years immediately after his death. In 1946, for instance, Ernst Schönwiese was able to resume publication of the journal *das silberboot* in Austria. Schönwiese had started this literary periodical in the 1930s mainly as an outlet for exiled German writers. Interestingly enough, its first issue (1935) had contained the chapter "General Stumm läßt eine Bombe fallen" (General Stumm drops a bomb) from Musil's work-in-progress *Der Mann ohne Eigenschaften*. Five numbers of *das silberboot* were secretly published and distributed in Nazi Germany before Schönwiese was forced to close down operations in 1937. After a hiatus of nine years, the journal resumed publication after the war with a German parallel edition under the title *Die Fähre* (edited by Willi Weismann), both editions again featuring texts by Musil. In 1946 Schönwiese began working for the Austrian radio station Rot-Weiß-Rot, where he produced a series of radio features on Musil. As head of the station's literary section Schönwiese later became a mentor of the young Ingeborg Bachmann, who was employed there between 1951 and 1953. Schönwiese, who had befriended Musil in the 1930s, thus helped create a kind of continuity in the reception of Musil's work in Austria and with the German-speaking literary public.

In various countries there were frequent attempts to keep Musil's memory alive. In the United States, for instance, Musil's erstwhile benefactress Barbara Church, who in 1935 had translated some excerpts from *Der Mann ohne Eigenschaften* into French for the literary journal *Mesures*, translated the same chapters into English and submitted them unsuccessfully to the *Sewanee Review* as early as 1945. In the following year, other chapters from Musil's novel were published in a French translation by Jean Rousset in the journal *Lettres*. Philippe Jacottet, a young Franco-Swiss author, emerged as a harbinger of Musil with his translation of "Die Amsel" published in 1948 in *La Licorne*. Other people to take up Musil's cause in the immediate postwar period by writing appreciative essays or helping to arrange publications of Musil's texts, sometimes assisting Martha Musil in her negotiations with publishers, included Franz Theodor Csokor, Oskar Maurus Fontana, Armin Kesser, and Willi Reich. One of the most notable journals that promoted Musil's cause in Germany in the postwar period was *Das Goldene Tor*, edited by Alfred Döblin at Baden-Baden in the French occupation zone.

In 1946 Martha Musil traveled to the United States, first to Philadelphia, where her daughter Annina Rosenthal lived, then to New York City, in the hope of interesting an American publishing house in Musil's work. These efforts came to naught, partly on account of the extraordinarily complex legal situation. Throughout her negotiations with publishing firms, Martha Musil retained the hope that her husband's work could return to the German Rowohlt Verlag, Musil's publisher from 1924 to 1937, and she was reluctant to relinquish international copyrights. What with trade restrictions and censorship enforced upon defeated Germany by the Allied powers, as well as paper shortages caused by the collapse of economic infrastructures, it was unclear whether Rowohlt would ever be able to rebuild his publishing company. In her negotiations with American publishing houses Martha appeared ambivalent, and the copyright situation remained unresolved. Since Musil's works had as yet not been translated into English, launching the work of an author virtually unknown in America required a major financial investment. Returns for such an investment were unsure: Musil's situation was unlike that of Thomas Mann, who already had international renown, or Kafka, whose discovery was causing considerable excitement at the time. In Musil's case, American publishers understandably were reluctant to take the risks involved.

Martha returned to Europe in March 1947 to live with her son Gaetano Marcovaldi in Rome. From there she made efforts to contact Rowohlt and various other German publishing houses, none of which brought about any results. In the same year she was approached by Adolf Frisé, a young German scholar and writer, who had written three appreciative essays on Musil during the 1930s that Musil had kept in his files. Frisé offered to mediate between Martha and Rowohlt. A meeting of the principal parties planned for April 1948 in Rome fell through; the question of publishing rights remained unresolved. Martha Musil, who all along had intended to oversee the republication of her husband's work herself, died unexpectedly on August 24, 1949. Her daughter Annina then turned to Rowohlt, entrusting Frisé with the task of editing Musil's work. Thus Frisé emerged as the bearer of Musil's torch in the German-speaking world.

Despite the collapse of all major forms of infrastructure following the defeat and capitulation of Germany and Austria, it did not take the academic world very long to rediscover Musil as a subject of scholarly investigation. Two doctoral dissertations came out of the University of Vienna in the immediate postwar period. The first, by Karl Riskamm, completed in 1948, offers little more than an appreciation of Musil's life and works for which the author was able to draw on the assistance of Musil's widow and others who had been close to the writer. Anna Maier's dissertation of 1949 places Robert Musil alongside Kafka in what the author labels the "ethical and moral trajectory" of modern prose. Both dissertations remained relatively obscure and had no noticeable impact on Musil scholarship. At best, they bear testimony to a kind of subterranean continuity in his scholarly reception.

On October 28, 1949, an article appeared anonymously in London in the *Times Literary Supplement*. Written by Ernst Kaiser and Eithne Wilkins, who were to become Musil's translators into English, it took the shape of a belated review of Martha Musil's edition of the third installment of *Der Mann ohne Eigenschaften*, used as a pretext to direct the attention of the British reading public to Musil, "one of the least known writers of the age." Kaiser and Wilkins seized the opportunity to persuade their readers of Musil's stature as "the most important novelist writing in German in this half century" (689). The tone of the article was uncommonly enthusiastic and triggered a considerable degree of interest in Musil: in response to it, British book dealers, as well as Annina Rosenthal, were confronted with a surprising number of inquiries about Musil's works. This suggests that Kaiser and Wilkins had struck a responsive chord in their readership. Yet it does not mean that the *TLS* article single-handedly reawakened interest in Musil or even that it marks the beginning of Musil scholarship: the two doctoral dissertations that preceded it belie this notion as do the editorial activities outlined above and investigated in greater detail by Renate Schröder-Werle in two articles of 1975 and 1976/77. In a way, Musil never completely disappeared from the literary landscape. To be sure, most of the activities documented by Schröder-Werle reached only a small audience. A year before the publication of article by Kaiser and Wilkins, Adolf Frisé had reminded the German reading public of the forgotten author in an article in the weekly *Die Zeit* (1948). What the *TLS* article probably achieved was to add pressure on the publishing house Rowohlt by highlighting the international prestige that could be gained by a republication of the work of such an eminent author. In this limited sense, the article by Kaiser and Wilkins marks Musil's rediscovery on the international level and the beginning of the subsequent widespread interest in his work.

One of the most tireless advocates of Musil's cause was his former friend the Austrian writer Franz Theodor Csokor. In an appreciative essay of 1950, written upon the occasion of what would have been Musil's eightieth birthday, Csokor mixes personal recollections with an appraisal of Musil's work, doing his part to remind the reading public of Musil as the chronicler of the sickness of a bygone civilization. Csokor stresses the contribution to Musil's literary endeavors of Martha Musil, who had provided the one element of stability in her husband's precarious existence.

With the financial support from Rowohlt, Frisé was able to travel to Rome to study Musil's unpublished manuscripts for his projected edition of a complete *Mann ohne Eigenschaften*. Frisé spent fourteen weeks in Rome in the fall of 1951, a period that turned out much too short in view of the complexity of the undertaking. Musil's posthumous writings comprise over ten thousand pages of manuscripts in dozens of portfolios, more than half of which concern *Mann ohne Eigenschaften*. It is possible that Frisé initially had no idea of the enormity of the task he had set out to do. Given the time constraints, he could at best skim through the enormous mass of material to gain some general sense of orientation. His achievement is all the more remarkable for having been made under such severely limiting circumstances. He was able to present an edition of Musil's novel in 1952, just a few short months after his sojourn to Rome (Frisé 1980).

With Frisé's edition, Musil's main work again became available to the reading public, some twenty-two years after the publication of the first volume and nineteen years after the publication of the second installment. The history of the reception of Musil's work is thus highly discontinuous and closely interconnected with the political and economic history of central Europe. Fascism, exile, war, and the economic and social postwar chaos all played their part in preventing his literary voice from being heard. Despite the efforts of a handful of people who knew Musil personally or had a sense of his literary stature, he had largely been forgotten in the academic world and by general readers.

3: "Collateral Campaigns" (1952 to the Early 1970s)

ADOLF FRISÉ'S EDITION OF *Der Mann ohne Eigenschaften* appeared in 1952, making available Musil's magnum opus to the general reading public for the first time after a hiatus of almost twenty years. This edition, initially widely acclaimed as a towering achievement, effectively marks the beginning of Musil scholarship in the German-speaking countries. Not surprisingly, Musil was thus rediscovered almost exclusively as the author of this unfinished novel at the expense of the rest of his oeuvre.

The dissertations by Riskamm and Maier notwithstanding, it was Frisé's edition that put Musil back on the literary map. Within a few months, Gerhart Baumann published the first major scholarly study on Musil. Under the modest title "Eine Vorstudie" (A Preliminary Study), Baumann focuses on the dissolution of linear narrative in Musil's novel, viewing the narrative method as the correlative of a specifically Austrian mentality. *Der Mann ohne Eigenschaften* appears to Baumann as a veritable "Austrian encyclopedia" (1953, 296). In many ways, Baumann's essay anticipates both the tone and the sometimes questionable method of much of the Musil criticism that was to come: observations and personal associations, often brilliant, are freely combined with aphoristic paraphrases of Musil's texts, frequently alternating with lengthy quotes. Baumann's approach is largely affirmative, making Musil the advocate of the critic's own perspective.

The impact of the rediscovery of Musil's unfinished novel is documented by a flurry of reviews and appreciations; it can be measured, for instance, in the 1954 inaugural issue of *Akzente*, a journal which was to become one of the most prestigious periodicals in the German language. This issue featured no fewer than three articles on Musil, including one by Ingeborg Bachmann, who at the time was emerging as one of the most significant poets of the postwar period. In his opening essay, Karl Markus Michel reflects on the utopian elements of Musil's style, a satirical one that explores the uses and abuses of language, its limits and possibilities. To Walter Boehlich, Musil's chronicle of the collapse of the Habsburg monarchy becomes an analysis of the "general fate of the modern world" (39). Boehlich also draws connections between Musil's thinking and various philosophical traditions, from the sociological theories of Max Scheler to the mysticism of Emanuel Swedenborg. Ingeborg Bachmann's essay is of particular interest: she stresses the ethical implications of Musil's aesthetic project, insisting on Musil's insightful critique of the connection between the corrupt use of language and a social practice that leads to the catastrophe of war. Bachmann credits Musil with the discovery of a new ethics that construes moral values as variable functions rather than fixed entities. In Bachmann's reading, *Mann ohne Eigenschaften* constitutes "the most comprehensive effort at a philosophy of history"; moreover, it offers "the most relentless critique of world views since Voltaire's *Candide*" (50). Bachmann's essay is written in a tone of ethical urgency, prompted by the realization that the collapse of European civilization in the First World War chronicled by Musil was followed by the renewed double catastrophe of the Holocaust and the Second World War. To a certain extent Bachmann here anticipates, though as yet without a specifically political focus, the interest in Musil's *Ideologiekritik* that came to the fore in the late 1960s in the wake of the German student movement.

In the United States, the rediscovery of Musil turned out to be a complicated affair. In 1952 Helmut R. Boeninger had tentatively attempted to remind the academic world of Musil in a brief introductory article in *Modern Language Forum*. Outside the community of Germanists, critical response to Musil was anything but enthusiastic. The English translation of *Der Mann ohne Eigenschaften* by Ernst Kaiser and Eithne Wilkins met with general incomprehension or downright hostility among American critics. Siegfried Mandel, in the *New York Times Book Review*, represents the more conciliatory end of the spectrum; while conceding that Musil's "talents are undeniable," he complains of the "self-indulgent reflective verbosity" of Musil's protagonist Ulrich (1953, 7). Wolfgang Freese (1983) gives an overview of the more polemical responses. The anonymous reviewer writing for *Newsweek*, for instance, dismisses Musil as an "almost intolerably bad writer" and "a sort of jet-powered literary no-good." Similarly, Stanley Cooperman of the *New Republic* dismisses the novel as "a rather bumbling mass of Teutonic metaphysics." Anthony West, in the *New Yorker*, raises objections to the enthusiastic response Musil had received in Great Britain, insinuating that the laudatory review of Kaiser and Wilkins in the London *Times Literary Supplement* of October 1949 amounted to a kind of literary hoax (Freese 1983, 103).

After such devastating advance publicity by critics who wield a considerable influence on American intellectual tastes, it is perhaps no surprise that Musil, unlike Thomas Mann, Kafka, and later Hermann Hesse, did not have much of a discernible impact on the American book-buying public. Even in the German-speaking countries, it has to be noted, Musil was and is appreciated only by a small number of readers, mostly academics. In academia, though, a sizable interpretive community developed relatively quickly within a few years of the republication of *Der Mann ohne Eigenschaften*. Gerhart

Baumann's study and the three *Akzente* essays, the first significant pronouncements on Musil after the war, had set the tone; these contributions are paradigmatic of much of Musil criticism over the following two decades: for the longest time, affirmative assessment and programmatic reappropriation went hand in hand. The more detached critics endeavored to assign Musil his due position in the literary pantheon. Those with a sense of mission undertook their rediscovery with the intention of highlighting the relevance and pertinence of his work and thought to the contemporary situation. Musil often served — as is particularly evident in Bachmann's case — as a spokesperson for pressing ethical and existential concerns, as yet not articulated in clearly political terms.

Such tendencies to see in Musil a precursor of current concerns prevalent in the German-speaking countries in the West found interesting parallels in East Germany. In 1955, on the occasion of the seventy-fifth anniversary of Musil's birth, Rolf Schneider published the first assessment of Musil to appear in the GDR. Schneider implicitly defends Musil against the charge that he is a supposedly decadent writer: as a person, Schneider argues, Musil may have remained closely attached to a bourgeois value system, yet in his works he emerges as the prime critic of decadence and bourgeois corruption. While conceding that Musil lacks the appropriate awareness of the class nature of society and that he shows little sympathy for the working class, Schneider maintains that Musil still offers "unrelenting criticism of society" (108). As the essay's title "Die Tragik des Alleinseins" (The Tragedy of Isolation) indicates, Schneider attributes the failure of Musil's aesthetic project mainly to the author's self-induced isolation from the objective social and historical forces of his time. Schneider clearly attempts to claim Musil as part of the "humanist heritage" of the GDR. Moreover, the impassioned defense on behalf of Musil, the author of "perhaps the most accomplished German prose of this century" (111), can also be read as a programmatic plea for independence outside the official party lines for Schneider himself in his own efforts as a creative writer. In the increased tensions of the Cold War, Schneider's words and those of others who pleaded Musil's cause, such as Eduard Zak (1955) and — most notably — Austrian Reform-Socialist Ernst Fischer (1957), found little resonance in the GDR.

It has to be noted that all three East German publications, though devoting most of their attention to *Der Mann ohne Eigenschaften*, try to address Musil's oeuvre in its entirety. All three accord special positions to *Törleß* on the one hand (as an analysis of societal decadence) and "Tonka" on the other, viewed here as the only instance in which Musil approximated a depiction of the confrontation between two classes. By way of contrast, Musil scholars in the West had little interest in his shorter fiction. A notable exception is the 1954 Tübingen dissertation by Inge Jens that places the two *Vereinigungen* novellas in the context of the development of German expressionist prose. As a whole, however, Western Germanistik appeared to be less interested in Musil as a writer than in his stature as a thinker. This focus was aided by the publication in 1955 of the second installment of Frisé's edition of Musil's works. Under the title *Tagebücher, Aphorismen, Essays und Reden*, Frisé made available a sizable collection of Musil's critical writings that provided new and fascinating insights into the intellectual makeup of the author. Two years later, Frisé presented the third and final installment of his edition of Musil's works, *Prosa, Dramen und späte Briefe*. The volume offered most of Musil's shorter works, including his plays, and provided the basis for a future exploration of his overall oeuvre.

By the late 1950s Musil had thus been more or less fully rediscovered, although *Der Mann ohne Eigenschaften* clearly remained the main focus of interest. Ingeborg Bachmann's series of lectures on poetics at the Goethe-Universität Frankfurt of 1959/60, entitled "Probleme zeitgenössischer Dichtung" (Problems of Contemporary Literature), marks a milestone in the general reception of Musil's work: Bachmann repeatedly invokes Musil as one of the most important advocates of a fusion of ethics and aesthetics. First and foremost, Bachmann here highlights the utopian dimension of Musil's writing, a dimension gaining in significance in the age of the Cold War and the potential threat of global nuclear annihilation (Bachmann 1960).

At the 1958 World Exposition at Brussels Musil was featured as one of the authors who had shaped the modern mind. The display prompted inquiries with local officials at Klagenfurt, who found themselves embarrassed when they could not answer questions about that city's most illustrious son. Karl Dinklage, a historian based there, was entrusted with the matter. This task, during which Dinklage not only identified Musil's long-forgotten birthplace but also unearthed a large number of official documents and personal memorabilia, marked the beginning of Dinklage's subsequent lifelong devotion to Musil's cause. With unfailing energy, Dinklage organized a conference that managed to unite most of Musil's close personal associates still alive then with important Musil scholars. Papers presented on this occasion were published in 1960 under the title *Robert Musil: Leben, Werk und Wirkung*. The volume, which under the abbreviation *LWW* became a cornerstone of Musil studies, assembled a wide range of reminiscences of persons close to Musil, such as his friend Johannes von Allesch; some of his helpers, including Bruno Fürst and Pastor Robert Lejeune; and fellow writers like Oskar Maurus Fontana and Franz Theodor Csokor. It also featured a range of essays that were to provide important impulses for Musil scholarship. Marie-Louise Roth, for instance, presented a short introduction to Musil's intellectual and artistic development as reflected in his works. Dinklage contributed an article based on his painstaking research on Musil's biographical background; this was the main source of factual information on Musil's life until Karl Corino's monograph appeared in 1988.

The book is still useful today as a document of Musil reception and, with some reservations, as a source of biographical information.

The celebratory tone of Dinklage's volume belied the rather hostile atmosphere created by a controversy that already preoccupied much of Musil scholarship at the time, the protracted debate over the reliability of Frisé's 1952 edition of *Der Mann ohne Eigenschaften*. The dispute was set in motion by Ernst Kaiser (1957), who with his wife Eithne Wilkins had translated Musil's novel into English. Kaiser and Wilkins are to a large extent responsible for the turn Musil scholarship took from the late 1950s onward: critics either thrust their energies into the debate over the definitive edition of *Mann ohne Eigenschaften* or preferred to work on isolated aspects of Musil's oeuvre removed from scholarly controversy. Albrecht Schöne's classic 1961 essay on Musil's use of the subjunctive and Werner Hoffmeister's 1965 contrastive investigation of *erlebte Rede* — the stylistic device known in the English-speaking world as free indirect discourse — in Musil and Thomas Mann (based on his 1962 Brown dissertation) are good examples of what critics have been able to accomplish when they concentrated on textual analysis rather than theoretical speculation.

In this context it is perhaps not surprising that the first major comprehensive study on Musil did not originate from the German-speaking world but rather from the outside: in 1961, Burton Pike's book-length introduction to the author appeared in the United States. Pike's book is written with the general reader in mind and goes a long way toward making Musil accessible to an English-speaking audience. Most notably, Pike does not share the quasi-obsessive focus on *Der Mann ohne Eigenschaften* that was characteristic of most European scholars at the time. Instead, he approaches each of Musil's texts as a work in its own right. This leads him, for instance, to appreciate *Die Schwärmer*, at that time still widely dismissed as a failed literary five-finger exercise, as one of Musil's supreme artistic achievements. Some of Pike's readings would need to be modified now in the light of more information that has become available over the decades; however, his level-headed independence of mind and the elegance of his style still make the book stimulating to read.

The controversy over Frisé's edition of *Der Mann ohne Eigenschaften* came to a climax in 1962 with the publication of a monograph by Ernst Kaiser and Eithne Wilkins, which, like Pike's book, was subtitled an introduction to Musil's work. The designation is rather misleading, though, since Kaiser and Wilkins devote most of their energies to a comprehensive polemic against Frisé, not always free, it has to be noted, of malicious ad hominem attacks. Frisé's edition was based on the assumption that, although Musil meticulously and obsessively crafted every single chapter he decided to publish (sometimes rewriting entire chapters twenty times or more), the basic constellation of plot and overall structure remained largely unchanged throughout the writing process. A number of general deliberations indicate that the two main plot strains, that of the *Parallelaktion* (translated by Kaiser and Wilkins as Collateral Campaign) and that of Ulrich and Agathe, were to converge in a dual catastrophe: brother and sister were to consummate their love during a joint trip; thrust into a personal crisis after their incestuous union, they were to be surprised by the outbreak of the war. Frisé's edition, then, culminates in the chapter "Die Reise ins Paradies" (The Journey into Paradise), a draft from the mid-1920s that describes the incestuous sexual union of brother (here still called Anders) and sister and the ensuing crisis. Following Musil's own technique of frequently taking recourse to material written a long time previously and integrating it into a current context, Frisé had changed the name of the protagonist to Ulrich, creating the impression of a seamless continuity. Changes like these, made in the interest of increased accessibility and readability, provided the basis of Kaiser and Wilkins's severe criticism of Frisé's edition.

The two critics took issue particularly with Frisé's method of "contaminating" texts from various developmental phases without indicating their chronological origin and status within the genesis of Musil's novel. The couple effectively embarked on a crusade against what they charged were practices at once unscholarly and unethical. At that time Kaiser and Wilkins were the only critics with unrestricted access to Musil's unpublished manuscripts; their critique of Frisé appeared to gain authority from the fact that since 1954 they had been working on Musil's literary estate in Rome, where Musil's stepson Gaetano Marcovaldi kept the manuscripts. Their work as translators of the English edition of *Der Mann ohne Eigenschaften*, supported by a grant from the Bollingen Foundation of New York, involved overseeing an Italian translation, whose final volume was to feature an arrangement of the *Nachlaß* material based on their own editorial criteria. Musil's novel, they proposed, could not be understood properly on the basis of what had been published by Frisé; the *Nachlaß* materials supposedly offered insights into the genesis of the novel and the projected continuation that required a radical revision of previous interpretations of the book.

The crucial claim was that the *Nachlaß* manuscripts indicated that Musil had fundamentally altered his conception of *Mann ohne Eigenschaften* in the mid-1930s: the focus on a critique of a dying society was supposed to have receded in favor of a more positive countermodel embodied in the spiritual union of Ulrich, the protagonist, and his sister Agathe. In this light, Kaiser and Wilkins argued, the only responsible editorial policy was to disregard the extensive and frequently contradictory material pointing to incest, war, and global catastrophe. Kaiser and Wilkins went on to speculate that, given the chance, Musil would have continued the novel toward a kind of apotheosis of the mystical union between brother and sister, one they insisted was entirely devoid of sexual implications. The chapter "Atemzüge eines Sommertages"

(Breaths of a Summer's Day), on which Musil was working at the time of his death, in their opinion represented what could be known of the author's final intention. Consistent with this view, the edition of the Italian translation of *Der Mann ohne Eigenschaften* in which they collaborated culminated in the chapter in question, followed by an appendix that featured *Nachlaß* texts with their explicative commentaries. Thus a rather absurd situation arose: in the early 1960s the Italian reading public was supposedly in possession of a more "authentic" edition of Musil's masterpiece, an edition, it was claimed, that reflected the author's intentions more accurately than the German one.

In their monograph, Kaiser and Wilkins read Musil's entire oeuvre as a confessional autobiography, attributing to motifs and images the significance of depth-psychological symbols in the tradition of Carl Gustav Jung. Strong tendencies to set Musil up as a kind of spiritual guru, reflected in their emphasis on his mysticism, are offset by critical observations concerning Musil's alleged lack of control over his subject matter. Kaiser and Wilkins attack the standard notion of Musil's intellectual precision by pointing to what they regard as oversights, inconsistencies in his imagery, and even grammatical and stylistic errors, all of which they attribute to unconscious psychological forces at work in Musil that allegedly led to lapses of his intellectual control. Their insistence that Musil's intellect was far from infallible lends their book an aura of critical neutrality, a characteristic sadly missing in their handling of their subject matter.

Despite a great number of shrewd and insightful observations, one cannot help feeling that the mystical-psychoanalytic reading of Musil proposed by Kaiser and Wilkins — to a certain extent indeed supported by much of Musil's novel — is in large part a function of their own personal biographies: it would appear that Ernst Kaiser, the exiled Austrian, and his wife Eithne Wilkins, the woman from New Zealand suffering from severe medical problems due to a physical handicap, found in Musil a spokesman for their personal hopes and desires, their own existential concerns. They took up their author's cause with a missionary zeal that provided little room for the kind of detached discussion one would hope for in a scholarly exchange. In their eagerness to advocate their views of the "authentic" Musil, the couple often committed the very same errors and omissions they attacked in others. Kaiser and Wilkins have been found to tamper with their material, inadvertently or intentionally misquoting sources or misinterpreting texts in order to support their own highly idiosyncratic views. Indeed, Eithne Wilkins partly revoked some of these ideas shortly before her death in 1975. While the couple rightfully pointed to errors and inconsistencies in Frisé's approach, the implicit charge that Frisé consciously falsified Musil's text was clearly exaggerated. Although their book provided some valuable and stimulating insight into *Nachlaß* materials not generally available at that time, it remains an odd hybrid that has to be approached with extreme caution.

Eithne Wilkins and Ernst Kaiser deserve unqualified credit for making Musil's works available to the English-speaking world with their translations, and many of their arguments are based on serious scholarship. At the same time, however, with their interference in the debate about definitive editions they severely hindered the development of Musil scholarship. For almost three decades the chimera of the *historisch-kritische Ausgabe* continued to hover over Musil scholarship. Adolf Frisé had in fact never claimed that his edition was to satisfy scholarly criteria. He had not been trained in the intricate methods of editorial textual criticism and had merely attempted to provide the reading public with a reasonably reliable text based on the parts that Musil had completed and published during his lifetime, augmented by selections that were to indicate the direction the project might have taken. Largely because of the difficult circumstances and the time pressure under which he was working, Frisé had indeed made mistakes in transcribing manuscripts and taken liberties in smoothing out what he considered to be inconsistencies in the text. He freely admitted to such shortcomings and, in the fifth edition of *Der Mann ohne Eigenschaften* (1960), corrected most of them on the basis of the objections raised by Kaiser and Wilkins. With regard to their ideas about the ending of the novel, however, he understandably was more adamant.

In leaving his magnum opus unfinished when he died, Musil "bequeathed," as David S. Luft so aptly put it, "to the critics the author's own neurosis about how to finish his novel" (1980, 213). The dispute over Frisé's edition of *Der Mann ohne Eigenschaften* spilled over from the academic world into journalistic media, most notably in a series of articles in *Frankfurter Allgemeine Zeitung*. In September 1962, Frisé's response to the charges elicited a polemical reply from Kaiser and Wilkins, whereupon several scholars, including Wolfdietrich Rasch, sprang to Frisé's rescue in the same newspaper. Rasch pointed out that Frisé's method of "contaminating" text segments from different phases in the interest of constructing a coherent and readable text was in fact common editorial practice. Moreover, he dismissed the notion of a profound reorientation in Musil toward a mystical position, as proposed by Kaiser and Wilkins. All the same, the polemical debate split Musil scholars into separate camps, engendering endless debates and sometimes creating scholarly *Parallelaktionen*, uncoordinated collateral campaigns — ironically enough — not unlike those ridiculed in Musil's grand novel.

Most of the community of Musil scholars viewed the ideas of Kaiser and Wilkins with reserved suspicion, while Karl Dinklage, who, though not a literary scholar, had become a central figure in Musil studies as the founder of the Klagenfurt Vereinigung Robert-Musil-Archiv, largely sided with Kaiser and Wilkins, as did Joseph Strelka to a certain extent (1976). Wilhelm Bausinger, a young scholar trained in the methods of genetic *Textkritik* by Friedrich Beißner at Tübingen, found himself in the same camp by default, since his studies on editorial problems associated with *Der Mann ohne Eigenschaften* had shown just how many mistakes Frisé had apparently made. Bausinger's focus, however, was different from that of Kaiser and Wilkins in that he largely abstained both from speculation with regard to the continuation of Musil's book and from personal invective against Frisé. His 1962 dissertation, published in book form in 1964, assembles material for a projected *historisch-kritische Ausgabe* of the novel based on Beißner's methodology. Yet in this dissertation of over seven hundred pages he was able to analyze only some twenty-four chapters of the book in the kind of detail called for; this gives an indication of the enormity of the proposed undertaking.

In hindsight, the debate over the edition of *Der Mann ohne Eigenschaften* and the ensuing squabbles and tensions in the community of Musil scholars sometimes appear to be full of farcical elements. One of the more bizarre incidents in Musil scholarship, for instance, concerns the mysterious disappearance of two portfolios from Musil's *Nachlaß* (the manuscripts are now available only in photocopies, since Eithne Wilkins and Ernst Kaiser lost the originals in Rome on August 17, 1970 under unexplained circumstances). At the same time, however, the history of Musil criticism is not devoid of elements bordering on tragedy. In the early 1960s, several meetings were held involving Kaiser and Wilkins, Frisé, Bausinger, Dinklage, and the publisher Ledig-Rowohlt, in which different editorial strategies and programs were discussed with little result. In early 1964 Bausinger withdrew from the project in frustration. In October of that year in Rome, however, an agreement between Frisé and Kaiser and Wilkins on a complete scholarly edition was reached. With bitter irony, Bausinger died a few days later in a car accident. The community of Musil scholars had thus lost perhaps the only person who on account of his training, his experience, and the work he had already invested in the project might have been capable of making the envisaged comprehensive historical-critical edition a reality. Tragedy likewise struck in the sudden death of another young Musil scholar, Wilfried Berghahn, a Germanist of exceptional intellectual promise and a close friend of the philosopher Jürgen Habermas. In 1963 Berghahn had contributed what many to this day consider to be the finest general introduction to Musil in German, a volume in the popular *Rowohlt Bildmonographien* paperback series. The deaths of these two scholars represent a great loss both to Musilians and to the community of German studies at large.

The spirit of stocktaking after about a decade of Musil scholarship is reflected in the 1965 issue of *Deutsche Vierteljahrsschrift* devoted exclusively to Musil. Alongside contributions by Ingo Seidler on Musil and Nietzsche, Wolfdietrich Rasch on the genesis of *Der Mann ohne Eigenschaften*, and Heribert Brosthaus on the concept of the "other condition," the volume features an extensive bibliographical essay by Ulrich Karthaus. Karthaus gives a detailed critical account of the development of Musil studies to that date, including the debate discussed above concerning editorial and textual problems. He admonishes Musil scholars to widen their focus and address Musil's other works instead of concentrating almost exclusively on his grand novel (Karthaus 1965b, 61). In the same year, Marie-Louise Roth published a volume of Musil's theater reviews and essays on drama, revealing a facet of Musil's oeuvre thus far virtually unknown. The first major publication on Musil by a scholar who was to assume a central role in Musil criticism, Roth's book also contains a comprehensive commentary on Musil's ideas based on far-reaching research of contemporary sources. Roth's collection was enthusiastically greeted by critics, some of whom even argued that it revealed that Musil equaled Brecht in stature as a theorist of modern drama (see Kohlhase 1968). Roth intended the volume as the first in a series of publications that were to make available to the reading public little-known texts by Musil, yet the publishing house Rowohlt, eager to protect the interests of its own editor, Frisé, was reluctant to collaborate in questions concerning copyrights.

In the public imagination, Musil's work came into a different focus in the mid-1960s on account of Volker Schlöndorff's film version of Musil's literary debut piece, released in 1966 under the title *Der junge Törleß* (Young Törleß). Although Schlöndorff had not been one of the cosignatories of the famous Oberhausen Manifesto of 1962, in which a group of young film directors had launched their critique of the derelict West German movie industry, his film was hailed as an indication of what the new generation of directors could contribute to a revitalization of German cinema. Schlöndorff took a decidedly political approach to Musil's debut piece, in effect presenting Musil's analysis of the rituals of oppression in a Habsburg cadet school as a microcosmic anticipation of the mechanics of Austro-German fascism. Schlöndorff was among the first to stress a political reading of Musil, even before such a perspective was fully developed in Musil criticism.

All in all, the 1960s were a period of extensive basic research in Musil scholarship: alongside Musil's editor Frisé, people like Karl Dinklage, Wilfried Berghahn, and Karl Corino assembled most of the factual information regarding the biographical circumstances of Musil's life; scholars like Helmut Arntzen, Albrecht Schöne, Werner Hoffmeister, and Jörg Kühne published seminal stylistic studies, while critics such as Renate von Heydebrand, Heribert Brosthaus, and Ulrich Karthaus focused on *Geistesgeschichte*, investigating the wide range of intellectual influences that informed Musil's writing. In 1968 Jürgen C. Thöming provided two critical overviews of Musil studies; one is an annotated bibliography in the series *Text + Kritik* and the other a separate small book, both documenting the significant progress that had been made by Musil scholarship in the preceding one and a half decades.

Musil thus appeared to be firmly established in the domain of Germanistik, when in May 1968 the scholarly community was shaken by a public scandal in the shape of an article entitled "Die Bob-Hansen-Story" (The Bob Hansen Story), published in the West German satirical magazine *Pardon*. Thirty-two publishing houses and twelve major literary critics had been sent part of chapter 119 of Musil's *Der Mann ohne Eigenschaften* as a sample of an alleged novel-in-progress by an aspiring author named Bob Hansen. The point of this whimsically irreverent experiment, for which famous controversial reporter Günter Wallraff later claimed credit, was to test whether unknown authors were treated fairly by the literary establishment (Wallraff 1987). Much to the dismay of Musil scholars, none of the readers recognized the passage, although Wallraff had left Musil's text virtually unchanged. To make matters worse, none of the literary editors — not even the one at Rowohlt-Verlag, the house that actually publishes Musil's works — considered the text worthy of publication. The passage describes the bizarre sexual encounter of Ulrich and Gerda Fischel; with supreme irony, Wallraff had renamed the protagonists Jürgen and Helga in the manner of the then popular *Aufklärungsfilme*, the pseudo-documentary films on human sexuality à la Oswald Kolle. This may, at least partly, explain why most readers found the sexual focus of the passage limited and mannered, admonishing the supposed fledgling author to broaden his perspective beyond sexual aberrations.

To some scholars, this embarrassing incident marked the nadir of the reception of Musil's works (Albertsen 1968). Given the accolades bestowed upon Musil in academia as one of the great masters of modern fiction, the results of the experiment indeed appear disconcerting. It would, for instance, have been quite unthinkable that comparable groups of French or Anglo-American readers would fail to recognize a passage from Proust, Faulkner, or Joyce. Yet as Peter Henninger has pointed out, the apparent lack of familiarity with Musil's work may tell us as much about the nature of the process of reading Musil as it does about the potential ignorance and arrogance of critics: it is clear that even those who obviously *had* in fact at some point read Musil's novel did not remember the passage. To Henninger, this suggests that notions concerning the overall significance of the whole work are retained in the reader's mind at the expense of sometimes disturbing particulars. Within the context of the novel, details that resist being subsumed into a cohesive master reading recede into the back of the reader's mind. It is only when such details are presented in isolation, as was the case in Wallraff's experiment, that their disturbing impact is felt: the reader is impelled forcefully to reject them — in psychoanalytic terms, to repress them (Henninger 1981).

The incident shows that for all the extensive research on Musil, the critical image of Musil prevalent in the 1960s was largely sanitized and streamlined, an image that ignored the rough edges and contradictions in oeuvre and person alike. It was not until the iconoclastic impulses from the student movement of the mid-1960s made an impact on Musil scholarship that a less harmonious image of Musil began to emerge.

The politically polarized climate of German academic life translated itself in the early 1970s into an extensive *Methodendiskussion*, a debate concerning the validity of methodologies of literary criticism. In the ideologically tainted field of Germanistik, with its disavowed Nazi past and its allegedly unpolitical stance, this debate was carried out with particular urgency. One of the results of this reorientation was that a young generation of scholars rediscovered Musil and began either to criticize him for his supposed shortcomings or to claim him as a spokesperson of their own political and ideological concerns. Klaus Laermann's 1970 monograph on *Eigenschaftslosigkeit* (absence of qualities) is one of the earliest and most significant efforts to apply criteria developed from neo-Marxist *Literatursoziologie* in the vein of the so-called Frankfurt school to an examination of Musil's work. Sociopolitical perspectives were actually nothing new to Musil criticism; Arntzen's monograph on satire (1960), though political only by implication, is a case in point. As early as 1962, Irma Hanke-Tjaden had endeavored to define Musil's political views in her Freiburg dissertation, some results of which were published in an article of 1964. Likewise, Frank Trommler applied a sociopolitical approach to Musil's works in his chapter on Musil in a monograph on the modern novel (1966). None of these early critics, however, employed a stringent comprehensive theoretical model. Within a few years, Frankfurt school *Kritische Theorie* appeared to provide scholars of German literature with a finely tuned critical methodology. The reverse side of this methodology was a proliferation of jargon, a sometimes excessively cerebral conceptual terminology.

Frankfurt school thought was first introduced into Musil studies by Ulf Schramm (1967) and Stefan Reinhardt (1969). Contributions like theirs, though by no means themselves above criticism, gave important new impulses to Musil scholarship. At the very least, they compelled critics to reflect on their own affirmative stance: it became obvious that it was insufficient merely to attempt to understand or summarize what Musil had supposedly intended in his art or to identify and classify the sources of his ideas. Both Musil's aesthetic position and the critic's methodological approach, these young scholars argued, needed to be reexamined before new insights could be gained beyond mere paraphrase and the repetition of clichés.

This is not to say that mainstream Musil scholarship had altogether disappeared or lost its usefulness. The best of traditional Musil criticism of the period is perhaps represented by two books that appeared in 1972 and that sum up what could be said about Musil on the basis of methods emphasizing the empathetic reconstruction of the author's conscious intention. In her monograph of that year, Annie Reniers-Servranckx presents, in chronological sequence, a general overview of Musil's shorter works. She emphatically rejects the tendency to view Musil essentially as the author of one book (namely *Der Mann ohne Eigenschaften*). Instead, she uses *Törleß* as a starting point to illustrate how a series of central motifs and issues permeates Musil's entire literary output. Each work is seen not as a preliminary step toward the grand novel but rather as a valid and autonomous artistic solution to Musil's overriding thematic and aesthetic concerns. Reniers-Servranckx is virtually the first critic writing in German world to devote close attention to all of Musil's "lesser" works, such as *Vereinigungen*, the plays, and *Drei Frauen*. Her approach stresses development, modification, and continuity over rupture and discontinuity. In her focus on the motivic connections between Musil's literary works, Reniers-Servranckx offers a fine complement to Berghahn's intellectual biography of 1963. Alongside Berghahn's monograph, the book by Reniers-Servranckx remains one of the most useful general introductions to Musil, accessible not only to the specialized scholar but also to the interested reader.

Marie-Louise Roth's comprehensive *Ethik und Ästhetik* (1972) continues on a large scale the work begun by Berghahn's project. It also represents a summing up of much of the research on Musil that had been conducted during the previous two decades. Roth attempts to understand Musil's intellectual world on his own terms, tracing the development of his philosophical ideas and his artistic approaches in his diaries, his essays, and his literary texts. Always sympathetic to Musil's endeavor to unite the ethical and the aesthetic dimension of art in his work, Roth's study never seeks to approach Musil's views from a methodologically defined critical position. It thus shares the problem associated with affirmative Musil criticism in general: the critic's discourse largely redoubles that of Musil. Today Roth's book may appear more like a large-scale compilatory effort than a grand synthesis, but at the time of its publication it was a highly valuable contribution to scholarship. For instance, it made available for the first time a wide range of unpublished materials, enabling and encouraging critics to undertake a more comprehensive analysis of Musil's aesthetic and theoretical views.

In this first phase of Musil reception, from 1952 to the early 1970s, impressive achievements go hand in hand with missed opportunities. All in all, the dispute over Frisé's edition brought about a rift in the community not conducive to creating a spirit of collaboration. One need only look at the history of the various institutions established during that period to promote Musil research to see a disconcerting lack of coordination. Until 1972, Musil's *Nachlaß* remained in the possession of his stepson at his private home in Rome. This was obviously not an ideal situation, though Marcovaldi made every effort to allow interested scholars access to the materials. As early as 1961, Karl Dinklage had founded the Vereinigung Robert-Musil-Archiv at Klagenfurt, intended as a clearinghouse for anyone interested in Musil's work. In 1968 Eithne Wilkins left Rome to assume a lectureship at Reading University in England and took with her the materials collected during her extensive studies of Musil's *Nachlaß*, including a set of microfiche copies of Musil's manuscripts. She established a Musil Research Unit at Reading, but with Wilkins's health failing in the years before her death in 1975, little use was made of this valuable collection. In 1970 Marie-Louise Roth opened the Arbeitsstelle für Robert-Musil-Forschung in Saarbrücken. After the death of Gaetano Marcovaldi in 1972, Roth helped arrange the transfer of Musil's literary estate to the Österreichische Nationalbibliothek in Vienna. A set of microfiche copies of the manuscripts was made and taken to Saarbrücken with the intention of dividing labor between Saarbrücken and Vienna: Saarbrücken was supposed to pursue a critical edition of Musil's shorter writings, while a separate Forschungsstelle Robert-Musil-Nachlaß was founded in Vienna under the direction of Elisabeth Castex (later Castex-Rieger) to work on an authoritative edition of *Der Mann ohne Eigenschaften*. As early as 1973 Castex presented a long-term project for cataloging Musil's unpublished original manuscripts with the help of computer technology. In addition to this, for a while Karl Corino and Elisabeth Albertsen ran a small archive in Frankfurt that made material on Musil available to the interested scholar. They, too, were working on the *Nachlaß*, publishing their own pagination of Musil's papers (Danner 1973). Several universities, most notably Tübingen and Münster, had emerged as major centers for Musil research. Last but not least, in 1976 Musil's birthplace in Klagenfurt, which had been rescued from demolition in a quasi-heroic effort by Dinklage, became the official home of the Robert-Musil-Archiv. With several research facilities operating alongside one another with little or no sense of coordination, it is not surprising that Musil scholarship during the 1960s and early 1970s was characterized by a certain degree of organizational confusion. The irony of repeated bungled collateral campaigns — efforts unnecessarily duplicated and energies wasted — would surely have amused Robert Musil.

    The early phase of scholarly Musil criticism, then, comprises four major fields of activity: first, there is the area of textual criticism, with the quarrels and quibbles over an authoritative edition of *Der Mann ohne Eigenschaften*, the negative side effects of which I have tried to outline. The second emphasis is on stylistic studies that aim at defining the specific nature of Musil's writing. The third field of interest during this early phase can be described as basic research: with considerable diligence critics began to assemble factual information that sheds light on Musil's life and his works, such as the sources that contributed to his intellectual development and inspired his literary techniques.

The fourth emphasis is on largely essayistic appreciative assessments of the significance and stature of Musil and his works. In this field Musil's tremendous quotability creates a peculiar problem, namely a glut of publications that do little more than mix strings of quotations with paraphrase. Such largely affirmative criticism frequently fulfills a useful function for purposes of orientation. At the same time, however, it contributes to a mushrooming of exegetic literature that can hinder rather than facilitate access to Musil's works.

4: Toward the Age of CD-ROM (Early 1970s to the Present Day)

MUSIL CRITICISM ENTERED A new phase in the early 1970s. Most of the basic research concerning factual information had been accomplished, and the various centers of research activity had been established. Musil scholarship, until then largely affirmative and explicatory, became enriched and diversified through the influx of new approaches: different concerns and methodologies emerged in the context of the intellectual reorientation brought about by the antiauthoritarian student rebellion of the late 1960s. Scholars now subjected Musil and his works to a different kind of scrutiny, sometimes producing results highly critical of the author and his aesthetic and ideological stance. Various kinds of sociologically and politically oriented approaches permeated the academic world in the German-speaking countries, above all based on neo-Marxist ideas in the vein of Georg Lukács on the one hand and, on the other, the aesthetic and political theories derived from Frankfurt school *Kritische Theorie* of thinkers like Max Horkheimer, Theodor W. Adorno, and Jürgen Habermas.

Gert Mattenklott's 1973 essay on *Törleß* (discussed in greater detail in my chapter on the short novel) ranks as one of the best and most influential examples of the *ideologiekritisch* approach, which examines the ideological implications of Musil's texts and his sociopolitical position. Mattenklott argues on a level of high theoretical sophistication, making differentiations free from the crude basis-superstructure dialectic sometimes employed in neo-Marxist studies. The most comprehensive reorientation along the lines of *Ideologiekritik*, however, was undertaken by Hartmut Böhme in his 1974 book *Anomie und Entfremdung*, combining sociological and psychoanalytic perspectives in one of the most multifaceted and stimulating readings of the interconnections between Musil's theoretical essays and his grand novel.

Different in nature and approach, though no less valuable in their own terms, are two dissertations that were published in the same year as Böhme's book, though both in fact date back to 1969. These take a more traditional tack. The first, Karl Corino's extensive study on the genesis of *Vereinigungen*, is significant for two reasons. Like Wilhelm Bausinger before him, Corino was trained in Friedrich Beißner's genetic methods of textual criticism. Based on extensive studies of Musil's *Nachlaß*, Corino made available material that broadened the discussion on a historical-critical edition of Musil's works beyond the confines of the quarrels over *Der Mann ohne Eigenschaften*. Moreover, in a series of interpretive chapters, Corino offered a reading of the two novellas that effectively reminded Musil scholars of texts thus far largely ignored. The second monograph, by Dietmar Goltschnigg, presents an extension of part of Renate von Heydebrand's work on the intellectual influences upon Musil's magnum opus. Goltschnigg shows how Musil integrated material from one primary source, Martin Buber's 1909 collection of mystical writings, *Ekstatische Konfessionen* (Ecstatic Confessions), in the mystical reflections and conversations of Ulrich and Agathe.

In the early 1970s, while young scholars were attempting to challenge or to refine the image of Musil, Musil criticism as a whole appeared to be stuck in an institutional quagmire, with collaboration rendered difficult by personal animosities and by uncoordinated research activities taking place in various locations. It was Marie-Louise Roth who finally made an effort to resolve a situation that was threatening to turn into an academic impasse: she secured the sponsorship of Austrian Chancellor Bruno Kreisky and founded the Internationale Robert-Musil-Gesellschaft, based in Vienna. Roth collaborated closely with one of Kreisky's personal advisers, Wolfgang Mayer-König, who was to serve as the society's secretary. Austrian scholars and bureaucrats apparently felt rebuffed by such a close alliance of politics and academics: they objected that no Austrian scholar was slated to be part of the society's governing board. With true Musilian irony, another collateral campaign ensued; the Austrian Musil specialists founded a separate Musil-Forschungsverein, also based in Vienna. The question of Austrian representation in the international Robert-Musil-Gesellschaft was to a certain extent resolved when Friedbert Aspetsberger of Klagenfurt joined its governing board. The actual inauguration of the society in Vienna in June 1974 was, however, marred by further controversy. Charges of overspending were raised against the organizers from Saarbrücken, who in turn argued that the funds were depleted largely by excessive financial demands from the Klagenfurt Musil Archive, which had provided an exhibit on Musil for the occasion (see Corino 1975). The precarious unity so painstakingly achieved seemed to evaporate once again in bureaucratic infighting. The tensions were later resolved, but they did affect the climate in the community of Musilians, an international assemblage still trying to recover from the debate between Kaiser and Wilkins and Frisé a decade earlier.

In an atmosphere of collateral campaigns in Musil criticism, it is perhaps fitting that there are two series of publications focusing on the author. In 1971 the first volume of *Musil-Studien* appeared, edited by the Klagenfurt Archive. It is primarily a series of book-length monographs on Musil, sometimes alternating with volumes presenting the proceedings of the Internationales Robert-Musil-Sommerseminar held annually at Klagenfurt. A journal entitled *Musil-Forum* was launched by the Saarbrücken Arbeitsstelle in 1975 as a clearinghouse for Musil studies. In its early stages it differed from other scholarly journals in that it offered space for interested readers outside of academia to give voice to their views on Musil and his works. Interesting as this idea is, it sometimes produced rather bizarre results, with some readers seizing the opportunity to pontificate on their author with almost religious zeal. In many ways, the lay readership was thus reproducing critical directions within Musil criticism of the preceding two decades, tendencies that the new theoretical and methodological impulses had largely rendered obsolete. From a scholarly point of view, another innovative idea was more fruitful: books submitted for review were usually reviewed by several critics, and the author was given an opportunity to respond. For a while, this fostered a climate of true discussion of issues and viewpoints. Sour notes were sometimes struck, however, as for instance when Frederick G. Peters, obviously hurt by the rather outspoken criticism of his 1978 book, *Robert Musil. Master of the Hovering Life*, resorted to somewhat ill-tempered personal invectives against his three reviewers. The idea of multiple reviews was later dropped altogether, mainly because coordination turned out to be too complex and time-consuming. For a while there was a risk that the Saarbrücken journal would overlap with the Klagenfurt series. *Musil-Studien* now no longer includes collections of essays; it consists only of book-length studies. Thus the risk of potentially duplicating formats has been eliminated.

The political polarization of universities in the Western German-speaking countries during the early 1970s was accompanied, or to a certain extent counterbalanced, by a call toward greater *Wissenschaftlichkeit*: literary studies were supposed to aspire to scientific rigor, with scholarly methods derived above all from modern linguistics. Such tendencies, advocated primarily by proponents of French and American structuralism, on the whole had little impact on Musil studies. One of the few examples of this kind of approach is Wolfgang Frier's 1976 study of emotional aspects in the language of *Törleß* that draws on theories of applied text linguistics. It is perhaps not surprising that this attempt to tackle the complexities of Musil's work with the help of statistical charts and diagrams found few followers in Musil criticism.

At first glance, it is striking that *Rezeptionsästhetik*, the tradition known abroad as reader-response criticism and widely acknowledged as the main contribution to international literary criticism to emerge from German culture, has not had a considerable impact on Musil studies. This lack of impact may partly be attributable to the unusual circumstances associated with reading Musil. Most readers will agree that Musil's works, *Der Mann ohne Eigenschaften* in particular, place extraordinary demands on the intellectual alertness of the reader, to say nothing of the time commitment involved. Once one has mastered the task of becoming acquainted with his unfinished novel, it is nearly impossible to reconstruct in retrospect the peculiar nature of the reading experience. As a rule, scholars of Musil show little patience with the concerns proposed by reader-response criticism, such as structures of expectation, audience address, and the implications of form and style. Few Musil scholars ever reflect on the nature of their own reading experience. Instead, most critics aim for an interpretation of what they regard as the overriding crucial issues, often at the expense of attention to the manner in which these issues are presented. In a climate of immense professional pressures it is understandable that there is a tendency toward favoring the grand statement over a painstaking analysis of detail: errors on the level of the small and the factual are easy to identify, whereas grand assertions have the advantage of being difficult to criticize while also creating an aura of competence that can enhance the critic's prestige. One rather sad side effect of this is that much of the literature on Musil appears to have been written without any concern for a potential readership in mind; a great deal of Musil scholarship could indeed serve as a particularly striking example of a literary criticism that has turned largely into a self-serving and self-preserving enterprise.

When Musil scholars address the reading experience, they tend to do it in manners different from mainstream reader-response criticism. A notable specimen is Norbert Groeben's volume (1981) on the reception of Musil's short prose text "Hasenkatastrophe" (Hare Catastrophe) from *Nachlaß zu Lebzeiten*. The project of conducting quasi-scientific experiments on "lay" readers' responses to Musil's texts was formulated in the early 1970s as part of a program designed to render literary criticism more "empirical" (9). The discussion of the findings is contrasted with a series of essays by "professional" readers illustrating different interpretations derived from some of the major hermeneutic theoretical paradigms (here, formal analysis, *Geistesgeschichte*, psychoanalysis, and Marxism). Groeben's objective is to synthesize the findings into a structuralist theory of the reading experience. Despite some competent contributions by first-rate scholars such as Renate von Heydebrand and Werner Faulstich and some interesting results regarding the reading strategies of uninformed readers, the volume represents a tendency that had become largely obsolete by the time the project was finally published in 1981, when German literary scholarship had again turned its back on so-called empirical studies.

By and large, then, Musil criticism has not emulated the theoretical impulses generated by reader-response criticism. Groeben's enterprise derives its inspiration mainly from efforts to apply aspects of empirical psychology to literary studies. For instance, Groeben makes no attempt to utilize Wolfgang Iser's theories concerning the aesthetic structuring of texts. Nor does he draw on Hans-Robert Jauss's theses on the embeddedness of a given text in a variety of contexts created by literary conventions and culturally determined expectations. The only major Musil scholar to work with a methodology derived from German *Rezeptionsästhetik* is Jürgen C. Thöming. His 1974 book

Zur Rezeption von Musil- und Goethe-Texten is indebted both to Iser and Jauss and to the aesthetic theories of literary reception of their joint predecessor, Roman Ingarden. In his book, Thöming tests whether ideas developed in reader-response criticism can be applied to Musil's writing by focusing on the aesthetic function of specific metaphors in a variety of Musil's texts. For instance, he takes up the issue of the alleged opaqueness and difficulty of "Die Vollendung der Liebe" and fruitfully examines the way in which the novella opposes traditional reading strategies. One example is that Musil withholds a great deal of information the reader usually expects from a self-contained narrative (such as pointers to the location and the temporal duration of events), creating gaps which the reader has to fill. In particular, Thöming shows how Musil creatively dissolves a petrified literary trope, the motif of the heart, to achieve a "dissolution of linguistic and emotional clichés" (319). Musil, he argues, does this in an effort to sensitize the reader. Thöming concedes, however, that few readers are willing to follow Musil's invitation to call into question what they expect from literature. The problem is compounded by questions of literary genre: Musil's prose, Thöming concludes, requires of the reader a degree of attentiveness and sensitivity usually associated with reading poetry. The apparent failure of Musil's literary experiment has much to do with the lack of an adequate reading public; if this text is, as Thöming maintains, "at the mercy of the few readers of poetry that there are" (310), it is not surprising that there should be virtually no audience ready to appreciate the particular quality of this work by Musil.

While *Rezeptionsästhetik* had little impact on Musil scholarship, interest in Musil was given a fresh boost in 1976 with the publication of a revised edition of his diaries. Musil used his journals as repositories of literary ideas, sometimes keeping several notebooks simultaneously to jot down observations and reflections related to different projects. In his 1955 edition, Frisé had attempted to give a chronological selection of this material. With the exception of a few notebooks containing mainly sketches and drafts for published essays (see Roth 1987a, 283), the new edition features virtually all that has been preserved of Musil's diaries. It also provides extensive annotations and commentaries on all sorts of issues.

Valuable as this edition of Musil's diaries is as a scholarly resource, it met with rather mixed responses. This is due in part to the intricate nature of the texts themselves. For instance, Frisé's edition makes it very difficult to establish the exact chronology of a given entry; the various diary portfolios are printed separately in sequence according to the date of their earliest entry, and as a result, entries relating to the same time period are spread out over the pages. Frisé initially separated Musil's text from his own annotations into two volumes. Unfortunately, Frisé appears to have discovered considerable amounts of new information after most of the text had already been typeset, which made necessary the addition of a lengthy appendix. Consequently, the two volumes are somewhat difficult to use, though Frisé went out of his way to provide all conceivable sorts of indexes and cross-references. While praising Frisé's self-sacrificing diligence in this colossal undertaking, critics found fault with his method of annotation and cross-referencing, which sometimes sets the reader off on a frustrating circular search for information. In Frisé's defense it has to be said that Musil never intended to have these diaries published as something to be handed down to posterity neatly wrapped. Rather, they represent his personal archive, often organized in an ad hoc and erratic fashion. Perhaps there is in fact no way in which Musil's manner of multi-dimensional note-keeping can adequately be represented in the two-dimensional format of the printed book; this, it seems, is the conclusion drawn by the editors of Musil's *Nachlaß*, now available on CD-ROM (Eibl 1991).

Despite the difficulties associated with using Musil's unwieldy journals, scholars quickly began to draw on Frisé's edition because of its vast resources that shed light on Musil's intellectual makeup. To this day there is hardly a study that does not use the material collected here to illuminate points or support arguments.

In 1977 Sibylle Mulot's Tübingen dissertation on Musil's formative years, covering his life before his studies in Berlin, was published as a book. Giving close attention to contemporary sources, Mulot provides fascinating insights primarily into the cultural life of the period and the kinds of intellectual and artistic impulses to which Musil was exposed during the years that he lived in Brünn (from 1898 to 1902). She explores the impact that local writers now largely forgotten exerted upon the young Musil, authors such as Richard Schaukal, Karl Hans Strobl, and Franz Schamann, who were as influential as they were well known at the time. Brünn, it turns out, was quite a lively cultural center in Habsburg Austria at the turn of the century, eager to emulate the latest tendencies of the European avant-garde in general and German culture in particular. Mulot's book is as unpretentious in its approach as it is valuable as a resource concerning the formation of Musil's aesthetic and philosophical views.

Two years after the publication of Musil's diaries, Frisé's thoroughly revised new edition of Musil's works, entitled *Gesammelte Werke*, appeared simultaneously in four hardback volumes and as a nine-volume paperback edition with identical pagination. This 1978 edition, hailed by most critics as a substantial improvement over the volumes published in the 1950s, is generally considered to be Frisé's crowning achievement as an editor of Musil and has become the standard edition. Frisé was able to include a large number of unknown or obscure writings by Musil that had been rediscovered since the publication of the 1952 edition. He also augmented the texts with extensive notes, similar in nature to those contained in his commentary to the diaries. The most significant changes in the new edition, however, are in the presentation of *Der Mann ohne Eigenschaften.* Frisé obviously took the criticism of his 1952 edition to heart, now refraining from any arrangement that might suggest a clear linear order of the envisaged continuation of the unfinished novel. He first presents all the chapters finished and approved by Musil. These are followed by the chapters on which Musil was still working at the time of his death, sometimes with several variants. The final part of the edition features selected chapters, drafts, and, in small print, notes from the *Nachlaß* pertaining to the novel. No attempt is made to gloss over discrepancies and inconsistencies. Musil had, for instance, tried out similar scenarios by interchanging one or more personages from his array of characters. In Frisé's edition, the *Nachlaß* material is arranged in reverse chronological order, representing material from the late 1930s back to the 1920s. The reader is thus invited to make up a personal version of what Musil may have retained or taken up again in the course of his novel-in-progress.

By making his editorial principles known, identifying his insertions with diacritical signs, and refraining from suggesting any definitive solution, Frisé made a serious effort to address the criticism leveled earlier against his editorial practices. Though the response to the 1978 edition was mostly positive, especially with regard to Frisé's dedication and commitment, some critics were not entirely satisfied with the result. A few argued that this improved and annotated edition, for all its merits, did not eliminate the need for a historical-critical edition (Zeller 1982). Others suggested that the criteria for the selection of the *Nachlaß* materials were still unclear: on what base, for instance, did Frisé decide which texts to include out of the more than five thousand pages of manuscripts pertaining to *Der Mann ohne Eigenschaften*? Still others asked why he had left out Musil's doctoral dissertation on Ernst Mach, surely of great significance for an understanding of the author, while including his largely perfunctory contributions to various military publications during the First World War. Some critics charged that Frisé had over-annotated the texts and that the new arrangement of *Der Mann ohne Eigenschaften* discouraged the reader rather than facilitating access to Musil's most important work. One blithe spirit even went so far as to express a longing for the "good old days" of the 1952 edition, which, as far as he was concerned, provided a clear and readable text, whether or not it accurately represented Musil's novel (Schmitz 1980). The suggestion triggered a minor debate in *Musil-Forum.* Frisé clearly intended his annotated and amended *kommentierte Werkausgabe* as a compromise between a popular reading edition and a scholarly historical-critical edition; he did not presume to present more than an interim solution, yet the responses show that the conflict over what constitutes Musil's text had not been resolved. On the whole, however, the 1978 edition was warmly received by the vast majority of Musil scholars. In 1980 a reprint of Musil's doctoral dissertation on Ernst Mach was published; a year later Frisé was able to present an edition of Musil's letters, effectively completing his project of making all of Musil's known and creatively significant writings available to the reading public.

In the late 1970s a discussion intensified in Musil studies regarding the question of the relationship of Musil's work to psychoanalysis, an issue raised originally by Karl Corino's work. There had, of course, been earlier efforts to address Musil's indebtedness to psychoanalysis, among them Kaiser and Wilkins's curious efforts to psychoanalyze Musil the author, as it were, in terms of Jungian depth psychology (1962) and Erhard von Büren's well-balanced study of Musil's affinity to contemporary psychological theories (1970). Often, however, such efforts were based largely on mere conjecture, such as Harry Goldgar's methodologically flawed attempt of 1965 to read Musil's *Törleß* as an epigonal literary representation of Freudian insights. The discussion reached a new plateau of theoretical sophistication with the publication in 1979 of Johannes Cremerius's large-scale investigation of Musil's attitude toward Freudian psychoanalysis. Cremerius, a noted psychotherapist, puts forth a wide range of material from Musil's diaries and unpublished *Nachlaß* manuscripts to show that Musil kept abreast with a great deal more of Freud's publications than had hitherto been assumed. The underlying thesis is that Musil actively attempted to counter the overpowering impact of Freud's ideas by establishing an alternative psychology to rival or perhaps even surpass that of Freud. Cremerius directly relates Musil's notorious problems in writing to this supposed project, which was doomed to fail.

Musil, Cremerius maintains, was a highly neurotic person only too aware of the validity and accuracy of Freud's insights. For this reason, he found it necessary to obscure any indebtedness to psychoanalysis by eradicating and camouflaging any traces of Freud's ideas in his own writing. In a manner of speaking, Cremerius reiterates Corino's thesis that Musil's literary output represents documents of a gigantic "defensive battle" waged against the overpowering impact of psychoanalysis. He somewhat polemically contends that Musil, as an artist interested in matters of the psyche, found himself in the position of a "Columbus, who upon setting foot on American soil has to find out that he is the second person to get there" (740). Musil here emerges as the most significant example of the comprehensive rivalry between literature and psychoanalysis that, in Cremerius's view, all creative writers of the period had to confront. Cremerius is certainly correct in defining the emergence of psychoanalysis as an intellectual discipline that potentially intruded upon the traditional domain of literature, the realm of the human psyche. Yet the implication that Freud's ideas somehow rendered obsolete all forms of poetic psychological investigation is highly questionable in that it bestows upon Freud's theories the status of unchallengeable truth. In Cremerius's reading,

Freud is not so much part of an ongoing process of theorymaking as he is a kind of prophet who uncovered unchanging universal verities.

While scholars continue to explore the complex interconnections between Musil's ideas and those of psychoanalysis, they do not necessarily share the assumptions underlying Cremerius's polemical comparison. The most recent contributions (Lobner 1990 and Giampieri Deutsch 1990) tend to focus less on Musil's alleged feelings of rivalry toward Freud than on an examination of potential parallels and affinities between Musil and psychoanalytic thought.

Two books published in 1980, a year after Cremerius's study, carry the debate initiated by Corino and Cremerius in a different direction by bringing poststructuralist ideas to bear on a psychoanalytic interpretation of literature. Drawing on recent psychoanalytic theories of thinkers like Jacques Lacan and Julia Kristeva, Peter Henninger, in his monograph on Musil's *Vereinigungen*, and Dieter Heyd, in his "psycho-semiological" study of *Der Mann ohne Eigenschaften*, expressly question preconceived ideas concerning the nature of the processes of writing and reading. Henninger seeks not only to redefine Musil's position vis-à-vis Freudian psychoanalysis but also to challenge the manner in which Musil's works are approached by Musil criticism, placing his own enterprise in polemical opposition to the general tendencies of Musil studies. In its initial period, Henninger stresses, scholars hailed Musil as a timeless "thinker"; in the 1970s the focus shifted to an image of Musil as a critical "ideologue." Both tendencies, Henninger contends with some justification, focus virtually exclusively on Musil's late work *Der Mann ohne Eigenschaften*, downplaying the significance of his early or "minor" writings (190); scholars thus uncritically accepted the image that Musil sought to project of himself to the public rather than investigating the unconscious truths concealed in his texts. Henninger argues that the key to a psychoanalytic understanding of Musil's works comes precisely from phenomena traditionally ignored or considered unimportant, from elements in the works that escape the author's conscious control.

Instead of essentially reduplicating what Musil overtly "says" in his works, Henninger focuses on minute details (such as contradictions, gaps, or recurring patterns) in Musil's published texts and in the various preliminary drafts that reveal what for various reasons cannot be put into words. In a series of highly original and sometimes idiosyncratic analyses, Henninger interprets Musil's writing as an eroticized activity. This sexual aspect of Musil's work, Henninger proposes, is of necessity repressed both by the author and by most readers. Particularly stunning is Henninger's exploration of recurring textual elements (such as specific letters, words, images, or syntactic structures). For instance, he highlights the significance of the "grapheme V," a signifier that in Lacan's sense "insists" in Musil's texts: as number (triangular five-part constellations that point to Oedipal fantasies and castration anxiety), as letter ("V" with its obscene — that is, unacknowledgeable sexual — connotations in German), and as shape (as an unconscious representation of the female genitalia). In analogy to Freud's famous notion of *Traumgedanken*, or "dream thoughts," Henninger develops the concept of *Textgedanken* (75), the psychic content that escapes the author's conscious control and, against and despite the author's manifest or proclaimed intentions, forms the actual motivating impetus in the writing of a given text.

To Henninger, Musil's neurotic difficulties as a writer are attributable to a paradoxical psychosexual constellation: on the one hand, erotic reminiscences and desires provide the subject matter of Musil's writing; on the other hand, the process of writing becomes itself a highly eroticized activity, the significance of which has to be repressed by unconscious self-censorship. To Henninger, Musil's excessive use of metaphoric images and his obsessive insistence on rewriting represent a repetition compulsion involving contradictory impulses toward simultaneous self-disclosure and repression. Henninger concludes that erotic desire thus constitutes both the motor and the impediment to Musil's art, resulting in a self-destructive logic of intermittent creative outbursts and increasing periods of creative paralysis.

As in the case of Cremerius, there are obvious methodological problems associated with Henninger's approach. Again, the most basic one perhaps concerns the underlying assumption that the truth claims of psychoanalysis (in this case in its Lacanian variant) are not subject to the logic of "scientific" revision and refinement but that they are somehow mere descriptions of "truth." Witness, for instance, Henninger's apodictic statement that Lacan's theories offer a "description of concrete factual actualities" rather than mere theoretical constructs (116). Be that as it may, Henninger's contribution is highly thought-provoking in the best sense of the term. Henninger is among the first Musil scholars to raise profound questions that go way beyond a literary interpretation or evaluative assessment of Musil's works: what is it that makes Musil (or any other author) write, and what is it that makes us — critics as well as readers — read Musil's works (or those of any other author)? Which unconscious mechanisms propel a writer to focus his or her energies on a given project; which unacknowledged interests bring a critic to devote his or her intellectual resources to a given work of literature? Whatever one may think about Henninger's ideas, after reading his book one will read any text with different eyes.

The year 1980, marking the hundredth anniversary of Musil's birth, brought about a flurry of activities: more than a dozen symposia were held to commemorate the author at places as diverse as Vienna, Berlin, Rome, Paris, London, Barcelona, and Warsaw. Some of the proceedings of these conferences were published, with the usual delay, in book form. The most interesting of such volumes is perhaps the one edited in 1982 by Dieter P. Farda and Ulrich

Karthaus, which documents the 1980 convention at Berlin and features illuminating articles by writers including Helmut Arntzen, Maximilian Aue, Hartmut Böhme, Peter Henninger, Claudia Monti, Walter H. Sokel, and Rosmarie Zeller.

While Musil scholars during the 1950s had largely ignored the political dimension of Musil's thinking and writing and during the 1960s and 1970s had attempted to present Musil as a harbinger of *Ideologiekritik*, the 1980s brought efforts toward a more comprehensive assessment of the contradictions and ambivalences that characterize Musil's political views. Those who had addressed Musil's politics earlier had reached widely different conclusions: In his 1974 book *The Broken Eagle* C. E. Williams detected in Musil an alleged proclivity toward fascism, an opinion echoed by Rolf Kieser in his 1984 essay on Musil's Swiss exile. Yet it will be remembered that none other than Georg Lukács — despite his professed aversion to Musil as a "bourgeois" avant-garde author — had generously, if somewhat grudgingly, granted Musil the status of "antifascist" (1958, 69). Likewise, Beda Allemann argued that on account of his intellectuality Musil was more immune to a contamination by the "Ungeist des Nationalsozialismus" than any other writer (1983, 90). Jürgen C. Thöming (1970), Hartmut Böhme (1974), and Roger Willemsen (1984) could stress Musil's sympathies for left-wing anarchist activism during the period following the First World War.

A more differentiated perspective emerged during the 1980s. Josef Strutz (1981), for instance, emphasizes that the political dimension of Musil's work lies in the manner in which he examines the "basic conditions which underlie human action in a given culture in their anthropological and historical diversity" (109). Guntram Vogt (1984, 1986, 1993) endorses and refines this view, adding that it is Musil's very reluctance to embrace a party-political program that makes Musil a political author. Musil's analytic intellect, Vogt proposes, compels him to confront any ideology and to recognize its respective internal contradictions as well as its potential practical implications. What appears as political ambivalence, then, turns out to be a symptom of Musil's intellectual and political integrity.

The question of Musil's integrity was at issue in a controversy that flared up in the mid-1980s. In an essay on Musil's diaries for *Die Zeit* (1986), literary critic Fritz J. Raddatz reiterated the suggestion that Musil's attitude toward National Socialism was not beyond reproach. The insinuation, based on conjecture and a willful array of quotations taken out of context, drew an angered response from Musil's editor, Adolf Frisé. Frisé showed that Raddatz had used quotations from early periods to make points about Musil's alleged political position in the 1930s. Moreover, Frisé argued that Raddatz's essay consisted of little more than ideas culled (and misappropriated) from an earlier essay by Werner Fuld (1983), whom Raddatz had not credited and whose ideas he had in fact grossly misrepresented (Frisé 1991). A few years later, a similar debate arose when Peter C. Pfeiffer's appearance at the 1988 Klagenfurt Sommerseminar caused a minor scandal: some members of the audience took his polemical remarks about Musil's political views in the 1930s to imply that Pfeiffer thought Musil harbored protofascist views (see Strutz 1988). In the introduction to his 1990 study of Musil's use of aphorism in *Der Mann ohne Eigenschaften*, Pfeiffer is at pains to dispel the charge that this was what he wanted to suggest. Nevertheless, in the main part of his book, he employs potentially incriminating designations to characterize Musil's ideological position, such as "Nietzsche disciple" (77) and "right-wing intellectual" (92), that fall short of the level of discourse reached in Strutz and Vogt concerning the question of politics. David S. Luft rightly notes that the problems associated with an assessment of Musil's political stance perhaps reflect the larger issue of the inner affinities between a wide variety of political positions in the first half of this century that on the surface seem to be radically opposed to one another (1980, 137).

On a less controversial note, the early 1980s mark a period of stocktaking in Musil studies. One of the most notable examples of this tendency is Renate von Heydebrand's collection of some of the most influential essays on Musil in the prestigious series *Wege der Forschung* (1982). The excellent volume features an introduction in which von Heydebrand gives a concise and insightful assessment of the history of Musil criticism thus far. Von Heydebrand's collection is complemented by a two-volume set of commentary on Musil's works edited by Helmut Arntzen. The first such *Musil-Kommentar* (1980) deals with all of Musil's shorter writings, while the second volume (1982) concentrates on *Der Mann ohne Eigenschaften*. Together the three volumes provide a useful resource for Musil scholars. They also represent a culmination of certain traditions of mainstream *Germanistik*, marking a moment in the history of the discipline before the impact of new theoretical paradigms, primarily French poststructuralist thinking, made itself felt in the field.

Liliane Weissberg's essay on Musil's narrative technique (1980) skillfully negotiates the methodological divide between traditional *Geistesgeschichte* and poststructuralist narrative theory. On the one hand, Weissberg places Musil in the large cultural context of the dissolution of the notion of a stable subject — diagnosed, for instance, by Nietzsche and Mach — as well as the discussions conducted by Hofmannsthal, Walter Benjamin, and Theodor W. Adorno, among others, about the resulting disintegration of linear narrative. On the other hand, she relates Musil's preoccupation with language as a necessarily limited but nevertheless indispensable medium of expression and exploration to Lacanian theories concerning the formation of identity. Musil's rejection of mimetic narration, Weissberg notes, bears traces of narcissistic constellations, resulting in an essentially monologic mode of discourse (480).

Among the young scholars to embrace poststructuralist theories was Roger Willemsen. In his dissertation, published as a book in 1984, Willemsen gives a detailed analysis of Musil's poetic theories. He addresses a wide range of sources for Musil's aesthetic ideas, ranging from Plotinus (the concept of "emanation") to Béla Balázs (the pathbreaking analysis of the impact of film upon the perception of modern reality). Out of the most heterogeneous literary, philosophical, psychological, anthropological, and aesthetic theories, Willemsen argues, Musil fashioned his own definition of the epistemological and utopian function of literature. Musil's writing is characterized by conglomerations of images (1984a, 290) that serve to eliminate conventional means of literary mediation by touching a level of consciousness that precedes categorical thinking (292). Literature, then, is on the one hand an epistemological tool that reaches spheres of knowledge not accessible to discursive reason; on the other hand, it opens up a utopian space in which alternative perspectives of reality appear in the euphoric experience of the work of art. Musil, Willemsen maintains, attempts to give special legitimacy to *Dichtung*, the art of writing, a field of human endeavor all too often relegated to the status of mere diversion or entertainment.

Roger Willemsen's 1984 book marked the auspicious debut of a Musil scholar of extraordinary promise. In the same year, Willemsen found himself embroiled with Helmut Arntzen in one of the controversies that from time to time shake up the small world of Musil studies. In the *Göttingische Gelehrte Anzeigen*, Willemsen published a review of Arntzen's two monographs mentioned above, launching an all-out vicious surprise attack. He complained that Arntzen had failed to provide the community of Musil scholars with what had allegedly been promised, namely a set of source books that would bring together everything that was known about Musil and which could form a factual resource for Musil study. Instead of providing, for instance, a "stocktaking of the interpretive perspectives" (1984c, 232), Willemsen contended, Arntzen had essentially offered his own idiosyncratic and outdated views on Musil, thinly camouflaged as commentary or objective information. Given the considerable achievement that the two volumes represent, Willemsen's argument, spiced with flourishes of heated rhetoric, may indeed appear to be grossly unfair. It all but pales, however, against Arntzen's angered response. No stranger to controversy (witness his attacks on Elisabeth Albertsen on charges of alleged plagiarism, 1968c), Arntzen picked up the gauntlet and retorted with a lengthy pamphlet, published privately at his own expense (1985), in which he tried to set the record straight by virtually tearing his younger colleague limb from limb. Both Willemsen's oddly biased review and Arntzen's venomous response display a degree of personal malice that suggests that there was a subtext to the clash of these two Musil scholars that involved ideological, generational, and methodological components — as well as institutional and personal aspects, perhaps — none of which fully came out in the exchange. In the end, it would appear that the controversy in effect destroyed the academic career of one of the most brilliant and promising of a young generation of Germanisten: Willemsen eventually gave up his academic position and has since achieved considerable success as a journalist for the prestigious weekly *Die Zeit* and on German cable TV. What is a severe loss to Germanistik in general — and Musil studies in particular — turns out to be a gain for private television.

Willemsen primarily has to be viewed as a representative of a new generation of German literary scholars: in the early 1980s developments in poststructuralist criticism profoundly changed the nature of the entire discipline of German studies. In France, prominent poststructuralist thinkers had, as it were, already enlisted Musil in their project of dismantling the "logocentric" *epistémes* of the Western tradition: in his seminal *La condition post-moderne*, for instance, Jean-François Lyotard quotes Musil's famous comments from *Mann ohne Eigenschaften* on the dissolution of linear narrative, turning Musil into a harbinger of his own notion of the disappearance of the *grand récit*, the narrative ordering of experience in language (Lyotard 1979, 30). In increasing numbers, scholars of Germanistik began to address Musil's works from a variety of approaches indebted mainly to French theoretical models. Among the thinkers who became profoundly influential are Jacques Lacan (Henninger 1980), Julia Kristeva (Heyd 1980), Jacques Derrida (Eisele 1982, Wagner-Egelhaaf 1989, Nadermann 1990, Völse 1990), Michel Foucault (Pott 1984, Cejpek, 1984), Gilles Deleuze (Allais 1987), and Roland Barthes (Pekar 1989), alongside Mikhail Bakhtin (Meisel 1991).

Often critics not merely adopt one critical model of thinking but draw on a whole range of poststructuralist ideas in their interpretations of Musil, sometimes combining them with ideas drawn from the German intellectual tradition. In some cases, such eclecticism produces highly readable and stimulating contributions to Musil studies, with regard both to particular works (such as Pietsch's level-headed analysis of self-reflexivity in *Der Mann ohne Eigenschaften*, 1988) and to Musil's oeuvre as a whole (like Thomas Pekar's monograph on the problem of love, 1989). On occasion, the theory boom inspires critics to challenge established conventions of academic discourse and develop their own idiosyncratic personal style, resulting in a strange hybrid of expository and creative prose: Thomas Zaunschirm's intriguing comparison of Musil and Marcel Duchamp (1982), Ingram Hartinger's semiconfessional piece on Musil and anti-psychiatry (1984) or Manfred Moser's ruminations on memory and irony in Musil (1985), for instance, are difficult to classify as literary criticism in any traditional sense of the term. Hubert Thurnhofer even concludes his idiosyncratic assessment of Musil's significance as a philosopher (1987) with a fictional story of his own, reminiscent of "Tonka." All secondary literature can be called parasitic insofar as it nestles in the space created by other authors; this should not, however, be viewed as an invitation to blur the distinctions between the object of analysis (a given literary work) and the critic's striving for self-expression.

On a different note, an ambitious theoretical orientation sometimes produces new forms of blindness that reenact and reinforce conventional — and largely unacknowledged — aesthetic value judgments. For all their intellectual sensitivity, for example, both Hans-Georg Pott (1984) and Gerhard Meisel (1991), who attempt to address Musil's oeuvre in its entirety in a highly sophisticated manner, do not so much as mention Musil's dramas. In light of the revival of Musil's plays at successful productions in Vienna (1980, 1985), Berlin (1981), and elsewhere, failure to acknowledge Musil's interest and involvement in drama indicates a conspicuous bias, suggesting the limitations of methodologies that tend to separate literary works from the contexts of genre issues and literary history.

Roger Willemsen's second book, a 1985 introductory monograph on Musil, is thus far perhaps the boldest effort to give a concise and complex assessment of Musil's life and works from a multiplicity of poststructuralist perspectives. Willemsen explores above all the connection between Musil's aesthetic preoccupations and his ethical ideas. Willemsen's style is elliptic and allusive rather than discursive: whereas literary criticism usually makes points by way of citation and commentary, Willemsen offers aphoristic statements that tend to be as enigmatic as they are illuminating. The book contains some of the most brilliant insights into Musil, yet, in its extreme density, it also marks the limits of readability. Though part of a series by a publishing house not primarily specializing in academic publications, Willemsen's book can be read and appreciated by only a handful of readers who not only share the author's detailed knowledge of Musil but are also initiated into Willemsen's theoretical and methodological background.

Alongside a generation of young critics eager to assimilate international theoretical models of literary criticism, there exists a sizable contingent of young Musil scholars that prefers to take recourse to more traditionally philosophical approaches. During the late 1980s, such efforts to draw on the German philosophical tradition produced some of the lengthiest (and also some of the most unreadable) contributions to Musil studies. Since such contributions, almost invariably doctoral dissertations, for the most part deal exclusively with *Der Mann ohne Eigenschaften*, I will discuss them in the chapter on the critical reception of the novel.

The dilemma that faced Musil criticism from its very beginning in the early 1950s manifested itself in altered, but more acute, form in the second half of the 1980s: while early "affirmative" Musil critics had found it difficult to distinguish between paraphrase and critical commentary, the later generation of Musil scholars fell into a similar trap, either producing high-powered *wissenschaftlich* discourse or else creating a peculiar kind of appreciative secondary "poetic" prose. While the jargon-ridden poststructuralist or philosophical contributions represent an eagerness to display scholarly prowess, the parasitic quasi-literary writings reflect an impulse to reject academic writing altogether. Once again, both tendencies raise the question of readership: why should anyone who, inspired by an interest in Musil, turns to Germanistik for guidance be expected to plow through a quagmire of excessively scholarly or pseudocreative prose? The disconcerting situation in Musil studies reflects on a small scale the current quandary of German studies. Unlike the debate of the 1970s, the current crisis is not about questions of methodology but rather reflects a much more fundamental disorientation concerning the legitimacy and function — the point, as it were — of *Literaturwissenschaft* altogether. It is perhaps not surprising that a recent volume on the crisis of Germanistik, edited by Frank Griesheimer and Alois Prinz (1992), features contributions by many critics who are prominent Musil scholars, such as Arntzen, Laermann, Mattenklott, Stern, von Matt, and Willemsen.

Undaunted by the pervasive sense of disorientation and crisis, Musil scholars still produce fruitful and impressive results. For instance, the publication in 1988 of Karl Corino's monumental pictorial biography of Musil marked the culmination of several decades of dedicated research. The abundance of information Corino collected in this volume makes it an indispensable source book for any consideration of the interconnection between Musil's personal life and his creative concerns. For instance, the photographs Corino identifies as the sources for scenes or motifs in Musil's texts make it possible to analyze the peculiar manner in which Musil drew on visual aides for inspiration in his writing. The increased awareness of the visual element of Musil's writing, initiated in part by Helmut Lethen (1987) and Arno Rußegger (1988), has received valuable stimuli from Corino's book: Martina Wagner-Egelhaaf in her investigation of photographic elements (1991b), Rolf Günter Renner in his discussion of affinities between Musil and postmodern forms of narration (1991), and my own work on Musil's attitude toward the medium of film (1992), gratefully draw on the material brought into focus by Corino's volume.

After the publication of Corino's massive biographical monograph on Musil, it seemed as though everything that could be known about Musil's life had finally been assembled. Yet there still appears to be room for nuances and the occasional interesting detail to surface. For instance, Cornelia Blasberg's 1989 account of Musil's sojourn to Stuttgart during the years 1901 and 1902 remains somewhat anecdotal, while Gesine Bey (1989) and Silvia Bonacchi (1992) shed an interesting light on his formative years of study in Berlin from 1903 to 1908. The latter two particularly stress Musil's close proximity to contemporary developments in experimental psychology and Gestalt theory, both of which, as the authors cogently show, play an important role throughout all of Musil's works, including *Der Mann ohne Eigenschaften*. Bonacchi assembles highly useful factual information that helps trace Musil's intellectual development, such as a list of the lecture courses in which he enrolled as a student.

While Musil scholars had always been fond of comparing Musil to other authors of international stature — see, for instance, Gerhard Kaiser's monograph on Musil, Proust, and Joyce (1972) — it was not until the 1980s that comparative literature specialists seriously began to address Musil's literary achievement in an international context. There are, for instance, several studies that compare Musil to Proust: Gene M. Moore (1985) and Anne Longuet-Marx (1986, 1990) stress the affinities of the two authors' aesthetic and ethical positions.

A different comparatist perspective is introduced by Warner Berthoff (1986), who examines the way in which *Der Mann ohne Eigenschaften* first sets up and then transcends expectations associated with the novel genre, comparing the genre shift to that in Goethe's *Elective Affinities* on the one hand and the bipolar philosophy of Lao-Tsu on the other. Marike Finlay (1990) places Musil in the context of an international epistemological reorientation in the natural and social sciences at the beginning of the twentieth century. In her assessment, Musil's thinking displays affinities with the semiotic theories of Charles S. Peirce and Werner Heisenberg's reflections on the epistemological implications of quantum physics. All three thinkers, Finlay observes, share a rejection of the traditional *epistéme*, the notion that an object of knowledge exists independently of an observing subject. Instead, they advocate an essentially tripartite structure in which language (as a medium of reflection and a structuring principle of cognition) is always present in, and constitutive of, the interaction between subject and object. The three models, Finlay suggests, lead to a rejection of the notion of a stable, suprahistorical notion of truth. Like Peirce's semiotics and Heisenberg's physics, Musil's essayism and irony replace *truth* with the concept of *validity*, implying a social consensus on the preliminary acceptance of statements that can always be revoked in the face of new evidence. Closed, stable systems of thought (what Finlay calls "classical discourse") are thus replaced with open-ended and dynamic models ("modern discourse"). Combining a multitude of theoretical impulses from a wide variety of disciplines, including discourse analysis (Michel Foucault), cybernetic anthropology (Gregory Bateson), and communicative ethics (Jürgen Habermas), Finlay ascribes to modern discourse in general — and to Musil's irony and essayism in particular — a politically emancipatory potential. In this fashion, Finlay attempts to combat the playful arbitrariness of postmodernism by stressing the pragmatic and ethical implications of intellectual activity.

Finlay's study, though severely marred by capricious typographical errors, is a stimulating attempt to rescue Musil from international oblivion by assessing the significance of his work outside the established contexts of literary criticism. Likewise, even within the field of Germanistik, scholars are adopting an essentially comparatist perspective that transcends not only traditional divisions of national literatures but also those between academic disciplines. Perhaps the most brilliant and original comprehensive study of Musil of recent years is Gerhard Meisel's monograph of 1991. Meisel attempts an interpretation of Musil's entire oeuvre (with the exception of *Törleß* and the dramas) based on a highly complex version of intellectual history informed by recent developments in literary criticism such as Mikhail Bakhtin's concept of the essentially dialogic nature of literature. At the core of Meisel's project is the thesis that Musil's works engage in an "intertextual dialogue ... with virtually all of the tendencies of reflection and modes of cognition of his period" (9). While Meisel in principle concedes the usefulness of psychoanalytic categories for an interpretation of Musil's texts and frequently draws on notions developed by Freud and some of his French followers, he rejects Peter Henninger's speculative Lacanian approach as too restrictive. The "intertextual" aspects of Musil's writing, Meisel emphasizes, can be understood only if one does not lose sight of the intellectual context from which Musil's views originate. Contemporary intellectual concerns leave their imprint upon Musil's creative works, his theoretical reflections, and his personal writings, all of which must be drawn upon for an elucidation of a given work. Meisel skillfully synthesizes many of the factual aspects known about Musil and his intellectual context with sometimes highly original and insightful readings that I will outline in the chapters on the works concerned.

Meisel's contribution represents a welcome effort to overcome the sense of disorientation and fragmentation engendered by the existence of a multiplicity of discourses in Musil studies, which in return reflect the confused state of Germanistik in general in the early 1990s. What was welcomed in the 1970s as *Methodenpluralismus* is in danger of turning into a situation that spins out of control. In literary studies, as in most academic areas, diversification has reached a point at which communication across the discipline has become difficult, if not impossible. Both the mushrooming of theoretical discourse and its opposite, a resistance to theory, are symptoms of an overall crisis that affects academic enterprises. In Musil studies, this crisis is mirrored in a coexistence of traditional approaches with new and sometimes excessively cerebral theoretical methods. The former are frequently naively or disdainfully ignorant of recent theoretical developments and of the methodological complexities involved in studying Musil, while the latter are often prone to jargon-ridden intellectual posturing. As is to be expected, *Der Mann ohne Eigenschaften* is receiving by far the most attention in the debates concerning

Musil's stature as a writer. While this is fitting, it should not produce a disregard of Musil's oeuvre as a whole, an oeuvre that includes a series of shorter works that in my estimation equal or surpass in artistic rank many of what have become the canonical texts of German-language literature.

In 1992, on the fiftieth anniversary of Musil's death, several symposia were held, in places like Klagenfurt, Vienna, Brno, Düsseldorf, and Geneva. It would appear that such activities signal the recognition of Musil as a major author. Yet his emergence as a figure of public admiration is not without its ironies. One of the more bizarre events staged to honor Musil was a reading from his works in the Austrian parliament in Vienna on April 15 (the day of his death). Musil would, I am sure, have cherished the supreme irony of such a celebration which enthroned, in the very center of political powermongering of the former "Kakania," an author largely marginalized throughout his life: in his satirical story "Märchen vom Schneider" (The Tailor's Tale) of 1923 Musil had portrayed a luckless writer who in his works wants to "blow up his age." The writer — who is deemed a harmless eccentric — actually manages to place an allegorical "bomb" in parliament; he is even able to light it, only to find to his dismay that the "wind" produced by the ceaseless speeches of the parliamentarians quickly extinguishes the "revolutionary" fire. The writer is then taken to court, not for his subversive activities, but for committing the worst crime in a commercialized society, that of not making any money.

In order to write, a writer has to live. In order to live, a writer has to gain recognition for his work. In order to gain recognition, Musil once noted sardonically, a writer has to die first. Fifty years after his death, Musil appears to have accomplished what he called the "ontological feat" (*Briefe* I, 1083) of belated recognition after death. Musil's posthumous fame is a strange case of enshrinement born out of a mixture of adulation and ignorance. Despite the overpowering scholarly output, Musil remains, in the words of Michael Kowal (1966), an "unread master"; he is still for the most part the object of veneration of a rather small coterie of literary cognoscenti. Musil is too much of an individualist to be marketable on a large scale, which is not to say that he is in any way esoteric or elitist: I cannot help thinking that Musil and his work are fundamentally opposed to the institutional structures that govern academic interaction, both on the level of research (with periodicals, organizations, governing boards, membership fees, conferences, and symposia) and on the level of teaching (with lectures, seminar papers, and exams). Musil is an author who asks to be read by an individual reader willing to invest emotional and intellectual energy in an infinitely rewarding and enriching process of exploration. Such an author does not lend himself to the mechanisms of public adoration, with plaques or monuments unveiled (witness his satirical "Denkmale" [Monuments] in *Nachlaß zu Lebzeiten*), public speeches accompanied by chamber music and culminating in polite chitchat over wine and cheese. In fact, such public homage perhaps finds its most perceptive critic in the Musil who described in minute and merciless detail the goings-on of the *Parallelaktion* in Diotima's salon. The relationship between Ulrich and Agathe in *Der Mann ohne Eigenschaften* can be viewed as embodying Musil's idea of readership as a process of intimate communication of individual minds in an ongoing (and unending) exchange of ideas and experiences. Musil is no *Großschriftsteller* after whom streets or schools should be named; he is an author who establishes and demands intimacy with the reader.

Readers in the English-speaking world have at best obtained a rather skewed picture of Musil's oeuvre. For decades, the translations by Eithne Wilkins and Ernst Kaiser offered access only to a selection of Musil's prose works. The situation began to change in the 1980s with the translation of his doctoral dissertation (by Kevin Mulligan, 1982); his first play, *Die Schwärmer* (by Andrea Simon, 1983); and his lesser known short prose (by Peter Wortsman, 1987). Perhaps the most significant contribution to the advancement of Musil criticism in English is the translation of selected essays of Musil by Burton Pike and David Luft (1990), an excellent collection that highlights the tremendous scope of Musil's critical intellect. These translations are soon to be complemented by a new English version of *Der Mann ohne Eigenschaften*, begun by Sophie Wilkins (see Wilkins 1988) and completed by Burton Pike, and by a selection from Musil's journals prepared by David Luft. With the publication of these volumes, virtually all of Musil's oeuvre will be available to the English-speaking reader. These translations, it is to be hoped, will render Musil's work accessible to a whole new generation of readers.

What then, is the situation in Musil studies in the early 1990s? At the beginning of the present decade, the two centers for Musil research find themselves in a period of transition. Following the retirement of Marie-Louise Roth in 1991, the Arbeitsstelle für Robert-Musil-Forschung at Saarbrücken has begun a process of expansion into a research facility for Austrian literature and culture in general. Likewise, there are plans to convert Musil's birthplace at Klagenfurt (which houses the Robert-Musil-Archiv as well as the Ingeborg-Bachmann-Museum) into an ambitious cultural center for the province of Carinthia. Josef Strutz, the successor of Karl Dinklage as head of the archive, is engaged in an effort to establish a large-scale *Literaturhaus* there which is to integrate the collections on Klagenfurt's two most famous authors into a general meeting place featuring a café, an auditorium, and exhibition spaces for regional artists. In 1991 the Klagenfurt archive began publication of *Rapial*, a new journal that is intended to bridge the gap between the specialized scholars and the general reader interested in Musil and in the cultural diversity of the region. On account of its flexibility, the journal has the potential for providing a forum for communication in critical exchange.

Forty years of Musil scholarship have accomplished a great deal: his works are available in editions that are, if not perfect, for the most part reasonably reliable, augmented by Adolf Frisé's copious notes. We can also consult his diaries and his letters in equally helpful editions. Vast amounts of information have been amassed on the biographical, intellectual, aesthetic, and historical background of his literary oeuvre. Musil's labyrinthine *Nachlaß*, comprising over ten thousand pages of manuscripts and notes, is now available on CD-ROM, giving scholars unparalleled access to the intricacies of Musil's thinking (Rußegger 1992). Critics today have a kind of control over Musil's notes that in a way far surpasses that of the author himself. But what would Musil, the obsessive, meticulous craftsman, have said if he had been confronted with an army of researchers that tackle the complexities of his manuscripts armed with a text-processing program somewhat menacingly called Word Cruncher? Perhaps the academic community, for all its good intentions, is doing Musil a disservice by rendering his literary world an object of scholarly control rather than the stimulus of critical reflection. The usefulness of such innovations notwithstanding, it seems to me that perhaps what Musil needs is not "scientific" boldness but a sense of readerly humility, not more researchers equipped with high tech but more readers — attentive and open-minded.

Criticism of Individual Works

5: *Die Verwirrungen des Zöglings Törleß*

MUCH AS MUSIL'S CONTEMPORARIES had viewed *Törleß* almost exclusively as an autobiographical novel about the sexual aberrations of an adolescent, Musil criticism after the Second World War downplayed the sexual aspects of the text. Drawing on Musil's statement that the depiction of sexual pathologies was but a pretext for an exploration of more profound issues (*TB* I, 723), critics have with few exceptions attempted to define the nature of these issues in philosophical, aesthetic, sociological or psychological terms. This is not to say that they overlooked the sexual dimension of the book. Rather, this dimension at best receives second billing in most readings.

Given that Musil had to be rediscovered after the war, it is understandable that the early efforts of critics were concerned with placing him and his works in the familiar contexts of literary history. Walter Jens (1957), for instance, takes *Törleß* as evidence of the *Sprachkrise*, the crisis and redefinition of poetic language in the literature of the early twentieth century, a concern highlighted by the motto from Maurice Maeterlinck's *Le trésor des humbles* (The Treasure of the Humble) that opens Musil's novel. The problems that Musil's protagonist has in expressing his inner emotions thus find their place alongside Hofmannsthal's "Chandos-Brief" (Letter of Lord Chandos) and works by Rilke and Kafka as manifestations of the erosion of the subject-object relationship, a development that culminated in the radical destruction of poetic language in expressionist writing, for which Georg Heym serves Jens as an example.

Ernst Kaiser and Eithne Wilkins (1960) touch on the epistemological problems raised in the book: they view Törleß's preoccupation with the square root of minus one as a central motif in Musil's thinking, emblematic of his concern to explore in his writing an elusive inner unknown quantity. Their essay is surprisingly undogmatic compared with the chapter on *Törleß* in their later book (1962), in which they give a psychological interpretation of *Törleß* as a study in abnormal behavior, an interpretation betraying a certain sense of moral indignation with Musil's sympathetic treatment of the allegedly deviant and degenerate.

Theodore Ziolkowski (1961) was the first to stress Törleß's predisposition to become an artist: his overall sensitivity enables Törleß to experience moments of "inversion," spiritual revelations akin to Joyce's epiphanies. Like Jens, Ziolkowski sees an affinity between Musil's *Künstlerroman* and the depictions of artistic crises in Hofmannsthal and Rilke.

Robert Minder's short 1962 essay relates Musil's first book to the wave of turn-of-the-century literature on puberty and adolescence, a phenomenon later examined in detail in a large-scale comparative study by Peter Grotzer (1991). Minder links Törleß's sexual perturbations and his concern with power with the philosophical (Cartesian) quest to form an identity in a repressive environment. Wilfried Berghahn adopts a similar perspective in his influential 1963 monograph on Musil. The view that the sadistic rituals in Törleß's *Kadettenhaus*, the Habsburg military academy, anticipate the horrors of the Nazi regime also underlies Volker Schlöndorff's famous 1966 film adaptation of the novel. This perspective is partly supported by Musil's own statement that the novel depicts future dictators *in nucleo* (*TB* I, 914) — often quoted in political readings of the novel. Critics who cite this statement usually do not differentiate between the three protagonists; Dietmar Goltschnigg (1981, 24) proposes that Musil's pronouncement refers only to Reiting and Beineberg and not to Törleß. Minder, Berghahn, and Schlöndorff anticipate the sociologically oriented approaches of the late 1960s that view the novel as a significant document of a protofascist mentality latently present in the Habsburg Empire. Most outspokenly, Thomas Brasch (1979), as a creative writer outside of literary criticism adopting a perspective of anarchist individualism, endorses the assessment of Musil's debut piece as a profoundly political work.

In marked contrast to such politically oriented readings, Wilhelm Braun (1965a) views the book as the depiction of a successful process of maturation. Braun shows no interest in the sociohistorical context evoked by Musil's novel. Instead, he approaches the fate of the protagonist exclusively in terms of personal psychology. Törleß's adolescent crisis, he maintains, should be viewed against the backdrop of an earlier childhood trauma (the experience of having been abandoned as a child). When Törleß learns to accept and express his emotions, he "emerges from his tribulations as a cured and sensitive human being" (116; the notion was convincingly refuted by Wolfgang Düsing 1982, 54). The problem with what Braun somewhat too confidently offers as the "proper interpretation" of the novel is that it assumes a stable (wholesome, normal, natural) value system into which Törleß successfully integrates himself. Such a reading neglects the critical distance the narrator maintains from the protagonist and the society portrayed, which in Frank Trommler's view makes *Törleß* the first instance in Musil's lifelong project of giving a critical analysis of the consciousness of the period (Trommler 1966).

Harry Goldgar (1965) expressly approaches the book from a psychoanalytic angle: the manner in which the novel presents an analysis of transitional homosexuality in puberty as well as the significance accorded to childhood experiences, he argues, show Musil to be a perceptive student of Freud, who developed his theories around the same time. Interesting as this reading may be, it suffers from unpardonable methodological laxness. Goldgar infers that Musil, as an Austrian trained as a psychologist, necessarily must have been familiar with Freudian theories. Yet Musil's ideas emerge from a radically different intellectual context: he studied experimental psychology (later to become the basis of Gestalt theory) in Berlin, while Freud was laying the ground for his psychoanalytic theories in Vienna. Although Musil's novel contains material that can fruitfully be analyzed along psychoanalytic lines, the psychological models Musil himself employed derive from a different tradition. Erhard von Büren (1970) stresses the young Musil's independence of contemporary psychological theorems such as those of Freud. Goldgar's claim that Musil knew Freud's theories at the time he wrote his novel and that he more or less deliberately set out to illustrate in his own text Freud's insights into the Oedipus complex, amounts to little more than unsubstantiated conjecture and has been refuted by Annie Reniers-Servranckx (1969, German version 1970).

Drawing on research conducted by Ernst Kaiser, Karl Corino (1968) is able to identify the historical models for most of the novel's characters, showing how closely the text is based on Musil's personal experience. Corino's evaluation of the transformation of the autobiographical material into literature tentatively suggests the psychoanalytic approach he was later to adopt in all of his writings on Musil. Corino credits Jürgen C. Thöming with the idea that the name Törleß might derive from the word *türlos*, the motif of the absence of doors connoting a convergence of the psychological and philosophical dimensions of the novel. This view was taken up by Lars Freij (1972) and much of Musil scholarship. Later, several alternative interpretations of the protagonist's name were proposed: Henry Hatfield, for instance, suggests a different interpretation: Musil's protagonist overcomes his sexual and intellectual perturbations, ending up free of his folly ("der Torheit los," 1969, 37). Lynda Hoffmann adds another speculation, using a linguistic approach to explain the protagonist's name. The suffix *-less*, she argues, derives from a South German diminutive, indicating that Törleß indeed discovers a "little door" within himself (1989, 9). Neither Hatfield's nor Hoffmann's suggestion appears to have been adopted by Musil criticism.

Elizabeth Stopp (1968) presents a detailed study of the novel's form to complement Braun's 1965 psychological interpretation of its thematic content. Above all she attempts to reconstruct the author's conscious intentions in the structural choices he made, relating motivic aspects of Musil's text to a wide variety of intellectual and literary traditions. She takes issue with the notion prevalent in Musil criticism that the Maeterlinck motto opening the novel evokes a resigned acceptance of the failure of language. Instead, she argues, it expresses a challenge to overcome the limits of language, one that Musil successfully met in the artistic form of his book. Stopp's essay, sensitive and well informed, is still one of the best traditional studies of Musil's first book.

Two studies published in 1971 shift the focus away from psychological considerations toward the intellectual content of the novel. Jan Aler reads *Törleß* as a philosophical work that complements Musil's dissertation on Ernst Mach. He sees parallels between Musil's and Edmund Husserl's critique of Mach's notion of the dissolution of the subject and the implications this dissolution brings about for epistemology. In Aler's view, the novel marks Musil's first effort to embark on a comprehensive examination of the limitations of Western rationality. Gerd Müller, taking up Walter Jens's idea of Musil as *poeta doctus*, shows how the novel resonates with a broad range of ideas prevalent at the period, in effect encapsulating the "intellectual substance of [Musil's] time" (10). Müller differs from Aler in the emphasis he places on the manner in which philosophical ideas are mediated in literature. Musil, Müller notes, must be placed in the general shift from positivist science toward a *geisteswissenschaftlich* orientation that occurred around 1900. Musil derived his philosophical subject matter from the positivist Ernst Mach, while his style echoes the proliferation of poetic images in the impressionist writer Maurice Maeterlinck. Müller shows how the novel's narrative style blurs the distinction between narrator and character, formally mirroring Mach's notion that subject and object are ultimately indistinguishable and form a continuum in the process of perception. To Müller, in its critique of the limitations of Mach's scientific reductionism, *Törleß* marks the first manifestation of Musil's mystical tendencies: Törleß experiences that there is a central *Seinsbereich*, a sphere of existence that lies beyond what can be articulated in language. This insight is derived from a multitude of influences, among them the Romantic tradition (Novalis), current *Lebensphilosophie* (Bergson), and its popular derivative (Ellen Key).

Lars Freij's 1972 monograph on *Törleß* represents an oddity in Musil criticism: with scrupulous diligence Freij records the frequency with which certain stylistic devices and images occur in Musil's text. Anyone looking for statistical information of this sort will find Freij's study an extremely useful reference tool, particularly his analysis of the novel's supposed key words. At the same time, his impressive "microanalysis" of Musil's poetic language is sometimes oddly myopic, since he makes few attempts to use the amassed material to draw interpretive conclusions, instead anchoring Musil's images firmly among the "contemporary stock of symbols" (24), a concept that is never defined or delineated.

Two studies published in 1973 reflect — though in very different manners — the reorientation of Germanistik in the wake of the political upheaval in the late 1960s. Both Uwe Baur (1973b) and Gert Mattenklott approach Musil's novel as a document of the bourgeois mentality of the period during which it was written. Baur rejects the notion that the novel is an autobiographical confession, stressing instead its significance as a social case study: on one level, it targets the exclusion of sexuality from bourgeois society in its alleged propriety. In Baur's reading, Musil presents the violence and oppression occurring at the boarding school not as an aberration but as a function of the economic order and the class structure of the Habsburg monarchy. He concedes that Musil did not always overcome the ideological strictures he set out to expose: the flash-forward describing Törleß's later development, for instance, Baur argues, is the least artistically convincing part of the text. Here Musil unsuccessfully attempts to distance himself from his protagonist's detached aestheticism through the use of irony.

Gert Mattenklott views Törleß as a representative of the disoriented intellectual at the turn of the century. His analysis centers on three crucial episodes in the novel that illustrate Törleß's position in the bourgeois family (in his separation from his parents) and his opposition to different social classes (the upper class in his friendship with Prince H., the proletariat in his association with the prostitute Bozena). To Mattenklott, Törleß's subjectivity is thus conditioned by class ideology. Much as bourgeois ideology attempts to obfuscate its own class interests by presenting its problems as expressions of an allegedly universal human condition, Törleß experiences his predicament as an ontologically fixed problem. In Mattenklott's reading, Törleß's sexual, ethical, and existential crisis is tied up with a lack of a historical perspective of those segments of the middle class that had become marginal in the development of capitalism toward increased monopolization. To be sure, Mattenklott's essay is perhaps overly dense and poses some methodological problems: his concept of a "non-monopolistic bourgeoisie," for instance, unduly equates Wilhelminian Germany and Habsburg Austria, whose economic and social structures around the turn of the century were quite different. Despite minor reservations, Mattenklott's seminal, if somewhat speculative, essay provides Musil scholarship with valuable impulses, ultimately elevating the level of critical discourse. It offers a critical, nonaffirmative reading based not on matters of taste or on psychological speculation.

By way of contrast, Lothar Huber takes a more traditional approach in his article of the same year. Huber again raises the familiar issue of a *Krise der Sprache*, at the same time qualifying Braun's overly positive evaluation of Törleß's development: while a resolution of Törleß's crisis seems possible, Huber maintains, it is not presented as a condition actually achieved in the present but is rather projected into the future as Törleß's potential ability to express his conflicting emotions.

Like Jan Aler (1971), Yvon Desportes (1974) assumes a close connection between the novel and Musil's dissertation, viewing the novel's style as a transformation of Mach's philosophical ideas into literature. Following Mach, Musil places the emphasis on fluctuating sensations rather than a stable self. Desportes's reading culminates in the slightly overstated aphoristic assertion that *Törleß* in its unity of form and content constitutes Musil's "actual dissertation."

In her somewhat oddly focused volume on the motif of the attic in German literature (1974), Margret Rothe-Buddensieg insists on the importance of the sexual theme. Musil's text, which she regards as a novella rather than a novel, primarily provides an example of a problematic quest for a male identity: in the attic — a demonic clandestine counteridyll to a repressive social reality — Törleß is confronted with the subversive potential of his own sexual urges. His adolescent crisis represents a form of male narcissism in which both Törleß and Basini are implicated as subject and object of mutual sexual repression, mirroring the male-dominated social structures around them. As far as I can tell, Rothe-Buddensieg is the first critic to raise the issue of gender in Musil criticism, pointing to Törleß's crisis as a specifically male predicament rather than a gender-neutral concern. In tentative and cursory fashion she thus touches on aspects of Musil's work that merit further consideration.

David Turner (1974) also focuses on the sexual aspects of Musil's book and their political and moral implications, though in a radically different fashion. His point is programmatically expressed in the title of his article: he views Törleß's perturbations as the "Evasions of an Aesthete." Explicitly rejecting any readings that attempt to trace the text's inner logic — be it biographical, formal, psychological, sociological, or philosophical — Turner embarks on a moralistic critique of Törleß's ethical position. He emphasizes the active involvement of Musil's protagonist in the torture of an innocent victim, an indication of the detached aesthete's ambivalent fascination with violence and oppression. For Turner, Törleß thus becomes the quintessential a-moral decadent: his development does not follow the wholesome path of self-cultivation — *Bildung*, in Goethe's sense — but instead culminates in a politically dangerous form of aestheticism. Turner's heartfelt moral indignation with Musil's hero is most apparent when he suggests that Törleß belongs to the kind of intellectuals who would later opt for political appeasement and accommodate themselves in *innere Emigration*, a withdrawal to the ostensibly apolitical private sphere, during the Nazi regime (41).

In Turner's reading the sense of moral outrage critics had voiced when Musil's novel first appeared thus returned, almost seventy years later, in different form. Refreshing as the polemical energy of his style may be, Turner displays a surprisingly naive trust in the existence of timeless "normal moral and social patterns" (33); the novel, in its assessment of the duplicity of the society it depicts, actually calls into question such allegedly stable social values. Starting from radically different premises, GDR writer Rolf Schneider (1975) appears to reach conclusions surprisingly similar to those of Turner; his ostensibly orthodox Marxist reading leads him to argue that Musil's protagonist emerges from his moral and epistemological crisis as an aesthete potentially sympathetic to fascism (32). Unlike Turner, however, Schneider does not confuse the author with his character, attributing to Musil a higher degree of nascent political awareness than that of his protagonist Törleß. In its failure to distinguish between the narrating instance and the depicted fictional world, Turner's reading falls short of achieving its task. Turner fails to account for the thematic significance of the novel's form. For instance, issues concerning the narrative structure of Musil's book, such as the variations in the narrator's attitude toward the protagonist, are hardly ever addressed. A careful examination of such issues might have induced Turner to qualify his negative assessment.

Walter Sokel's comparison of Hesse's *Demian* and Musil's *Törleß* (1976) implicitly refutes Turner's charge of Musil's complicity with an amoral stance. Not unlike Turner, Sokel argues that both books depict a quasi-Nietzschean "intellectual atmosphere which facilitated the birth of Fascism" (38). Yet Sokel is quick to point out how Musil transcends the ambivalence of fascination and repulsion to which Hesse largely remains attached. Unlike Hesse, Sokel maintains, Musil actually displays a keen sense of the ethical implications of adolescent power politics in a larger sociohistorical context.

Whatever the limitations of Turner's moralistic approach or Schneider's ideological one may be, the two authors at least display an awareness of a general political perspective. Such awareness is sorely missing from Hertwig Gradischnig's 1976 study, which aims to address a crucial topic discussed by Turner and Schneider, the question of Törleß's aestheticism. Unfortunately, Gradischnig offers little that is new or original. Törleß appears as one of the first manifestations of Musil's images of the creative writer: his development is characterized by an epistemological crisis that goes hand in hand with a crisis in language. The crisis of the "seeker for knowledge" (113) is ultimately overcome by an acceptance of the limitations of rational thought. Gradischnig makes little effort at embedding the discussion of familiar insights in a larger theoretical frame.

In contrast, Wolfgang Frier (1976) uses a clearly delineated theoretical model in his investigation into the poetic representation of emotionality in Musil's novel, a textual linguistics derived from a combination of transformational grammar (Noam Chomsky) and semantic theories (A. J. Greimas). Frier's study thus covers much of the same ground as that of Freij (1972), though on a methodologically more ambitious — and ultimately more fruitful — level. Frier's approach reflects the endeavor, typical of parts of the community of Germanistik scholars in the mid-1970s, to render *Literaturwissenschaft* truly scientific. Such efforts did not have a widespread impact, and much of Frier's terminology appears dated now. Still, he goes beyond merely giving a taxonomy of linguistic and stylistic phenomena in Musil's novel, frequently addressing such diverse issues as the strategies Musil employed to depict corporeality and mental processes.

In his study on the connection between memory and identity formation in Musil, Wolfgang Düsing (1982) once again traces the origins of Musil's narrative technique to the familiar turn-of-the century *Sprachkrise*. Düsing sees a correlation between the nonlinear structures of memory and the novel's narrative form, rejecting Braun's (1965) thesis that Törleß undergoes a successful process of growth. In the end, Düsing writes, Törleß's identity remains problematic: "Törleß has discovered a problem; he has not, however, solved it" (54).

Gilbert Reis (1983) stresses the self-reflexive aspects of all of Musil's works. *Törleß* for him is an example of Musil's overall concern with defining the creative artist's attitude to reality. Törleß's attempts to express aspects of reality that are excluded from everyday discourse converge with Musil's definition of a writer's true objective (61). Reis's reading, resting largely on paraphrase and commentary of familiar material, culminates in the thesis that Törleß — like Musil in his writing of the novel — comes to realize what the task of the creative artist is: to investigate the spheres of existence that lie outside the control of scientific rationality. While this may be correct, the conceptual premises that underpin Reis's approach are questionable; he equates the literary project with "Musil's efforts to assign to poetic thinking a place within the *one*, general, objective reality" (11; emphasis in the original). Such a thesis presupposes a monolithic view of "objective" reality fundamentally alien to Musil. In 1987, Reis refined some of his ideas, placing Musil and his narrative technique in the context of the modern crisis of subjectivity. Here Reis notes that Musil's assertion of subjectivity is problematic since it denies the objective factors that determine the very conditions that make subjectivity possible. Reis concludes that while Musil's first novel maintains a rather conventional relationship between the protagonist and a distanced narrator who vouchsafes for the validity of the narrative, his later texts display a profound change in the subject-object relationship, culminating in *Der Mann ohne Eigenschaften*, in which the attempt to effect an intellectual synthesis of subjectivity and objectivity (achieved in *Törleß* in a series of ecstatic experiences) is shown to fail vis-à-vis the unyielding objectivity of reality.

Several critical traditions converge in Hans-Georg Pott's chapter on *Törleß* in his 1984 monograph on Musil. Drawing on insights from Gert Mattenklott and psychoanalytically oriented poststructuralist theory, Pott places the novel in the overall context of the "discovery" of sexuality and adolescence around the turn of the century. He also develops on a sophisticated theoretical plane some of the ideas about the connection of sexuality and power anticipated in rudimentary form by Rothe-Buddensieg. In its male protagonists, Pott argues, Musil's debut piece illustrates the complex problem of male socialization into the bourgeois family. In Pott's view, this socialization is subject to the mechanisms of social control formulated by Michel Foucault: the sadistic manner in which Reiting, Beineberg, and Törleß treat Basini represents an attempt to sublimate tendencies that are excluded from societal discourse, from the symbolic order that is established through rules of speech and behavior. In its violent aspects, this sublimation parallels both the theses concerning the formation of the "authoritarian personality" developed by Horkheimer and Adorno and the characteristics of the "male fantasies" described by Klaus Theweleit in *Männerphantasien* (Male Fantasies, 1978), the influential book on German male elites of the early twentieth century. Pott emphasizes that the manner in which one speaks about the world — the "discourse" — is more important in Musil's novel than the characters' actions. Törleß is removed from school not because he has participated in any unsanctioned activities but because, in his efforts to communicate the essence of his disturbing experience, he violated the rules of acceptable speech. It is a lapse into a poetic mode of speaking, a "deviant discourse that resists assimilation" (15), that brings Törleß into conflict with the representatives of the social symbolic order, the school authorities. Pott suggests that Törleß, in his confrontation with sexual desire and violent impulses, has actually discovered not something that is beyond the social order and threatens it from outside, but something that makes up the very fabric of that social order: the fractures within Western rationality itself (23). Pott's stimulating essay represents a major effort at combining German critical traditions (Freud, the Frankfurt school) with French thought (Lacan, Foucault) in Musil studies.

Starting from different premises, Aldo G. Gargani reaches similar conclusions in his essay on *Törleß* included in *Wien 1870–1930 — Traum und Wirklichkeit* (Vienna 1880–1930 — Dream and Reality), the catalogue of the highly successful 1984 exhibition. In this dense and insightful essay, Gargani on one level associates Musil's novel with the overall cultural crisis of the period. On another, he interprets the childhood memories of the protagonist (centering on Törleß's infantile trauma of having been abandoned) as a largely unconscious manifestation of Musil's Oedipal rivalry with Heinrich Reiter (the live-in companion of Musil's mother, somewhat speculatively identified here with Reiting, the character in the novel). In a crisis brought about by a complex conglomerate of childhood recollections, sensual confusions, ecstatic experiences, and a frustrated rational quest for something ineffable, Törleß comes to discover the gaps in traditional rationality. He thus participates in the discovery of a "new logic," characteristic of turn-of-the-century thinking, a realization that the supposedly contradictory spheres of existence cannot be isolated but must be regarded as intricately intertwined.

In sharp contrast to Gargani, Erich Meuthen (1985) explicitly rejects readings that view *Törleß* as a document of a cultural crisis. Instead, he introduces some rather unusual ideas into the discussion of Musil's debut piece. Meuthen identifies the labyrinth as a motif that tacitly underlies the entire narrative. Other motifs, such as those of automatism and role-playing, stress the artificiality of the text, which is reinforced, in Meuthen's view, by Musil's stilted language. Elements like these lead Meuthen to read the novel as a manneristic piece, little concerned with a representation of phenomena based on empirical experience. Drawing on Northrop Frye's typology of comic devices, Meuthen analyzes the unwittingly "comic" elements of the text and finds that Törleß's erotic and existential upheavals place him in the tradition of the naive fool, the "tumbe tôr" (130). In his quest for truth, Törleß does not arrive at a serious answer, merely at the insight — as laconic as it is trivial — that "everything happens." To Meuthen, the banality of Törleß's revelation signals that the entire text ultimately presents us with a comedic "Much Adoe about Nothing" (143, Meuthen's spelling). It is difficult to do justice to Meuthen's reading, which is more complex and less self-assured than this summary may perhaps suggest. In my opinion his polemical effort to read the text against the grain of virtually the entire tradition of Musil criticism goes too far: for one thing, Meuthen unduly limits the motifs he analyzes to the comic sphere; yet the images of labyrinth, theater, and dissembling also belong to the common stock of motifs expressing irreality and the existential threat of the uncanny. While it is possible to criticize Törleß's perplexity as a manneristic pose, one should not disregard the real suffering of Basini, the victim whose dehumanization gives the narrative a potentially tragic dimension (compare the association some critics draw between the novel and the sociopsychological roots of Fascism). I think that Meuthen's concept of the comic does not address the nature of the actual reading experience, which — as the moralistic objections frequently raised against the book suggest — can encompass an element of existential dread. From the lofty vantage point of Meuthen's Heideggerian reasoning, it seems to me, every work of art, including Picasso's *Guernica* and Peter Weiss's *Die Ermittlung* (The Investigation), would likewise turn into "Much Adoe about Nothing."

Where Meuthen restricts his focus on questions of genre, Volker Knüfermann (1986) attempts to combine aesthetic concerns with larger sociopsychological issues. Knüfermann compares formal aspects of Musil's debut novel with Thomas Mann's *Death in Venice* along lines suggested by Heinz Kohut's psychoanalytic theories on narcissism. Both Mann and Musil, Knüfermann argues, link identity formation with the activity of writing: language appears simultaneously as the medium in which a sense of self is narcissistically formed and as the means by which the self aims to transcend its narcissistic encapsulation. This paradoxical constellation has repercussions on the literary endeavors of both authors not only in thematic terms but above all on a formal level: whereas Mann's Aschenbach, in his erotic escapade, succumbs to the destructive postulates of the Protestant work ethic, Musil's Törleß overcomes his existential crisis in a precarious arrangement with the given social conditions of moral duplicity; he consciously assumes the position of the detached aesthete. His role-playing marks his relative success in establishing a self-sufficient identity through aesthetic self-creation. In this fashion, Knüfermann suggests, Törleß becomes an emblem of Musil's dynamic self-creating aesthetics, which bears resemblances to the "progressive transcendental poetics" advocated by early Romanticism (94).

For all their methodological differences, both Meuthen and Knüfermann, in the refusal to widen their focus of enquiry to include political and historical aspects, remain within the parameters of relatively traditional Germanistik. By way of contrast, Joseph Vogl, in his 1987 discussion of Musil's first novel, attempts to stretch the limits of literary criticism towards a comprehensive critique of civilization. Meuthen's reading of *Törleß* as "comedy" was prompted by the sense that Törleß's tribulations lead to nothing; Törleß's quest does not produce a discovery that would resolve his confusions. Vogl takes this absence of a revealed truth as the starting point of a complex examination of the work's anthropological dimension. The motif of the gaze that finds no reciprocity, Vogl argues, indicates that the novel questions the notion that a self is formed in a process of interaction between a subject and an objective world. For Törleß, the quest for a self-image takes on the form of a quest for something that promises a resolution of his conflicts yet remains out of reach. Törleß seeks affirmation through transgression, through an exploration of the limits of human experience. Yet his sexual, existential, psychological, and philosophical crisis leads not to affirmation but only to a kind of double negation. He finds that there is no positivity in which he could anchor his existence, the apocalyptic interplay of a mystery sought for and a promised revelation yields only an awareness that the object of the quest lies outside the confines of cognition and of language. Vogl views this antimetaphysical component of Musil's book as a radicalization of the Enlightenment project of a demystification of belief systems (73). Musil, like Nietzsche before him and Foucault after him, Vogl suggests, is engaged in an effort to establish a new anthropology, an image of human nature based in immanence rather than transcendence. Vogl's essay is a fascinating blend of theoretical sophistication and attention to detail, an example of which is the author's linking the failure Törleß experiences concerning his treatise "De natura hominum" to Musil's overall project of an anthropology that does not presuppose any aspects of human nature as universal and transhistorical givens (71).

Like Meuthen, Thomas Söder (1988) is indebted to Heidegger's notions on the concept and function of literature. The centerpiece of Söder's study is a discussion of the Kant episode in *Törleß*, based on Heidegger's interpretation of Kant's *Critique of Pure Reason*. Musil, Söder notes, differs from Kant in his view on the nature of imagination and his rejection of the Kantian concept of causality. To Musil, Kant's systematic philosophy is based on too limited a range of empirical experience. By rejecting as "ossifications" Kant's interest in comprehensive systematic order, Söder maintains, Musil misses the point of Kant's critical enterprise. To Söder it is no surprise, then, that Törleß's confusions mirror the inability properly to distinguish the three Kantian notions of observation, reflection, and imaginative faculty, (*Anschauung, Denken*, and *Vorstellungskraft*, 120). Such a reading, while acknowledging the differences between Musil and Kant, potentially reinstalls Kant as an absolute authority, a move that the novel and Musil's implicit critique of Kant clearly do not support.

Karl Pestalozzi (1989) places *Törleß* in a different philosophical context, that of turn-of-the-century mysticism. He maintains that critics have traditionally underestimated the significance of the motto from Maurice Maeterlinck's *Le trésor des humbles* that opens Musil's novel. Maeterlinck's ideas, Pestalozzi stresses, are indispensable as "keys" to an understanding of Musil's text (498). Pestalozzi attempts to trace resonances of Maeterlinck in a variety of motifs, characters, and situations. The protagonist's very name evokes the door metaphor that in Maeterlinck designates the separation of the spheres of ordinary and mystical experience: in his spiritual crisis, Musil's protagonist lacks access to his innermost self; he is indeed "doorless" (503). To Pestalozzi, Törleß's experience of infinity when he is confronted with the vast expanse of the sky, Bozena's function as mystagogue, and Basini's ability to inspire in Törleß an intimation of experiences that lie beyond language all find their origin in Maeterlinck's mysticism. Pestalozzi's speculations go even further when he suggests that the very page layout of the original edition of *Törleß* is indebted to Maeterlinck: punctuation and blank spaces are employed, he proposes, to create a sense of the inexpressible, a juxtaposition of language and silence that is crucial to Maeterlinck and that Musil emulates in this novel. It should be noted that most of the features which Pestalozzi singles out are elements common to turn-of-the-century mentality; the images and ideas were part of the discourse of the time. Thus Pestalozzi's implicit thesis that Musil derived them from a single source such as Maeterlinck is less than completely convincing.

In a short essay of 1990, Robert von Dassanowsky-Harris discusses the novel's philosophical and sociopolitical aspects in the context of the Austrian tradition of empiriocriticism. He contends that Musil undertook to point to the politically dangerous implications of Ernst Mach's notion of the dissolution of a stable subject. Törleß, in this reading, is a person whose identity is as yet not fully established — what the author, somewhat unfortunately, calls a Machian *Nicht-Ich*. Törleß's epistemological and moral detachment from the mechanisms of violence that surround him anticipates the political apathy of the "masses" in the Habsburg Empire weaned on Ernst Mach's "*Impressionist philosophy* of Monism" (22; emphasis in the original), since the notion of a substanceless self (Mach's *Unrettbares Ich*) can be taken to imply an absolution from individual moral responsibility. Musil's novel, the author proposes, shows the protagonist emerging out of the moral quagmire with a realization that Mach's theories lead to passivity and appeasement in the political world. Unlike Jan Aler (1971), Gerd Müller (1971), and Yvon Desportes (1974), von Dassanowsky-Harris views Musil's novel not primarily as a philosophical critique of Mach but as a moral one. Thus the author confronts essentially the same issues as David Turner does (1974), yet he reaches diametrically opposed conclusions by assuming a firm moral stance in Musil where his predecessor had seen nothing but moral equivocation. Von Dassanowsky-Harris also shares with Turner some methodological problems, compounded here by the very brevity of the essay, which leads him to make the occasional shortcut and oversimplification.

Renate Schröder-Werle (1991), in her useful overview of some of the main interpretations that *Törleß* has so far elicited, attempts to avoid the kind of narrow focus that characterizes the approaches of Pestalozzi and von Dassanowsky-Harris. She acknowledges that there is no single interpretation that addresses the entire text in all its complexity. At the same time, however, she implicitly sets out to define the limits of methodologically legitimate approaches. At the core of her argument is her belief that Musil tries to develop in *Törleß* a comprehensive philosophy of the world (196). That Musil anchored his project in the context of the identity crisis of a young person has led critics, Schröder-Werle argues, to misunderstand the novel as primarily of sociological or psychological interest. She rejects both sociopolitical and psychological interpretations, since they unduly narrow the focus: the one to the genesis of fascist oppression, the other to the analysis of adolescence. Likewise, philosophical approaches tend to reduce the novel to its epistemological aspects. Schröder-Werle clearly favors an approach that aims to reconstruct the author's conscious intentions, maintaining that Musil himself is his own most competent reader (193). She thus has no sympathy for critics who examine the unconscious aspects potentially contained in the novel. Her effort to establish a master interpretation sanctioned by recourse to the author's pronouncements is problematic, as becomes evident in her polemical charge that Hans-Georg Pott's (1984) reading amounts to a "conflagration of misunderstandings" (223). Her ostensibly descriptive approach to literature, developed out of a sense of exasperation with what she regards as a growing "conceptual anarchy" in Musil criticism (192), thus reveals a potentially dogmatic normative dimension.

It is ironic that her article was published alongside a reading, in the same volume, that might be classified by Schröder-Werle as an example of the kind of conceptual anarchy she rejects: Andrew Webber's essay in many ways complements the Lacanian reading of the *Vereinigungen* narratives undertaken by Peter Henninger in 1980. Webber focuses on the recurring motif of beholding and being beheld, a motif linked with the Romantic traditions of the veiled mystery and the Doppelgänger figure. These traditions, associated with Freud's concept of the *Urszene* (primal scene), link the eye with the phallic order, where the phallus functions as a symbol of both the desired object and its inaccessibility; the male hero's "visual compulsion" and his quest for identity are interpreted as the impossible desire to merge with the other. Törleß's mother (veiled at the beginning of the book) becomes the object of Törleß's oblique gaze at the end of the novel, suggesting that this compulsion is linked with a desire to return to the mother's womb. Webber's reading is stimulating in its attention to details whose implications sometimes escape attention. However, Webber's emphasis on a latent psychic economy allegedly encapsulated in the text potentially erases the difference between the author and his protagonist.

This latent psychic economy is the subject of Stanley Corngold's essay of 1992. Corngold poses a question that is as original as it is simple: why is it that readers generally respond to Musil's text with a great deal of respect for the thematic substance when it contains material that, encountered in a different context, is potentially offensive in moral terms? Corngold seeks the answer in an examination of the novel's defensive narrative strategies, which serve to undermine the reader's elaborate defense mechanisms against disturbing subject matter and are designed to win him or her over. Corngold's reading, intelligent and inspiring, in a way brings Musil criticism full circle, addressing the nexus between ethical and aesthetic aspects, the very questions that Musil's contemporaries found either fascinating or morally objectionable.

6: *Vereinigungen*

THE TWO SHORT NARRATIVES that make up Musil's second book, the slim volume *Vereinigungen* (1911), were long neglected by Musil criticism. For decades, many critics shied away from texts reputed to place inordinate burdens on the reader. In 1974 Dorrit Cohn called the *Vereinigungen* novellas "two of the world's most unreadable stories" (154). Cohn's statement — made not without a sense of ironic sympathy for Musil and his artistic cause — apparently met wholehearted endorsement by the majority of Musil scholars. This does not mean, however, that the two stories were entirely overlooked. There is, for instance, Inge Jens's effort in her 1954 Tübingen dissertation to assign these novellas a position within the development of expressionistic prose. However, it was not until the early 1960s that Musil scholars seriously began to address these texts. Burton Pike's reappraisal of *Vereinigungen* as "one of the most interesting experiments in modern fiction" (1961, 70) marks a clear turning point.

The focus of most early interpretations is largely on psychological themes: to Pike, the novellas are part of Musil's lifelong investigation into the nature of love. The two texts form a unity, presenting complementing attitudes about love. One of them Pike calls "yea-saying" (in "Die Vollendung der Liebe"), the other "nay-saying" (in "Die Versuchung der stillen Veronika"). In their focus on the inner world of psychologically unstable female characters, the two novellas, Pike argues, anticipate Musil's depiction of problematic femininity in *Der Mann ohne Eigenschaften*, especially the nymphomania of Bonadea and the schizophrenia of Clarisse. Pike also introduces a term that was to dominate the discussion of *Vereinigungen* for a long time when he compares Musil's novellas with "clinical case studies" (58).

Hans Geulen (1965) echoes Pike's criteria when he approaches "Die Versuchung der stillen Veronika" as a psychological case study. Geulen identifies a series of structural segments of the text that correspond to phases of the inner development of the female protagonist. Despite his sympathy for Musil's interest in experimental writing, Geulen raises questions about the artistic success of the experiment. To him, Musil's attempt at "exclusively representing abnormal emotions" (186) in effect undermines the status of the story as a work of literary art. Geulen seems to have in mind the bizarre association suggested in Musil's text between Veronika's spiritual aspirations and her quasi-sodomitic sexual fantasies. It is clear that moralistic objections, not unlike those raised by critics with regard to *Törleß*, come into play in interpretations of Musil's early novellas.

In sharp contrast, Gerhart Baumann (1965) leaves aside any consideration of the potentially disturbing psychosexual content of Musil's short narratives. He is among the first to shift the focus away from individual psychology toward an attempt to define Musil's narrative style. In "Die Vollendung der Liebe," with its nonlinear presentation of accumulated images, he detects a "spatialization of time" comparable to Paul Valéry's notion of *chronolyse*. The story thus has to be seen in the context of a general tendency toward mysticism around 1900. While Baumann's reflections contain many valuable observations, his essayistic approach does not allow him to focus on specifics.

Jürgen Schröder's seminal 1966 essay on *Vereinigungen*, on the other hand, does display a willingness to address specific aspects. Instead of merely reiterating the complaint frequently voiced by critics that Musil's short narratives are opaque and inaccessible, Schröder investigates what makes these texts so difficult for the reader. He takes issue with the notion that difficulty makes the texts artistic failures, proposing that Musil was fully aware of the degree of irritation his stories would create in the reader and that this irritation was precisely what the author aimed for. In a series of detailed analyses of particular aspects, he shows how Musil pushes poetic language to the limits of expression. Musil does not subsume human experience under the familiar headings of psychology or philosophy. Instead, his language hovers between "precision and indeterminacy" (reprint 1982, 383). Musil's language is based upon quasi-mathematical principles: his excessive similes, metaphors, and comparisons are like mathematical equations that are left for the reader to resolve. The narratives, Schröder suggests, call for a new way of reading that is attentive both to detail and to overall structure, an "art of reading microscopically and synoptically at the same time" (393).

Schröder offers one of the most comprehensive analyses of Musil's language, supplemented by statistical information on the frequency with which certain stylistic figures and tropes occur in these novellas. He bases his discussion on a series of close readings of specific instances in the works, describing how the texts resist traditional attempts to evaluate such aspects as character development, plot, and the exposition of a theme. In many ways, Schröder thus lays the groundwork for later interpretations that would explore the peculiar mixture of fascination and repulsion created by the two novellas. The criteria he developed here helped Musil criticism out of a double impasse: Schröder exposed the largely unacknowledged normative notions of much literary criticism regarding what makes a story artistically successful; and he questioned the essentially moralistic bias that underlies ideas about what kind of subject matter is admissible in a literary work of art. Shifting the focus to the reading experience envisaged by Musil opened up valuable new avenues of interpretation. Schröder's essay remains one of the most insightful analyses of *Vereinigungen* as well as one of the most significant contributions to Musil scholarship as a whole.

In her 1968 Bochum dissertation (published as a book in 1973), Brigitte Röttger examines the experimental writing style of both *Vereinigungen* novellas. Her introduction contains a useful critical assessment of the scholarly reception of Musil's early writings. Röttger takes issue with Schröder's reading of the opening of "Die Vollendung der Liebe" as a quasi-ideal scene, instead stressing the elements of tension, artificiality, and entrapment suggested by the images Musil employs. Musil's writing is characterized by a shift from a linear, chronological presentation of narrative elements toward a nonlinear, associative logic. The two novellas feature, on the formal as well as the thematic level, a "Grundfigur des Kreisens, der Einkreisung," a narrative technique of encircling something that eschews clear articulation (89). Both texts are characterized by essentially cumulative methods. The female protagonists undergo climactic experiences that Röttger describes as experiences of "spatial inversion" (125). Renate von Heydebrand (1966, 96) had already related these phenomena to experiments in the psychology of perception of Gestalt theorist Erich Moritz von Hornbostel, with which Musil was familiar.

In 1969 Karl Corino completed his Tübingen dissertation on the genesis of Musil's *Vereinigungen*. The prime value of this expansive study, comprising over 460 pages when it was published in book form in 1974, lies in the author's detailed account of the complex transformations the novellas underwent during the two and a half years it took Musil to give them their final shape. Corino sees in the evolution of the various versions of the texts an effort on Musil's part to downplay the overpowering impact of psychoanalysis on his outlook on life and to camouflage the validity of Freud's ideas with regard to his own psychosexual situation. What sets *Vereinigungen* apart from the novella tradition, Corino argues, is that here metaphoric imagery become the primary constitutive element of writing rather than a functional device (413). All the same, in Corino's opinion, the two *Vereinigungen* novellas are little more than documents of Musil's "desperate defensive battle against psychoanalysis" (242).

The problems associated with Corino's approach are obvious: for one thing, he uncritically accepts as axiomatic Freudian ideas that are to this day hotly contested in the field of psychology; moreover, he presents psychoanalytic theory as a monolithic entity, ignoring both the development of Freud's own thinking and the modifications debated by the different psychoanalytic schools during Freud's lifetime and after his death. All the same, unlike more essayistic interpreters of Musil's writings, Corino proceeds from a clearly delineated methodological vantage point. With its abundance of details on the background and the evolution of the two stories, Corino's study provides an invaluable source of information that no serious student of Musil's *Vereinigungen* can afford to ignore.

Drawing upon concepts developed in structuralist narrative theory, Dorrit Cohn (1971 and 1974) places "Die Vollendung der Liebe" in the context of the manifold ways in which modern authors tried to render mental processes in prose fiction. Musil's approach to mental phenomena differs from the interior or narrated monologues favored by other modern masters like James Joyce or Arthur Schnitzler in that Musil does not attempt to present us with the inner discourse of a fictional character. While he essentially maintains a third-person narrative situation, his unidentified narrator allows the reader access to strata of Claudine's mental activity that escape the character herself. Musil's focus is on a layer of the psyche which "bypasses not only self-articulation, but also self-consciousness and self-understanding" of the female protagonist (1971, 292). The text features a preponderance of images and other poetic devices that only rarely can be identified as having their origin in Claudine's mind. Musil's use of such images creates a "fusion between the narrating and the figurative consciousness by blurring the line that separates them" (1971, 294). Cohn suggests the term *psycho-analogies* as a designation for this narrative technique, which lends a largely static and atemporal quality to Musil's prose. In the 1974 article she explores in greater depth the significance of spatial metaphors in Musil's depiction of the states of an individual psyche. The mythical qualities of the text do not reside in the thematic subject matter but are brought about through the narrative form: "Where Musil's contemporaries, and Musil himself in his later works, used myth, magic, dream, lyrical statement, philosophical dialogue, or ideational superstructures to convey the problematic of the human condition, the author of 'Die Vollendung' was bent on diagramming it in the depth of a single consciousness" (1974, 168). Cohn's analysis of narrative form does more to elucidate Musil's singular achievement than most traditional efforts in Musil scholarship to understand the novella and its central character in psychological or thematic terms. Rosmarie Zeller (1981a) provides a structural analysis of "Die Versuchung der stillen Veronika" that complements Cohn's reading of "Die Vollendung der Liebe" while explicitly rejecting any effort at a directly psychological interpretation.

Lisa Appignanesi (1973a) approaches *Vereinigungen* in the context of a general investigation of the depiction of femininity in modern prose. Musil's stories enter the debate about the nature of femininity that was initiated in the nineteenth century by Johann Jakob Bachofen and was picked up in highly divergent ways in turn-of-the-century Vienna by thinkers as diverse as Sigmund Freud, Otto Weininger, and Ludwig Klages. In marked opposition to the predominantly negative myths about the feminine propagated by these authors, Musil's two novellas, in their focus on the problematic psychological and erotic identity of their female protagonists, depict "femininity in search of itself" (15).

Claudine, for instance, undergoes a journey toward a realization of her femininity, her bodily and spiritual identity, which Appignanesi describes in terms of Bachofen's notion of *hetaerism* (23). Her bodily desires cannot be subsumed under the masculine rule of order. In sharp contrast to the moralistic objections frequently raised against the two novellas, Appignanesi stresses the positive and liberating aspects of the texts. In her interpretation, "Die Vollendung der Liebe" turns into an almost therapeutic text. It would appear that she fully endorses the cathartic effect of the presentation of a female protagonist who "must relive her experience as a woman and be reborn into a fuller being" (20). While one should welcome a reading that addresses Musil's novellas from a decidedly feminine perspective, Appignanesi's method poses profound problems. For one thing, her interpretive quest for the "mythological and primeval depths of femininity" (19) displays oddly mystical tendencies. Moreover, her thinking involves a somewhat crude juxtaposition of allegedly universal male and female principles, viewed as a largely static and timeless opposition without any social, historical, or political specificity. Likewise, it is not clear what would make Bachofen's concept of the "hetaerean core" of femininity a category of unquestioned validity. In retrospect, Appignanesi appears as a representative of an early, emphatic phase of feminism, characterized by an attempt to claim parts of the literary canon for its own objectives. All the same, she was among the first to insist that issues of gender are of crucial importance in Musil's work, a point that to this day is widely neglected in Musil scholarship.

As late as 1974 Jürgen C. Thöming could polemically label the history of the reception of these works a "history of a lack of impact" (304). Since the publication of Thöming's stimulating and provocative theses there has been a remarkable resurgence of interest in the novellas among Musil scholars, owing partly to Corino's exhaustive volume of the same year on the background and origin of the texts. During the late 1970s a wide range of perspectives began to be developed. Perhaps the most traditionally psychological, but by no means unsympathetic, contribution is Wilhelm Braun's 1976/77 analysis of the water imagery in "Die Vollendung der Liebe." Braun shows how imagery associated with water permeates Musil's entire narrative on a multitude of levels. He views the story essentially as the psychological profile of a schizoid person (29) and believes the water imagery is ideally suited to convey the complex shifts in Claudine's subjective experience in its wide variety of manifestations (motion, stillness, turbulence, peace).

In contrast to Braun's empathetic reading, Dietrich Krusche (1978) focuses not so much on character psychology as on modes of interpersonal communication. Krusche derives his concepts partly from models developed by American theorists of communication psychology like Gregory Bateson and Paul Watzlawick, whose ideas became very popular in Germanistik in the German-speaking countries in the 1970s. While critics in their emphasis on individual character psychology or on Musil's narrative style had repeatedly stressed the difficulty of the *Vereinigungen* novellas, Krusche maintains that they feature patterns of interaction that can be identified quite easily. The stories, he observes, initially raise the question of whether there can be an intersubjective experience of love. In a subsequent shift to a literary representation of a single subjectivity (that of the respective female protagonists), they explore the general problem of identity formation (321). Both women are ambivalent toward the tension between the "spiritual" and the "animal" aspects of love (a relationship with a specific individual as opposed to participation in the universal, deindividualized rituals of mating). It is precisely the absence of any real interaction with the loved partner that allows the women to reconcile the two aspects in a subjective experience of union, the title concept of *Vereinigung*. Although Krusche criticizes psychological or stylistic interpretation as inadequate, he paradoxically arrives at a thematic interpretation not very different from the ones he rejects, namely an explication or description of the issues he assumes Musil wanted to convey to the reader.

The problem of an author's conscious intention receives a radical twist in what is perhaps the most significant contribution to a reassessment of the *Vereinigungen* novellas: Peter Henninger's provocative 1980 volume on the texts, the first — with Dieter Heyd's monograph on *Der Mann ohne Eigenschaften* — major attempt to bring ideas derived from Lacanian psychoanalysis to Musil studies. Henninger takes the extreme difficulties Musil experienced while he was writing the novellas as an indication that the author was dealing here with material of crucial personal importance. What interests Henninger in his psychoanalytical method of criticism is "the role played by the Unconscious in the genesis of texts" (20). This leads him to focus on what the stories conceal rather than what they ostensibly aim to convey.

I have discussed earlier the innovative dimension of Henninger's project and its significance for Musil studies in general. In the present context it suffices to point out several specific aspects in Henninger's work that help elucidate Musil's *Vereinigungen* novellas. Karl Corino (1974) had already suggested parallels between "Die Versuchung der stillen Veronika" and ideas put forward by Josef Breuer and Sigmund Freud in their *Studies on Hysteria* (1895). It is documented that Musil read the book before 1913. In detecting surprising verbal traces of Breuer and Freud's work in Musil's story, Henninger challenges the dating of Musil's exposure to Freudian thought and proposes a direct influence as early as 1910. His discussion of the psychosexual implications of Musil's attempts to solve structural and stylistic problems posed by the story is also highly interesting, especially with regard to the permutations of the preparatory "Vorspruch" that opens the text. In his readings, Henninger implies that at the core of Musil's writings lies the author's problem of coming to terms with his male identity: his empathy with the sexual experience of a woman in "Die Vollendung der Liebe" signals his desire to accept the feminine aspects of his identity that go against socially acceptable notions of masculinity. However, the efforts at opening oneself up to the Other are subject to strict societal control that permeates the male psyche. On one level, both *Vereinigungen* novellas, with their focus on the female experience of sexual desire, turn into manifestations of Musil's unconscious attempt to come to terms with his own ambivalent sexual desires and fears. For a less author-centered reading of the same aspect see Joseph Strelka (1983a), who views the *Vereinigungen* narratives primarily as literary stylizations of Martha Musil's experiences, complementing the earlier autobiographical focus of *Törleß*. Moreover, Henninger detects another basic structure in Musil's texts in which an excluded third party frequently is found overhearing and witnessing the eroticized interactions of two others. This feature evokes Freud's theory of the significance of the primal scene in the sexual fantasies of the child. Henninger relates this and other phenomena to a complex set of aspects in Musil's biography. There is, for instance, the Oedipal constellation complicated in the Musil household by the presence of two father figures, one weak (Musil's father, Alfred), one strong (Heinrich Reiter, the friend of Musil's mother, Hermine, who lived in the Musil household for extended periods of time). On this level, the two *Vereinigungen* novellas reflect Musil's unconscious preoccupation with his own coming into being, the question of the identity of his father and the sexual nature of his parents. Henninger's work was later complemented by that of Andrea Köhler, Christine Adam, Horst Hamm, and Joachim Pfeiffer in a collective essay on "Die Versuchung der stillen Veronika" (1985). Adopting a more orthodox Freudian position, they examine and compare the various versions of the story, noting that in his revisions Musil aimed at camouflaging overtly sexual aspects. To them, Veronika — a woman caught, like Musil's mother, between two men — represents Musil's effort to address his pre-Oedipal mother fixation in a narcissistically regressive identification fantasy.

In two articles published in 1980, the same year as Henninger's speculative study, Michiko Mae gives an outline of Musil's concept of the nature and function of the novella genre. She contradicts the notion, suggested by Renate Rieth (1964), that Musil was unaware of the rich history of efforts to define the genre. Musil, Mae shows, attempted to use the aesthetic potential inherent in the novella genre to achieve a series of specific effects on his intended audience, among them subliminally suggestive effects, empathetic understanding, and an experience of existential reorientation (1980a, 36). Mae concurs with Corino that the *Vereinigungen* novellas are based on a new aesthetic principle, that of employing images as the main constitutive elements — an insight, she rightly points out (38), anticipated by Béla Balázs in his

1923 essay on Musil. Unlike Corino, however, Mae refrains from attempting to speculate on the psychological reasons for Musil's rejection of academic psychology, focusing instead on purely aesthetic motivations.

An early version of what was to become "Die Versuchung der stillen Veronika" was published in 1908 under the title "Das verzauberte Haus" (The Enchanted House) in Franz Blei's journal *Hyperion*. In a detailed comparison, Dietmar Goltschnigg (1981) combines aesthetic and psychological considerations in his discussion of the transformation of the early text into the final version. Musil's focus, Goltschnigg argues, was to explore the question of a union of sexual and spiritual love. The changes in narrative perspective and in a wide variety of details show that Musil intended the ultimate version to mirror the logic of dreams (47). In a polemical aside, Goltschnigg takes issue with Corino's implicit interpretation of "Die Versuchung der stillen Veronika" as the "simple pathography of a hysteric" (45). Instead, he proposes, the novella highlights the psychotherapeutic effect of the fantasies the female protagonist experiences. Goltschnigg stresses that the novella's latent significance lies in the analogous therapeutic effect it may have on author and reader alike.

Like Goltschnigg, Jacqueline Magnou (1982 and 1984) sharply distinguished between psychology and psychopathology. Musil, she maintains, is less concerned with the workings of the psyche in interesting "special cases" than with the incommensurable aspects of psychic life in general as they manifest themselves in the marginal or pathological. Magnou shows that Musil was familiar with the theories on altered personalities set forth by A. Binet, whose study *Les Altérations de la Personnalité* (1892) features a negative definition of personal identity that anticipates Musil's preoccupation with an undefinable core. Like Binet, Musil saw a close affinity between mysticism and pathology, and this helped him steer clear of flat psychological realism in his writing. Instead of merely depicting psychopathological issues, Musil employs "the very mode in which insanity itself operates" (111). In Magnou's view, the two *Vereinigungen* novellas suggest that the experiences of the female protagonists, which in traditional terms border on the insane, have a logic and a validity of their own. In this fashion, Magnou argues, Musil anticipates the radical ideas of modern "anti-psychiatry" (R. D. Laing) and of thinkers like Michel Foucault, who challenge conventional notions of normalcy. Musil shows that in a deformed social organization the formation of a so-called normal personal identity is an impossibility. In this context, Magnou subtly hints at a political dimension of Musil's novellas: the protagonists' desire to forfeit their restrictive identities can be viewed as a subversive gesture of protest aimed at a politically and psychologically repressive social order.

We can see that a profound shift has taken place in Musil scholarship in the assessment of *Vereinigungen*: the supposed abnormality of its characters, which had frequently provoked moralistic objections, is now no longer seen as a personal preoccupation of Musil. Instead, the psychopathological aspects of Musil's texts appear as symptoms of larger issues, as indicators of the pathology of a profoundly problematic civilization. What early critics rejected as bizarre and deviant or attempted to explain away in philosophical or metaphysical terms, a new generation of Musil scholars embraces as inspiring and illuminating aspects of Musil's work.

Roger Willemsen's 1983 essay on "Die Vollendung der Liebe" displays this reorientation most clearly. Willemsen focuses on the identity of G., the fictional character who is the topic of the conversation between Claudine and her husband at the beginning of the novella. Willemsen identifies him as Gilles de Rais, the mass murderer eulogized in Joris-Karl Huysmans's *Là Bas* (1884) and featured in Franz Blei's *Prinz Hippolyte und andere Essays* (Prince Hippolyte and Other Essays) of 1903. Willemsen tries to show a close correspondence between G. (or Gilles) and Claudine; her interpretation of G. at the beginning of the text forms a distinct thematic substratum that sets the stage for her subsequent infidelity. Claudine replaces the fixed norms of social morality with a functional ethics in which each variable is subject to contextual variations, an operation that makes possible the breach with what is socially acceptable. This breach, Willemsen argues, takes place not only on the level of the redefinition of erotic emotions (infidelity as the perfection of love) but also on that of the female protagonist's latent propensity for criminality, as suggested by her sympathy for the notorious erotic villain. In Claudine's mind Gilles's crimes betoken a "passionate quest for knowledge" (35). His acts of violence and Claudine's adultery represent transgressions that can be viewed as attempts to break out of the constraints of socially determined identities in a quest for a new identity. This quest turns both into "exceptional human beings," a necessary intermediate stage, Willemsen maintains, in the Nietzschean evolutionary development "from normal to new human being" (46).

Apparently independently of Willemsen, Dietmar Goltschnigg (1986) offered a similar derivation of the character of G. as Gilles de Rais in "Die Vollendung der Liebe." Like Willemsen, Goltschnigg stresses Musil's fascination with criminality as a manifestation of what is socially marginal and psychologically problematical, the most significant illustration being the figure of Moosbrugger in *Der Mann ohne Eigenschaften*. Unlike Willemsen, however, Goltschnigg sees a reorientation on Musil's part away from the essentially decadent decisionist morality in the early narrative toward an acutely responsible social ethics in the later novel.

Willemsen's reading is highly speculative and runs the risk of uncritically glorifying the medieval mass murderer Gilles de Rais beyond the treatment of this historical figure in Huysmans and Franz Blei and of the fictional G. in Musil's novella. Mae (1988) has taken issue with the manner in which

Willemsen glosses over the disturbing aspects of the historical Gilles, whose actions apparently were characterized by extreme brutality. In Gilles's reported sexual abuse and ritual murder of innocent children Mae finds little that would warrant a quasi-philosophical reading of his acts as expressions of a metaphysical quest that provokes Claudine's sympathetic identification.

Catherine Wilson (1984) aims to address what she regards as the moral and philosophical paradox at the center of "Die Vollendung der Liebe," namely that an instance of marital infidelity is presented as the alleged intensification of love between Claudine and her husband. Wilson seeks the solution to the "evident inscrutability" (222) of Musil's story in the problem of human volition that has haunted Western philosophy since Descartes. In Claudine, she contends, Musil illustrates the unresolved contradiction between *willing* (implying a subject essentially in control of its actions) and *wanting* (implying a subject controlled by appetites and desires) that lies at the center of the Cartesian tradition (227). Wilson concedes that the story may be designed to induce the reader to abandon preconceived notions of morality in favor of an openness to the inner logic of emotional and mental states. Yet she finds it difficult to question her own preconceptions on love and the manner in which they may be determined by social codifications (an issue ably addressed by Thomas Pekar, 1989). Through the absence of such methodological reflection Wilson's ostensibly detached philosophical essay acquires an oddly moralistic personal tone.

Wilson's moral scruples vis-à-vis Musil stand in sharp contrast to the enthusiastic appropriation of Musil's alleged anarchic subversiveness by young critics such as Roger Willemsen. His tendency to speculate on Musil's texts from a perspective informed by poststructuralist ideas is radicalized in Kai Allais's 1987 reading of "Die Versuchung der stillen Veronika." Allais views the novella as Musil's "most modern and most radical work" (79), because it dismantles textual meaning altogether. Traditional literary hermeneutics, Allais argues, is compelled to presuppose in a literary work an essential unity that is to be uncovered in the process of interpretation. Allais attempts to show how Musil's novella resists the reconstruction of a unified meaning that refers to something outside of the text. For this purpose, he traces a number of related repetitive clusters (such as the motif of concealment) throughout Musil's text, which intersect and create a friction instead of fashioning a single unified narrative: the "serial" principle of Musil's writing creates an infinite number of possible narratives. In semiological terms, Allais proposes, this produces a "disturbance" which enters between the "message" and the "decoding" of the text; he calls such disturbance "noise" (91). This "noise," he proposes, makes it impossible to determine a center or essence as the object of the interpretive enterprise. Fascinating as this interpretation of the self-deconstructing qualities of Musil's literary experiment may be, Allais's reading is prone to severe methodological problems: for instance, he traces the series associated with the motif of the "Glocke" (bell) and that of the "Tier" (animal) to their intersection in the image of the "Glockentierchen" in Musil's novella. In a footnote, he acknowledges that, when he gave an earlier version of his essay as a paper, members of his audience pointed out that this is a little-known term for a real maritime animal (94). All the same, Allais goes on to interpret the Glockentierchen as a nonexistent creature that has no referent in empirical reality, arguing that Musil's novella displays a "fundamental absence of a referent" (89). Such assertions, made here in benign disregard of information to the contrary, would seem to confirm charges frequently leveled against the deconstructive approach: the combination of Heideggerian etymological speculation with a Derridean fascination with the contradictions inherent in the act of writing runs the risk of postmodern arbitrariness. It would appear that any given text can be made to say whatever the critic wants it to say, regardless of its specific nature or structure. Allais is certainly focusing on an important aspect of Musil's writing. However, he discredits his own method and undermines his own enterprise of criticizing the unacknowledged presuppositions underlying hermeneutics when he bends his material to fit his own preconceived notions.

To be sure, Allais only reenacts in a rather blatant way what we can find in a great deal of Musil criticism from the very beginning, a tendency on the part of critics to appropriate Musil's works for their own purposes. While the Musil scholars of the first generation (in the 1950s and 1960s) had, for moral and aesthetic reasons, great difficulties accepting the *Vereinigungen* novellas, from the 1970s onward new generations of critics clearly found some of their own existential concerns articulated in Musil's challenging novellas.

Every now and then, amid the clamor of idiosyncratic personal appropriations of Musil's works, a reading emerges that displays intellectual skill while maintaining the necessary critical distance to its subject. One such contribution is Lorna Martens's perceptive 1987 essay on "Die Versuchung der stillen Veronika," in which she discusses in detail the possible connections between Musil's text and Breuer and Freud's *Studies on Hysteria*, proposed earlier by Corino (1974) and Henninger (1980). Her examination of the various drafts of the story leads her to assume that Musil was familiar with the psychoanalytic theory of hysteria even earlier than those two critics had assumed, as early as 1906 or 1908. Martens argues that Musil borrowed from Breuer and Freud the notion of repressed traumatic memory to enrich his original idea, expanding the theme in each successive version of his story (103). Yet Musil, Martens cautions us, did not wholeheartedly accept the theory of etiology of psychic illness underlying early psychoanalytic theory. Martens shows how Breuer and Freud's theory is essentially monistic: in their model, a state of psychic health is interrupted by an outside force that lodges itself in memory as traumatic shock; a recollection of the affect accompanying the troublesome impact, Breuer and Freud assert, can release the traumatic emotion, purging memory and restoring psychic health. Martens convincingly argues that Musil opposes such a straightforward tripartite model of wholeness–disturbance–wholeness restored. Instead, she notes, he assumes that the psyche is subject to conflicting tendencies at any time, be it in a healthy or afflicted state: psychic illness is thus not primarily the product of a pathogenic impulse from outside but rather a particular manifestation of the configurations of conflicting desires that are always present. This aspect runs parallel to the later development of Freud, who embraced a conflict-centered model of the psyche after his break with Breuer. Yet Musil remains skeptical toward the therapeutic claims of psychoanalysis. As Martens writes, Musil "is willing to posit a traumatic experience as the *origin* of psychic conflict, but is not willing to grant that the expulsion of the memory means the conflict's end" (112; her emphasis). In the case of Veronika, in whose psyche the rejection of Johannes's sexual advances are linked with the memory of a confrontation with animal sexuality in an encounter with a dog, the psychic constellation precludes the kind of healing through recollection that is the object of psychoanalysis as therapy. In contradistinction to Freud, Martens shows, Musil asserts in his story that psychic conflicts remain present even after they have been released from repression and into consciousness. Despite her repeated epiphanic ecstatic experiences, Musil's female protagonist is not cured but relapses into her former psychic condition.

Another important contribution that shuns facile appropriation is Maximilian Aue's discussion of "Die Vollendung der Liebe" (1987/88). Aue draws on a seminal article by Walter H. Sokel (1984) that defines Musil's writing style as a response to the aesthetic postulates of naturalism. On the one hand, Aue notes, Musil rejects the mimetic impulse of naturalism with its interest in a depiction of empirical external reality. On the other hand, he remains indebted to the naturalistic ideal of scientific accuracy: for instance, Musil's observation of minuscule gradations of emotional states displays affinities to the naturalistic *Sekundenstil*, the attempt to conflate narrated and narrating time (37). Musil, Aue shows (following Sokel), transfers mimesis onto the sphere of the human psyche. This shift of focus from a representation of the external world to an exploration of an internal reality — constituting both a logical extension and a reversal of the naturalistic enterprise — has profound aesthetic implications. By radicalizing the postulates of naturalism, Musil paradoxically achieves not only a narrative style diametrically opposed to naturalism but also a dissolution of traditional narrative methods altogether. Kathleen O'Connor was later to explore the poetological implications of Sokel's and Aue's ideas in greater detail in her study of Musil's stories in the context of the novella genre (1992).

The most impressive indication of the extraordinary fascination the *Vereinigungen* novellas have had upon a young generation of Musil scholars is Michiko Mae's 1988 monograph *Motivation und Liebe*. More that five hundred pages long, the book is by far the most comprehensive attempt to date to analyze in detail the peculiar nature of Musil's two novellas. Mae's key concept is that of the aesthetic experience Musil aimed for in his readers. His poetics, Mae argues, postulates a dialogical relationship between text and reader. Mae's treatment of Musil's stories draws on an extraordinary range of theoretical reflections on the nature of love and the problem of motivation. Motivation, the multidimensional logic of the *Vereinigungen* narratives, is intended to induce the reader to engage in the process of dissolving petrified psychological, moral, and philosophical concepts. According to Mae, for instance, the movement toward opening up that Claudine experiences in "Die Vollendung der Liebe" ideally runs parallel to a similar process of reorientation in the reader. In attempting to provide the basis for a near mystical participation of the reader in the literary work, Musil aims for *Liebe*, love as a holistic human experience that transcends the fragmentation of alienated modern individuals. Mae concedes that this project has failed with the majority of readers, who instead feel excluded from Musil's fictional world, which they perceive to be hermetically closed (75).

Mae's monograph displays her uncommon willingness to analyze Musil's texts on their own terms. This does not mean that she uncritically accepts Musil's ideas. For instance, she takes issue with his tendency to restrict his female characters to the sphere of the erotic. Mae views this as a severe limitation, rejecting Appignanesi's positive evaluation of Musil's insights into the allegedly hetaerean nature of femininity. In her analysis, as her previously discussed polemic against Willemsen shows, Mae takes seriously the interplay between Musil's aesthetic and ethical concerns. For Musil, she insists, these concerns always have to do with a concrete moral and material reality outside the fictional world of literature.

In 1990 Hartmut Böhme accompanied an edition of *Vereinigungen* with a reflective essay that ranks among the most thoughtful and most sensitive treatments of Musil's two novellas. Like Henninger (1980), Böhme takes as his starting point the extraordinary difficulties the two novellas posed for Musil. The biographical and psychological dimension of the stories (as depictions of Musil's encounter with Martha in her Otherness) correlate with the poetological and epistemological aspects: Musil sets out to explore the limits of what is sayable and what is knowable. As a result, the stories acquire an esoterically hermetic quality. Böhme examines the spatial metaphors in "Die Vollendung der Liebe" and concludes that the story establishes an experimental space for the examination of a process that leads Claudine, the reader, and the author from one condition to its opposite. Underlying the story, Böhme suggests, is a desire for mythical unity reminiscent of the notion, familiar from Plato's *Symposion*, of an androgynous wholeness predating the differentiation into two genders. In Böhme's reading, "Die Versuchung der stillen Veronika" replaces ancient myth with Christian mythography, such as the motif of a temptation and the legend of St. Veronica. Musil's aim here is to achieve a congruence of poetic language with the experience of femininity; like St. Veronica, who captured an imprint of the face of Jesus on her cloth, Musil aims to capture in language something that can be represented only through its absence. Böhme stresses the etymology of the heroine's name as *vera ikon*, signifying the "true image" that is the objective of Musil's literary undertaking. In his literary epistemological experiments, Böhme proposes, Musil accords to his writing a quasi-sacral significance, endeavoring to turn reading into an act of contemplative communion.

Gerhard Meisel, in his study of Musil's prose narratives, *Liebe im Zeitalter der Wissenschaft vom Menschen* (1991), addresses the two novellas from a multitude of angles, laying particular emphasis on the relationship of Musil's writing to psychoanalysis and contemporary science. Some of his views echo Böhme's conclusions. For instance, the description of a bourgeois interior that opens "Die Vollendung der Liebe," with its emphasis on abstract geometric patterns, colors, sounds, and angles, according to Meisel opens up a "semantic space" (29) in which Musil aims to conduct his inquiry into human nature (the "Wissenschaft vom Menschen" of the title of Meisel's book). The story initially appears as a kind of literary analogue to Ernst Mach's empiriocriticism. Yet Musil's incessant use of comparisons, similes, and metaphors creates a "surplus of meaning" that explodes the space designated by positivist science (30). Musil's literary project of "continuing the task of science with different means" (37) involves a kind of existential experiment which Claudine, as it were, conducts with her own body (51). Psychically and physically she experiences the problematic nature of marriage as a contractual relationship. The authenticity of the emotion underlying such a contractually defined union can be measured only against a third party, an element that both defines and undermines the nature of the love between two people. Meisel, following Gilles Deleuze, views masochism as a form of contract that both creates and eliminates a third party. Through her masochistic association with a stranger Claudine achieves the perfection of her love in a simultaneous affirmation and annihilation of the initial (marital) contract through entering into a different contract (49). This leads Meisel to reject the notion, put forward by Mae (1988), among others, that the man with whom Claudine finds herself involved is essentially an arbitrary stranger. Meisel maintains that it is significant that he is a *Ministerialrat*: as someone who holds a high public office he is a prime representative of the codified — male — law that Claudine seeks to transgress. It is only through an involvement with such a representative of law that the symbolic order can be suspended for Claudine.

Meisel's reading of "Die Versuchung der stillen Veronika" is just as innovative and stimulating, again closely paralleling that of Böhme. Meisel relates the name of the title character to the dispute raging at the turn of the century over the authenticity of the Shroud of Turin, the cloth with which St. Veronica supposedly captured an image of the face of Jesus Christ. Like Böhme, although apparently independently of him, Meisel stresses the etymological implications of the name as *vera ikon*, as a true image of a woman's selfhood that goes beyond what can be expressed in language. In Meisel's assessment, other details of the story, such as Veronika's bizarre sexual fantasies, are not symptoms of sodomitic desires but rather point to an identification with nature beyond what Lacan defines as the symbolic orders of culture and language.

Like Allais and Meisel, Anna Burmann (1991/92) draws on Lacanian ideas in her three-part essay on *Vereinigungen*. Yet Burmann does not attempt to "interpret" the two novellas; instead, she focuses on Musil's literary experimentation. She downplays the sexual aspects of the stories, assigning sexual matters a functional role in Musil's aesthetic enterprise that has to do with "bringing-to-language a consciousness that is unlived, because it is interdicted by the language of self-consciousness" (part I, 13). Musil became aware that the "aesthetic desire" that propelled his literary experiment is by definition unfulfillable. In sharp contrast to a wide range of psychoanalytically oriented critics, Burmann asserts that the best assessments of the aesthetic significance of the stories come from Musil himself. His essays and diaries of the period contain valuable insights into the construction of subjectivity through language; such insights, Burmann seems to imply, anticipate and run parallel with ideas developed much later by Jacques Lacan. Burmann clearly favors "Die Versuchung der stillen Veronika" as the more daring of the two novellas and as the one in which Musil's self-professed "abhorrence of narrative" (part III, 8; see also *GW* II, 1315) reaches the highest degree of independence of traditional narrative patterns. Burmann's essay culminates in an almost mystical apotheosis of writing as an activity that opens up space for an expression of that which cannot be expressed in the language accessible to consciousness. Once again, a critic embraces Musil as the purveyor of a personal message, in this case Burmann's own mission as a creative writer.

Compared to Allais, Böhme, Meisel, and Burmann, Sabine Kyora's discussion of the psychoanalytic dimension of "Die Versuchung der stillen Veronika" (1992), also combining Freudian and Lacanian ideas, is less enterprising. Following Lorna Martens (1987), she emphasizes the parallelisms between the story and Breuer and Freud's theories on hysteria. Veronika's near mystical experiences, which prefigure Musil's concern with the "other condition," she contends, display parallels to the notion of a *condition seconde*, the altered state of consciousness characteristic of hysteria as defined by Breuer and Freud. Kyora links her psychoanalytic approach with a comparatist perspective, establishing interesting interconnections between Musil and the tradition of French surrealism as defined by Walter Benjamin (188). Moreover, she uses Gustave Flaubert's "Temptation de Saint Antoine" as a foil for her reading of Musil's story. In contradistinction to Flaubert's religious mysticism, Kyora writes, the sexual subtext of Veronika's experience of self-transcendence in Musil's story signals "a loss of the metaphysical plain" (174). Kyora sees the innovative aspect of the story primarily in Musil's attempt to assume in his depiction of hysteria the position of the hysterical female subject itself (166). This, in turn, she interprets as a symptom of unconscious conflicts within Musil that find their full manifestation in the incestuous fantasies featured in *Der Mann ohne Eigenschaften*. With Kyora, psychoanalytic interpretation of Musil's texts seems to lead back, though with a different perspective, to the claim introduced by Karl Corino that Musil found himself enmeshed in a net of dependencies upon psychoanalysis that produced symptoms of rivalry and denial.

In marked contrast to the speculation centering on depth psychology that were prominent from the late 1980s onward, Kathleen O'Connor adopts a more traditionally literary approach. In her 1992 monograph, she seeks to define the status of the *Vereinigungen* stories in the context of the history of the German novella. The genre, she notes, features a dual structural opposition, the "tension between objectivity and subjectivity" on the one hand and the "claim to exemplify truth about experience" on the other (56). In his short narratives Musil attempted to render these tensions aesthetically productive. Focusing on the subjectivity of his protagonists, he pushed to their logical limit certain tenets of naturalism concerning the exploration of internal reality. But the extreme introspectiveness of *Vereinigungen* radically departs from the naturalistic preoccupation with external reality, with its emphasis on specific sociohistorical situations. To O'Connor, the two narratives mark Musil's break with mimesis, the depiction of individualized characters according to traditional norms of psychological plausibility. They also represent the first step in a process that would lead Musil toward modes of writing oriented upon mythical models of thinking. Combining impulses mainly from intellectual history and narratological theories, O'Connor's pragmatic and level-headed discussion of the context of Musil's *Vereinigungen* in literary history is a welcome addition to a field littered with psychological speculation, philosophical rhapsodizing, and flowery paraphrase.

The history of the reception of *Vereinigungen* shows a fascinating shift in the assessment of these early Musil stories. To the majority of Germanists trained in traditional forms of literary criticism from the 1950s to the 1970s, the two novellas were a source of provocation and irritation, partly perhaps because they resist facile attempts at subsuming them under any convenient classification. To a subsequent generation of critics weaned on Freudian and other forms of psychoanalysis and on the intricacies of poststructuralist thinking, however, these texts have attained a special status to the point of becoming ideological manifestos. It is interesting to see that psychologically oriented critics seem to favor "Die Vollendung der Liebe," whereas on the whole those with a more philosophical focus prefer "Die Versuchung der stillen Veronika," indicating a clear connection between a critic's aesthetic judgment and his or her underlying world view. Once dismissed as failed literary experiments, Musil's early novellas are now seen as some of his most important contributions to the literature of modernity. The two *Vereinigungen* narratives remain as iridescent and as intriguing as ever.

7: *Die Schwärmer*

EAGER TO ASSIGN ROBERT Musil a permanent position in the literary pantheon on account of *Der Mann ohne Eigenschaften*, scholars in the 1950s and 1960s for the most part paid little attention to his efforts in drama. For a long time, Musil's extraordinary involvement in the genre — spanning over twenty-five years — went unnoticed. Besides the two published plays, Musil drafted several dramatic projects and wrote dozens of theater reviews as well as a series of important theoretical essays on the nature and function of drama.

To most critics, Musil's first play, *Die Schwärmer* (1921), was at best of interest for the manner in which it prefigures thematic issues developed more fully in his grand novel. During the first one and a half decades of scholarly Musil criticism after the war, the few critics that devote attention to Musil's first drama agree that it is a work that may have its merits as a piece of literature but that is not suited for the stage. The play's failure at its disastrous first production in 1929 seemed to prove that Musil's drama was indeed but an unperformable *Lesestück* (reading play; Kaiser and Wilkins 1962, 102). On the whole, Musil scholars were content to dismiss his dramatic writings as negligible and to view Musil as a writer who had quickly come to realize that his approach to writing was not compatible with the demands of the theater.

This attitude prevailed even in the face of efforts on the part of practitioners of theater to rediscover Musil's play. In 1955 director Gustav Rudolf Sellner, generally acknowledged as one of the most important directors in postwar German theater, mounted a production of *Die Schwärmer* at the Staatstheater Darmstadt. Within a few years, small-scale productions at Bremen (1956) and at Vienna (1958) followed (see Schneider 1973, 265). In a review of the Vienna production, Friedrich Torberg (1958) bemoaned the lack of irony in the performance. This failing, he felt, turned the play into "Neo-Gartenlaubismo," a coinage typical of Torberg's inimitable — and untranslatable — panache that alludes to the sentimental family idylls found in the popular German nineteenth century periodical *Die Gartenlaube*.

The Darmstadt production was accompanied by a program booklet that featured essays by Paul Fechter and Karl Otten (1955), who both stressed the innovative aspects of the play. Yet with the exception of a review by Walter Karsch, the production at Darmstadt was greeted with incomprehension on the part of theater critics. Karsch, instead of rejecting the apparent verbosity of the play's dialogues, suggests that Musil's use of dramatic language effects a dissolution of the traditional concept of dramatic character. In Musil's play, Karsch notes, the characters are no longer individuals sketched along lines of psychological realism; they appear no longer as the sources of their utterances but as functions of them (1962, 296). Neither Karsch's observations nor the Darmstadt production had any immediate impact on the community of Musil scholars. However, Karsch's review, tentative as it was, anticipated ideas that were to be developed later in Musil criticism, first by Michael Scharang (1964 and 1965) and more fully by Bianca Cetti Marinoni in a series of essays (1986, 1989, 1990, 1991) and a book (1988/92).

The lamentable lack of response associated with the 1955 production of *Die Schwärmer* at Darmstadt underscores a general dynamic operating in literary criticism, one that is shared by Germanistik as an academic discipline: most twentieth-century critics tend to regard drama as a genre intrinsically less important than the novel. Whereas Hegel could still place drama at the pinnacle of his aesthetic system, modern critics display a lack of patience with an art form ostensibly tainted by its association with the ephemeral and trivial world of the theater. One need only compare the impressive achievements of narrative theory with the rather lackluster efforts of drama criticism, a field that in the German-speaking world was focused for some twenty years on rather rudimentary ideas such as Volker Klotz's venerable distinction between "open" and "closed" forms of drama. It was not until the 1980s that the field gained some fresh intellectual energy from the semiology of theater, in itself a relatively new discipline groping for self-definition. Musil's plays do not fit any of the deceptively neat categories adopted by Germanistik, such as Epic Theater or Theater of the Absurd. Nor could they be easily assimilated into the thematic and aesthetic issues upon which Musil scholars in the 1950s and 1960s chose to focus. It is no surprise, then, that Musil's interest in drama long went neglected even by Musil scholars.

Musil's play found greater resonance among artists with an interest in the theater. For instance, Austrian poet Ingeborg Bachmann, noted also for her contributions to radio drama and for several libretti for works by composer Hans Werner Henze, in the late 1950s adapted both of Musil's plays for the radio. This would suggest that she, as a creative artist in her own right, found in these works qualities that were compatible with her own artistic concerns and that she deemed relevant for a contemporary audience. Bachmann, in highlighting the role of Regine and in other changes, gave *Die Schwärmer* a pessimistic, protofeminist twist (Rogowski, 1990a). In 1961 Musil's first drama received a successful production in Paris at the Théatre Moderne under the title *Les Exaltés*. The director, Sacha Pitoëff, was assisted by a young intern from Germany, Volker Schlöndorff, who was later to make his debut as a filmmaker with his version of Musil's *Törleß*.

Notable exceptions to the general disregard for *Die Schwärmer* among critics during the early decades include Marianne Kesting, whose seminal study *Das epische Theater* (1959) features a brief discussion of the significance of the play's structure as an example of an "epic" dramaturgy. Paul Fechter (1958) likewise acknowledges Musil's contribution to the dramatic genre, mainly presenting his approach to drama as a rejection of expressionism. Not that all acknowledgments of Musil's involvement in drama were helpful: for instance, theater historian Margret Dietrich struck a rather bizarre note when she detected in his two plays a "streak of nostalgic homage, of love for the Austrian type" (63) in her influential book *Das moderne Drama* (1961).

If Musil criticism can be said to begin with Frisé's edition of *Der Mann ohne Eigenschaften* in 1952, it is striking that it took almost a decade for a critic to defy the tacit consensus that Musil's involvement in drama was of marginal importance and that, consequently, *Die Schwärmer* was a second-rate work. In 1961 Burton Pike broke the silence in a chapter on the play in his introductory monograph on Musil. Pike boldly asserts that, the undeniable importance of *Der Mann ohne Eigenschaften* notwithstanding, Musil's first play "may one day be considered his finest work" (71). With his reading, sympathetic to Musil's ethical and aesthetic concerns, Pike helped pave the way for a greater acceptance of *Die Schwärmer*.

Wilhelm Braun was the first Musil scholar to devote several articles to *Die Schwärmer*. First, he attempted to provide an overall thematic interpretation of the play (1962a, 1965b) before focusing on particular characters — Anselm (1967) and Stader (1992) — and on problems of translation (1988). The 1962 article includes a useful discussion of the names of the characters in Musil's drama, expanding and clarifying some suggestions and speculations put forward by Ernst Kaiser and Eithne Wilkins in their monograph on Musil of the same year. All in all, Braun's readings remain largely on the level of affirmative commentary, placing the play in the familiar context of thematic constellations in Musil's oeuvre. More significant for the elucidation of the text as a drama is the work of Michael Scharang, who in two essays (1964 and 1965a) and in his doctoral dissertation (1965b) seeks to define Musil's contribution to twentieth-century drama. In his first article, Scharang convincingly shows how Musil places his own dramatic effort in direct opposition to prevailing standards of realism, particularly as advocated by proponents of its extreme variant, German naturalism. In his second essay, Scharang notes that Musil in effect dissolves Hegel's concept of drama: the notion of dramatic character as individual agent of larger forces is eroded as is the notion of dramatic action as a conflict based on a clash of such supra-individual forces (1965a).

Scharang stops short of drawing a significant conclusion, namely that both tendencies — the opposition to naturalism and the dissolution of dramatic character — place Musil squarely in the center of what Peter Szondi has described as the "crisis of modern drama," a conclusion that I have pursued in my own work on the play (Rogowski 1993). Szondi (1956) had shown how a wide variety of playwrights attempted to respond to the question of whether modern reality, in its extreme sociopolitical, technological, and psychological complexity, could adequately be represented on the stage within traditional dramaturgical parameters.

For almost a decade, Karsch's and Scharang's observations found hardly any resonance among Musil scholars. Those few critics who took on *Die Schwärmer* approached it from an angle that effectively disregards its nature as drama and its association with the theater, addressing it mainly in the context of Musil's overall thematic concerns. Sibylle Bauer (1966), for instance, views it as an investigation of the problem of *Wahrhaftigkeit* — ethical integrity and emotional authenticity — arguing that Musil's position on these issues resembles that of Jean-Paul Sartre. Michael Oczipka (1972) analyzes the play in the context of Musil's overall quest for the *anderer Zustand* ("other condition"). Annie Reniers-Servranckx (1972) devotes a chapter to the play in her introduction to Musil, stressing its motivic and thematic interconnections with the rest of Musil's oeuvre. Lisa Appignanesi (1973b) discusses it as one illustration of Musil's investigation into femininity. Studies like these, despite their authors' willingness to acknowledge a lesser known work of Musil's, potentially perpetuate the assumption that *Die Schwärmer* represents little more than a stepping-stone in Musil's creative development that culminated in *Der Mann ohne Eigenschaften*.

After the two dissertations by Scharang and Oczipka, Günther Schneider's monograph on Musil as dramatist (1973) provides the first comprehensive effort to take Musil's involvement in drama seriously. Schneider gives a detailed thematic reading of *Die Schwärmer*, taking his cue from one of Musil's comments on the basic idea of the play as "a quite ordinary plot set among people of significance" (*TB* I, 495). While Schneider is attentive to a wide range of facets of Musil's drama, he pays little attention to the more general aesthetic dimension of Musil's quest for a new form of drama. Instead, he engages in an extended polemic against Scharang's attempt to examine the dramaturgically innovative aspects of Musil's play (238–41). Schneider's aversion to the theoretical impulses provided by Scharang appears to reflect an unwillingness on the part of a typical Germanist to address the manner in which a literary work may relate to the theoretical and practical traditions of theater. He does not reflect on the dual nature of drama as literary text and performance piece; thus his close reading of the play represents a relapse to positions that Scharang's reflections had rendered obsolete. In view of the singularity of Musil's *Die Schwärmer*, Schneider's classification of it as a "typical transitional drama" (159) is an unsatisfactory conclusion. The main value of Schneider's book thus lies in the many insights on particular details yielded by his textual analysis and in the vast amount of factual information he assembles concerning the genesis and reception of the play.

Murray G. Hall's article "Der Schwärmerskandal" (1975c) provides a useful account of the historical and biographical context that influenced the critical reception of the play. Drawing on an abundance of contemporary documents, Hall contrasts the positive response to the publication of *Die Schwärmer* in book form in 1921 with the difficulties Musil experienced in trying to see the play performed by a reputable theater company. Together with Schneider's book, Hall's essay will remain an indispensable source for anybody interested in a serious analysis of Musil's first drama.

During the remainder of the 1970s, it must have appeared to Musil scholars as though Schneider had said everything there was to say about *Die Schwärmer*. For almost seven years, no Musil specialist felt called upon to examine Musil's play — quite a remarkable gap in Musil studies, an area that had by that time turned into a veritable interpretive industry. The silence was broken only tentatively: in 1980 Jürgen Kaizik discussed Musil's play briefly in his examination of the mathematical aspects of Musil's oeuvre. David S. Luft, in his intellectual biography of Musil of the same year, includes a sympathetic treatment of Musil's first play, viewed here largely from the perspective of individual character psychology more appropriate, perhaps, to Arthur Schnitzler than to Musil.

In the early 1980s *Die Schwärmer* was rediscovered not by the scholarly community, but by the theater. Whereas a few years earlier, an attempt to stage the play in Polish translation in Poznan (1977) met with relatively little success (see Naganowski 1985, 75), Erwin Axer's 1980 production of the play at the Akademietheater, the smaller venue of the Vienna Burgtheater, elicited general critical acclaim. Only a few months later, Hans Neuenfels directed the play at the Schloßparktheater Berlin (1981), likewise scoring a success. Axer's approach was conservative, concentrating on psychologically nuanced ensemble acting; the director attempted to remain faithful to Musil's text by refraining from textual cuts. Neuenfels's production was more adventurous, stressing the play's emotional extremes. The two productions showed the wide range of possibilities Musil's drama offered to the theater. All of a sudden, the piece reached an audience of unprecedented numbers: the Vienna production was shown on Austrian and German television, while Neuenfels in 1985 did a television adaptation of his Berlin production. Other stagings in German followed in Basel (1982) and Hamburg (1983); in translation it was produced, for instance, in Brussels (1983), Rotterdam (1985), and Craców (1988), among other places. In Freiburg the play was staged in 1987 as part of a project entitled "Das Pompeji der Gefühle" (The Pompeji of Emotions) coupled with Ibsen's *Hedda Gabler* — a fascinating choice given the intertextual connections between the two plays (Rogowski 1993). More recent stagings in Germany include a second production in Darmstadt (1988) and one in Hannover (1989), a production that apparently was a major artistic achievement (Thöming 1989).

Drama critic Peter von Becker (1980) assesses the Vienna production, suggesting that Musil's play had previously met with incomprehension mainly because it stands isolated in the history of German drama. He names Georg Büchner's intellectual comedy *Leonce und Lena* as a predecessor and argues that *Die Schwärmer* anticipates tendencies in recent German-language theater, notably the intricately cerebral plays of Peter Handke and Botho Strauß. Despite its brevity, von Becker's essay establishes a wide range of associations useful for an interpretation of Musil's drama.

Jürgen C. Thöming (1981) is among the first Musil scholars to view the success of the productions in Vienna and Berlin as an indication of the play's viability on the stage. Interpretive problems, he suggests, are due in large part to the different modalities of reception involved in reading the text as opposed to watching the play performed. Thöming offers a detailed analysis of the motif of the wardrobe in the third act of *Die Schwärmer*. Both in the stage setting and the characters' dialogues, it metaphorically defines the imaginary space in which the action is supposed to take place. In reading, the motif recedes in the recipient's mind, thus losing its potential significance; in a performance, however, it is visually present all the time, so its dramaturgical function is highlighted. The stage space closes in on the characters, indicating both a loss of room in which to move and a regression into childlike patterns of behavior in response to the encroachment of their existential dilemmas.

Thöming's essay is an important effort to examine the manner in which Musil creatively anticipates and responds to the demands of the stage in the dramaturgical structure of his play. Not all critics, however, agree that Musil succeeds. Martin Esslin (1982), for instance, despite a certain sympathy for Musil's thematic concerns, is quick to dismiss *Die Schwärmer* as an altogether "flawed play" (24). Paul Stefanek (1985b) counters this position by discussing the presuppositions that tacitly underlie the rejection of the piece as an unperformable *Lesedrama*. The notion that there are fixed norms concerning what is and what is not suitable for the stage, Stefanek observes, is based on a cultural consensus that is subject to historical change. Stefanek shows how such standards have changed over the last few decades: recent dramatic experiments such as the interminable soliloquies of Nova, the female protagonist in Peter Handke's 1983 *Über die Dörfer* (Across the Villages), he argues, have made audiences more receptive to and appreciative of the intellectual verbosity of Musil's characters, formerly rejected as excessive. Stefanek salvages Musil's play as a drama that dictates its own standards regarding performability.

In the preface to the published script of his television adaptation of *Die Schwärmer* (1985), director Hans Neuenfels fervently presents his case that

Musil's first play represents a major achievement in the history of German drama. To Neuenfels, it is a highly political play, addressing the disillusionment of a group of exceptionally gifted and aspiring people who stood in opposition to society but whose failed efforts at revolt resulted in existential despair and petty infighting. Neuenfels's essay culminates in the passionate assertion that *Die Schwärmer* is "one of the most important dramas of the twentieth century, if not the most important one that literature in the German language can so far call its own" (7). It would appear that Neuenfels's strong sense of identification with Musil's drama reflects at least in part the political and existential disillusionment of his own generation, that of the rebels and would-be rebels of 1968.

The impact of the rediscovery of Musil's piece on the stages of Vienna and Berlin made itself felt in the scholarly community at the Klagenfurt Musil seminar in the summer of 1984. The volume of papers presented on this occasion, which came out a year later, includes four essays on *Die Schwärmer*. Karl Dinklage (1985) attempts, not too convincingly, to establish parallels with the play's inconclusive ending and the de facto conclusion of Musil's unfinished novel, the chapter "Atemzüge eines Sommertages" (Breaths of a Summer's Day) of *Der Mann ohne Eigenschaften*. Erwin Naganowski (1985) makes an emphatic case for the play's suitability for the stage, detailing some of its productions to that date.

The two remaining contributions in the volume that address *Die Schwärmer* infuse discussion of the play with intellectual energy derived from recent currents in literary criticism, most notably discourse analysis. Drawing from ideas raised in the debate about postmodernism, Marianne Charrière-Jacquin (1985) describes the structure of the play as analogous to that of a musical score. She focuses on the motif of the deck of playing cards that underscores the internal affinity of various characters: the ideological position of each character appears as the reverse side of that of another character. Charrière-Jacquin detects a symmetry in the play's structure, centered around Thomas's soliloquy in the second act. The symmetry mirrors the "duplicity" (34) of human beings, split into intellect and body, an existential tension intensified in the experience of modernity. The antagonism between Thomas and Anselm is representative of a rivalry between two "discourses of modernity" (35), both of which represent responses to internal divisions and external conflicts that have become difficult if not impossible to resolve. Of the various binary oppositions that Charrière-Jacquin discusses, her observations on the tension between the extreme intellectuality of the dialogues and the underlying animal-like, physically violent impulses in the characters are the most fruitful aspects of her essay.

Gerda Ambros (1985) draws on Jacques Derrida's observations concerning the function of writing in our culture. Ambros traces the circulation of written documents in the play, including Josef's letter and Regine's allegedly incriminating diary. Such references to writing in a literary text, Ambros contends, highlight the problem of interpretation, rendering the drama a self-referential "play about its own interpretation" (79). In subverting the authority of written documents, the play calls into question any effort to interpret signification. What remains in Ambros's reading of *Die Schwärmer* as self-deconstructing artifact is what she, somewhat cryptically, calls an "aesthetic utopia of writing. A writing which no longer presents or represents anything" (94).

The essays by Charrière-Jacquin and Ambros indicate an increased interest on the part of Musil scholars to take *Die Schwärmer* seriously as an autonomous work of art by approaching it in terms of recent developments of literary theory. This tendency continued throughout the 1980s in discussions of the play. Most of these readings are informed by theoretical models that draw from psychological theories. Christel Zahlmann (1986), for instance, detects narcissistic traits in the psychological makeup of the characters that can be analyzed in terms of the psychoanalytic theories of Heinz Kohut. For instance, Zahlmann emphasizes that the characters in their conflicts frequently regress to infantile modes of behavior. She suggests that, psychologically speaking, their inability to relate to one another in mature terms is based on a narcissistic choice of love objects that precludes genuinely reciprocal interpersonal relationships.

Peter Henninger (1986) shifts the focus from the psychological disposition of the play's characters to the psychological dimension of the interaction between text and recipient; he addresses the interpretive problems the play poses to readers or spectators. For instance, Henninger argues, there are no indications in the text that the relationships between the characters in the play are sexual in nature, yet critics and theatergoers alike take it for granted that the play is about matters involving adultery or sexual infidelity. To Henninger, this indicates once again that people gloss over the unusual and problematic aspects of Musil's texts by taking recourse to their own preconceptions about external reality rather than focusing on what is contained in the actual text. From Henninger's Lacanian perspective, such tendencies to subsume the recalcitrant aspects of a text into the familiar constitute a misreading.

The respect for the complexity of *Die Schwärmer* evidenced by these 1980s readings contrasts sharply with a lack of interest in the play on the part of some Musil scholars. Eckhard Heftrich, for instance, in his introductory monograph on Musil (1986), devotes merely a few sentences to the play in a chapter whose very brevity indicates the impatience of the author to move on to "important" and more "substantial" things, namely a discussion of *Der Mann ohne Eigenschaften*. Philip Payne (1987) appears to be so exasperated by the complicated background of the play's plot that he feels compelled to suggest that Musil should have introduced a spoken prologue to clarify the intricate entanglements that provide the backdrop for the dramatic situation so the reader or spectator could "concentrate on what the characters say" (132). A younger generation of Musil scholars, however, is more sympathetic to the play in all its complexities. Roger Willemsen has some fascinating, albeit brief, things to say about the piece in his 1985 monograph on Musil. Lowell A. Bangerter treats it with sympathy in his book (1989). Thomas Pekar (1989) gives a short but illuminating discussion of the topic of love in *Die Schwärmer*, while Claus Erhart (1991) places the drama in the context of Musil's development away from aestheticism toward a more ethical perspective.

Peter Horn (1990) employs *Die Schwärmer* as the starting point for a highly personal reflection on the significance of literature and the function of literary criticism. He defines literary language as the vehicle in which what Lacan has termed the Real (the actual psychic and bodily desires) bypasses the dual censorship of the Imaginary (the presence of such desires in the mind) and the Symbolic (the social and linguistic codes that determine what can be expressed and how). The proliferation of metaphors in Musil's play, in Horn's view, is a correlative of the complexity of the psychosexual issues involved: the Lacanian Real can find expression only in poetic metaphor, in a language that does not conceal or deny that all language is intrinsically metaphorical. In view of this constellation, Horn proposes, any attempt to assert a position of *Literaturwissenschaft* detached from and superior to the object of interpretation amounts to a reduction of the truth contained in a given text to preconceived, inappropriate categories. Notwithstanding his conclusion that the task of interpretation would then be to acknowledge the manner in which a literary work refuses to be interpreted (105), Horn ventures an interpretation of some aspects of Musil's text: in particular he focuses on the motif of the brother-sister relationship in the play. Men assume a position in a social order through entering a relationship with women; women, in turn, circulate in a social order as the objects of a logic of exchange. Horn views the relationship between Thomas and his imaginary sister Regine, which parallels that of Ulrich and Agathe in *Der Mann ohne Eigenschaften*, as a rejection of the imperatives of male socialization. He rightfully points out the autoerotic component of the quasi-incestuous desires of Musil's male protagonists, who seek in the bodily or imaginary sister above all a mirror image of themselves (100). Yet for all his awareness of the reductive nature of theoretical concepts, Horn reinstalls just such concepts — here, those of Lacanian psychoanalysis — as apparent harbingers of eternal truth.

The sophisticated readings of *Die Schwärmer* produced during the last ten years or so are an indication that the play is gaining acceptance in Musil criticism as a work worthy of serious consideration. All the same, not unlike the contributions of the previous decades, these readings sometimes display a tendency to ignore genre-specific points; the majority of critics fail to address the play as a work written for, and intricately associated with, the theater. One of the few critics to combine theoretical reflection with a focus on the aesthetics of the dramatic genre is the Italian scholar Bianca Cetti Marinoni. Her fascinating reconstruction of the long and complex genesis of *Die Schwärmer* (in a monograph first published in Italian in 1988) is now available in German (Cetti Marinoni 1992). Analyzing a large number of unpublished notes and drafts, Cetti Marinoni traces the manner in which Musil attempted to solve the crucial dramaturgical problems in writing the play. The final version, in her view, evidences a shift from a "syntagmatic" structure of drama (the unfolding of a sequence of logically related events) to a "paradigmatic" one (the essayistic working through of thematic issues).

Cetti Marinoni defines as the germinating idea and thematic center of the play the notion of the dissolution of the self that Musil developed in the wake of Ernst Mach: all characters in Musil's drama partake to a greater or lesser extent in the problem of establishing selfhood. Following the narrative theories of Gérard Genette, Cetti Marinoni shows how Musil replaces "characters" in the Hegelian sense with dramatic "figures," ideological positions that may comprise several personages: instead of conflicts between individual agents, Musil's play presents us with an interplay of theoretical positions. These positions are "essayistically" distributed over the various dramatic personages. One reason that Musil spent more than ten years wrestling with the dramaturgical problems of writing *Die Schwärmer*, Cetti Marinoni suggests, is that this constellation renders dramatic conflicts in the traditional sense impossible. It was only when Musil had clarified the nature of the ambivalent relationship between the two male antagonists (finally named Thomas and Anselm) that he managed to create a suitable dramaturgical structure. Moreover, at a relatively late stage he inserted a comic figure, the detective Stader, as a motor to propel the external action. He also contrasted Anselm more clearly with Thomas: while both still share their awareness of the basic existential problem, Anselm's narcissistic self-aggrandizement is now unmasked as a false gesture, whereas the skepticism of Thomas emerges as an authentic response to the situation.

In many ways, my own work on Musil as a playwright (Rogowski 1993) complements that of Cetti Marinoni and some of the other critics discussed above, notably Scharang and Thöming. My main focus is on the self-referential aspects of *Die Schwärmer*. Partly following ideas on the "crisis of modern drama" during the first third of the twentieth century as outlined by Peter Szondi (1956), I examine the way in which the play defines its own problematic position in the context of the history of the genre. The underlying thesis is that Musil was profoundly interested in exploring drama precisely because he viewed it as a genre that could potentially help reconstitute some form of collectivity. In a variety of ways, both *Die Schwärmer* and his second play, *Vinzenz*, profoundly question the viability of drama as an art form capable of conveying intellectual substance. My approach traces a number of related elements in a series of concentric rings centered on a pivotal issue, both dramaturgical and thematic. In *Die Schwärmer*, intertextual allusions to the formal and dramaturgical conventions of the Austrian *Konversationsstück* (the "well-made" conversation drama) of successful authors such as Anton Wildgans and to the mimetic realism of the naturalistic tradition inaugurated by Henrik Ibsen point to the question of whether there can be a modern form of tragedy. Similarly, at the core of *Vinzenz* there is the question of whether there is an audience for the kind of drama Musil thinks is existentially necessary and aesthetically appropriate. In focusing on this self-questioning substratum of Musil's plays, I attempt to situate his efforts in drama in the context of the overall development of European drama of the period, marked on the one hand by realism (the attempts at verisimilitude of authors like Strindberg, Ibsen, and Gerhart Hauptmann) and on the other by various forms of experimentation (of such playwrights as Brecht, Artaud, and Pirandello).

In her bibliography overview of the scholarly reception of *Die Schwärmer* (1989), Chiara De Tullio stresses the necessity of placing the play in the larger context of modern drama. The contributions emerging from Musil criticism in the second half of the 1980s have begun to do just that. It is clear that the significance and the extent of Musil's interest in drama is finally being recognized and that the community of Musil scholars no longer ignores a text that, as Bianca Cetti Marinoni succinctly put it, constitutes, alongside *Der Mann ohne Eigenschaften*, "Musil's most significant contribution to contemporary literature" (1992, 7).

8: *Vinzenz und die Freundin bedeutender Männer* and Drama Criticism

TO THE EXTENT THAT Musil's interest in the drama was overlooked by critics during the first two decades of Musil scholarship, his second play was mostly brushed aside with a few perfunctory remarks or ignored altogether. Felix Holländer, in his review of the first production of *Vinzenz* in Berlin in 1923, had labeled the comedy an "insignificant work of a significant author" (1932, 11). In similar fashion, Ernst Kaiser and Eithne Wilkins were quick to dismiss *Vinzenz* as Musil's weakest work (1962, 106). Wilfried Berghahn, in his 1963 Musil biography, adopts a more benevolent tone, suggesting that Musil's *Posse* (farcical comedy) anticipates the theater of Friedrich Dürrenmatt, the Swiss representative of the Theater of the Absurd, an idea more fully developed by Egon Naganowski (1973, 1981). For the longest time, however, critics were content with seeing in Vinzenz merely, as Wolfdietrich Rasch put it, a "younger brother" of the protagonist of *Der Mann ohne Eigenschaften* (1969, 166).

In the world of the theater, Musil's second play met with moderate interest in several reasonably successful productions. It was first revived in Cologne in 1957 in a production directed by Friedrich Siems that featured as Vinzenz the great Austrian actor Romuald Pekny, by all accounts a performer capable of conveying the mixture of ironic playfulness and wistful melancholy of that character. Reviewer Walter Karsch praised the comedy as a "grand intellectual jest" (1957). In his review of the Cologne production for the *Frankfurter Allgemeine Zeitung*, Albert Schulze Vellinghausen (1957) relates a fascinating anecdote: during the intermission, the story goes, a gentleman — mispronouncing Musil's name as though it were that of a French author — innocently inquired who had translated the piece so brilliantly into German. Schulze Vellinghausen rightly uses this telling anecdote as a springboard for a rumination on the disturbing discontinuities of German intellectual history: while a handful of experts was busy proclaiming Musil as one of the greatest novelists of the twentieth century, the general public seemed to be totally unaware of his existence. All the same, the Cologne production was well received. A staging in Vienna followed in 1958; a series of smaller productions at places such as Freiburg (1958), Munich (1960), Oldenburg (1960), and Tübingen (1962) led to a revival of the piece in Berlin (1963) and a French production in Paris (1969; see Schneider 1973, 264–68). Other productions are documented for Poznan, Poland (1972) and Mannheim (1974), as well as a second staging in Paris (1986); in Austria the comedy was subsequently produced at Klagenfurt and Graz. The two theaters where *Die Schwärmer* had been "rediscovered" in the early 1980s returned to Musil and produced his second play to complement their earlier productions. Yet neither Erwin Axer's staging at the Akademietheater Vienna (1985) nor that of Dietmar Pflegerl at the Schloßparktheater Berlin (1989) could repeat the success of the respective previous productions of *Die Schwärmer*.

As was the case with Musil's first drama, the scholarly community took a long time to develop an interest in *Vinzenz*: it was not until 1962 that the first two scholarly articles devoted to a discussion of Musil's comedy appeared. Wilhelm Braun (1962b) approaches the play as a variation of Musil's overall thematic concerns that culminate in *Der Mann ohne Eigenschaften*: Alpha and Vinzenz are typically Musilian *Möglichkeitsmenschen* ("possibilitarians," 133). The play's central thematic issue, according to Braun, is that of the "division of the human psyche into masculine and feminine archetypes, into reason and imagination, logic and love," a division which the characters must try to overcome with the help of a "metaphorical quality of mind" (125). The play, Braun contends, ends on a note of failure since no synthesis of the polar oppositions has been achieved. Braun has some very useful things to say, for instance on the possible origins of the name of Alpha's husband, Apulejus-Halm (122). It seems to me, however, that Braun operates with categories of interpretation that remain alien to the play. For instance, his application of the concept of psychological archetypes — drawn from C. G. Jung's depth psychology — misses the ironic aspects of the comedy. In a later article (1983), Braun modifies his reading to concentrate on the subject of love, arguing that Musil's play illustrates the impossibility of achieving a lasting union even between two people of like minds.

Unlike Braun, who pays little attention to the dramatic structure of the play, Helmut Arntzen (1962) focuses on the play's position within the context of contemporary comedy. He places *Vinzenz* alongside two comedies by Georg Kaiser to analyze some general characteristics of early twentieth-century German comedy. In response to the increasing theatricality of modern reality, the genre, Arntzen demonstrates, displays a tendency to satirize the tradition of tragedy by way of self-referential devices. Vinzenz's theatrical intrigues represent attempts at overcoming universal existential alienation in a world that has become histrionic: we are made aware that what governs the theater is not genuine dramatic action but rather the same laws of commodity exchange that characterize the operation of industrialized capitalist society as a whole. As Arntzen aphoristically phrases it, commerce ("Handel") replaces dramatic action ("Handlung"; 550). Arntzen stresses the critique of social reality that is implied in Musil's satirical unmasking of societal constructs: businessman Bärli, for instance, is "healed" of his passions in a "cathartic" experience (prearranged and duly paid for) that mocks the supposed effect of tragedy. Society generates fictions that nevertheless determine actual reality (557). Arntzen's essay is highly stimulating. His focus on the problem of satire highlights important aspects of the play. For instance, Arntzen was the first to note that it was in his plays that Musil developed, as David S. Luft later put it, "his ironical voice and the satirical emplotment" that were to become the hallmark of *Der Mann ohne Eigenschaften* (1980, 177).

In 1965 Marie-Louise Roth published a collection of Musil's theater reviews and theoretical reflections on the nature and function of drama, accompanied by a series of essays on the background and context of Musil's writings about drama that display her great sympathy for his concerns. The volume made evident the extraordinary degree of Musil's interest in the genre: contrary to accepted opinion, it occupied Musil for over two and a half decades. In the light of these resurfaced materials it was no longer possible to dismiss this side of Musil's literary enterprise as immaterial. Among those who recognized its importance was theater critic Siegfried Melchinger, who, in his 1965 review of the Roth volume, showed himself highly impressed by the range and depth of Musil's reflections on the theater.

The impact of Roth's publication made itself felt in the late 1960s in general assessments of Musil's significance as playwright and theorist of drama by Annie Reniers-Servranckx (1967), Norbert Kohlhase (1968), and Jörg Jesch (1968). Kohlhase enthusiastically hails Musil's theoretical reflections on the genre as equal in significance, if not superior to, those of Bertolt Brecht in terms of their potential impact on the development of modern theater. Jesch, in his article on Musil in the influential series *Text + Kritik*, primarily presents in condensed form ideas outlined by Roth in her commentary on Musil's writings on drama. Taking Musil's own concept of *Ideendrama* or "ideographic drama" as his cue, Jesch emphasizes the way in which Musil's completed plays complement his theoretical reflections; both *Die Schwärmer* and *Vinzenz* are specimens of Musil's new "ideographic" drama, contributions toward a utopian form of theater that, rather than portraying psychological conflicts, explores intellectual issues. Like Berghahn (1963), Jesch invokes Friedrich Dürrenmatt as a dramatist whose work could be seen to represent a realization of some of the innovative aspects of Musil's ideas (28). Musil's essentially narrative ("epic") approach to drama, Jesch maintains, turned out to be incompatible with the restrictive demands placed upon drama by the stage. The notion of an epic quality of Musil's plays, already introduced by Marianne Kesting (1959) was later to be endorsed by Ursula Tiebel (1980). Towards the end of his essay, Jesch intimates that the modern media of film and radio drama display affinities to Musil's epic brand of theater — but he fails to develop the idea further.

Jesch does not engage in an interpretation of Musil's second play. Instead, he refers the reader to Braun's and Arntzen's studies on the comedy. Indeed, it seems that to most Musil scholars during the 1960s and 1970s it appeared as though after Braun and Arntzen nothing was left to be said about *Vinzenz*. Even Günther Schneider, in his monograph on Musil as playwright (1973), dismisses the necessity for a close reading of Musil's second play citing the work already done by Braun and Arntzen (IX). Schneider's chapter on the *Posse* thus remains largely perfunctory, reducing the play to a mere satirical foil for the first drama, a "Satyrspiel" that parodies the thematic issues treated more seriously in the first play.

Wolfdietrich Rasch (1969) aims to place the comedy in the dual context of the history of the genre and of Musil's overall work. His focus is on the notion of playfulness. Rasch interprets Vinzenz's histrionics, his stage managing of other people's desires, his gambling schemes, and his lack of seriousness as indications of despair, reactions to a reality that has become devoid of significance (174). The underlying seriousness of the play's thematic focus, Rasch emphasizes, belie the apparent shallowness and frivolity of its surface. To Rasch, Musil's often neglected play is a "Komödie von Rang" (178), belonging among the best of German comedies — a genre, to be sure, not exactly represented in great abundance.

In his 1972 Vienna doctoral dissertation Michael Oczipka undertakes the first discussion of a wide range of Musil's unfinished dramatic projects as found in the manuscripts of his *Nachlaß*. The drafts include sketches for a play called "Die Schildkröte" (The Turtle), in which a jealous conflict between two brothers over a woman is placed against the backdrop of political revolution; the only element of stability in the existential and social turmoil appears to be the title character, an old servant woman known as Schildkröte. Oczipka deserves credit for drawing attention to this and other unfinished dramatic works that document Musil's intense interest in the genre. In an article of the same year, Egon Naganowski examines three of these, a draft of a satirical comedy from 1919/20 (referred to as "Satyrspiel" or "Tempora Meier" in Musil's diaries), a social satire under the title "Panama" about conditions in the Austrian officer's staff during the First World War, and a large-scale allegorical piece of which Musil actually published an excerpt entitled "Vorspiel zu dem Melodrama *Der Tierkreis*" (Prologue to the Melodrama *The Zodiac*). In some ways, Naganowski's appraisal of the texts is problematic. He regards the prologue as a serious exercise in expressionism — a view that misses the savage irony of the piece, as I have argued elsewhere (Rogowski 1993, 64).

With his 1973 article on *Vinzenz*, Naganowski became one of the most important advocates of Musil's second play. He outlines the play's position in

Musil's overall work, drawing insightful thematic and structural connections between it and Musil's other writings, notably *Der Mann ohne Eigenschaften*. More important, however, is that he examines the play's dramaturgy with an eye to theatrical and dramatic traditions. Unlike Musil's contemporaries, who had associated the play's bizarre humor with Wedekindian social comedy, Naganowski emphasizes its affinity to different traditions, namely those of surrealism and dadaism, contending that Musil's comedy anticipates what became known as the Theater of the Absurd (94). Naganowski was later to explore further the play's affinity to the spirit of dadaism (1983).

The Viennese theater historian Paul Stefanek, who shared Naganowski's interest in *Vinzenz*, also emerged in the early 1970s as a champion of Musil's cause as playwright and drama theorist. In his first contribution to Musil studies (1973), Stefanek proclaims Musil emphatically as the first theorist in the history of European drama to call into question not just particular aesthetic traditions but the very societal underpinnings of theater (304). With this bold assertion, Stefanek moves Musil from the periphery of drama criticism to its very center. Like Kohlhase (1968) before him and Cetti Marinoni (1986) after him, Stefanek places Musil in direct opposition to Bertolt Brecht. Brecht, Stefanek notes, with his political and ideological agenda, aims at a pragmatic reform of theater; Musil focuses on a more fundamental level, that of the very anthropological basis of writing and performing that underlies our theater culture. The alienation effects that Musil employs in his plays differ from Brecht's in that they do not serve to make sociopolitical conditions transparent, but function as dramatic correlatives of intrapsychic conflicts (315). In Stefanek's opinion, *Vinzenz* represents not an epigonal rewriting of comedic clichés but rather a profound ironic critique of the formal conventions of *Effekttheater* (319), the kind of theater that has lost its anthropological mission of exposing the audience to an existential experience of reorientation. In Stefanek's reading, Musil emerges as the most perceptive critic of the commodification of the theater experience and of the stifling impact of the theater apparatus — dominated, as it is, primarily by commercial concerns — upon drama as a literary art form. Observing the overall development of twentieth-century drama, Stefanek suggests that the general success of authors like Beckett, Ionesco, and Witold Gombrowicz has paved the way for a reappraisal of Musil as a playwright of major significance.

Vinzenz, traditionally regarded as a minor work of an author with little interest in the theater, is shown in Naganowski's and Stefanek's assessments to be a piece that addresses some of the crucial issues confronting drama in the twentieth century. Likewise, Musil is treated as one of the sharpest and most significant critics of the genre. Stefanek was later to examine Musil's comedy in greater detail in several articles, particularly with regard to its place in the tradition of German and Austrian comedy (1980a and 1981). He also explored affinities between *Vinzenz* and the self-referential ironic dramaturgy of Luigi Pirandello (1980b) before returning to Musil's drama criticism in an essay of 1985.

In 1979 Elisabeth Albertsen presented the results of her research into the biographical background of Musil's comedy in a two-part article in *Musil-Forum*. All the characters, she demonstrates, are based on real people in Musil's circle of acquaintances. Alpha, for instance, is in large part a portrait of Ea von Allesch (the wife of Musil's friend Johannes von Allesch). She also shows that Marek, the young student, is an unflattering representation of Hermann Broch, then still unknown as an author. Karl Corino (1985) complements Albertsen's findings, pointing out that the basic plot constellation mirrors an affair Gina Kaus had with Musil's mentor Franz Blei. Both Albertsen's and Corino's articles are useful for placing the play in a contemporary social and biographical context, although the authors tend to reduce the play to a mere *pièce à clef* satirizing Viennese personalities.

In the late 1970s two dissertations dealt with Musil's involvement in drama from the perspective of *Theaterwissenschaft*. Ursula Tiebel's study (1978), appeared in revised form as a book in 1980. Monika Meister's dissertation (1979) was not published, but some of her key ideas are available in a series of essays. Tiebel delineates Musil's poetics of drama on the basis of his pronouncements in his reviews and essays, showing how certain dramaturgical concepts correlate with the two published plays as well as the *Tierkreis* fragment. She discusses the various practitioners of theater who may have had an impact on Musil's ideas, such as Adolphe Appia and Edward Gordon Craig (on set design), and Max Reinhardt and Leopold Jessner (on production practices). She cites as literary influences on Musil's approach to drama such writers as Georg Büchner, Maurice Maeterlinck, and Paul Claudel and notes the productions for which Musil expressed his admiration, in particular Stanislavsky's Moscow Arts Theater. She also notes Musil's interest, first pointed out by Marie-Louise Roth (1965), in cabaret-like theater groups, primarily Yiddish or Russian *Kleinkunst* ensembles. Tiebel seems to be eager to dismiss any notion that Musil may have seen drama as an art form with a potentially political function. This leaves open the crucial question of why he decided his hand at drama at a time that was marked by profound political turmoil in the wake of the First World War and the collapse of the Habsburg Empire — clearly reflected both in his *Panama* and his *Schildkröte* drafts. It should be remembered that Musil's involvement with drama coincides, for instance, with his close association during the years 1918 to 1924 with Austrian activist Robert Müller and the secret organization Katakombe, of which both were members. That Musil refrained from endorsing a party-political program in his plays does not mean that he did not reflect upon the political aspects of drama, the theater's potential to engender a collective experience, or the theater's position in a concrete sociopolitical context.

Monika Meister's work on Musil's poetics of drama addresses just such issues from a broad theoretical and aesthetic perspective. In her first essay (1980a), for instance, Meister presents the surprising parallels between Musil's critique of the theater of his time and aesthetic ideas developed slightly later by thinkers of the Frankfurt school. Although Musil did not share the neo-Marxist ideological background of proponents of *Kritische Theorie*, Meister notes, his observations on the nexus between social alienation and contemporary performance practices bear remarkable resemblances to ideas developed by Theodor W. Adorno and Max Horkheimer. One such parallel is the notion of the commodification of the aesthetic experience in what Adorno and Horkheimer labeled in their *Dialectics of Enlightenment* (1947) the "culture industry" of capitalist society. In a series of articles that followed, Meister explored Musil's attitudes towards contemporary dramatists (1980b), his drama criticism (1981), and the connection between the concept of the *andere Zustand* and Musil's ideas on the effect of art (1983). In the last essay Meister suggests an affinity between Musil's concept of art as both vehicle of criticism and catalyst for existential reorientation with the aesthetic theories of Theodor W. Adorno. In stressing the crucial importance of what Adorno calls *Erschütterung* and *Betroffenheit* in Musil's reflections on the effect of art, Meister is among the first to address Musil's interest in the *reception* of literary works of art as opposed to considerations involving the aesthetics of *production*.

Jürgen Kaizik's (1980) examination of mathematical aspects in Musil's works, based on his 1978 Saarbrücken dissertation, contains a brief discussion of Musil's involvement in drama from a somewhat unusual perspective. Kaizik outlines Musil's negative attitude towards naturalism and expressionism, endorsing the view that his critique of contemporary theater in many ways parallels, or even transcends, that of Brecht (70). Musil's interest in "exactitude" in art, Kaizik contends, reflects his mathematically trained mind. Mathematics remains an analogy of the usefulness as well as the limits of the role of scientific methods in Musil's investigation into human concerns.

With the critical writings of Tiebel, Meister, and Kaizik, the early 1980s clearly mark a resurgence of interest in Musil's involvement in drama. Most prominently, Helmut Arntzen's comments on Musil's poetics of drama in his comprehensive *Musil-Kommentar* of 1980 indicate a recognition in mainstream Musil criticism of the extraordinary significance that Musil had attached to the drama. Here Arntzen introduces some concepts that help the reader appreciate the specific nature of Musil's dramaturgy. He observes that in Musil's plays there is a tension between a self-consciously mechanistic plot structure, which he calls *Handlungsdrama*, and a stratum that touches on a deeper level of significance, for which he coins the term *Bedeutungsdrama*. Arntzen reads

Vinzenz as a play that addresses the problem of alienation in modern industrialized society: it presents a satirical critique of the manner in which prefabricated ideological ideas (derived largely from misunderstood literary models) determine people's actions in a world in which money constitutes the only reliable value. In Arntzen's assessment Musil's play demonstrates how life turns theatrical by emulating *kitsch*, an idea he later explored more fully in a separate essay (1983).

In his 1980 commentary, Arntzen mentions some of Musil's unfinished dramatic plans. Marie-Christine Pila examines these unpublished drafts in detail in two brief articles (1980 and 1981). Of particular interest are her remarks on projects that display Musil's interest in dramatic experimentation: "Das Doppel-Ich oder der Verlust der Persönlichkeit oder das Erlebnis eines Zigarrenhändlers" (The Dual I, or Loss of Personality or Experience of a Cigar Vendor), a whimsical exercise in "epic" theater; the complex of manuscripts entitled "Panama/Der kleine Napoleon," an ironic rendition of Musil's wartime experiences; and a draft for a comedy satirizing social disorientation after the First World War. Michael Oczipka (1972) discusses these and other projects in greater depth, and I touch on them in my monograph on Musil as playwright (1993). Pila's focus is mainly on problems involving a critical edition of these writings, yet her essays serve as a reminder of Musil's intense involvement with the dramatic genre.

More than the efforts of critics like Tiebel, Meister, and Pila, the successful productions of *Die Schwärmer* in the early 1980s helped rekindle scholarly interest in Musil's second play and in his contribution to a poetics of drama. Among the first to give an appraisal of Musil as a playwright after this watershed in Musil studies was Axel Fritz (1981), who restricts himself mainly to a commentary on Musil's two finished plays. Lynda J. King (1983) explores the sociopolitical dimension of Musil's *Vinzenz* from a highly original angle, addressing the play in the context of the debates about femininity during the Weimar Republic. Alpha, in her estimation, is a portrait of the New Woman who emerged out of the chaos of the First World War to challenge the established male order, most notably on the basis of her newly gained economic and sexual independence. This assessment, however, overlooks certain ironic aspects of the play: Alpha may be playing with the erotic desires of her admirers, yet it is clear that her economic status depends on the men around her, since she does not hold a profession. Likewise, she does not escape the institution of marriage; at the end of the play she accepts the proposal of a certain Baron Ur auf Usedom. Musil does not endow Alpha with the kind of intellectual and economic autonomy that would warrant King's reading. All the same, King's contribution represents a welcome change in Musil studies insofar as it highlights the necessity of a feminist critique of Musil's views on gender roles.

Gilbert Reis (1983) touches on such issues in his examination of the self-referential aspects of Musil's comedy. He approaches *Vinzenz* as a complement to *Die Schwärmer* that provides a satirical critique of the serious issues raised in the first play. Among the self-referential techniques that challenge a rigid notion of reality are the swapping of gender roles and the various theatrical intrigues stage-managed by Vinzenz. "Reality" in *Vinzenz* turns out to be the "reality of the cliché" (140). All the same, Reis contends, the comedy acknowledges the overpowering force of this reality in which money and sexuality are the only fixed values. Reis presents a thematic reading of Musil's play sensitive to a wide variety of details but one that, on account of its central focus on the depiction of reality (*Wirklichkeitsdarstellung*), can offer little that goes beyond traditional Musil criticism.

In his essay on Musil's concept of theater, Ulrich Karthaus (1985) stresses the author's indebtedness to Aristotle, whose theories on tragedy Musil critically emulated in his reflections on the ethical effect of theater. Musil, Karthaus writes, saw the ethical task of theater not in an improvement of individual conduct but in an overall spiritual enhancement (12). This idea is clearly related to the concern with the *andere Zustand* that permeates Musil's entire work. To Musil, Karthaus points out, the theater is one of the few socially sanctioned spaces in which an experience of existential reorientation is potentially possible by way of the suspension of everyday experience. Musil's aim in drama is to change human consciousness through "testing and developing new modes of feeling and seeing" (22). Karthaus's essay is perhaps the most concise summary of some of the key issues of Musil's poetics of drama, especially useful in the way it places Musil's ideas in a broad context ranging from Aristotle to Schiller and the normative theories of Gustav Freytag. One component missing in Karthaus's presentation is a discussion of Musil's attitude toward the tradition of mimetic realism that dominated the stage at the time he came of age intellectually and artistically. All the same, the essay, written by one of the most important and influential Musil scholars and culminating in the emphatic assessment "Musil's theater is *Poesie* made visible" (22), is an encouraging sign that by the mid-1980s mainstream Musil criticism had come to recognize Musil's status as dramatist.

Roger Willemsen, a representative of a younger generation of Musil scholars, provides perhaps the most interesting thematic discussion of Musil's *Vinzenz* in a brief but stimulating chapter on Musil's plays in his 1985 monograph. In a few highly condensed phrases, Willemsen identifies the thematic core of the comedy as the tension between *unentschiedene Liebe* (a love uncertain of its object love) and *liebender Betrug* (betrayal in or through love; 176). Like much of Willemsen's book, the chapter on Musil's plays is a veritable tour de force of a brilliant essayist who makes few if any concessions to his readers.

Generally speaking, the contributions by Karthaus and Willemsen, alongside those of Naganowski, Stefanek, and Meister, signal a heightening of the level of discourse on Musil's plays and his poetics of drama during the 1980s. Bianca Cetti Marinoni is another critic who has added significantly to a more differentiated assessment of the innovative aspects of Musil's dramaturgy. In an article of 1986, for instance, she emphasizes an affinity between Musil and Brecht with regard to the use of *Verfremdungseffekte*, devices that defamiliarize phenomena in order to induce in the recipient a reassessment of ideas usually taken for granted. The crucial difference between the two authors, she suggests, is that whereas Brecht employs defamiliarization in the interest of a reorientation towards a specific political worldview, Musil refuses to establish such new reassurances, dismantling ideological constructs altogether. Thus *Verfremdung* encompasses the very structure of his plays. With Musil, Cetti Marinoni observes, the *ideologiekritisch* impulse aims not merely at petrified worldviews but also at the notion of a stable autonomous subject (the precondition of drama as defined by Hegel). The disappearance of dramatis personae in the traditional sense (noted already by Karsch 1962 and Scharang 1965) requires a shift from what Cetti Marinoni calls a "syntagmatic" dramaturgy — one based on a plot structure propelled sequentially by conflicts between characters — toward a "paradigmatic" dramaturgy, which revolves around a gradual unfolding of thematic issues. Cetti Marinoni describes Musil's new dramaturgy as "essayistic" (119), an idea more fully developed in her monograph on the genesis of *Die Schwärmer*. In Cetti Marinoni's view this shift endows Musil's poetics with extraordinary potential with regard to the future development of the dramatic genre.

The reorientation regarding Musil's status as theorist and practitioner of drama indeed represents a dramatic reversal of opinions that is clearly correlated with questions of methodology. During the first three decades of Musil criticism, most Musil scholars had been content with dismissing Musil's dramatic efforts as marginal. In the mid-1980s, the methodology employed by Cetti Marinoni, combining *Ideologiekritik* with a Hegelian theory of drama enriched by structuralist concepts, propels Musil to the very forefront of the development of modern drama. If Paul Stefanek (1973) stresses the significance of Musil's contribution to the theory of modern drama, Cetti Marinoni advances a similar claim on behalf of the praxis: in her assessment, Musil emerges as one of the most important dramatists of the twentieth century.

Old and new Musil criticism meet halfway in Marie-Louise Roth's interpretation of *Vinzenz* (1987b). Ideas explored by Cetti Marinoni on an abstract level are here recast in more traditional terms in a reconstruction of the aesthetic intentions that underlie Musil's comedy. In its dadaistic elements, such as the repeated disruption of the theatrical fiction in situations that are unmasked as vacuous coups de théâtre, Roth detects a therapeutic impulse:

Musil aims to challenge rigid worldviews and awaken in his audience the utopian notion of a transformation of reality. Roth relates the comedy to Musil's overall concern with the "other condition," which she interprets as an ethical postulate relevant to society at large, a utopian notion that bears a resemblance to Schiller's hopes for a brotherly human community (440).

Outside the limited circle of Musil specialists, *Vinzenz* has received relatively little recognition. Notable exceptions include Manfred Pfister, who in his seminal book *Das Drama* (1977) cites Musil's play as providing an example of a particular variant of comedic endings. Likewise, Reinhold Grimm (1978) draws on Musil to illustrate the emergence of a new type of grotesque humor in the comedy of the Weimar Republic. Christopher Balme echoes this focus in a 1988 article on grotesque farce in the Weimar Republic, in which he places Musil's *Vinzenz* alongside early one-acters by Bertolt Brecht and Ödön von Horváth's *Rund um den Kongreß* (Round about Congress, 1927) as a specimen of grotesque comedy as a vehicle for social criticism.

In my work on Musil as dramatist, I have attempted to approach *Vinzenz* as a play of considerable complexity. My discussion of the play's ending (1989), for instance, draws on a series of typologies developed in German literary criticism to describe endings of comic dramas. Many different thematic and structural strands converge in the ending of *Vinzenz*. Depending upon which of these strands one focuses on, it appears that each of the various typological categories can be said to apply. The ostensible triviality of the play's plot permutations goes hand in hand with a surprisingly subtle dramaturgical organization. In combination with the play's many self-referential devices, I contend, this mixture creates a disorienting effect on the recipient: the play in effect cancels itself out, closing itself off from its potential audience.

In another article (1990b) I explore the intertextual connections between Musil's comedy and August Strindberg's *Miss Julie*. A structural parallelism (both dramas center around a sexual encounter taking place offstage) points to a surprising richness of correspondences between the two plays. On the thematic level, Musil's piece features a variety of further allusions to Strindberg's text. To a certain extent, Musil's irreverent farce can be read as a rewriting of Strindberg's drama. What is of particular interest here is that Strindberg devised *Miss Julie* as a paradigmatic modern tragedy. Various self-referential devices in Musil's play — the subplot surrounding Bärli's abortive murder-suicide, for example — satirize such efforts to revitalize tragic drama. In what appears to be a seemingly innocuous comedy, I suggest, Musil takes issue with Strindberg's demonization of relations between the sexes. Moreover, he questions the precepts underlying Strindberg's attempt to establish a modern form of tragedy. The two essays on Musil's *Vinzenz* have since been incorporated into a book on Musil as dramatist (1993), which focuses on the modes of audience address implied in the dramaturgical structure of his plays.

Two recent contributions to Musil criticism share a similar focus in that they address the self-referential aspects of *Vinzenz* as well as their dramaturgical implications. Dietmar Goltschnigg (1991) delineates the play's position within the system of the genre of comedy, stressing the connection between social criticism and "metaliterary" self-reflection in Musil's piece. The anti-illusionistic playfulness of the *Posse*, Goltschnigg points out, engenders laughter that enables the viewers to recognize their own limitations and opens up "a utopian perspective of an authentic life, liberated from prefabricated action patterns and props" (163f.). Goltschnigg reads the ending of *Vinzenz* as a parody of the conciliatory ending of Hofmannsthal's famous comedy *Der Schwierige* (The Difficult Man, 1921), in contradistinction to Wilfried Berghahn (1963), who had viewed the ending of Musil's play as a gesture of homage on Musil's part to the work of his elder colleague.

Rosmarie Zeller (1991) examines the connection between *Vinzenz* and the history of German drama in the twentieth century. Like Goltschnigg, she proposes a "poetological reading" of Musil's comedy, in which the piece is seen as a realization of the aesthetic views that Musil had put forth in his theoretical essays on drama. In particular, Zeller stresses Musil's radical rejection of illusionistic theater, which led to aesthetic results different from both Brecht's epic theater and the symbolist tendencies of the period. In both *Vinzenz* and *Die Schwärmer*, Zeller suggests, Musil may have inaugurated and anticipated tendencies in recent drama that have as yet not come to full fruition (150).

Goltschnigg's and Zeller's essays are too short to address in greater depth any of the issues raised and to a certain extent they echo opinions already expressed by such critics as Arntzen and Stefanek. All the same, they provide evidence that Musil's second play is gaining increased recognition in the community of Musil scholars. Agata Schwartz (1991) offers a more exhaustive general assessment of Musil's poetics of drama. She outlines his theoretical views, treats some of his unfinished dramatic works ("Die Schildkröte," "Tempora Meier," and the *Tierkreis* fragment), and discusses his two completed plays. As the thematic core of Musil's efforts in drama she defines his concern with the loss of unity that characterizes modern man. Musil, Schwartz argues, aims to reconstitute the lost unity in the aesthetic experience of drama, an art form involving the totality of human faculties. On the thematic level, he addresses the question of a new form of love as a microcosmic emblem of the societal changes he envisages as necessary on the macrocosmic level if modern fragmentation of experience is to be overcome. Whereas *Die Schwärmer*, in the nascent relationship between Thomas and Regine, points to the possibility that this fragmentation can be overcome, *Vinzenz* offers a more resigned assessment of the difficulty, if not the impossibility, of a "new kind of love" (38). In

Schwartz's opinion, *Vinzenz* is more traditional than Musil's first drama, for instance in the way existential contradictions are located on the level of interpersonal tensions rather than within the dramatic personages themselves. It thus, she contends, falls short of realizing Musil's theoretical postulate of a creative new form of drama. Schwartz reaches conclusions that are diametrically opposed to those of Cetti Marinoni, largely dismissing the comedy as a second-rate play.

While I would not argue that *Vinzenz* is one of Musil's most important artistic achievements, I would like to stress that even this apparently innocuous comedy displays an unusual degree of complexity that should not be underestimated. German-language theater, and the culture in which it is embedded, did not prove to be congenial to Musil's aesthetic and thematic aims. Yet his theater reviews and theoretical reflections on drama identify him as a shrewd and perceptive observer who, circumstances permitting, could have had a significant impact on the theater of his day. *Vinzenz*, written with apparent ease and — for Musil — uncharacteristic speed, at the very least is an indication of what its author could have achieved if he had been able to pursue his interest in drama more fully. Such ruminations in the subjunctive mood concern mere possibilities, perhaps, but possibilities that may be quite appropriate for Musil, the *Möglichkeitsmensch*.

9: *Drei Frauen*

OF ALL OF MUSIL'S shorter works, the three stories collected under the title *Drei Frauen* have always been treated with a considerable degree of respect. Like all of Musil's short texts, they attracted critical attention rather belatedly. In the 1950s they received only cursory treatment in comprehensive studies of Musil, such as that of Baumann (1953); and some efforts were made to place them in the context of the overall development of twentieth-century German short prose (Reiss 1955). Right up to the mid-1960s most scholars viewed the three stories primarily as texts anticipating *Der Mann ohne Eigenschaften* (Kaiser and Wilkins 1960; Loebenstein 1960).

The few critics who focused on the stories in greater detail as individual works approached them primarily in a fashion that was known in the 1950s and 1960s as the *werkimmanent* method. This approach, based on a rejection of theoretical models exterior to a given text, supposedly eliminated an interpreter's bias by locating the meaning of a literary work in a description of its aesthetic form or in a reconstruction of the author's ostensible intention. Correspondingly, *Drei Frauen* elicited mainly three types of readings during this period: the first concerns stylistic issues (addressing, for instance, Musil's use of images); another focuses on questions of content from a philosophical perspective (sometimes mixed with theological issues); the third consists of psychological interpretations (sometimes taking recourse to psychoanalytic ideas). Especially in the case of the latter two types, it is clear that the methodologically naive effort to avoid ideological biases frequently allows a critic's unreflected *Weltanschauung* to enter, as it were, through the back door.

Among the early discussions of Musil's *Drei Frauen* narratives, Paul Requadt's essay on "Die Portugiesin" stands out (1954/55). This study of specific motifs places the story in the context of views and perceptions of Italy as the embodiment of a culture of sensuousness and allure, a longstanding tradition in German literature. Like Requadt, Gerhard Friedrich in his essay on "Tonka" (1960) stresses the complexity of Musil's imagery, but with a somewhat more philosophical bent: to Friedrich, the story shows the failure of language when confronted with the mysterious, a situation in which probability replaces the notion of a verifiable truth. Friedrich has some interesting things to say about the problem of memory highlighted in the story. On the whole, however, his essay is representative of the general tendency in Musil criticism of that period to mingle paraphrase with sometimes moralizing commentary.

Such moralizing tendencies in Western Germanistik were complemented in the East in a decidedly political fashion. In the GDR, "Tonka" was the one shorter work of Musil singled out to warrant a great deal of appreciation. In 1955, Rolf Schneider, for instance, suggests that it is in this story that Musil comes closest to overcoming his bourgeois limitations in sensing the magnificence of simple (read: lower-class) people — without, however, fully comprehending it. This failure to see the class-based nature of society, Schneider asserts, is what causes Musil's tragic isolation (112). Two years later, Ernst Fischer echoes this assessment when he criticizes Musil's short works *Vereinigungen*, *Die Schwärmer*, and *Drei Frauen* as failed literary experiments (1957, 856). Fischer exempts only "Tonka," concurring, however, with Schneider that the underlying social aspects of the conflict in the story are insufficiently brought out. Schneider's and Fischer's cautious comments clearly indicate the narrow limits of what could then be said in East Germany about Musil, the "bourgeois" author suspected of "decadent" tendencies.

Critics in the West were more concerned with placing the *Drei Frauen* novellas in the context of Musil's artistic and intellectual development. Wilhelm Braun (1961) reads "Tonka" as an indication that Musil realized the kind of rationality characteristic of the natural sciences could ultimately not be transferred to the realm of human experience. This realization, Braun argues, necessitated a profound reorientation in Musil involving a redefinition of scientific reasoning, a project carried out with great acuity in the novel *Der Mann ohne Eigenschaften*.

Jost Hermand (1962) introduces new terms into the debate about Musil by subjecting "Grigia" to a reading informed by speculative depth psychology. Three interrelated mythological notions, Hermand suggests, underpin Musil's narrative, the motifs of the mine, the quest for gold, and the mystery of the feminine. Hermand associates the three motivic strains with a multitude of cultural traditions, his depth-psychological speculations sometimes stretching the limits of what was then accepted as *Literaturwissenschaft*. As concerns the literary context, Hermand's idiosyncratic approach leads to a rather surprising conclusion: he argues that Musil's "Grigia" engages in a critique of literary expressionism in a manner that parallels Thomas Mann's exploration of decadence in *Death in Venice*.

Lida Kirchberger (1963) is one of the first critics to approach the three stories of *Drei Frauen* as a trilogy, a unified whole. Using Bachofen's concepts on the ages of humankind, she sees represented in each story a different version of the "conflict of the sexes," arranged in a sequence ranging from the archaic through the medieval to the modern period. This sequence, according to Kirchberger, runs parallel to Freud's interpretation of the psychological significance of object choice in his 1913 essay "The Theme of the Three Caskets." Interesting as this attempt to combine mythography with psychoanalysis is, it brings with it severe methodological problems. For one thing, it would appear that a desire to fit the stories into a preestablished interpretive scheme leads to somewhat skewed readings (Kirchberger argues that "Grigia" displays the archaic variant of the central conflict, although the story clearly takes places in a contemporary setting). Moreover, it remains unclear what makes these Freudian ideas valid as interpretive tools for these particular stories; and the alleged correspondences between Musil's story and Freud's theories here are hardly substantiated in Kirchberger's essay.

Two readings of the late 1960s present Musil as a kind of precursor to existentialism. Walter H. Sokel (1967) focuses on the question of faith in "Tonka" by drawing parallels between Musil's text, Kleist's "Die Marquise von O...," and Kierkegaard's *Fear and Trembling* as three works in which an extraordinary experience challenges men to a "suspension of common sense in favor of an irrational and absurd trust" (505). To Sokel, Tonka represents "an indeterminacy that eludes the categorizing and causality-conscious thinking" of the male protagonist (513). Sokel seems to suggest that the narrator's experience with Tonka leads him to insights similar to those expressed by Wittgenstein at the end of his famous *Tractatus Logico-Philosophicus*, where Wittgenstein pointed out that there are mystical aspects of life that elude language and cannot be resolved by reason but have to be delegated to the realm of faith. Sokel argues that this realization shows that Tonka has had "a transforming impact upon her lover" (515). What escapes Sokel in his focus on the spiritual crisis of Musil's male protagonist is that Tonka herself is destroyed in the process, an aspect that undermines his essentially positive reading of the story. Sokel does not address the fact that the inexplicability of Tonka's condition is clearly overdetermined: either a pregnancy or a venereal disease unaccounted for would have sufficed to motivate the crisis of faith in the protagonist, yet here they are combined in a manner that suggests that more is at stake than the question of trust in the other in the face of evidence that such trust may be unwarranted.

Elizabeth J. Boa (1968) draws parallels between "Tonka" and Kleist's story "Die Marquise von O..." that are similar to Sokel's. Also, like Sokel, she argues that Musil's story prefigures the concerns with personal authenticity later addressed by existentialist philosophers. All three *Drei Frauen* narratives emerge in Boa's reading as illustrations of a typically Austrian preoccupation with the difference between illusion and reality (119). Whereas other critics stress the metaphysical and mystical implications of Musil's short texts, she sees an almost comically detached irony at work. She altogether doubts the seriousness of Musil's literary undertaking by stressing what she calls the "purely destructive irony" of "Grigia" and the "rather whimsical 'miracle' solution" of "Die Portugiesin" (126). Few critics, I suspect, would be willing to follow Boa's assessment that in *Drei Frauen* we already see at work Musil the "biting satirist and virtuoso stylist" of the first sections of *Der Mann ohne Eigenschaften*.

From the late 1960s onward, readings of *Drei Frauen* emerge that in their focus on issues of gender represent decidedly feminine, if not feminist, perspectives. Annie Reniers-Servranckx illustrates this tendency in her 1972 monograph. Christine Oertel Sjögren (1969) questions the psychological disposition of the unnamed narrator in Musil's "Tonka," while Lisa Appignanesi (1973b) views the three stories as parts of Musil's quest into the nature of femininity. Given the highly problematic nature of gender relationships in *Drei Frauen*, it is surprising that such readings found relatively little resonance. It was not until the mid-1980s that critics such as Hans-Georg Pott (1984), Todd Kontje (1987), and Thomas Pekar (1989) began to address the stories as problematic representations of male encounters with the Other.

On a more traditional note, Erich Heintel (1973) offers a theological reading of "Tonka" as an illustration of a dual dilemma that, Heintel maintains, preoccupied Musil above all in his *Der Mann ohne Eigenschaften*: the story addresses the contradiction between religious faith and secular historiography on the one hand and the contradiction between faith and scientific thinking on the other. In an analogy to the biblical miracle of Maria's immaculate conception, Heintel identifies Musil's unnamed male protagonist as a Joseph figure who is unable to reconcile the opposing modes of experience in his narrow rationalism (73). Heintel's systematic approach induces him to skirt some of the more problematic aspects of the story. Like Sokel, he focuses exclusively on the problem of Tonka's mysterious pregnancy (which alone would support his theological analogy), altogether leaving out the additional issue of her equally mysterious venereal disease. Psychoanalytically speaking, Musil's story here is clearly overdetermined, calling into question Heintel's neat categorizations. Interestingly enough, as far as I can tell, this overdetermination is also overlooked in all of the psychoanalytically oriented readings of the story, which should address this issue as one of prime importance.

Jochen Schmidt (1975) takes a view diametrically opposed to Heintel's in his discussion of Musil's concept of *Eigenschaftslosigkeit*, the "absence of qualities." The opposition is an indication of a profound shift that occurred in mid-1970s in the reception of *Drei Frauen*. Like previous critics, Schmidt is concerned with the position Musil's early narratives occupy in his oeuvre. Unlike his predecessors, however, Schmidt places Musil's thematic and aesthetic concerns in a broad sociohistorical context. This leads him to single out "Grigia" as a text of crucial significance. The story, Schmidt argues, prefigures most of the major aspects that were to preoccupy Musil in his main novel. In particular, Schmidt focuses on the intrinsic logic of the male protagonist's inner development, a process that mirrors what Nietzsche called the *große Loslösung* (9), the profound crisis brought about by the dissolution of traditional value systems in the experience of modernity. Schmidt stresses the politically problematic implications of Homo's depersonalization: Musil endorses a mystical transfiguration of the dissolution of individuality in a kind of nihilism that displays affinities, Schmidt argues, with irrationalist antidemocratic tendencies of right-wing intellectuals in the Weimar Republic. With few reservations, Schmidt's reading is to be welcomed as one of the first directly to address the historical and political dimension of *Drei Frauen*, a collection of stories all too often approached from a supposedly timeless, neutral perspective.

A special 1976 issue of *Modern Austrian Literature* features three articles on the *Drei Frauen* narratives that reflect in their different methodologies the broad spectrum of approaches to Musil studies in the 1970s. Christine Oertel Sjögren (1976) aims at resolving the "enigma" of Musil's "Tonka." She stresses that readings addressing the story's alleged philosophical, mystical, and metaphysical aspects tend to identify Musil's narrator with Musil the author. Oertel Sjögren follows Annie Reniers-Servranckx (1972), who pointed out that the unnamed narrator of the story is unreliable and that Musil, through a series of satirical devices, maintains a critical distance toward this figure. The reader ought to focus, Oertel Sjögren argues, on the manner in which the narrator recollects his own past actions. On this level of human interaction, the main thematic concern of the story is that of a failed relationship between a man and a woman. Tonka's enigma, then, is easily resolved: it rests in the narrator's inability to accept Tonka and to face the "challenge of any love-relationship, namely redemption of the ego at the price of commitment to another person" (110).

In a somewhat more mundane manner, Maximilian Aue (1976) investigates the residues of German Romanticism in *Drei Frauen*. Focusing primarily on "Grigia," he argues that one of Musil's chief aims is to subject central concepts of Romantic thinking to a rigorous critique. In particular, Aue detects parallels between Musil and Novalis, the author who most clearly epitomizes the subjective idealism of early German Romanticism. By virtue of overt and covert references to his Romantic predecessor (such as the role played by Novalis's diaries in the story), Aue maintains, Musil scrutinizes two key concepts of Romantic thinking: on the one hand, there is the concept of death as a transcendent unifying force; on the other, there is the notion that Man can overcome his alienation from Nature. Musil's protagonist, Homo, however, dies a pointless death in utter isolation. His death lacks the elements of transfiguration through love and integration into universal harmony characteristic of Novalis's thought. In Aue's reading, "Grigia" most clearly encapsulates Musil's rejection of these ideas of early Romanticism, a negative attitude that underlies all three *Drei Frauen* novellas.

The third essay, by Peter Henninger (1976), pays particular attention to lapses in the stories, moments in which the flow of the narrative is interrupted by unclear formulations. In "Tonka," for instance, a reference to the separation of the lovers is phrased in such a way that it remains unclear whether it was the narrator or Tonka who went away on a trip. The reader routinely and inadvertently supplies such missing information by way of recourse to his or her knowledge of the world. Such narrative anomalies can produce insurmountable problems for the translator, who is faced with the dilemma of either reproducing Musil's ambivalent phrasing or else smoothing out the text's rough edges in a manner similar to the unconscious operations of the reader. Henninger argues that such moments of indeterminacy, when the author's control over his narrative material appears to fail, mark an intrusion of the actual issues that on a depth-psychological level motivate Musil's writing: to Henninger, Musil is always unconsciously "speaking about himself," even when he is ostensibly engaged in telling a story about fictional personages (83). Musil's narrative technique, which blurs the distinction between narrating voice and narrated characters, indicates a split in the author's subjectivity. In Henninger's reading, the *Drei Frauen* narratives illustrate Musil's efforts to come to terms with his problematic male identity vis-à-vis his wife Martha, who on an unconscious level is the absent (yet implied) main character and addressee of the three stories. Henninger's ideas have not remained uncontested (see Eibl 1978), yet his discussion of the manner in which readers, by ignoring anomalies in Musil's text, construct meaningful, streamlined, "stories" goes right to the heart of what makes Musil's narratives so fascinating and so irritating at the same time.

In 1978 Karl Eibl published an edition of *Drei Frauen* that contains extensive annotations and commentary alongside the text of the stories. Unlike Henninger, Eibl is not interested in fathoming any unconscious significance. Instead, he firmly locates the meaning of Musil's works on the level of thematic concerns. In his afterword to this edition, Eibl links the three novellas above all to Musil's lifelong investigation of the problem of the *andere Zustand*. Eibl's account differs from traditional approaches in that it does not seek to arrive at a definition of the nature and the genesis of this central concept through recourse to Musil's writings. Instead, Eibl invokes the intellectual context at the turn of the century, when a crisis in the rationalistic positivism brought about an interest in metaphysics. Musil, Eibl notes, participates in the endeavor to bridge the gap between rationalism and mysticism, seeming opposites that upon closer analysis turn out to be two complementary aspects of the same epistemological crisis (132). Musil differs from other representatives of the period such as Mach, Mauthner, and Wittgenstein in that he insists that *Dichtung* is the privileged domain in which a solution to the problem can be attempted through a combination of what Musil in his famous statement from *Der Mann ohne Eigenschaften* called "precision and soul" ("Genauigkeit und Seele"; see *MoE* 583). *Drei Frauen*, then, represents three instances in which a rationalistic male protagonist experiences a profound *Lebenskrise* (157) upon being confronted with the experience of a mystical Other, embodied in the woman he encounters. Eibl shows how Homo in "Grigia" loses interest in the day-to-day reality through an ecstatic experience in which erotic and self-destructive aspects intermingle. "Tonka," in which the unnamed protagonist attempts to arrive at an interpretation of incommensurable past experience, foregrounds for Eibl the problematic nature of remembrance itself (the underlying thesis of a nexus between remembrance and personal identity in "Tonka" was later developed in greater detail by Wolfgang Düsing, 1982). Eibl refrains from psychological speculation and is attentive to the narrative presentation itself, making good general points about the nature of Musil's poetic language such as his narrative technique and his use of images, described by Eibl as a principle of a paratactical arrangement of images (139). The connection Eibl draws between the medievalism of "Die Portugiesin" and medieval *Mirakeldichtung* is a little less convincing. This does not, however, detract from the usefulness of the volume as a valuable resource book.

Wolf Wucherpfennig (1978) undertakes an investigation of the interconnection between philosophical and psychological issues in "Tonka" from the perspective of Freudian psychoanalysis. In his view, a peculiar mixture of rational empiriocriticism and irrational *Lebensphilosophie* characterizes both the "fear of knowledge" (233) of Musil's narrator and the epistemological poetics of Musil himself. According to Wucherpfennig, such attitudes have their roots in childhood experiences: like Hamlet, Musil's narrator is caught up in an Oedipal rivalry, which here involves both his feeble father and his mother's "manly" friend Hyazinth. The simultaneous identification with and rejection of the father prefigures the narrator's ambivalent attitudes toward Tonka. His yearning to reconcile conflicting logics in the mystically transcendent sphere of the "other condition," Wucherpfennig maintains, is a symptom of a narcissistically regressive desire for unification with the mother.

Wucherpfennig's relatively orthodox Freudian approach is complemented by readings informed by the psychoanalytic theories of Jacques Lacan. In an essay (1981) and a monograph (1982), Ronald M. Paulson explores Musil's use of symbols from an idiosyncratic poststructuralist perspective. Paulson focuses on what he calls the "ineffable," signs that resist being subsumed under a traditional rational heading, such as elements associated with myths and fairy tales. Rather than attempting to reconstruct a symptomology of the psychic condition of an individual (that of a character, of the narrator, or of the author), Paulson concerns himself with general psychic structures as they allegedly manifest themselves in Musil's narratives. Paulson's approach, drawing on the cultural psychoanalysis of C. G. Jung and the ethnological study of mythologies of James G. Frazer, is highly speculative, displaying little regard for the reader who may not be familiar with — or inclined to accept — the theoretical concepts underpinning his ideas.

Manfred Sera's essay on "Die Portugiesin" (1980) covers more familiar terrain. Sera associates Musil's story with Nietzschean ideas: the development of Musil's male protagonist toward self-recognition parallels the path described in the first speech of Nietzsche's *Zarathustra*. Sera does not indicate whether he assumes a coincidental parallel or a concrete intertextual link; rather, he appears to assume that Nietzsche's notion of the "three transformations" (146) expresses some timeless universal truth.

Rosmarie Zeller has written a series of articles on the stories collected in *Drei Frauen*. Perhaps her most incisive one is her 1983 essay on Musil's narrative techniques, in which she argues that attempts at defining the narrative situations in the three stories based on traditional narrative theory have failed to capture the essence of Musil's style. Instead, she proposes an approach that draws on the models of structuralist narratology of theorists like Gérard Genette and Dorrit Cohn. She shows how Musil's effort to present familiar material in a new light led him away from using traditional forms of first-person narration and toward his own particular blend of an unspecified narratorial voice and a focalization of narrated events that approximates, yet never fully reaches into, a character's consciousness. "Tonka," with its narrator reflecting on the experiences of his former self, is a special case. Instead of vouchsafing for the authenticity of a recollected experience, the narratorial voice actually destabilizes the reader's position: conflicting and contradictory assessments of events, emotions, and situations are given; this technique, in conjunction with excessive use of metaphors, renders it impossible for the reader to piece together a sense of factual reality. In this fashion, Zeller suggests, Musil anticipates narrative strategies explored much later by proponents of the French *nouveau roman* and in the more experimental writings of Peter Handke (43). (The affinity between "Tonka" and *nouveau roman* modes of writing had been stressed before by Rudolf Schier in a short essay of 1977).

Susan J. Erickson (1983) approaches "Tonka" in the context of an examination of Musil's writer's block. She focuses on the narrator's relationship with his mother, which closely mirrors Musil's own situation as revealed in his notebooks. The professed task of literature as defined by Musil, the quest for knowledge, is related to the ambivalent nature of Musil's relationship with his parents. The questions of paternity and trust at the center of "Tonka" (the problem of knowing the identity of the father and the true nature of the mother) parallel the confusion engendered by the presence of two father figures in the Musil household, Alfred Musil and Hermine Musil's lover Heinrich Reiter.

This constellation, with its ensuing Oedipal rivalries, Erickson suggests, produced a particularly thwarted set of parental attachments in Musil: "An erotic attachment to the father is inadmissible, and the mother, as a force that obstructs desire, becomes a 'de-eroticized object'" (83). At the core of Musil's writing paralysis, Erickson concludes, lies a masked incestuous desire that is both "the hindrance of the poetic instinct and its deepest source" (75). This is perhaps a surprising conclusion to be drawn from a reading of "Tonka," but similar to one that other Musil scholars have reached in different contexts (see Henninger 1976 on "Die Amsel").

Michael Jennings (1984) draws on observations about Musil's narrative style made by Brigitte Röttger (1973), Dorrit Cohn (1974), and Peter Henninger (1976) to provide a thematic interpretation of "Grigia" as a novella concerned with the existential and ethical problem of constructing an identity in a post-Niezschean world without stable values. Jennings rejects affirmative readings that assert a resolution of the story's central thematic conflict (Kaiser and Wilkins 1962, Tober 1966, Reniers-Servranckx 1972, and Eibl 1978). The experimental nature of Musil's narrative technique, with its unstable narrative perspective, Jennings argues, precludes the possibility that Musil's protagonist may be viewed as reaching a new, stable sense of identity. The narrator's frequent interventions, sometimes contradicting Homo's views and perceptions or subjecting them to irony, illustrate to Jennings the protagonist's fundamental disorientation, a "deficiency in his ability to order reality" (64). Homo is shown to lack the ability to structure his perceptions temporally and spatially so that the borderlines between him as the observing subject and the world of objects around him become blurred. Instead of reconciling the tension between inner and outer world, Jennings emphasizes, Homo altogether rejects outer reality "in favor of absolute interiority" (70). Jennings relates this negative assessment of Homo's development to Musil's critical attitude toward his experiences in the First World War that provide the biographical basis of "Grigia"; the mining expedition and Homo's abortive solipsism metaphorically represent the conflict that profoundly shook the foundations of old systems of beliefs, the First World War as "the final state of a society composed of isolated individuals dependent upon an imagined mystical mission" (75).

Jennings's reading is distinguished in its concern for the formal aspects of Musil's writing, which it places in a larger sociohistorical context. In many ways, Hans-Georg Pott's discussion of *Drei Frauen* (1984) provides Jennings's approach with a complement from a poststructuralist anthropological perspective. Among other sources, Pott draws on ideas developed by ethnologist Hans-Peter Duerr. In his seminal book *Traumzeit* (Dreamtime) of 1978, Duerr explored the residues of archaic forms of consciousness found in modern civilization such as myths, rituals, and other practices now generally grouped under the label superstition. Duerr argued that the line that allegedly separates rational civilization from primeval "wilderness" is less clearly drawn than is normally assumed. As he showed, the tradition of witchcraft, for instance, continues on a subterranean level throughout our culture, which is ostensibly informed by Christian religion and scientific rationality. For Duerr, "witches" represent human beliefs and practices that cannot easily be subsumed into a rational system; they are women who appear to reside on the borderline between what we call civilization and wilderness, thus representing a projection onto the female of fears associated with the continued presence of "wilderness" within our civilization. Hans-Georg Pott views the female protagonists of *Drei Frauen* as witches in Duerr's sense. Pott combines such an anthropological focus with theories derived from Freudian and Lacanian psychoanalysis, without, however, speculating on Musil's personal preoccupations, as critics such as Corino, Henninger, and Wucherpfennig tend to do. Instead, Pott interprets the three novellas of *Drei Frauen* as a unity that represents a kind of revocation of the rationalistic tradition of the occidental Enlightenment (68). For instance, Homo's willingness to submit to self-destruction in his relationship with Grigia, Pott argues, contrasts sharply with the famous interpretation of Odysseus in *The Dialectic of Enlightenment* by Max Horkheimer and Theodor W. Adorno: the cunning Odysseus displays in resisting the lure of the Sirens through an act of self-control had appeared to Horkheimer and Adorno as a parable of the self-domestication propagated by the Enlightenment. Musil, Pott maintains, shows that such self-domestication is an impossible ideal, since the body ultimately reasserts itself.

In a short essay, Joseph P. Strelka (1985) points to interesting correspondences between Musil's early novella "Die Vollendung der Liebe" and "Grigia." Unfortunately, the limits of space do not permit Strelka to explore the parallels and differences beyond rather general poetic and biographical considerations: the later work in many ways presents a complement, from the male perspective, to the thematic issues raised in the earlier piece, centered on the problem of infidelity in marriage. In Strelka's estimation, the most significant new components in "Grigia" are the integration of a mythic perspective and a return to a more traditional mode of narration. The former element lends the story a greater universality than Musil's earlier literary experiment, while the latter makes it more accessible to the reader. Both aspects, Strelka contends, make "Grigia" the greater artistic achievement.

While Pott asserts the interplay between literature and other human activities and Strelka stresses the connections between Musil's various works, Renate Homann, in her examination of "Tonka" (1985) appears to claim for the work of literature a status of absolute autonomy. Homann emphatically rejects readings of the story that place it in extraliterary contexts — for instance, the theological reading of Heintel (1973) or sociological ones such as Arntzen's (1980). The significance of Musil's text, she contends, rests not on the level of the male protagonist nor indeed on that suggested by the narrator figure (498). Instead, she asserts that self-referential devices such as overt and covert literary allusions establish a third level on which the text conducts an investigation into the nature and function of literature (499). In this context, Tonka's predicament is of interest mainly as a metaphorical representation of the manner in which literature provides a unique form of *Erkenntnis*, knowledge created by and in the medium of literature alone. While the concern with literature as a vehicle of *Erkenntnis* is, of course, an issue crucial to Musil, it is odd how Homann, in a series of rather surprising moves, manages to eliminate any sense that the story might refer to a reality outside and beyond itself. By way of recourse to Schiller's theory of an opposition of *naiv* and *sentimentalisch* literature, for instance, the motif of Tonka's miraculous pregnancy comes to stand for the unaccountable fertility of the literary imagination ("die Zeugung im literarischen Sinne," 510). Homann proposes that the male protagonist, a *sentimentalisch* thinker in Schiller's sense, is unable to understand Tonka (representing "the naive voice of *Poesie*," 509) because he makes the categorical mistake of attempting to interpret his relationship with her with the help of an inappropriate paradigm (515).

Homann's essay, for all its sophistication, raises severe methodological problems. In her reading, Homann provides ingenious allegorical explanations not only for Tonka's pregnancy but also for such elements of the novella as Tonka's death and the protagonist's scientific invention. Once again, however, not a single thought is wasted on the crucial issue that would complicate this interpretation — Tonka's unexplained venereal disease. This suggests that, for the sake of presenting the story as an instance of the self-examination (or even the self-celebration) of literature, Homann is compelled to select certain elements that she fits into an allegorical mold, neglecting in the process anything that would call into question such an abstract allegorical reading.

Methodological problems of a different nature are evident in Rae-Hyon Kim's monograph on Musil (1986). In his book, originally a dissertation written at Bonn under Beda Allemann, Kim places "Tonka" in the context of a discussion of Musil's overall poetological enterprise. In his writing, Musil, he argues, was interested in analyzing history in its structural dimension, an approach based on a functional-mathematical mode of thinking (22). This necessitated a mode of writing in which the historically limited meaning of words was transcended and the "structural-paradigmatic" qualities of words were allowed to emerge (89). To Kim, "Tonka" illustrates this endeavor of uncovering a dimension of the ineffable underneath the quotidian. Musil displays a tendency "to reduce ostensibly obvious incidents to their inexplicability" (155). In this fashion, according to Kim, he achieves autonomous *Dichtung*, poetic writing that cannot be subsumed under any other form of discourse. The Heideggerian resonances of such a concept of *Dichtung* are easy to see. Problems arise in Kim's unreflected use of Heidegger's concept of *Geschichtlichkeit* (historicity). Kim's insistence on the "incommensurability ("Nichtverfügbarkeit") of literature" (175) leads him to ignore the concrete biographical, social, and historical aspects of material reality upon which Musil draws in his project of poetic transformation.

Albrecht Classen (1988) takes the obvious biblical motifs in "Tonka" as a starting point for a discussion of the supposed religious significance of the story. He contends that Musil's text centers on a problem crucial to modern man, the tension between faith and rationality (182). Classen makes some interesting points, for instance, on the connection between the medieval legend of St. Mary and the snow motif in the story. However, his effort to search for parallel biblical citations for a wide variety of details in Musil's story is not always convincing. Classen appears to overlook the fact that biblical resonances belong to the general cultural inventory of Western civilization; biblical parallels thus do not necessarily have to reflect Musil's alleged "central theme of the quest for God" (180). In the context of the autobiographical background of the story (Musil's problematic relationship with Herma Dietz), a reading that views "Tonka" primarily as religious allegory underemphasizes the psychological factors that appear to motivate the very endeavor of storytelling. This would suggest that it is perhaps less a quest for a deity than a quest for absolution from guilt that constitutes the novella's religious dimension.

Cornelia Heering-Düllo (1988) pursues several aims in her reading of "Die Portugiesin." On one level, she attempts a thematic interpretation of the story as an illustration of how a sense of personal identity ultimately cannot be communicated. She tentatively places this problem in the historical context of the social and political upheavals in the wake of the First World War. She also stresses the story's position in the history of the German novella. Moreover, her reflections on the theoretical definitions of the genre lead her to suggest that Musil's story represents a *Metanovelle* (50), a narrative text that reflects on the limitations of narration, since it renders problematic the very narrative conventions on which the novella genre is based.

Judith Ryan (1989) addresses similar aesthetic points in a brief but thought-provoking essay that links "Tonka," alongside Gertrude Stein's "Melanctha" and André Breton's *Nadja*, with Peter Bürger's theories of the avant-garde. She argues that in some ways Musil's seemingly traditional story provides a greater challenge to the ideological underpinnings of Western art than ostensibly more experimental texts, such as openly provocative works of dada and surrealism, the two avant-garde movements that to Bürger most clearly signify the rebellion against traditional art in bourgeois society. Ryan's focus here is less on the dual enigma of Tonka's pregnancy and illness than on the significance that the process of recollection and narration has for the narrator. The narrator is ultimately unable to make sense of the past, to resolve the inner conflicts that apparently prompted his writing. "Tonka," Ryan concludes, thus calls into question "the notion of the therapeutic function of artistic self-reflection" (105), a key assumption about the function and purpose of literature in Western bourgeois societies.

Drei Frauen occupies a central position in Thomas Pekar's 1989 study of love relationships in Musil's works. The three stories continue Musil's quest for a heightened form of love initiated in his *Vereinigungen* while also anticipating the comprehensive analysis of love as a socially encoded mode of behavior that comes to full fruition in *Der Mann ohne Eigenschaften*. Whereas the societal codes of love are violated in Musil's grand novel by the choice of a partner who is "too close" (Ulrich and his sister Agathe and the ensuing problem of incest), in the three early narratives problems arise out of the "remoteness" of the women whom the male protagonists encounter. "Grigia" embodies the clash between a male order of relationships (equated here with civilization and aggressiveness) and a female order (associated with nature and submissiveness). Homo's confrontation with the archaic-exotic *Liebesordnung* of Grigia's world turns out to be self-destructive: his paradoxical quest for the mystical transfiguration of his love for his wife in his relationship with Grigia leads to his death. "Die Portugiesin" is concerned with the "creation of intimacy" (123) in the sense of the social psychology of Niklas Luhmann, a reciprocal communication that bridges the gap between two partners from different spheres. The Portuguese lady, at first a mere object of von Ketten's possession, acts as a catalyst of his transformation: his mystical illness and recovery signal von Ketten's emergence out of the male world of warfare and into the sphere of reciprocal love. "Tonka" shows that subjective intimacy and the societal construct of the "good family" are irreconcilable. In his relationship with Tonka, the male protagonist attempts to escape the rigidly codified order of the family. His inability to shed the inhibiting constraints of this social order leads him to reject and ultimately destroy Tonka, a woman who on account of her dubious social origin cannot be integrated into the *Familienordnung*. The male protagonist retreats by transfiguring Tonka's suffering in his imagination into a redemptive mystical experience. Pekar reads Musil's texts primarily as symptoms of an ongoing debate with the effects of socially imposed internalized norms, throughout refraining from criticizing him for his potential complicity in the perpetuation of such norms.

Eichiro Akashi (1990) suggests a similarity between Musil's use of poetic images in "Tonka" and the paintings of Paul Cézanne. Both artists, he argues, attempted to break away from impressionism (Cézanne from the painting style of Camille Pissaro, and Musil from the "impressionist" philosophy of Ernst Mach) in a quest to depict the effect of the world of objects in the consciousness of the perceiving subject. This focus is mirrored in Musil's peculiar narrative technique, which is based on the recollections of an individual who reflects in the third-person voice on his past experience. Akashi highlights the innovative aspects of Musil's style by contrasting it with Dostoyevsky's "The Gentle One," a story with thematic concerns similar to those of "Tonka" but in which the process of remembrance is represented more conventionally in a first-person narrative.

Whereas Akashi explicitly rejects any attempt to interpret "Tonka" in terms of speculative psychology, Hildegard Lahme-Gronostaj (1991) devotes an entire monograph to a discussion of the novella based on an investigation of the psychoanalytic concept of *Erkenntnis*. Following Melanie Klein's theories regarding the formation of subjectivity and object relations in the infant, Lahme-Gronostaj defines *Erkenntnis* as a sense that it is possible to acquire knowledge about the external and internal world. Underneath the Oedipal level of the story (the narrator's ambivalent love relationships with Tonka and with his mother), Lahme-Gronostaj detects another level reaching back to the pre-Oedipal stage of subject-object division. The story centers on the irresolvable question of paternity; the narrator's obsession with the identity of the father of Tonka's child reflects his insecurity about his own origins. The narrator's religious ruminations about Tonka's "mystery" represent narcissistic fantasies of omnipotence that correlate with his insecure sense of self. In its irregularities (for instance, the blurred distinction between third-person narration and first-person narrator), Musil's text both enacts and participates in the narrator's inability to reach *Erkenntnis*. Lahme-Gronostaj combines the psychoanalytically oriented approaches of Oertel Sjögren (1969 and 1976) and Henninger (1976, 1980, 1981) with Röttger's (1973) and Schier's (1977) analyses of the story's formal structure. Her conclusion, which reintroduces the notion of authorial intentionality, remains somewhat incongruous; to her, "Tonka" represents Musil's "endeavor to reestablish an undivided state of being" (182) — understood here, presumably, as an archaic sense of identity between infant and parent that predates individuation. Although, like Oertel Sjögren, she employs the notion of narcissistic regression, Lahme-Gronostaj is not interested primarily in developing a psychopathology of the narrator figure, nor does she follow Henninger's speculations about the psychosexual disposition of Musil the author.

Gerhard Meisel's (1991) reading of *Drei Frauen* carries the speculative psychological approach — tentatively implied in Lahme-Gronostaj's reading — further in a tour de force of brilliant and baffling interpretive moves. Meisel sees a dual correspondence between Musil's three stories and ideas drawn from Immanuel Kant and Johann Jakob Bachofen. The sequence of stories in *Drei Frauen*, he proposes, reverses Kant's famous three questions concerning human nature in his *Critique of Pure Reason* and runs parallel to the three stages of the development of human society that Bachofen outlines in *Das Mutterrecht*. "Grigia" corresponds to Kant's question "What may I hope?" and to Bachofen's notion of a rule-free "hetaerean" stage of society; "Die Portugiesin" mirrors Kant's "What ought I do?" and Bachofen's notion of a Demetric (matriarchal) phase; "Tonka," finally, represents "What can I know?" and the Apollonian (patriarchal) era. Meisel refrains from making Kirchberger's (1963) mistake of equating Bachofen's typological stages with actual historical time periods. The association of "Tonka" with the Kantian problem of faith was, in part, anticipated in an essay on the novella by Rainulf A. Stelzmann (1975). Meisel's argument, rhetorically enlivened with metaphors drawn from chess, is too complex and too original to do justice to here. Of particular interest is his interpretation of the scientific and rationalistic dimension of "Tonka." He argues cogently that in accepting at face value the male protagonist's ostensible central dilemma — that of reconciling rational evidence and subjective sympathy — Musil's critics remain caught up in the same patriarchal dynamic, imposing rules of mathematical probability on what actually lies outside the sphere defined by Musil as the "ratoïd." The female body, with its cycles of menstruation and reproductivity (which, as modern medicine well knows, are subject to extreme variations), fundamentally eschews the "ratïod" — the patriarchal sphere of rational logic. Meisel suggests that the preoccupation of Musil's male protagonist with the cause of Tonka's pregnancy points to an insecurity regarding his own origin: the story ultimately centers around the protagonist's questions concerning the identity of his father (115; see also Erickson 1983). Meisel's conclusion does not, however, induce him to speculate about Musil's psychosexual disposition. In many ways, Meisel's thoughtful and highly stimulating interpretations call into question the entire tradition of affirmative readings of *Drei Frauen*, which attempt to come to an understanding of Musil's stories through a mixture of paraphrase and recourse to Musil's own pronouncements.

Alongside innovative and enterprising efforts such as Meisel's, studies continue to appear that represent more traditional approaches found in Germanistik and that still prove to be of value. Kathleen O'Connor (1992) pragmatically discusses Musil's short narratives in the context of the tradition of the novella in German literature. She defines as the crucial structural tension of the genre an opposition between what she calls "mimetic" and "subjective" tendencies. In *Drei Frauen*, she maintains, Musil continues the move away from a mimetic representation of a referential reality toward a subjective exploration of mythical modes of thinking. According to O'Connor, Musil achieves a perfect balance of these two opposing tendencies in "Tonka" with its combination of realistic and mythical elements.

Ursula Meier Ruf (1992) focuses on the "dissolution" of the identities of the male protagonists in the three stories. This central thematic issue, she notes, finds its correlative on the formal level in the proliferation of poetic images and in a narrative technique that dissolves traditional notions of time, space, and causality. The three male protagonists undergo different experiences of crisis and ecstasy that result in a profound reorientation ("Peripetie," 12). Both O'Connor and Meier Ruf reject psychological speculation yet only too often implicitly assume ideas of psychological plausibility in their discussion of the stories' characters that are oddly reminiscent of the *werkimmanent* interpretations of Germanistik in the 1950s and 1960s. O'Connor counterbalances this tendency with an insightful analysis of the aesthetic limits and possibilities of the novella genre at the beginning of the twentieth century. Meier Ruf uses models on the nature of narrative that were developed in the 1960s and 1970s by scholars like Eberhard Lämmert and Franz Stanzel, thus ignoring some twenty years of international developments in the theory of narrative. All too often, she reverts to paraphrase so that her study, though well presented and clearly structured, offers little new that would illuminate Musil's enigmatic *Drei Frauen*.

Peter Stephan Jungk (1992) addresses the alleged enigma at the center of Musil's "Tonka." Jungk rightly points out that both the story and most of its interpreters conflate two events that were distinct in Musil's life: the pregnancy of his lover Herma Dietz and her abortion on the one hand, and her death from an apparent syphilitic infection on the other. Jungk's research shows that the first incident happened in February 1906. Musil's diaries dating from late 1906 contain drafts of the story in which Herma's death is envisioned. According to Musil's biographer Karl Corino (1988), Herma is presumed to have died in the fall of 1907, more than one and a half years after the crisis over her pregnancy. In the story "Tonka," however, the time frame is compressed so that the two events appear to occur almost simultaneously with an implication of a causal connection. Jungk suggests that the obfuscation of temporal division in the literary version of the personal experience clearly indicates the mechanisms of guilt and repression at work in Musil; in his writing, he camouflages his own responsibility for Herma's fate and for her death. The "mystery" at the core of "Tonka," Jungk concludes, lies more in the psyche of the creator than in the supposedly irresolvable enigma surrounding the fictional character. Jungk's essay is a refreshing reminder that it is still possible to discover interesting new aspects of a work by sidestepping the well-worn paths of Musil criticism.

Alice Kuzniar's essay on "Die Portugiesin" (1993) develops some of the ideas suggested in Susan Erickson's semiotic reading of that story (1986). In a subtle and perceptive examination of modes of signification and recurring motifs, Kuzniar focuses on the tension between verbal and visual communication and its connection with the theme of interiority. Words are shown to be incapable of expressing the inner self, whereas gazes indicate that the self is constituted in an encounter with an Other. Kuzniar links Musil's novella with the Romantic tradition, especially with Novalis's notion of the discovery of the self in a *thou* (100). Von Ketten's miraculous recovery culminates in his reentry into his own castle (an emblem of his inner self), in which he finds his beloved wife. The Other, simultaneously familiar and foreign, is present within von Ketten. Interiority and exteriority are thus shown as mutually interdependent. Kuzniar deals with complex issues, yet she avoids both psychological speculation and the tendency to subsume Musil under the heading of mysticism. While her approach is informed by semiotic theories, she does not succumb to the temptation to translate a literary text into theoretical jargon. Sensitive to the nature of Musil's language, Kuzniar allows the story to resonate in its complexity.

In 1979 Rosmarie Zeller complained that there was no tradition of research on *Drei Frauen* (248). Given the sheer volume of readings of the stories, even at the time when the pronouncement was made, such an assertion clearly appears to be a polemical overstatement. Yet it is true that, for the most part, writings about the three novellas up to that point were representative of the affirmative tradition of Musil studies, displaying the familiar mixture of commentary, quotation, and paraphrase that was the hallmark of much of Musil criticism before the critical debates initiated in the late 1960s and early 1970s. In this sense, it is true that readings dealing with the problematic aspects of Musil's short narratives emerge only in the late 1970s, starting perhaps with Peter Henninger (1976) and culminating in the work of Hans-Georg Pott (1984) and Gerhard Meisel (1991). Yet there is much that awaits illumination from the perspective of issues raised in recent theoretical debates concerning literary criticism (such as poststructuralist narrative theory, gender studies, and cultural anthropology). The interpretive problems posed by the contradictions and idiosyncracies of *Drei Frauen* are far from being resolved.

10: *Nachlaß zu Lebzeiten*

THE COLLECTION OF PROSE pieces that Musil published in 1936 under the bitterly ironic title *Nachlaß zu Lebzeiten* (translated as *Posthumous Papers of a Living Author*, 1987) is generally regarded as a work of minor importance. Although over the decades a sizeable body of work dealing with the texts has evolved, most of it remains on the periphery of Musil scholarship. Some general introductory works on Musil, such as those by Burton Pike (1961), Annie Reniers-Servranckx (1972), Gilbert Reis (1983), and Roger Willemsen (1985), contain chapters on the collection. Murray G. Hall, in his Vienna dissertation examining animal motifs in Musil (1975a), devotes considerable attention to the animal stories in *Nachlaß zu Lebzeiten*. Moreover, since Musil's short prose pieces are popular readings in high-school German classes, there are several commentaries dealing with the texts from a pedagogical angle (see Ingeborg Scholz 1978 and Klaus Zobel 1985). All in all, however, studies on the thirty prose pieces in Musil's collection remain sporadic; assessments and interpretations are hardly ever formed in a dialogue with other opinions. Only rarely, as in the case of Brigitte Röttger and her recourse to Soviet semiotics (1981), do studies reflect a deliberate effort to apply a particular methodology to a given text. More often than not, Musil scholars are content with making pronouncements on the texts collected in *Nachlaß zu Lebzeiten* without reflecting on their own, or anybody else's, theoretical position. This makes it difficult, if not impossible, to identify stringent developments or tendencies in this area of Musil criticism.

Throughout the 1960s, criticism of *Nachlaß zu Lebzeiten* by and large consisted of little more than paraphrase with added commentary. Most attention by far was focused on the short text "Das Fliegenpapier" (The Fly Paper) and the novella "Die Amsel" (The Blackbird). It was perhaps Benno von Wiese, eminence grise of West German Germanistik, who put the latter on the literary map, so to speak, by including a chapter on it in the 1962 edition of his influential volume on the German novella, *Die deutsche Novelle von Goethe bis Kafka*. In declaring the novella to be one of Musil's greatest artistic achievements, von Wiese put his stamp of approval on a short work of Musil's. Von Wiese stresses the mystical experiences that provide the core of the story's three internal narratives. These experiences, he maintains, inspire in Musil's protagonist a new sense of religious faith. Von Wiese strips Musil's novella of its historical and political dimension, thus establishing, as Jürgen C. Thöming notes (1974, 264), the parameters for the quasi-theological and psychological readings that were to follow. Erich Burgstaller (1972), for instance, explicitly presents his own interpretation of "Die Amsel" as but a modest modification and clarification of von Wiese's ideas; Musil's protagonist, he claims, is led to accept the extrasensual as a principle that dominates existence in an experience of "metaphysical rebirth." Sweeping generalizations like these are representative of tendencies within Musil scholarship to subsume Musil's writings under grandiloquent designs. As a rule, such interpretations pay little or no attention to the aesthetic organization of a given text.

During the 1960s there were only sporadic efforts to explore the richness of Musil's shorter prose pieces and place them within his oeuvre. Heribert Brosthaus (1964) was the first to argue that the short text "Triëdere" from *Nachlaß zu Lebzeiten* contains the key aspects of Musil's aesthetics in emblematically condensed fashion. Franz Hagmann (1969) reads "Das Fliegenpapier" as a kind of mystical allegory of a struggle for life, equating the fly's instinctual will to life with an indescribable inner force operating in human beings (17) — an interpretation echoed by Wilhelm Braun (1982). Yet it was not until the 1970s that critics began to focus more extensively on Musil's short prose pieces from a wide variety of perspectives.

The increasing diversification of perspectives is illustrated by three readings of "Die Amsel" that appeared in 1970 and were explicitly designed as responses to (and to a certain extent, rebuttals of) Benno von Wiese's 1962 essay on the piece. Frederick W. Krotz (1970) focuses on the psychopathology of the protagonist, Azwei. To him, Musil set out to depict the nature of an individual's psychosis, with the three embedded narratives representing aspects of the fictional patient's anamnesis (9). Krotz views Azweï's yearning for unconditional freedom, which leads him to abandon any ties to a stabilizing social order, as a symptom of madness (22), confirming the initial assessment that Azwei is a "victim of schizophrenic regression" (7). Krotz's reading is limited by the notions of psychic normalcy and illness he employs, which are ultimately alien to Musil's own conception of psychology. Karl Eibl (1970) offers an in-depth analysis of the narrative situation of "Die Amsel" in terms of structural linguistics. Eibl relates the narrative technique to Musil's conceptual opposition of the *ratioïd* and the *nicht-ratioïd* spheres, which the novella aims at mediating. The structural complexities of the piece, such as features that render the narrative fiction unstable, Eibl proposes, reflect Musil's central thematic concern. The three stories Azwei tells in an effort to give objective expression to his subjective mystical experience are intended to show that such attempts at objectivation are doomed to fail. What is left as a possibility is precisely the depiction of such failure. In a general discussion of Musil's narrative technique, Wolfgang Rothe (1970) briefly explores what he regards as affinities between "Die Amsel" and the contemporary literary context, in particular Kafka's writings, the prose narratives of the expressionist movement (Gottfried Benn and Georg Heym), and the narrative experiments in Hermann Broch's short prose.

Albert Berger (1970) singles out the "Unfreundliche Betrachtungen" (Unfriendly Meditations) collected in *Nachlaß zu Lebzeiten* to illustrate Musil's use of satire. These eleven essayistic prose vignettes, he argues, differ from Musil's theoretical essays in the manner in which they make allowances to the readers. In his essays, Musil attempts to do justice to the complexity of the issues addressed; this results in texts that sometimes place extraordinary intellectual demands on the reader. In the satirical sketches, Berger proposes, Musil intends to win over his audience by lacing his social criticism with a conciliatory spirit that aims to engage rather than provoke the reader. To Berger, the object of Musil's satire is to make his readers aware of the disparity between ostentatious claims and an underlying reality (567). Musil's relativism regarding world views, Berger contends, guards him and his works against appropriation by any kind of political ideology.

Albert Berger's view of Musil's status as ostensibly above politics, quite typical of Germanistik of the 1950s and 1960s, represents the kind of stance that a Marxist like Hans Sanders (1972) vehemently opposes. In his essay on "Die Amsel," Sanders has little sympathy for critics who read Musil's novella for its mystical, theological, philosophical, or psychological dimensions. Sander, because of his interest in *Ideologiekritik*, considers these various facets as symptoms of an overriding problem, that of the interrelatedness of individual experience and sociohistorical reality. In his mystical tendencies, Azwei emerges as a typical representative of the German bourgeois intellectual of the early part of the twentieth century. Azwei's indignation with urbanization, mass society, and the institution of marriage reveals his elitist bourgeois individualism. To Sanders, this elitism implies a rejection of the traditions of liberal democratic thinking that originated in the Enlightenment. Azwei's propensity toward mysticism is indicative of a withdrawal from concrete political reality: "Life as mythical primal force is declared an alternative to modern 'soulless' civilization" (89). Sanders contends that the illusory attempt to overcome the harsh realities of monopolistic capitalism in a mystical experience renders political reality a mere intrusion into a supposedly pure inner sphere. Political processes are not analyzed as the result of social forces but are experienced as acts of fate that are ultimately inaccessible to rational comprehension. To Azwei, for instance, the exposure to death in war turns into an existential experience that has erotic and aesthetic components. Following the ideas about the aestheticization and mythification of war in *Die Zerstörung der Vernunft* (The Destruction of Reason) by Marxist critic Georg Lukács, Sanders detects prefascist elements in the experience of Musil's protagonist. After the First

World War, Musil's story tells us, Azwei lived in the Soviet Union for a few years, yet he rejects the new system as inimical to his desire for individualism. Sanders views this stance as typical of the disorientation of bourgeois intellectuals of the period, torn between a realization that the old order has collapsed and an inability to embrace an emerging new order. To Sanders, the withdrawal into inwardness of the bourgeois intelligentsia effectively represents an abdication of the Enlightenment, the "capitulation of reason" vis-à-vis social reality (91). Occasionally, Sanders's argument is propelled in odd directions by the force of its own logic, for instance when he detects supposedly fascist and/or racist elements in Musil. At one point he engages in an abstruse speculative extrapolation of the possible overtones of Musil's image of the riding crop and its alleged association with Nietzsche's concept of the "blonde beast" (88; aptly refuted by Thöming 1974, 275). Sanders's insistence on the sociohistorical dimension of literature brings out important aspects of Musil's text; his staunchly Marxist position, however, endows his writing with disturbing self-righteousness and ideological certitude. In its mixture of intelligence and indignation, Sanders's essay is a fascinating reminder of the highly politicized academic climate in West Germany during the early 1970s.

Uwe Baur (1973a) contests the validity of Sanders's approach by stressing the elements within "Die Amsel" that are critical of Azwei. Baur begins with an assessment of previous interpretations of the story, in particular the three readings by Krotz, Eibl, and Rothe published in 1970. He stresses the close proximity of the short prose piece and Musil's novel-in-progress, *Der Mann ohne Eigenschaften*, which had reached a crucial stage when the novella was published in 1928. Baur takes the split of the protagonist into a narrating persona and a listening persona as an indication of a psychological crisis. Rejecting Krotz, who applies external standards of psychopathology to his interpretation of this point, Baur seeks to establish Musil's own views on the affinity between the mystical and the psychopathological experience. In a comparison of the novella with the unfinished novel, Azwei emerges as a more solipsistic variant of Ulrich. Unlike Ulrich, Azwei is unable to integrate his mystical experiences into a new definition of himself and a new attitude toward life. The third internal narrative of the novella, Baur notes, does not present a true mystical experience; instead, it emphasizes Azwei's unstable identity by showing how he creates a delusionary "surrogate reality" by totemizing the blackbird into a representation of his dead mother (250). Azwei's regression to an infantile self, which is paralleled by a withdrawal from society altogether, indicates that he has become incapable of experiencing the polarity of self and other that, according to Baur, is the hallmark of the true mystical experience (251). A detailed examination of the novella's structure with its frame narrative, which recedes as the three internal narratives unfold, leads Baur to conclude that Aeins and Azwei are to be viewed as figurations of the unidentified first-person frame narrator. The division of these two personages in turn reflects the identity crisis Musil experienced after the death of his mother in 1924. In distancing himself from Azwei, the frame narrator — and his author — achieves the new identity that eludes Azwei. Musil's working through of the problem in the short novella, Baur suggests, enabled him to develop a reconfigured personal identity, mirrored in the increased detachment of his new alter ego, Ulrich.

Jürgen C. Thöming (1974) takes the popularity of "Die Amsel" as an indication of tendencies on the part of Musil scholars (and high-school teachers) to obfuscate the problematic aspects of Musil's text. Thöming credits Sanders (1972) with breaking up the tacit critical consensus that regards "Die Amsel" as one of Musil's main works. Thöming differs from Sanders in rejecting the idea that Musil deliberately set out to discredit Enlightenment rationality and egalitarian democracy in his depiction of three existential experiences. Musil, Thöming emphasizes, cannot be accused of submitting to protofascist tendencies. He can, however, be faulted for publishing in the politically and ideologically volatile climate of 1928 a story that invites such a misreading. In the context of the crisis of democracy in the last period of the Weimar Republic, Thöming suggests, a novella that places much emphasis on a mystification of individual experience can easily be misconstrued as expressing sympathies for the antirationalistic tendencies of the political extreme right. Thöming singles out the second embedded narrative, the *Fliegerpfeil* episode, as an element in Musil's story that appears to endorse a mystification of the war experience in antidemocratic terms. He attributes the misunderstanding to a lack of artistic control on Musil's part, proposing three explanations for the author's decision to publish a text that fell short of his own aesthetic standards. "Die Amsel," Thöming speculates, may just be the product of financial necessity; it may represent a failed effort to put in practice a reductive theory of the novella; or it may have been intended as a testing ground for the mystical ideas with which Musil was preoccupied at that time in his novel-in-progress, *Der Mann ohne Eigenschaften*. In contrast to Baur, Thöming maintains that autobiographical material and thematic concerns are insufficiently mediated in Musil's story, an aesthetic flaw that renders the text vulnerable to erroneous kinds of ideological appropriation. He suggests that Musil counteracted the intrinsic deficiencies of his short novella by various means in his main novel, such as a more pronounced use of satire, more outspoken social criticism, and the introduction of a second main character (Agathe) to offset Ulrich's solipsism. The absence of such strategies, in Thöming's view, makes "Die Amsel" Musil's weakest text. The novella's ostensible accessibility and its popularity with readers and teachers, he argues, thus reflect profound misunderstandings of Musil's art.

Thöming's criticism of Sanders's rather extreme views is well taken, although Thöming himself, in his polemic against efforts to establish Musil as a classic above and beyond the dirty region of politics, sometimes appears to go too far. For instance, he speculates on whether Musil may have introduced the identification of blackbird and mother at the end of the story as a parodistic jibe directed against Jungian speculative psychology of myths (281). It is one thing to point to flaws in what may appear as Musil's tendency toward rash idealization; it is quite another in effect to discredit "Die Amsel" altogether as an inferior, perfunctory piece of writing. Still, Thöming's refreshing polemic and his keen sensitivity to Musil's use of language make his work one of the most significant attempts to combat literary hagiography and move Musil criticism beyond the confines of its affirmative stage.

Compared to Sanders and Thöming, Heinz J. Halm (1975) represents a staunchly traditional approach of mainstream Germanistik oblivious of methodological and ideological debates. In his discussion of three animal stories from *Nachlaß zu Lebzeiten* ("Das Fliegenpapier," "Die Affeninsel," and "Hasenkatastrophe"), Halm notes strong satirical overtones that arise out of a combination of neutral description and anthropomorphic comparison. The stories are not observed vignettes, Halm contends, but rather need to be read as satirical parables, as reflections on the human condition. The focus in all three stories is on certain aspects of collective human behavior. In Halm's view, the generally problematic position of Musil's narrator indicates the problem of individual complicity in and indifference to violence and oppression. Halm attributes to Musil a didactic intention: the stories compel readers to reflect upon their own ambivalent feelings concerning situations in their own lives that are analogous to the ones depicted here.

Alfred Doppler (1975) presents his examination of the narrative process in "Die Amsel" as a direct complement to Uwe Baur's sociopsychological reading of the story's subject matter. Doppler employs Eugen Coseriu's notion of *evocation* to describe the way in which Musil's text creates meaning out of the full semantic potential of the words, images, and ideas and their combination. In Doppler's view, the split between narrating persona (Azwei) and addressee (Aeins) highlights an antithetical principle in Musil's approach. Antithetical oppositions work on a multiplicity of levels, from the conceptual one down to that of syntax. The *Textsinn* — the "meaning" of Musil's text — Doppler maintains, thus resides in the very structure of Musil's enterprise, seen here as an "expedition toward truth" akin to that of Franz Kafka (136).

In his 1975 Mainz *Habilitation*, published in book form in 1982, Wolfgang Düsing takes issue with Baur's assertion that "Die Amsel" represents a study in psychopathology. To Düsing, Musil's main thematic concern lies in an exploration of the problem of identity formation, which is linked with a focus on the processes of memory. He places the novella in the overall context of the development of Musil's narrative technique from *Törleß* to *Der Mann ohne Eigenschaften*. "Die Amsel" serves as the clearest illustration of the nexus between *Erinnerungstechnik* and the quest for identity in Musil. Whereas Baur had argued that Musil's narrator pathologically totemizes his personal experience, Düsing insists that Azwei remains aware that the perception of personal experience in mystical or magical terms has a primarily symbolic function. Azwei realizes that his identification of the blackbird with his mother is a *Zeichen*, a sign or cipher (88): Azwei's narration represents a conscious attempt to constitute an identity in the process of recollecting past experiences. It thus not only has regressive elements, as was implied in Baur's reading, but displays, Düsing emphasizes, a forward-looking, utopian dimension.

Victor Lange, a leading Goethe scholar, offers the first in-depth analysis of "Das Fliegenpapier" in a short essay of 1976/77. Approaching the little prose vignette as an exemplary specimen of the author's narrative technique, Lange delineates the way in which Musil renders a subjective observation objective through his use of metaphorical similes. Lange rejects efforts to interpret the text as a direct allegory (such as the mystical reading of Hagmann 1969), emphasizing instead that it is an attempt on Musil's part to describe the very process of observation, in which sense perception and cognitive processing go hand in hand. As a manifestation of the labor of a perceiving consciousness, Lange suggests, Musil's text assumes a particular position in the history of subjectivity: Musil no longer resorts to preestablished philosophical, ideological, or moral concepts to describe an observed event but shows how both subjectivity and the world of objects are constituted in a process of perpetual interchange (reprint 1982, 459). In a brief but illuminating excursus, Lange contrasts this attitude with an example from the past, a poem of Goethe's from 1810 on the death of a fly. The striking similarity of subject matter only highlights the radical difference between the two authors' visions: Goethe's fly dies on account of a lack of circumspection and caution, intoxicated by the poison that leads to its destruction. The poem thus implies a stable universe in which unquestioned moral significance can easily be attributed to events. Lange concludes that, whereas Goethe presupposes an individual moral consciousness as given, in Musil such a consciousness has yet to be constructed in the process of perception. In its attention to detail and its range of vision, Lange's essay remains one of the most rewarding contributions to the study of Musil's *Nachlaß zu Lebzeiten*.

Peter Henninger (1976) addresses "Die Amsel" as the final link in the chain of Musil's seven short narratives that are usually labeled novellas, a series that begins with "Das verzauberte Haus" (1908) and includes the texts collected in *Vereinigungen* (1911) and *Drei Frauen* (1924). Henninger views all of Musil's writings as manifestations of the author's psychosexual predicament, his unstable identity revealing itself in manners that need to be examined psychoanalytically. Formal and stylistic peculiarities in Musil's texts mark moments when the ostensible aim of the writing process (that of an individual telling a fictional story) collapses and the actual writing situation (a subject, such as Musil the author, expressing its self-alienation) shines through. With its structural intricacies, "Die Amsel," in Henninger's opinion provides the clearest example of the nexus of autobiography and fiction in Musil: it reveals the fundamentally solipsistic nature of Musil's writing as camouflaged soliloquy (83).

Underlying Henninger's speculative reading is the thesis that Musil's unstable identity is the result of a pre-Oedipal mother fixation. This thesis, derived from complex Lacanian theories of self-formation, finds its more mundane complement in Karl Baedecker's reading (1976). Baedecker, who knew Musil personally, stresses the connections between "Die Amsel" and Musil's life. That Musil chose to place it at the end of his collection *Nachlaß zu Lebzeiten,* Baedecker believes, indicates that the story acts as a kind of summing up of Musil's entire existence (29). In particular, it focuses on the author's problematic relationship with his mother: "Die Amsel" was written, Baedecker points out, directly after her death in 1924. According to Baedecker, Musil's psychological development was hampered by the irregular situation in the Musil household; the presence of a rival father figure (Hermine Musil's friend Heinrich Reiter) induced in Musil ambivalent feelings concerning a lack of motherly love. In this context, "Die Amsel" represents an attempt on Musil's part to overcome his ambivalence and create a memorial to his mother (32).

Like Henninger and Baedecker, Wolfram Mauser (1978) bases his reading of "Die Amsel" on psychoanalytic categories. Unlike his two predecessors, however, he is not interested in the author's psychological makeup. His focus is primarily on the problem of identity formation in general. Musil's Azwei, Mauser contends, experiences a tension between his desire for self-development and pressures imposed from the outside (107). Rather than confronting and working through the psychic conflicts, Azwei escapes into narcissistic regression. It is only in isolated mystical moments of existential threat that he is able to experience a sense of self-fulfillment. The alternation between general despondency and moments of compensatory illusory fulfillment, Mauser argues, corresponds to the profile of narcissism. (This idea was anticipated by Henninger and later developed in greater detail, with recourse to Heinz Kohut's theories of narcissism, by Rudolf Hoppler in a somewhat sanctimonious essay of 1984). That the novella is open-ended indicates to Mauser that Musil comprehended the vicious cycle in which his protagonist was trapped and that the author ultimately distanced himself from the character he portrayed.

In 1980 Marie-Louise Roth published her *Habilitation,* a two-volume study comprising a detailed comparisons of all the variants of the texts contained in

Nachlaß zu Lebzeiten, most of which Musil had published several times in different forms in a wide range of journalistic and literary outlets before assembling them in his book. Roth's central focus throughout is on the manner in which subjective experience is rendered objective through Musil's manifold stylistic revisions of his writings. She combines the philological methods of meticulous *Textkritik* with interpretive commentary, always with a view toward clarifying the author's conscious intentions. Some portions of the work, which was originally written in French, are available in German in the form of short essays on selected texts. Though Roth's achievement is extraordinary, she sometimes relies perhaps too heavily on paraphrase in her interpretations.

Brigitte Röttger (1981) applies concepts developed by Soviet semiotician J. M. Lotman in her analysis of "Das Fliegenpapier." In particular, Röttger traces the way in which Musil turns an apparently irrelevant event (the death of a fly) into an issue of great relevance, a *sujet*, in Lotman's sense. Röttger shows how this *sujet* is created by a radical shift in narrative perspective: semantically neutral descriptive vocabulary is gradually displaced by emotionally charged language. Through the use of anthropomorphic images, for example, Musil suggests that sense perceptions are tantamount to acts of interpretation. The shift of focus to the attribution of meaning establishes the presence of an implied narrator who invites the reader to share his own vision. Musil's final metaphor of the eye, Röttger argues, emphasizes that the main point of the text is to show how the world is transformed through an act of "autonomous vision" (515).

Perhaps the most interesting contribution to the study of a particular text from *Nachlaß zu Lebzeiten* is the volume edited by Norbert Groeben (1981) that contains various readings of the short piece "Die Hasenkatastrophe" both by lay readers and by literary critics writing from different methodological approaches. Groeben's collection is a fascinating document of the *Methodendiskussion* that preoccupied West German Germanistik throughout much of the 1970s. It has to be noted that the professional essays are intended primarily as illustrations of the usefulness and the limitations of the respective methods employed and should not necessarily be viewed as readings that directly reflect their authors' views. The more traditionally hermeneutic approaches are represented by two contributions by Renate von Heydebrand (1981). In the first she gives a *werkimmanent* close reading of the piece as a literary work of art consciously crafted by its author. She compares the four different versions of the text published during Musil's lifetime and takes recourse to Musil's theoretical pronouncements to determine his intentions. Her findings, in conjunction with an analysis of the formal features and stylistic devices, lead her to conclude that the short text was written out of an impulse to criticize certain aspects of European civilization. Von Heydebrand's second essay, illustrating a *geistesgeschichtlich* approach, places the story in the context of intellectual currents of the period. The prose piece emulates a variety of views concerning man's relationship with nature that were prevalent during the first third of the century. Musil, von Heydebrand suggests, shares and critically reflects contemporary ambivalent attitudes of nature both as a refuge and as a potential threat to civilized man. Moreover, Musil shows how atavistic modes of experience erupt momentarily from underneath a thin veneer of civilization. This idea, von Heydebrand suggests, is linked with Musil's notion of the *andere Zustand*, which in turn resembles mystical tendencies in thinkers like Ludwig Klages and Max Scheler. Von Heydebrand concludes that "Die Hasenkatastrophe" is a depiction of a crisis in European civilization in which conflicting tendencies within civilized man wreak havoc (59).

Klaus-Dieter Schlüer (1981) provides a psychoanalytic interpretation of the piece in Groeben's volume. Perhaps not surprisingly, he detects unresolved sexual tensions in the unmotivated animosity that Musil's nameless narrator displays toward the "kleine Dame" who owns the feisty fox terrier. The narrator at first transfers his phallic-aggressive impulses upon the terrier, yet at the moment at which the hare becomes the victim of the dog's violent attack, the hare is metaphorically changed into a child, indicating a switch in identification. The narrator, Schlüer proposes, resorts to an infantile status in order to avoid direct confrontation with those aspects of his psyche that he cannot consciously acknowledge. Schlüer's reading, if occasionally somewhat strained, is supported by intriguing reflections upon the psychosexual connotations of Musil's metaphors. In many ways Schlüer spells out on the individual level what von Heydebrand tactfully labels general ailments of civilization: to Schlüer, the "catastrophe" of the piece lies in the narrator's inability to reach an awareness of his own psychosexual conflicts; he cannot relate positively to his anima (74).

The other contributions in Groeben's volume are of less interest. Elmar Lochner's short essay sketchily outlines a Marxist approach to Musil's prose piece. The focus is on the ambivalent attitude of the narrator toward the social environment he depicts: on the one hand, he is hostile toward his fellow tourists, yet at the moment of crisis he is just as unwilling or unable to act as they are. To Lochner, this signals a typically bourgeois predisposition, which combines limited critical awareness with a socially conditioned paralysis. In effect, Lochner polemically attributes to Musil's text the kind of political specificity a mainstream critic such as Heinz J. Halm (1975, discussed earlier in this chapter) is at pains to avoid. Hermann Greisinger illustrates a structuralist methodology, which in this case consists largely of classifying words, concepts, and motifs into clusters of "lexemes" in an effort to provide a solid "material base" for a comprehensive interpretation. Attempts at empirical approaches are represented by Werner Faulstich and Hartmut A. Oldenbürger, who seek to fathom the nature of the reading experience of actual readers with the help of questionnaires, cloze procedure tests, and the like. Both articles feature elaborate statistics, graphic diagrams, and flow charts that present "empirical results" in a truly *wissenschaftlich* if somewhat overbearing manner. The volume and its findings led to an interesting polemic debate between Werner Faulstich and Wilhelm Solms (1986) that illustrates a rift that to a certain extent still permeates Germanistik.

Peter West Nutting (1983) takes the instability of the narrating voices in "Die Amsel" as an indication that the story has to be read ironically. He counters critics who attempt to view the characters Aeins and Azwei as aspects of one personality, insisting, instead, on the division between these two distinct personages and the frame narrator. Drawing on Mikhail Bakhtin's notions of the dialogic nature of narrative, West Nutting sees in Azwei's attempts at storytelling a comic, carnivalesque component. Azwei's production of images and similes in a quest for self-discovery, he contends, reveals him to be clown or a fool who wears a "self-ironic smile" (52). West Nutting polemically rejects readings of the story as concerned with the mystical experience or with psychopathology. While Azwei generates signs in an unending process of narration, he refuses to settle for a "final signification" (56). In West Nutting's opinion, this precludes any direct attribution of serious significance to the stories Azwei tells. West Nutting's unorthodox view implies that generations of Musil scholars have missed the novella's comical and ironic elements. Though such a conclusion is quite plausible in a field less in tune, perhaps, with subtle ironies than with grand philosophical and psychological speculation, I find it in this particular instance less than convincing.

If West Nutting takes a provocatively inquisitive approach that does not shun interpretive risks, Marie-Louise Roth stands at the other end of the spectrum as a firm proponent of interpretive orthodoxy. Her reading of "Die Amsel" consists largely of a variation of ideas introduced by von Wiese. Roth's essay, originally written and published in French in 1979 and translated into German in 1984, once more seeks to establish Musil's conscious intentions. It differs from most other affirmative readings in that its author can draw on a detailed knowledge of the various drafts and manuscripts of the novella. Roth's main focus is on the protagonist's growing awareness and acceptance of a reality beyond everyday life. The three embedded narratives, Roth contends, confront Azwei with the existential challenge of redefining his existence vis-à-vis a metaphysical reality in a "primal decision" (1984, 182). The only parallel in Roth's reading to that of West Nutting is that, unlike most other critics, she does not view Aeins and Azwei as manifestations of a single personality. Instead, she suggests that Aeins is primarily a portrait of Musil's close friend and ally Franz Blei (177).

Joseph P. Strelka (1983b) is another advocate of a thematic approach based on a traditional notion of close reading. His discussion of the story "Geschichte aus drei Jahrhunderten" (Story from Three Centuries) addresses the three little narratives contained in the story as three humorous variations of the Amazon theme, involving the male fear of female violence. Strelka draws an interesting parallel between this underlying theme in its three manifestations (past, present, and future) and Othmar Schoeck's opera *Penthesilea*, which was performed in 1927, the year Musil wrote his story. At the core of Musil's story, Strelka observes, is a mythical dimension in which the acknowledgement of the polarity between the sexes mirrors the essential polarity of existence.

Starting in the mid-1970s, Gudrun Mauch (later Brokoph-Mauch) wrote a series of essays on various aspects of *Nachlaß zu Lebzeiten* that were later to become part of a monograph devoted to the book (1985). Unlike Roth (1980), Brokoph-Mauch does not deal with the complexities of the genesis of Musil's texts. Instead, she groups selected pieces into clusters according to a set of unifying themes. Like Brosthaus (1964), she singles out "Triëdere" as a text that illustrates Musil's general literary method, which she defines as a four-step sequence of identifying, approaching, distancing, and analyzing an object (1985, 152). Albert Berger had proposed a similar description of Musil's literary method in reference to "Triëdere" (1970, 569). One apparent aim of Brokoph-Mauch's study is to elevate Musil's short prose pieces to the status of literary works that anticipate or sometimes even equal in rank his main work, *Der Mann ohne Eigenschaften*. On occasion, this objective leads to overstatements, for example when she hails the short prose piece "Fischer an der Ostsee" (Fishermen on the Baltic) as a "miniature mirror image of the great novel" (51). Some of the issues Brokoph-Mauch addresses are important, however, and have largely been overlooked by Musil criticism. For instance, there is Musil's problematic attitude toward the emancipation of women; as she rightly notes, he fails to address the socioeconomic dimensions of the question (135). Brokoph-Mauch's overall conclusion that all of Musil's work represents an effort to reach a humanistic view of the world (191) is unsatisfying in its generality. In view of Musil's critical comments on the bankruptcy of the humanistic tradition in his address to the Paris Congress on the Defense of Culture, delivered in the summer of 1935 (a few months before the publication of *Nachlaß zu Lebzeiten*), such a view is difficult to maintain. While Musil wrestles with ethical and aesthetic questions in an endeavor to understand the human predicament in modernity, his thinking is too complex and too critical to be subsumed under what is commonly understood as humanism, with its advocacy of allegedly universal human values. Manfred Moser's (1989) discussion of "Ein Soldat erzählt" (A Soldier's Tale), a preliminary version of the *Fliegerpfeil* episode of "Die Amsel," implicitly refutes such a reading. Moser points to some disturbing tensions and contradictions in Musil's intellectual outlook, such as the combination of mysticism and Taylorist

Psychotechnik, that makes it impossible to place him unequivocally in the context of traditional humanistic rationality.

It will be remembered that only a year before Brokoph-Mauch's monograph appeared, Hans-Georg Pott had hailed Musil's work as a comprehensive critique of the European Enlightenment tradition — a view anticipated with regard to *Der Mann ohne Eigenschaften* as early as 1969 by Manfred Sera. In his chapter on "Die Amsel," Pott (1984) takes the description of Azwei, the story's internal narrator, as the starting point for his speculative interpretation of the psychosexual significance of the text. At the outset, Pott observes, Azwei is compared to a curved riding crop. To Pott, the comparison evokes the shape of an embryo and points to a regression into infantile experience. This regressive tendency, encapsulated in the embryo motif that appears several times in the text, is combined with reflections on narration as a means of creating and defining a self. This leads Pott to conclude that the three stories encompassed in "Die Amsel" have to do with a quest for the psychosexual mystery of existence, which extends from a preembryonic state to death and beyond (176).

To Rae-Hyeon Kim (1986), "Das Fliegenpapier" exemplifies Musil's interest in analyzing history in its structural dimension as a conglomerate of functional relationships; written before the First World War, the piece develops the metaphoric expression of people dying in the war "like flies" (107) into an image of the catastrophe of European civilization, which the war later appeared to Musil to be. Moreover, Kim detects self-referential aspects in the short text that are of direct relevance to Musil's poetology. The piece of paper upon which the fly is trapped, Kim suggests, evokes the author's confrontation with the proverbial blank piece of paper; and the author's involvement in the writing process is characterized by an ambivalent tension between fascination and entrapment. According to Kim, "Das Fliegenpapier" thus affords the reader a glimpse into Musil's own "language workshop" (118).

Helmut Lethen's fascinating examination of "Triëdere" (1987) draws on a wide range of theories of visual perception. Musil's short experimental piece, Lethen points out, belongs in the context of the debate about the act of seeing carried out during Musil's time in such diverse fields as psychology, philosophy, art history, the physiognomical theories of Ernst Kretschmer, and the dramaturgy of film developed by Béla Balázs. Lethen reads Musil's text as both an example and a criticism of what he calls the *szientifischen Blick* (211), a gaze of quasi-scientific detachment. He identifies E. T. A. Hoffmann's story "Des Vetters Eckfenster" (The Cousin's Corner Window, 1822) as the first instance in German literature of this gaze that characterizes the tradition of realism. In Lethen's assessment, Musil's prose piece marks both the culmination and the end point of this tradition. Musil emerges as a representative of tendencies in the European avant-garde to reflect on the contradictions inherent in the notion of central perspective, which presupposes a stable viewing subject with a fixed position, and is thus incompatible with the spreading awareness that the subject could no longer be thought of as a fixed entity with an identifiable substance. Lethen points to the aesthetic dilemma Musil faced: he belonged to a generation of European intellectuals who realized that the "scientific" gaze was untenable but who were also aware that there was no reverting to supposedly innocent or immediate ways of looking at the world. Though highly demanding of its reader, Lethen's essay is a welcome change from the myopic narrowness that sometimes characterizes close readings of Musil's short prose.

Peter Horn's essay on "Die Amsel" (1987) is perhaps less an interpretation of Musil's story than a rumination on the human predicament along lines established by such postmodern theorists as Michel Foucault, Gilles Deleuze, and Félix Guattari. Horn sees in Azwei's storytelling an attempt to escape the web of predetermination through "discourse" — the complex sets of symbolic orders (language, cognition, family, society, and the like) in which the self is embedded and which it is taught to accept as natural givens. Such orders, Horn contends, are constructs that both protect and entrap the self. Through his storytelling, Azwei engages in an endeavor to make sense out of contingency without subsuming experience under any of the given orders. At the core of this endeavor, Horn suggests, is a quest for the *Ursprung* of the self (398), the roots from which personal experience springs but which lie outside (beyond or before) the self. Horn seems to imply that this undertaking — difficult and endless, yet indispensable — is fundamental to the human condition.

Annette Fuchs (1988) examines some of the prose vignettes collected under the heading "Bilder" (Images) in *Nachlaß zu Lebzeiten* (in particular, "Triëdere," "Das Fliegenpapier," and "Slowenisches Dorfbegräbnis"). She counters any efforts to assign these short pieces an allegorical or symbolic significance with reference to a reality outside the texts. Instead, she argues, the pieces focus on the process of perception itself and establish a communication between the depicted object and the perceiving and narrating subject that undercuts categorical thinking. Musil's interest in a new way of seeing is akin to a general tendency of the period to seek to reclaim the fullness of experience by eliminating the limiting mediation of conscious thought — a tendency exemplified, for instance, in the efforts of Rilke's Malte to "learn seeing" (67). Musil's quest for an immediacy of perception, Fuchs suggests, represents an effort to overcome the loss of authentic experience. Fuchs locates the utopian dimension of Musil's writing in the insistence that this sense of loss, one of the main characteristics of modernity, can be overcome on the aesthetic level in the medium of literature.

Srdan Bogosavljevic (1989b) discusses the significance of childhood as a literary motif in Musil's works and its connection with the overriding inquiry into the nature of morality with reference to two of Musil's short prose pieces that had thus far largely been ignored. "Kleine Lebensreise" (Little Life Sojourn) of 1925 (a piece not included in *Nachlaß zu Lebzeiten*) and the whimsical "Kindergeschichte" (Children's Story) of 1926 link an experience of the extraordinary with the emergence of a socially conditioned morality. The fairytale elements of both stories, Bogosavljevic concludes, point to vestiges of childlike modes of experience, residues of the incommensurable within the allegedly rational world of adults that Musil accepts with a gentle, conciliatory sense of irony.

Like Bogosavljevic, Gerd-Theo Tewilt (1991) approaches Musil's short prose with an interest in issues of general significance. He uses the prose sketch "Inflation" as a starting point for a discussion of Musil's views on history. In Tewilt's reading, the prose pieces collected in *Nachlaß zu Lebzeiten* emerge as vignettes in which the structural aspects of historical constellations become evident as particular moments are arrested at a significant time. Musil refrains from attempting to impose any kind of predetermined rational pattern upon a given constellation. In this fashion, Tewilt argues, he makes visible the very "movement" of history without recourse to teleological notions such as *Rationalität* (rationality) or *Sinn* (meaningfulness; 363).

After the *wissenschaftlich* and rhetorical excesses of the 1970s and 1980s, studies of the pieces collected in *Nachlaß zu Lebzeiten* appear to take more traditional approaches once again. For example, Marie-Louise Roth (1992) uses the short prose sketch "Kann ein Pferd lachen?" (Can a Horse Laugh?) for an investigation of the development of Musil's use of irony. She traces the transformation of the text's central idea: it begins as an observed experience recorded in a diary in December 1913, reappears as a recollection contained in a diary of 1916, and later is reworked into the version included in *Nachlaß zu Lebzeiten* at the end of 1935. The transformation of personal experience to literary text, Roth observes, is marked by an increased presence of irony that bestows rich resonances of general significance upon an everyday occurrence and invites the reader to view matters in a new perspective. The prose piece thus illustrates the emergence of a writing strategy that Musil needed to accomplish his artistic and ethical aims and that culminated in the combination of essayism and irony in his *Der Mann ohne Eigenschaften*. Even in his ostensibly unassuming prose sketch, Roth suggests, Musil endeavors to challenge the reader's preconceived notions about the world.

In her examination of Musil's position in the history of the German novella, Kathleen O'Connor (1992) views "Die Amsel" as the end point of his development as a novella writer. In this text, the tension intrinsic to the genre (the juxtaposition of objective truth and subjective experience) leads to a dissolution of the form. A variety of formal features, such as the division of the text into three internal narratives, O'Connor proposes, reflects this dissolution that induced Musil to abandon the novella in favor of a different genre, the novel, as a forum for exploring his aesthetic and thematic concerns. For the most part, O'Connor steers clear of the kind of high-energy psychological speculation that dominates much of the criticism of Musil's short prose works. On occasion, however, she reverts to interpreting Musil's characters along lines oddly reminiscent of traditionally affirmative readings.

Nachlaß zu Lebzeiten will probably continue to occupy a marginal position in Musil scholarship. It is likely that "Die Amsel" will remain his one work most widely read by nonspecialists. The famous description of prefabricated life in a Berlin *Hinterhof* tenement featured in the first embedded narrative, Rudolf Hoppler informs us (1984, 190), has become required reading for students of architecture at the Eidgenössische Technische Hochschule at Zurich, presumably as a reminder of the potential social and political ramifications of architectural design turned practice. This is perhaps a fitting legacy of Musil, the engineer-turned-writer with an ethical mission who died in exile in Switzerland.

11: *Der Mann ohne Eigenschaften*

SCHOLARS OF GERMANISTIK SEEM to like books reputed to be difficult. Musil's *Der Mann ohne Eigenschaften* surely must rank among the books most written about in the field of literature in the German language. Ever since its republication under the editorship of Adolf Frisé in 1952, there has been a steady and incessant stream of articles, essays, and monographs on Musil's unfinished magnum opus from all sorts of different angles and perspectives. Given the sheer volume of criticism — now numbering in the hundreds, if not thousands, of works — it is surprising that there are few close readings of the novel that investigate its form or describe the nature of its language in detailed analysis. On the one hand, this probably has to do with the scope of the novel, which makes comprehensive analysis difficult. On the other hand, it is understandable that most critics seem eager to aim for a kind of master reading of the text rather than attempting to account for specific stylistic or poetic phenomena.

Serious study of Musil's complex and multifaceted work requires a considerable investment of time and intellectual energy on the part of the reader. To many scholars Musil's grand novel appears to present a kind of athletic challenge to display one's intellectual mastery. It is not surprising, then, that the novel is such a popular object for doctoral dissertations, leading to a proliferation of book-length studies that are as well-meaning as they are redundant: a limited number of topics is addressed time and again, with "new" methodologies frequently offering reworkings of familiar points rather than genuine contributions that open new vistas. The pressures of the academic world dictate that minute differences in accentuation be presented as radically new results, encouraging a tendency to subsume the complexity of Musil's text under a general overriding concept.

In the Cold War climate of the 1950s, the tendency of mainstream Germanistik was to downplay the political implications of Musil's art. A particularly telling example is the work of Hermann Pongs. In the second edition of his study on the modern novel (1956), Pongs added a discussion of *Der Mann ohne Eigenschaften* to supplement a work he had undertaken in 1952 in response to what he called "the current existential distress of the Germans" (reprint 1963, 7). Pongs emulates notions derived from Freudian psychoanalysis to describe Musil's protagonist, Ulrich, as a prime representative of the modern existential condition of ambivalence, a neurotic condition that is as acute, if not more so, after the Second World War as it was in Musil's time. While acknowledging Musil's predominantly critical attitude toward the sociohistorical situation depicted in the novel, Pongs renders this attitude essentially apolitical by presenting Musil's work as the diagnosis of a general "disease of the time" (326). In this fashion, he carefully avoids addressing the causal and functional background of the situation. Pongs ascribes to Musil a striving for *Einfalt* — unity and simplicity — that would resolve the polarizations and dichotomies that characterize the predicament of modernity (13). At certain moments in Pongs's writing there emerges a peculiar rhetoric that appears to belie the ostensible concern with existential crisis and mysticism: at one point, for instance, Pongs professes his exasperation with Musil's negative portrayal of the Habsburg military, although, Pongs exclaims, the admirable discipline of the Habsburg army had been the one element that provided cohesion in a society plagued by ethnic tensions, "truly a defensive eastern bullwark (*Ostwall*) of Europe" (329). Similarly, Pongs's rhetoric of distrust of "the whole range of the Eastern peoples" ("die ganze Skala der Ostvölker," 329), presumably representing forces of destruction and contamination, curiously harks back to those twelve years in the history of the German speaking countries that some representatives of Germanistik were all too eager to forget.

Sometimes the ideological or professional bias of a critic created oddly skewed readings of Musil's novel. Alfred Focke, for instance, writing from his perspective as a Jesuit theologian, eagerly follows ideas proposed by Gerhard Müller in his 1958 Vienna dissertation, hailing Musil's magnum opus as a philosophical and religious myth about the "fundamentally tragic status of human nature as such" (Focke 1957/58, 30). Such lofty ruminations culminate in the thesis that Musil's protagonist Ulrich represents modern man's alienation from God. Ulrich, Focke contends, fails to achieve a metaphysical trust in his maker, remaining unable to take the redeeming "leap into faith" (33). On a more mundane note, Gerhard Irle (1965) places Musil in the context of works by Kafka, William Faulkner, and Virginia Woolf that address the question of sanity in the modern context. Musil's portrayal of individual psychoses in the characters Clarisse and Moosbrugger, Irle proposes, turns the novel into a prime specimen of what Irle defines as a new subgenre, the "psychiatric novel" (148). Such reductive readings are by no means atypical during the 1950s and 1960s, the first two decades of academic Musil criticism.

There were, however, also serious efforts to provide a solid basis for the study of Musil's work. One of the first contributions to a more focused stylistic analysis came from Beda Allemann, whose influential monograph *Ironie und Dichtung* (1956) culminates in a lengthy discussion of Musil's use of irony in *Der Mann ohne Eigenschaften*. Allemann attempts to define irony as a self-conscious literary device that all but places literature in a sphere remote from the world of contingencies. His central metaphor is that of a *Spielraum* (4), a realm of poetic activity opened up by the self-canceling effects of ironic configurations. Allemann's notion of irony is indebted to German early Romanticism (particularly as typified by Novalis and Friedrich Schlegel) and is based in large part upon Martin Heidegger's concept of literature as *Dichtung*, a sphere of human activity that transcends everyday concerns. To Allemann, irony is a literary mode that contributes to the erosion of existential certainties by calling into question preestablished thought patterns. The comprehensive loss of certainties is one of the key features of the modern predicament. Musil's grand novel fragment serves Allemann as an ideal illustration of the connection between the experience of modernity thus defined and the essentially ironic nature of modern *Dichtung*. Allemann gives a series of examples from Musil's novel to describe his ironic style as "conciliatory" (173); Musil gently criticizes the world he describes, yet he never establishes a fixed vantage point from which to lay claim to a greater degree of authority. Each issue discussed or character portrayed is conceded a certain validity. Moreover, Musil's use of irony extends to his own poetic endeavor. Allemann argues that the irony in Musil's novel lies not so much in the manner in which particular statements are formulated but in the nature of the overall configurations, such as the relationships between the characters, which establish a network of finely tuned gradations in differences and correspondences.

Both Allemann's approach and his conclusions are highly questionable: he associates irony with the wistful self-awareness of a culture in its late phase, employing notions such as *Spätheit* (lateness) and *Spätzeit* (late phase), inspired by Martin Heidegger. From this Heideggerian perspective, history — in the sense of concrete material existence as reflected in the novel — evaporates and gives way to lofty notions of the privileged position of Musil as the wise poet-philosopher. Allemann in effect turns Musil into a modern version of the benign sage, very much in the manner of the public image of the late Theodor Fontane prevalent in West Germany in the 1950s. In his pronouncedly apolitical stance, Allemann is representative of a general tendency within Western Germanistik in the Adenauer era. In their insistence on a perspective that supposedly transcended politics (a stance that tended to amount to a general disavowal of the importance of politics altogether), literary critics directly mirrored the overall climate of restoration and conservatism.

Allemann's theses on irony spawned a debate in Musil criticism that in many ways continues to this day. Walter H. Sokel (1960/61) was among the first to respond publicly, noting that Musil's irony is far removed from the kind of all-encompassing conciliatory attitude Allemann ascribes to Musil. Sokel emphasizes Musil's critical attitude toward any kind of rash and superficial attempts at overcoming the existential, cultural, and political crisis depicted in his novel. Musil's irony, Sokel proposes, borders on satire whenever he unmasks and debunks efforts to combat the experience of fragmentation by way of a "feigned totality" (211).

It is easy to see why a younger generation immediately took issue with Allemann in social and political terms. Arntzen's 1956 dissertation on satire in Musil's work, published in book form in 1960, was written very much as a response to Allemann and as a rebuttal. Against Allemann's concept of irony as a literary mode transcending particular epochs and genres, Arntzen offers the concept of satire, stressing the element of hard-edged social criticism in Musil's novel. To Arntzen, Musil's main aim is an analysis of a culture in crisis, an investigation of the numerous factors that led to the collapse of civilization in central Europe. Arntzen is right in stressing that the critical impetus of Musil's project should not be overlooked. Yet his own critical stance, despite its sometimes brilliant rhetoric, lacks political concreteness: the key concept that runs through Arntzen's study is that of Musil's novel as a diagnosis of an unspecified societal *Schizophrenie*. The metaphor, taken from the sphere of psychotherapy, suggests that what Musil describes is a kind of organic illness devoid of concrete historical, political, economic, and ideological causes. Critics have since noted that Allemann's and Arntzen's approaches are not as dissimilar as Arntzen implies, turning much of Arntzen's polemic into a dispute over terminology (Karthaus 1965b, 466; Huber 1982, 99). Still, with his focus on *Gattungsgeschichte* (historical genre studies) and his insistence on what in the widest sense is a political reading of Musil, Arntzen provided useful impulses to Musil scholarship. Alongside a broad discussion of the nature and history of satirical writing, Arntzen presents a wide variety of examples based on close readings of passages from Musil's book. For this reason alone Arntzen's highly readable book remains one of the most significant contributions to Musil scholarship.

More limited in scope but just as fruitful is Albrecht Schöne's discussion of Musil's use of the subjunctive mood. Originally Schöne's inaugural lecture upon assuming a professorship at the University of Göttingen, it was published as an article in 1961. The essay has since been reprinted several times and ranks as one of the most impressive contributions to a stylistic analysis of Musil's work. In his eloquent and brilliant presentation, Schöne explores the significance of the subjunctive mode in Musil's novel, showing how aspects of grammar and style relate to overriding thematic concerns. He distinguishes the function and significance of the various types of subjunctive (*irrealis*, *potentialis*, and so on), all of which correspond to particular elements of Musil's overall poetics, such as his interest in experimentation or his focus on a utopian perspective. Such characteristics lead Schöne to place Musil and his work firmly in the tradition of the European Enlightenment. In his drafts and manuscripts, Musil sometimes experimented with putting different sets of characters in the same situation. Such variants, Schöne argues, possess the same degree of validity, since Musil's experimental attitude allows for — in fact, stresses — the coexistence of a variety of possibilities. Schöne does not take sides in the dispute over the continuation of Musil's unfinished novel: in his reading, the fragmentary and open-ended form of the book becomes a corollary of *Experimentiergesinnung*, the experimental attitude of Musil the trained scientist, from which springs the novelist's penchant for the subjunctive mood (reprint 1975, 304). Unfortunately, the scope of Schöne's essay does not allow him to develop his ideas at greater length. Yet the discussion of what superficially may appear to be minor grammatical issues yields a wide range of results of interest not only to the Musil scholar but to anyone concerned with the history of modern German prose.

Werner Hoffmeister's *Studien zur erlebten Rede bei Thomas Mann und Robert Musil* of 1965, based on his 1962 Brown University dissertation, is similar in approach. Like Schöne, Hoffmeister focuses on a particular stylistic phenomenon from which he draws general conclusions about the nature of Musil's art. This method, which Hoffmeister calls "inductive" and "empirical" (8), is enhanced here by an essentially comparative perspective. Musil employs *erlebte Rede*, the narrative technique known in English as free indirect discourse, with particular frequency. Hoffmeister places Musil's use of this stylistic device in the context of an overall tendency in modern literature toward an "interiorization of narration" (160), in which the focus shifts from the depiction of an outside reality to an observation of the operations of individual consciousness. Hoffmeister's book anticipates ideas that were later to be more fully explored in structuralist theories of narrative, such as Dorrit Cohn's *Transparent Minds* (1978), a monograph on modes of representing consciousness in prose fiction, which includes insightful comments on Musil's narrative technique.

Perhaps the most comprehensive thematic interpretation of Musil's novel to emerge from the first phase of Musil criticism is that of Wolfdietrich Rasch (1963). Under eight headings he addresses some of the crucial thematic and formal aspects that continue to occupy Musil scholarship to this day, such as the dissolution of linear narrative, the issue of utopianism, the tension between rationality and mysticism, the question of irony, and the relationship between Ulrich and Agathe. Rasch synthesizes much of the previous scholarship, including Wilfried Berghahn's 1956 Bonn dissertation on essayistic narration, and stresses the consistency of Musil's overall design in his discussion of the tricky questions about the envisaged continuation of the unfinished novel. Always mindful of the author's professed intention, Rasch manages to combine an affirmative stance with a perspective critical of the limitations and internal contradictions of Musil's narrative project.

The critical works of Allemann, Arntzen, Schöne, Hoffmeister, and Rasch remain exemplary achievements in Musil studies, regardless of the changes in interests, methods, and theoretical paradigms that Germanistik has undergone in the last thirty-odd years. They stand out in the incipient phase of Musil scholarship, when much energy was absorbed by the notorious dispute over the reliability of Frisé's edition and the need for a "definitive" version of the text, accompanied by innumerable essayistic reflections and appreciations of Musil and his work.

The 1960s brought a gradual reorientation in Musil studies toward *Geistesgeschichte* in the study of *Der Mann ohne Eigenschaften*, as scholars began to relate Musil's ideas to larger intellectual traditions or systematically explore Musil's intellectual background. Ulrich Karthaus, in his examination of the connection between the temporal structures of Musil's novel and the *andere Zustand* (1965a), represents the former approach. He employs notions derived from Kant's *Critique of Pure Reason* and Heidegger's *Being and Time* to examine Musil's treatment of time. The first two parts of the novel, he contends, are characterized by a suspension of linear time. Generally, the date and duration of fictional events cannot be easily identified. Instead, time appears as a polydimensional "playing field of poetic time" (156), filtered through the subjective experience of Musil's characters. This process allows a second kind of reality to shine through that eludes rationality. Part three, however, reasserts time as a chronological sequence of occurrences, highlighting the problem underlying Ulrich and Agathe's quest for the *andere Zustand* and showing their efforts to lend duration to a different mode of experience to be irresolvable. The only way for Ulrich and Agathe to transcend the contingencies of time, Karthaus maintains, would be to take recourse to the faith of an established religious tradition. Without recourse to religious dogma, their experiment is doomed to failure. To Karthaus, it is a sign of Musil's greatness and intellectual integrity that he refused to provide a fictional solution to a conflict that cannot be resolved in material reality. Karthaus thus stands in clear and diametrical opposition to the mystical tendencies of Kaiser and Wilkins (1962), who had claimed that Musil intended a kind of apotheosis of Ulrich and Agathe's spiritual union. At the same time, Karthaus's approach raises methodological problems concerning the applicability of philosophical theorems to an analysis of a literary work. Karthaus does not seem entirely to escape the pressure of systematization, the temptation to fit Musil's novel into a preconceived philosophical model.

Dieter Kühn (1965) is more attentive to the peculiar qualities of Musil's prose in his examination of Musil's characteristic stylistic devices of analogy and variation against the backdrop of some of the traditions that had a formative influence upon his intellectual outlook. To this end, Kühn correlates Musil's characters with the sources of their internal world. With Ulrich, for instance, it is primarily Ernst Mach's empiriocriticism; Nietzsche provides much of the substance that fuels the conflicts between Walter and Clarisse; and the watered down *Lebensphilosophie* of turn-of-the-century Swedish educational reformer Ellen Key is satirized in Diotima. Of particular interest is Kühn's discussion of the affinity between Gottfried von Strassburg and Musil's treatment of the relationship of Ulrich and Agathe, an issue later explored in more depth by Wolfgang Freese (1972). Kühn stresses the connections between Ulrich and the other characters, who all serve as foils of Musil's protagonist. Kühn's book stands out from other dissertations of the period in its focus, conciseness, and overall readability.

The most comprehensive and systematic attempt to place Musil's novel in the context of German intellectual history was undertaken by Renate von Heydebrand in her 1962 Münster dissertation, published in expanded form as a book in 1966. Here von Heydebrand provides a comprehensive overview of the textual sources that make up Ulrich's intellectual world. Though most of the sources and their authors had been known for a while, nobody had previously taken the trouble of actually identifying and analyzing specific references to works and ideas. Combining *Geistesgeschichte* with basic factual research, von Heydebrand assembles an impressive range of references to philosophical and literary works, showing that Musil transformed and assimilated a wide variety of sources. At the basis of Musil's concepts and images stand past thinkers like Nietzsche, Emerson, and Mach alongside divergent contemporary influences such as Gestalt theory, the experimental psychology of Ernst Kretschmer, Lucien Lévy-Bruhl's anthropology, the socio-philosophical theories of Georg Simmel and Max Scheler, and the mystical ideas of such diverse writers as Maurice Maeterlinck, Ludwig Klages, and Martin Buber. With an abundance of material, von Heydebrand convincingly illustrates a tendency in Musil toward what she calls an "escape into quotation" (96): Musil frequently resorts to citing pronouncements from predecessors whenever his own efforts at expressing something and at transcending the limitations of language threaten to fail. Because of this practice, his novel to a large extent amounts to a collage of citations. Unfortunately, von Heydebrand devotes little attention to the manner in which the material is integrated, the concept of intertextuality and a methodology for analyzing it systematically having not yet been developed when she wrote her study. Still, her study is much more than a positivistic exercise in identifying literary and philosophical interconnections. Rather, it places scholarship on the intellectual background of Musil's novel on a firm footing. To this day, von Heydebrand's book remains one of the most important contributions to the study of *Der Mann ohne Eigenschaften*.

During the late 1960s several studies appeared that complement the *geistesgeschichtlich* approach in aiming to explore in greater detail some of the standard poetological issues raised in the preceding one and a half decades. One such analysis is that of Peter Nusser (1967), who attempts to reconstruct

Musil's implicit theory of the novel by way of correlating the author's critical utterances from essays, journal entries, and letters with the novel *Der Mann ohne Eigenschaften*. Nusser attempts to describe the formal aspects of the novel, such as the dissolution of linear narrative and the way in which events are not described directly but refracted through a perceiving consciousness. Perhaps not too surprisingly, Nusser's essentially cumulative method yields the expected conclusion — familiar at least since Berghahn's 1956 dissertation — that the essayistic writing style reflects Musil's "possibilitarian attitude" (*Möglichkeitsgesinnung*).

Jörg Kühne's study on Musil's figurative language (1968) is more fruitful. Kühne shows what distinguishes Musil's use of the *Gleichnis* — a stylistic device that encompasses a wide variety of figurative modes of expression such as the simile, the metaphor, or even the extended parable — from that of other authors: a Musilian *Gleichnis* links two distinct notional spheres in a sometimes surprising juxtaposition; yet the analogies suggested do not serve to render the depicted phenomena easier to comprehend by adding plasticity and concreteness. Instead of mainly serving a decorative, illustrative, or explicatory function, Musil's metaphors, as it were, create the fictional reality itself (a view endorsed without significant modification by Gérard Wicht, 1984). On the one hand, linguistic images reflect the subjectivity of the characters. On the other, they make the presence of a narrating consciousness felt. However, this consciousness cannot be associated with a real personage, either within or outside of the fictional world depicted. Alongside theoretical interpolations and reflections, similes and metaphors construct what Kühne, in the tradition of German Idealist philosophy, calls a "transcendental" narrator, a narrating instance in which the distinction between empirical author, fictive narrator, and fictional character becomes blurred. The result is an amalgamation of the three into a narrative trinity that Kühne identifies as the crucial aesthetic basis of Musil's novel (35). This transcendental narrator, Kühne argues, renders impossible interpretations of the novel along the lines of individual psychology. Kühne counters earlier critics such as Michel (1954), who had stressed Musil's essentially ambivalent stance. In Kühne's view, ambivalence is a characteristic not of Musil's style but of the reality his style aims to address (55). Kühne's book is highly technical, but it offers a great deal of insight into the peculiar nature of Musil's style, which he always views as a direct correlate of Musil's philosophical and aesthetic vision.

In her book *Ratio und "Mystik" im Werk Robert Musils* (1968), Elisabeth Albertsen explores one of the novel's central conceptual polarities. Her thematic reading draws on Musil's other works as well as materials from the unpublished *Nachlaß* to show how Musil attempts to overcome the binary oppositions he creates. With the exception of Ulrich and Agathe, Albertsen contends, all characters in the novel represent false efforts at a synthesis. Yet even the true or authentic "mystical" experiment of brother and sister eventually leads to failure. Albertsen puts *Mystik* in inverted commas to emphasize the predominantly secular nature of Musil's mysticism, which is expressed not in a longing for unity with a deity but in the "conversational eroticism" (*Gesprächs-Eros*) of Ulrich and Agathe (107). She shows how Musil deferred the inevitable dual catastrophe that looms over the novel — the simultaneous failure of Ulrich and Agathe's spiritual union and the outbreak of the First World War — by expanding a segment of the novel from fifty pages in an early draft to well over a thousand pages. Albertsen stresses the irresolvable unity of Musil's writing and his thinking while denying him the status of a thinker who went beyond the intellectual parameters of his time (15), a notion heavily contested by a generation of scholars that emerged in the ensuing years to claim Musil as a prime spokesman of *Ideologiekritik*. Albertsen's contribution is uneven in quality; the chapter on language, for instance, which she added in the process of revising this Tübingen dissertation into a book, is not well integrated. The author appears to argue from a defensive position, as some of her polemical and combative asides indicate, primarily aimed against the sociopolitical ideas of Frankfurt school *Kritische Theorie* that were making their presence felt in Germanistik at the time.

Perhaps the most outspoken politically charged contribution to Musil studies of the period is the monograph by Klaus Laermann (1970). Laermann radically deviates from the traditionally affirmative approach, which consisted largely of collecting and commenting on a series of pertinent quotations. Instead, he examines Musil's novel from a decidedly neo-Marxist perspective by looking at the sociopolitical implications associated with the Musilian notion of an absence of qualities — *Eigenschaftslosigkeit*. Musil's protagonist Ulrich here emerges as a representative of a segment of the bourgeois intelligentsia at the beginning of the century. Ulrich's detached mode of existence, Laermann finds, is primarily a symptom of the overall alienation of marginalized intellectuals. Up to that point, few critics had so much as even noticed that Ulrich's existence is apparently free of all material concerns. Laermann argues that the fact that Ulrich is able to take one year's *Urlaub vom Leben* (leave from life) clearly indicates that he is economically privileged. That Musil downplayed the economic aspects of the society he portrayed implies to Laermann that the entire literary plan to present a comprehensive analysis of a culture in decline is seriously flawed, since it ignores some of the most important factors. Laermann integrates psychoanalytic concepts into his approach, identifying the predicament of Musil's protagonist with the Freudian notion of narcissism. Ulrich's detachment, which to most critics had thus far signified an enviable stance of openness and freedom from personal and political concerns, in Laermann's reading turns into a socially conditioned psychopathological condition. Laermann is highly critical of what he sees as the subjectivist and aestheticist bias of Musil's novel, implying that Musil did not fully comprehend the factors that determined his own position in the society he confronted. Perhaps the most fruitful discussion to emerge out of Laermann's study is that of Musil's position in the overall context of the various critiques of rationality that emerged in the latter half of the nineteenth century and continued into the twentieth, an issue explored later, with differences in emphasis, by Bernd-Rüdiger Hüppauf (1971), Götz Müller (1972), Hartmut Böhme (1974, 1986), Stephan Howald (1984), and Cornelia Blasberg (1984).

I have already remarked on the conspicuous dearth of contributions to Musil studies based on reader-response criticism. One notable exception is Hans Wolfgang Schaffnit's monograph *Mimesis als Problem* (1971), which views Musil's poetological reflections as an attempt to conceptualize a new kind of reader. Drawing on Roman Ingarden's notion of the essentially interactive process of reading, Schaffnit stresses the role assigned to the reader in the "concretization" of Musil's novel. Yet Schaffnit's discussion, replete with resonances of phenomenological criticism from Emil Staiger and Martin Heidegger, remains on a highly abstract level. Jürgen C. Thöming (1974) is one of the few Musil scholars directly to emulate reader-response criticism, whereas the philosophical component of Schaffnit's phenomenology found its continuation in the work of David Dawlianidse (1978), Dieter Fuder (1979), and Hartmut Cellbrot (1988), among others.

In the vein of *Ideologiekritik*, Götz Müller (1972) bases his analysis of Musil's novel upon Max Horkheimer's definition of ideology as false consciousness. In quoting and parodying pertinent contemporary modes of thought, Musil sets out to critique ideologies as inadequate responses to the social and philosophical problems of the era. To Müller, Musil's montage of heterogeneous linguistic material is "meta-linguistic" in that it reflects on the use of language as purveyor of world views. The dialogues of Arnheim and Diotima, for instance, are composed largely of direct quotations from the works of Walter Rathenau and Maurice Maeterlinck. Musil debunks the false pathos of these writers in placing their lofty ideas into an ironic context. Yet, at the same time, he acknowledges that the pathos of watered down *Lebensphilosophie* is not too far removed from the solutions that he himself is pursuing. Müller argues that this close affinity of ostensibly divergent thought patterns is evidenced, for instance, in the figures of Clarisse, whose madness consists of taking Nietzsche's ideas literally, and Moosbrugger, whose crime represents a thwarted version of the neoromantic quest for some primal unity of experience.

Musil's montage of quotations and allusions, addressed by Müller from a pronouncedly political perspective, is seen by Dietrich Hochstätter (1972) as a decidedly apolitical question of stylistic perspectivism. In retrospect, the central idea that Hochstätter proposes, that of a perspectivism that transcends ideological bias, appears as a correlate, on the level of textual analysis, to the general notion of a methodological pluralism that was advanced at the time by mainstream Germanistik in response to the challenges posed by the politically volatile climate in academia. All the same, Hochstätter develops his stylistic analysis primarily in opposition to traditional Musil criticism: he rejects Arntzen's notion of satire as well as Allemann's concept of constructive irony as too undifferentiated. Musil's method of citing and emulating a multiplicity of linguistic styles, Hochstätter contends, correlates with his multidimensional and "polyvalent" attitudes toward life and toward thinking (7). The examination of stylistic patterns culminates in a description of the "prismatic-essayistic" overall structure of Musil's novel (55). On the thematic level, Hochstätter's enterprise yields results similar to those of Elisabeth Albertsen (1968). Like Albertsen, for instance, Hochstätter stresses the essentially secular nature of Musil's mysticism and utopianism, while at the same time refusing to reflect on any concrete sociopolitical implications of Musil's ideas. In Hochstätter's reading, "interpretive multidimensionality" (147) appears to become a value in itself, posed against critical attempts to appropriate Musil in the interest of any specific ideological agenda.

In a climate characterized by politically charged polemics on the one side and recourse to lofty and supposedly timeless values on the other, Hartmut Böhme's monograph *Anomie und Entfremdung* (1974) marks a clear watershed. Steering clear of both political maneuvering and affirmative paraphrase, Böhme attempts to address the complexity of Musil's work in terms equally sensitive to aesthetic as to nonaesthetic issues. He takes as his starting point Musil's political essays and reads them as responses to the sociopolitical crisis of central Europe during and after the First World War. The project of confronting and analyzing this crisis continued in what was to become *Der Mann ohne Eigenschaften*. While Böhme in a way builds here on Marie-Louise Roth's work covering some of the same issues (1972), he develops a highly differentiated methodology. Throughout, he attempts to take into account the sociohistorical context both of his own theoretical position as critic and that of Musil's texts as the subject matter of the investigation.

First and foremost, Böhme takes issue with Laermann's one-sided reading of Musil's works as evidence of narcissistic and escapist tendencies. While Böhme acknowledges that such tendencies certainly are present in Musil, they do not make up the whole picture; in his essays and in the intricate ironic structures of his grand novel, Musil develops a critique of the very social conditions that produce the kinds of psychopathological deformations Laermann had identified. Böhme uses the sociopsychological concept of *anomie* to characterize Musil's analysis of central Europe in the first third of this century; technological developments, ethnic and social tensions, and other factors had eroded the established order and brought about a paradoxical situation in which hectic activity on the part of particular groups was coupled with the stagnation of the social system as a whole. In Böhme's reading, the psychopathology of Musil's characters is motivated by an essentially critical orientation: the extent of their individual alienation (*Entfremdung*) is a symptom of the overall societal *anomie*, the two concepts that make up the title of Böhme's study. Musil, Böhme argues, exposes the ideological causes of the current malaise, with its combination of social inertia and spiritual disintegration, in his portrayal of the array of representatives of the various discourses prevalent in the Habsburg Empire. As far as we know, Musil intended his novel to be divided into four major parts. Böhme identifies the death of Ulrich's father as the axis around which the novel is structured symmetrically. This construct gives the utopian experiments of Ulrich and Agathe the connotation of a rebellion against parental authority on the personal level, corresponding to a rebellion against patriarchy on the general level. To Böhme, Musil is far from advocating escapist withdrawal; rather, he develops critical countermodels in the shape of the various utopian projects envisaged by his protagonists. To do so, however, it is necessary first to probe the full extent of the existential implications of the sociohistorical situation for the individual.

Böhme draws on a multitude of concepts developed in sociology, psychology, and social philosophy. This makes for a multifaceted and highly differentiated discussion that aims to address the issues raised in all their complexity, in many ways already transcending the limitations of the sociopolitical approaches that were being developed at the time. Böhme's writing is dense and not entirely free of certain tendencies to favor jargon over accessibility. All the same, his book is one of the most theoretically sophisticated and fruitful studies of important aspects of Musil's oeuvre. His combination of a multitude of diverse intellectual traditions effectively raised the level of critical discourse on Musil's grand novel, synthesizing Hochstätter's notion of multidimensionality with a perspective that places Musil in a larger socio-historical context. Böhme's study represents a welcome change from the excessive adulation of Musil on the part of affirmative Musil criticism and from the potential hostility of neo-Marxist scholars. To be sure, his ideas have not remained uncontradicted: Stephan Howald (1984), for instance, takes issue with what he regards as Böhme's tendency to underestimate Musil's aesthetic achievement. Böhme later augmented his approach in a series of articles that have also had a lasting impact on Musil scholarship. Of particular interest in this context is his seminal essay on methodological issues involved in an analysis of *Der Mann ohne Eigenschaften*, first published in 1976 and reprinted several times in different contexts.

The more traditional method of *Geistesgeschichte* in German studies continued to yield productive results throughout the 1970s. For instance, Dietmar Goltschnigg's *Mystische Tradition im Roman Robert Musils* (1974) presents an extension of part of von Heydebrand's work on the intellectual influences upon Musil's novel. The conversations between Ulrich and Agathe draw heavily on the mystical sources from various centuries collected by Martin Buber in the anthology *Ekstatische Konfessionen* (Ecstatic Confessions) of 1909. Musil, as Marie-Louise Roth (1972) had demonstrated, made elaborate excerpts from a volume by Karl Girgensohn, who had based his reflections on the psychology of religion on material from Buber's anthology. Goltschnigg explores this interconnection in great detail, giving an extensively documented analysis of the manner in which Musil in his turn transformed, modified, and integrated the material into his novel. In this fashion, Goltschnigg provides fascinating insights into Musil's creative process. Goltschnigg is also the author of one of the best short introductions to Musil's novel, a concise essay published in a volume on the twentieth-century German novel edited by Paul Michael Lützeler in 1983.

Equally valuable for an understanding of Musil's novel is Jochen Schmidt's 1975 discussion of the concept of *Eigenschaftslosigkeit*, the "lack" or "absence of qualities" characteristic of modern man. Starting with an analysis of the novella "Grigia," Schmidt delineates the esoteric opposition Musil sets up between the isolated individual and a social reality that is rejected. In this antisocial stance of radical inwardness, Schmidt maintains, Musil's ideas display certain affinities to expressionism on the one hand and the contemporary tendencies of a "conservative revolution" on the other (27). Schmidt then outlines the intellectual sources of Musil's ideas on mysticism. He shows how Musil's reading in the mystic tradition ranged far beyond the Buber anthology singled out by Goltschnigg. For instance, the very concept of *Eigenschaftslosigkeit*, Schmidt proves, derives from the *Deutsche Predigten* (German Sermons) of medieval mystic Meister Eckhart, who rejects the concept of a personal God in favor of a notion of a deity without qualities — "âne eigenschaft" (48). Musil's concept, Schmidt continues, presents a secularized and intellectualized elaboration of Eckhart's idea of a transcendence of personhood in the experience of a *unio mystica*. Schmidt places Musil's interest in the mystical tradition within the context of the contemporary debates about inwardness, deindividuation, and abstraction, an intellectual spectrum ranging from Husserl's phenomenology and Kandinsky's aesthetic theories to the appropriation of mysticism by the protofascist propagator of the notion of a *Rassenseele* (racial soul), Alfred Rosenberg. Schmidt singles out the connection between artistic abstraction and *Eigenschaftslosigkeit*, correlates of Musil's interest in portraying in Ulrich a "prototype of modern man" (78). He also employs Kafka's "Description of a Struggle" as a foil to Musil's project, an alternative response to the challenges presented by modernity. Both authors, Schmidt contends, respond to the dissolution of stable social, spiritual, and psychological orders. In Kafka, the resulting existential uprootedness produces anxiety, whereas Musil views it as potentially liberating. Musil's philosophical leanings, then, give rise to a strange blend of conservative and anarchist tendencies; his excessively theoretical orientation, Schmidt concedes, leads to artistic problems in the integration of reflection into the narrative. Musil, Schmidt writes, seeks to merge abstraction and mysticism: "The theory of radical abstraction is the theory of *Mystik*" (84). Schmidt's study is an important contribution to Musil criticism, although it has to be noted that, while his discussion of the connection between aesthetic concerns and the anthropological question of deindividuation is stimulating, Schmidt has difficulties integrating the elements of irony and satire into his analysis.

In 1975, East German author Rolf Schneider supplemented his edition of *Der Mann ohne Eigenschaften* for the GDR with an accompanying introductory monograph on Musil. Since the 1950s, Schneider had been profoundly influenced by Musil in his own career as a creative writer. His book is thus interesting both as a personal homage to Musil and as a document of the situation of literary criticism in the GDR during the 1970s. Schneider's ideological bias, which was perhaps obligatory, is evident in the manner in which he dismisses the entire tradition of Musil criticism in the West as "bourgeois scholarship" (*bürgerliche Forschung*) supposedly oblivious of the historical and political components of Musil's work, a view that ignores the wide range of aesthetic and ideological positions (including explicitly political readings of Musil) that had already been developed by that time. Despite paying lip service to Georg Lukács's orthodox Marxist position, Schneider is deeply sympathetic to Musil as a writer. In his view, the social and political satire implied in Musil's depiction of the *Parallelaktion* (collateral campaign) makes Musil — alongside Brecht — the most astute critic of the cultural pretensions of bourgeois society. Grouping Musil and Brecht together in this fashion may be surprising, but it does signal an effort to remove the stigma of bourgeois "decadence" from the former. Schneider writes as a fellow author rather than a *Literaturwissenschaftler*, the result being a provocative and immensely readable book full of wit and panache.

Narratorial irony, the overriding concern of Schneider's decidedly unscholarly monograph, became the focus of a study by Alan Holmes (1978). Holmes systematically approaches a problem that long has — or ought to have — vexed critics of Musil's novel, namely the exact nature of the interaction between author, narrator, and protagonist. In his chapters on the genesis and transformation of the concepts of *Möglichkeitssinn* and *Eigenschaftslosigkeit*, Holmes covers much of the same territory as Jochen Schmidt (1975), though from a more pragmatic and text-focused angle. To the naive observer, it would appear that Holmes performs the kind of analysis that would constitute the prime task of Germanistik, an examination of the narrative organizing principles that inform the novel. In their interest in speculation and theorizing,

Musil's critics all too often tend to display disdain for the kind of solid and unassuming work of scholars like Holmes. At the same time, it has to be noted that Holmes relies on concepts that had already become outdated by the time of his writing; he does not employ the sophisticated methodologies developed by structuralist and poststructuralist narrative theory, nor does he adequately address the problem of irony. The lack of a differentiated conceptual framework lead Holmes to conclude that protagonist, narrator, and author are essentially identical, a highly problematic assertion (297). The value of Holmes's work is further impaired by the fact that, with the publication of Frisé's new editions of Musil's diaries (1976) and the novel (1978), and especially with that of Musil's entire literary *Nachlaß* on CD-ROM (1992), much material has become available that would render desirable a renewed analysis of the narrative technique of Musil's novel along the lines proposed by Holmes and his predecessors such as Wilfried Berghahn (1956) and Peter Nusser (1967). More recently, Peter-André Alt (1985) endeavored to address the problem of narratorial irony in *Der Mann ohne Eigenschaften* through integrating philosophical concepts of irony, once again neglecting the rich narratological research on literary irony. It can only be hoped that Musil scholars will begin to carry out the task outlined by Holmes on a more advanced level, in the light of the new materials and with the help of a more differentiated methodology.

Christiane Zehl-Romero (1978) is among the first critics tentatively to approximate a feminist perspective on Musil's novel. She places the love between Ulrich and his sister Agathe in the context of Romantic and neo-Romantic traditions ascribing to love a redemptory power that would allow the individual to transcend the limits imposed by reality. Musil's novel, Zehl-Romero argues, conducts a critical and comprehensive examination of this cultural construct, which predominates in all of Western civilization and is expressed most prominently in the myth of Tristan and Isolde (see Freese 1969 and 1972). While Ulrich and Agathe's story shares the element of active rebellion against reality, their relationship culminates not in an apotheosis of *amour passion* but in a realization that all human relationships are placed under the constraints of bodily and social existence. To Zehl-Romero, the issue of incest, which hovers over Ulrich and Agathe, is the clearest indication that Musil consciously attempted to avoid embracing a vacuous mysticism of love. Irrespective of whether or not the two consummate their love in a sexual union — as was suggested in the *Reise ins Paradies* (Journey into Paradise) complex from the mid-1920s — Zehl-Romero contends, Musil remains critical of the autistic and narcissistic nature of a relationship that never reaches the quality of a reciprocal encounter with a Thou in Martin Buber's sense. In contradistinction to Kaiser and Wilkins (1962) and Judith Burckhardt (1973), Zehl-Romero emphasizes that Musil dismisses the idea of redemption through love as a solipsistic myth by presenting it as a symptom of, rather than a solution to, the problematic condition of Western civilization.

Dieter Fuder (1979) takes the divergence and multiplicity of opinions on *Der Mann ohne Eigenschaften* as an indication that Musil's novel is designed as an "open" work of art that provokes essentially endless and multifarious processes of reflection. Focusing on the analogy as the basic figure of Musil's writing, Fuder extends the concept of mimesis from the primarily poetological concern it was for Schaffnit (1971) to a comprehensive anthropological principle. According to Fuder, analogical thinking in Musil's work is associated with a new concept of human nature; Musil's use of analogy characterizes a flexible "poetic logic" inherent in human experience that is different from the predominant, discursive logic of rigid binary oppositions (14). Musil's novel, Fuder notes, produces philosophical *Erkenntnis* on three interrelated levels. The openness of Ulrich's mode of thinking corresponds to the structural openness of the novel as a whole, which in turn is reflected in an experience of openness in the process of reading. This openness is the correlate of the force that motivates Musil's literary effort — the representation (mimesis) of human "subjectivity" as such (53). Fuder's study, relying heavily on Kantian philosophy, is perhaps not so much an interpretation of *Der Mann ohne Eigenschaften* as it is a plea for analogical thinking as a viable aesthetic principle that has, in Fuder's opinion, on account of its anthropological universality, claims to general philosophical significance.

In the early 1980s, poststructuralist ideas and methodologies were integrated into Musil studies and brought to bear in examinations of *Der Mann ohne Eigenschaften*. Alongside Peter Henninger's book on *Vereinigungen* (1980), Dieter Heyd's study of the novel (1980) is the boldest foray into speculative interpretation inspired by the psychoanalytic theories of Freud and Lacan. Drawing on Jacques Derrida's notion of *dissémination*, Heyd rejects a method of interpretation whose aim lies in a hermeneutic reconstruction of the author's conscious intention or a text's allegedly objective significance. Instead, he advocates a method of reading that unravels, as it were, the knots in the textures created by Musil's involvement with language. Musil's interest in the pathological, the imaginary, the mystical, and the erotically charged are of particular interest here. Heyd's "psycho-semiological" approach follows the operations of desire hidden in, or repressed by (though present in) Musil's text. On the psychological level, Heyd views recurring motivic patterns, image clusters, and thematic issues as evidence of unconscious forces that motivate Musil's writing. On the aesthetic level, Musil's dissolution of linear narrative techniques, rigid conceptual orders, and traditional ethical values, Heyd maintains, indicates that Musil engages in the *dissémination* of cultural constructs: Musil's work, in its multiperspectivity and its character as fragment, Heyd believes, occupies a crucial position in the critique of what deconstructionist philosophy has labeled "logocentrism," the assumption of the existence of a unified, rationally determinable, and essentially static concept of truth (290).

That poststructuralist theory and traditional academic rigor are not incompatible is shown, for instance, by the work of Walter Moser (1980), who emulates Michel Foucault in his discussion of Musil's novel. The emphasis here is on Foucault's notion of society as a sphere of competing "discourses," codified speech systems that proclaim merely to describe reality but actually create and control social order. Moser's thesis that Musil's novel, by way of essayistic appropriation, undertakes an investigation into the multiplicity of diverse forms of "discourse" in Foucault's sense is highly fruitful. In particular, it serves to place in a different conceptual framework a problem that has plagued Musil criticism from the beginning, that of the distinction between irony and satire and the ensuing terminological entanglements. Musil's novel, in Moser's model, provides a privileged sphere in which discourses from various disciplines (culture, politics, science, philosophy, jurisdiction, psychiatry, and so on) can be brought together and critically examined through various modes of juxtaposition. Moser presents a series of concrete examples to show how Musil's characters are not so much portraits of actual or possible personages, but rather serve as nodes where several types of discourse intersect. Concepts drawn from Foucault, Roland Barthes, and to a lesser extent Mikhail Bakhtin enable Moser to describe the aesthetic dimension of Musil's writing. At the same time, Moser does not fail to point out the limitations of Musil's experimental approach: on the one hand, the metadiscursive investigation into the mechanisms by which discourses circulate in society is in constant danger of turning into a mere pose; on the other hand, the encyclopedic preoccupation of Musil's work takes place in the social vacuum of the unfinished (and unfinishable) essay-novel, which in turn is in danger of becoming an expression of powerlessness vis-à-vis a reality in which discourses have actual practical and empirical effects.

The primarily philosophical and sociological applications of Foucault's discourse analysis in Moser are complemented by a more literary and aesthetic focus in Ulf Eisele. Eisele's contribution was written around the same time as Moser's and published first in Renate von Heydebrand's collections of essays on Musil (1982). Eisele emphasizes the self-referential aspects of the nexus between the writing process and the thematic core of the novel, the quest for meaning in individual existence. Ulrich's well-known ideal of "living the way one reads" (*MoE* 1936) is one of the manifold devices that according to Eisele indicate that the actual topic of Musil's novel is literature itself — its problematic status in society, the modalities of its coming into being, and its philosophical and aesthetic potential. Life and literary discourse, he maintains, are paralleled, and to a certain extent equated, in Musil's novel. In Eisele's reading, the opening chapter, with its extraordinary event (the traffic accident) and the appearance of characters (Diotima and Arnheim, whose presence at the site of the incident, however, is immediately called into question), evokes the impression of a kind of realistic novel that Musil's writing then proceeds to dismantle. The relationship between Ulrich and Agathe indicates a substitution of discourse for action: existence takes place in communicative exchange rather than in a sphere of activity. Ulrich and Agathe's "discourse eroticism" (*Diskurserotik*, 172) represents a sublimation of Oedipal sexuality transferred onto the level of speech. Musil's writing becomes dependent upon the suspension of what his characters experience: the prohibition against incest between Ulrich and Agathe coincides with Ulrich's refusal to become a writer. The nexus of *Inzesttabu* and *Schreibverbot* signals an "interference of the psychical/Oedipal problematic and the specifically literary one" (186). If, for instance, Ulrich himself had begun to write, Musil's novel would have turned into a kind of Bildungsroman, and the experimental nature of Musil's writing would have been destroyed. In highlighting the impasse of story and writing process alike, Eisele contends, Musil shows how a "realistic" novel has become impossible under the given sociohistorical circumstances; in its incompleteness, the novel thus addresses the "impossibility of the poetic" (193). Combining recent poststructuralist discourse theory with German Idealist aesthetics, Eisele's dense and complex essay is one of the most important contributions to a discussion of the relationship between Musil's writing and literary realism.

A monograph by Josef Strutz (1981) adds a welcome note of specificity to the study of the philosophical, aesthetic, and political dimensions of *Der Mann ohne Eigenschaften*. Strutz focuses on an ostensibly minor character, the pacifist poet Feuermaul, who emerges in the second part of Musil's novel as an advocate of lofty notions of human goodness and spiritual renewal. Feuermaul, Strutz demonstrates in a detailed exploration of biographical and intertextual allusions in the novel and in Musil's manuscripts, is an amalgam of expressionist writers like Leonhard Frank, Anton Wildgans, and above all Franz Werfel. In the context of the imminent catastrophe of the First World War and the subsequent collapse of the Habsburg Empire, Musil viewed Werfel's public success as poet and novelist and as pacifist activist as subject to multiple ironies. The significance assigned to the character Feuermaul indicates that despite Musil's preoccupation with the mystical notion of the *other condition*, he never lost interest in concrete historical reality. In fact, Strutz argues, Feuermaul — alongside such characters as the fervent young nationalist Hans Sepp, the mystagogue Meingast, and the racial researcher Bremshuber — becomes one of the indicators that Musil engaged not only in an examination of a past catastrophe but also conceived of his novel as a reflection upon the political realities of the 1930s: the second part of *Der Mann ohne Eigenschaften* in many ways represents a response to the emerging reality of National Socialism, a phenomenon that to a large extent has its historical and ideological roots in the Habsburg monarchy. Musil's observations in his notebooks and journals on Fascism in general and on Adolf Hitler as person and symbol, Strutz argues, provide the foil for the presentation of Feuermaul's empty antirationalist messianic fervor, a general intellectual attitude only too easily co-opted by National Socialism. Strutz has interesting things to say about Musil's assessment of the connection between the economic and ideological aspects of politics. In his focus on the political criticism contained in Musil's novel, he occasionally perhaps displays a tendency toward overstatement — for instance, when he one-sidedly labels Arnheim a money-hungry warmonger (a designation that does not do justice to the complex character of Arnheim nor to its historical model, Walter Rathenau). All the same, Strutz's insistence on Musil's persistent efforts to address concrete historical and political issues in his novel go a long way toward dispelling the myth of Musil as a world-weary mystic.

Like Strutz's study, that of Martin Menges (1982) indicates that, amid all the efforts at post-structuralist innovation, traditionally hermeneutic Germanistik can still produce impressive results. Continuing ideas introduced by Jochen Schmidt (1975), Menges defines the concept of abstraction as the overriding aesthetic and philosophical principle operating in Musil's novel. On three levels — the social, the aesthetic, and the mystical — abstraction indicates both the dissolution of rigid concepts of identity and the possibility of a renewed synthesis. This assessment leads Menges to take issue with Klaus Laermann (1970), who had accused Musil of escapism, and with Hartmut Böhme (1974), who had criticized in Musil a tendency toward viewing historically determined phenomena as ontological givens. Both interpretations, Menges contends, underestimate the critically utopian potential of Musil's aesthetic intentions. Menges proceeds to give the most detailed account of the various utopian models developed in Musil's novel, stressing that Musil himself reflects upon the failure of the attempt to bestow duration to the *other condition*. Musil, Menges notes, acknowledges that abstract reasoning requires both *Genauigkeit* and *Phantasie*, both an engagement with reality and imaginative reflection, to avoid ethical, intellectual, and spiritual impasse.

Like Menges, Gérard Wicht (1984) singles out one overriding issue as the focus of his analysis. His examination of the *Gleichnis* as the basic unit of Musil's writing to a certain extent complements, with a more philosophical accent, that of Jörg Kühne (1968), who had restricted himself largely to poetological considerations. Wicht evokes the intellectual context of Musil's interest in figurative language, discussing the various theories of the period on the limits and the potential of language. Wicht's broad and necessarily somewhat superficial survey includes the familiar exponents of *Sprachkrise* and *Sprachskepsis* in literature (for example, Hofmannsthal, Rilke, Broch, and Kafka) and philosophy (such as Nietzsche, Mauthner, Landauer, Klages, and

Wittgenstein). Musil, Wicht suggests, embraced the figurative potential of the *Gleichnis* as a linguistic device that promises to bridge and at the same time preserve the gap between linguistic expression and intended meaning. In this fashion, a *Gleichnis* fulfills an important epistemological function in that it points to something without subsuming it into a preexisting conceptual system; it creates the described phenomenon and allows it to shine in its uniqueness. The *Gleichnis* thus combines analytic and synthetic or philosophical and poetic capacities, becoming the "purveyor of the highest intellectual density" (111). Wicht defends Musil against charges that the use of figurative language implies a lack of precision and intellectual rigor by stressing that it is "the *object* of the narrative reflection which is polyvalent, not [Musil's] style!" (168, Wicht's emphasis). Wicht traces throughout the novel one particular set of metaphorical constructs, the semantic field centered on the image of the tree. This complex of images, Wicht argues, functions in a manner akin to lyrical poetry, evoking meaning in the interplay of linguistic signs rather than through reference to any extralinguistic belief system. This leads Wicht to the conclusion, among others, that the theological imagery Musil employs in his novel does not indicate that Musil held religious beliefs in the traditional sense (196).

Wicht's study shows that, even in the 1980s, approaches characteristic of mainstream Germanistik, in this case the history of ideas, continue to coexist with the innovative methodologies derived from poststructuralist thinking. The postmodern quasi-anarchistic tendencies latently present in Dieter Heyd (1980) are more pronounced in Lucas Cejpek (1984), who appears to abandon "methodical" literary criticism altogether in favor of a "mad" form of discourse. Taking his cues from the critique of Western rationality by thinkers like Nietzsche and Foucault, Cejpek presents Musil's novel as a reflection of the tension between "reason" and "madness" in European bourgeois civilization. In a collage of motley citations Cejpek freely moves in and out of all kinds of texts from the period in which Musil's novel originated. Cejpek defines this "historical field" of investigation as the "pre-War sphere" (referring to both world wars as one connected event) to distinguish it from his own context, that of a "post-War" perspective. In Cejpek's contention, war is not an unfortunate aberration from the true nature of European rationalistic civilization but a manifestation of it. Moosbrugger, for instance, appears in this light to embody the destructive essence of a male patriarchal system. Similarly, Clarisse illustrates how women internalize the male structures of violence and are driven to self-destruction. Musil, Cejpek suggests, displays in his novel an awareness of the "madness" at the core of Western rationality brought about by the marginalization of what cannot be subsumed under "reason," implying that all utopian models, including those involving the relationship between Ulrich and Agathe, remain confined within the destructive logic of European culture and therefore cannot be viewed as fruitful alternatives. For all his undeniable intelligence and imagination, Cejpek shows little regard for the reader. His book appears to preclude debate, since it does not offer a thesis supported by arguments but rather presents a rhetorical tour de force that the reader can either participate in or reject. Though it is full of fascinating insights and provocative ideas, Cejpek's book, with its pyrotechnic display of metaphors, is perhaps more an exercise in creative speculation than literary criticism.

Hans-Georg Pott (1984) manages to combine scholarly rigor in the traditional sense with an innovative approach that integrates poststructuralist ideas. On one level, he conducts his reading along lines similar to Eisele's, viewing Musil's novel as a laboratory for the examination of "discourses" (ideologies and their manifestations in different speech modes). On another, he focuses on the psychopathology of the characters as examples of failed modes of identity formation that Musil subjects to critical scrutiny. Pott synthesizes discourse analysis and Lacanian psychoanalysis to address the problem of the "ending" of Musil's novel in its aesthetic and psychosexual dimension. In Ulrich's conversations with Agathe, Pott notes, the topic of the exchange becomes secondary; instead, he writes, the endeavor to engage in an endless process of communication and communion through language "functions as the expression of their desire for union and loss of individual boundaries" (122). If the desired *unio mystica* were achieved, however, the conversations would cease, as would the process of exchange — and, ultimately, Musil's book. Pott proposes that a tension underlying Musil's impetus for writing subjects his novel to the paradoxical logic of deferral and postponement. In Musil's subjectivity, Pott suggests, the desire to keep alive is inextricably interwoven with the desire to keep the writing process alive. This constellation brings forth what Pott labels an "endless text," one that undermines the notion of a stable self by refusing closure: "Musil destroys the narrative model by dismantling the center of its meaning: the ending" (162).

Pott polemically denounces as "ideologues of alienation" (*Entfremdungsideologen*, 161) those critics who insist on the sociopolitical dimension of the aesthetic and psychosexual issues he addresses. However, at least one of the critics he dismisses in this fashion, Hartmut Böhme, has reached conclusions that are quite similar to Pott's, especially with regard to Musil's critique of Western rationality. In an important essay (1986), Böhme emulates recent poststructuralist theories in order to place Musil in the context of current debates on postmodernism. He finds in *Der Mann ohne Eigenschaften* a response to the collapse of European civilization in the First World War. On the aesthetic level, the cataclysm of an entire culture leads Musil to a rejection of realistic mimesis in favor of a semiotic approach: Musil's novel presents a semiotic panopticon in which ideas, ideologies, and values circulate as mere functions of discourse, "quotations" deprived of substance — "simulacrae," in the terminology of Jean Baudrillard. Musil's critique of Western rationality, Böhme contends, bids farewell to the notion that history is characterized by meaningful rational development, anticipating notions about the stasis of postmodern society developed by Michel Foucault and Jean-François Lyotard. In this context, Böhme views Musil's interest in the interconnections between love, mysticism, crime, insanity, and war as an effort to carve out a node of resistance to universal semiotization and commodification: "In a situation of world-wide rationalization Art offers the only space for an exhaustion (*Verausgabung*) and transcendency (*Überschreitung*) of the Ego — closely related to insanity, crime, and excess" (30). Musil's investigation of aspects of culture that resist closure, Böhme argues, places him alongside Georges Bataille among the "intellectual precursors of postmodernism" (25). Böhme's primarily philosophical focus was complemented later by Rolf Günter Renner (1991), for instance, who restricts himself to aesthetic considerations that link Musil's narrative technique with postmodern tendencies. Böhme's dense and stimulating essay goes far beyond the confines of traditional literary criticism in that it links Musil's aesthetic enterprise with a discussion of the situation of our civilization as a whole.

On a more mundane level, there is an abundance of smaller contributions that limit their focus on specific issues concerning Musil's magnum opus. Frequently such contributions have little impact on the discussion of *Der Mann ohne Eigenschaften*, where grand synthesis is usually favored over detailed analysis. A good example is Walter H. Sokel's (1988) essay on the legacy of the eighteenth century in Musil's grand novel. Sokel compares Musil with other important modernist novelists, such as Joyce, Dos Passos, and Döblin, and the manner in which their works represent a break with the realist tradition. According to Sokel, realistic mimesis is characterized by the author's attempt to increase to the fullest the reader's identification with the depicted world by way of eliminating distance and camouflaging the process of narrative mediation. Sokel identifies the origins of this tradition in Lessing's late-Enlightenment poetics of emotional involvement. What distinguishes Musil's critique of realistic mimesis, Sokel suggests, is that his writing in its combination of essayistic philosophical reflection and self-referential, playful irony harks back to the satirical novel of the first half of the eighteenth century by reemphasizing the distance between reader and fictional world.

Musil's novel, Sokel contends, displays affinities with early-Enlightenment authors like Swift, Fielding, Sterne, and Voltaire as well as their common precursor, Cervantes. When Sokel originally gave his paper in 1985, a discussion ensued in which respondents challenged both Sokel's central thesis and its underlying periodization. Yet it seems to me that Sokel's point that many elements of *Der Mann ohne Eigenschaften* can be related to eighteenth-century traditions is well taken (one need only think of the chapter headings, the division into books, the narrator's ironical interventions). Monika Schrader (1975) had anticipated some of Sokel's concerns in her study on Musil's novel within the Bildungsroman tradition. While her study is somewhat marred by an undifferentiated concept of *Bildung* and its historical permutations as reflected in the Bildungsroman genre, her comparison of Musil's work with Wieland's eighteenth-century novel *Agathon* yields a great deal of interesting insights that should be explored further. Perhaps it would be fruitful to place Musil's novel not primarily in the Bildungsroman tradition but, as Sokel suggests, in that of the picaresque novel (particularly with regard to questions of audience address). As far as I can see, however, such interconnections with literary traditions remain largely unexplored in Musil criticism.

In the late 1980s there was a series of attempts to approach Musil's work from a philosophical perspective. Most of these share the thesis that Musil's writing constitutes an intellectual enterprise that can justly be described as philosophical because Musil addresses far-ranging philosophical issues beyond the scope of fiction. Usually, the underlying assumption is that what remains unclear in Musil's thought and his writings can be clarified with the help of a particular philosophical method. Matthias Luserke (1987), for instance, stresses the unity of Musil's work as an "ideographic cosmos" (15) in his analysis of Musil's notion of "possibility" (*Möglichkeit*) with concepts drawn from Kantian modal theory. He proposes that this approach could provide a useful model for the interpretation of literary texts in general. In his enterprise, Luserke dispenses with traditional distinctions such as those between author and narrator and the idea that both narrator and fictional characters function as the sources of utterances in a narrative text. In their place, he distinguishes four abstract modes of representation at work in Musil's *Der Mann ohne Eigenschaften* that correspond to four "types of actuality" (*Tatsächlichkeitstypen*, 69). While Luserke consistently attempts to stress the affinity between these Kantian notions and Musil's intellectual environment (mediated, for instance, via Phenomenology and Gestalt theory), he operates on a level of abstraction that ultimately alienates the reader. Luserke's differentiation between the "really real" versus the "really possible" and the "possibly real" versus the "possibly possible" (74) — later augmented by elaborate charts and formulae — is likely to become a source of consternation even to the staunchest advocate of Musil's philosophical stature. Luserke might better have pursued the more interesting topic of the extent of Musil's indebtedness to Kant, which has — despite the contributions of Ulrich Karthaus (1981a) and Thomas Söder (1988) — thus far not received sufficient attention in Musil scholarship.

In a manner not unlike Luserke's, Ralf Bohn (1988) explores a different philosophical tradition; he seeks to establish parallels between Musil's works and ideas formulated in Romantic philosophy of nature, above all by Friedrich Wilhelm Schelling, that seek to collapse the distinction between philosophy and *Dichtung*. In Bohn's opinion, Musil's *Der Mann ohne Eigenschaften* illustrates, as a *Gleichnis*, the manner in which the philosophical subject constitutes itself as subject in the process of reflection by "inversion" — that is, by tracing its own development back to its origin. This *Ursprung* (73) is both the source and the goal of the intellectual effort. Bohn goes on to relate his notion of inverted conditions to a different idea of inversion, the altered perception of inside and outside relations characteristic of the mystical experience in general and Musil's *anderer Zustand* in particular. His observations may well be accurate, but in his opaque style Bohn tends to postulate rather than explicate such connections. His book is ambitious in scope, yet the lofty philosophical gloss is sometimes marred by slight factual errors — for instance, incorrect datings of some of Musil's diary entries.

Perhaps the most extreme example of a worthwhile topic mired in philosophical opaqueness is Dieter P. Farda's study of phenomenological aspects of Musil's work, originally a dissertation dating from 1982 and published in apparently unrevised form as a book in 1988. In phenomenological terms, the world does not exist as a single, given, "objective" reality. Instead, manifold "worlds" are constructed in a multitude of ways in a constant interaction between sense perceptions and a perceiving consciousness. Musil's notion of *Möglichkeitssinn*, Farda aims to demonstrate, acknowledges and illustrates this philosophical insight into the coexistence of "multiple worlds." The similar notion of "multiple realities" is explored in an interesting and engaging essay by Peter L. Berger (1983) with reference to the phenomenological sociology of Alfred Schütz. In Farda's case, however, an ultracerebral methodology, derived from Heidegger and somewhat presumptuously labeled "transcendental hermeneutics," leads to a convoluted allusive style that shows little regard for the reader.

The aforementioned studies and others, almost invariably doctoral dissertations, raise the question of the envisaged readership. On the one hand, it is unlikely that they will convince the nonliterary reader of Musil's stature as an intellect of significance; on the other, they operate with a specialized and sometimes rather arcane philosophical jargon that is likely to scare off most Musil scholars trained in mainstream Germanistik. The publication pressure on academics notwithstanding, it is a sad phenomenon to be confronted with book-length works that seem to be addressed to nobody in particular and that are destined to do little more than catch dust on library shelves.

One can, of course, write intelligently and intelligibly about Musil from a philosophical perspective. Cases in point are essays relating Musil to Mach (Claudia Monti 1979 and 1981; Manfred Diersch 1990) or to Wittgenstein (Aldo Gargani 1983; Friedrich Wallner 1983; Peter Kampits 1992) as well as some of the various explorations of Musil's indebtedness to Nietzsche (Aldo Venturelli 1980; Roberto Olmi 1981 and 1983; Friedrich Wallner 1984). Most interpretations of *Der Mann ohne Eigenschaften* and Musil's other works touch upon philosophical issues in one way or another, sometimes in highly sophisticated and enlightening manners. Manfred Frank, a student of Hans-Georg Gadamer who gained prominence as a mediator between the German hermeneutic philosophical tradition and the semiotically oriented (primarily French) poststructural approaches, also wrote several lucid essays on the connection between epistemological and mythological concerns in Musil (1981, 1983, 1988). Perhaps it should be no surprise that it is the mature professional philosophers who on the whole display a greater sensitivity to the complexity of Musil's thinking — and a greater regard for the reader — than do young, philosophically trained scholars in their doctoral dissertations.

Harmut Cellbrot's dissertation, published in book form in 1988, likewise proves that theoretical sophistication and readability need not be mutually exclusive. Cellbrot investigates affinities between Musil's work and the phenomenological theories of Edmund Husserl. It is documented that Musil read Husserl, above all the philosopher's *Logische Untersuchungen* (Logical Investigations, 1902), yet Cellbrot refrains from claiming any direct influence or dependence. Instead, he examines Musil's work as an enterprise that on a literary level in many ways parallels Husserl's philosophical ideas. The two thinkers, he points out, share an interest in the nature of cognition and perception; Musil's writing can be viewed as an investigation into the "movement of the processes of consciousness" (42). Musil's attentiveness to the minuscule gradations and shifts in modes of consciousness displays a kind of poetic complement to Husserl's philosophical rigor. Husserl acknowledges that perception and cognition are potentially endless processes, rendering it impossible to arrive at fixed conclusions. Because of its open-endedness, Musil's work, Cellbrot shows, constitutes a poetic analogue to this mode of thinking that is as legitimate and as fruitful as philosophy proper. Perhaps it is a sign of Cellbrot's sensitivity as a reader that he does not subsume Musil's literary enterprise under a supposedly superior philosophical construction.

The appropriating grip of a given theoretical or philosophical model is the focus of Reinhard Pietsch's deconstructive discussion of Musil's novel (1988). Like Eisele (1982), Pietsch draws on Jacques Derrida's notion of *dissémination* to describe the way in which Musil's text simultaneously invites and calls into question appropriative readings. In its discursive and poetic richness, Musil's novel contains a wealth of details that point in all directions and challenge the reader to integrate them under a unifying conceptual heading; yet at the same time, its character as a fragment renders impossible any attempt to arrive at a unifying interpretation. Pietsch concludes that Musil's text defies hermeneutic approaches that aim to interpret authorial intention or textual meaning.; he opts for an approach that focuses instead on the manner in which Musil's text addresses the creation and subversion of meaning in what Pietsch calls "self-implicating structures." He steers clear of the conceptual clichés that have predominated in Musil criticism for decades by developing his own metaphors to describe the peculiar character of Musil's writing, comparing the novel to a Moebius strip and the effect of Musil's prose to interfering "frequencies" (*Eigenfrequenzen*, 3). Pietsch traces the circularity of Musil's process of composition in two detailed analyses of what, because of Musil's untimely death, became the final chapter of Musil's text, "Atemzüge eines Sommertages." The excessive production of figurative language in ceaseless variation and repetition, Pietsch notes, dissolves the narrating instance: it becomes impossible to locate utterances in the text as coming either from the characters or from the narrator. The dissolution of the concept of narrating subject goes hand in hand with a sense of paralysis of the writing process; ending in stasis, Musil's novel seems a fragment bursting at the seams, both infinite and uninterpretable, a self-canceling artifact. While his approach is not free of the kind of totalizing gestures he criticizes in Musil scholarship, Pietsch nevertheless manages to present a refreshing look at Musil's novel. Of particular interest is his observation that the work includes, in addition to its reflections on the nature of the writing process, an extensive examination of the process of reading. Musil's investigation of the nature of reading, here only touched upon, is a topic that would merit closer attention.

The nexus between Musil's interest in mysticism and the processes of writing and reading is explored by Wagner-Egelhaaf, who includes a chapter on *Der Mann ohne Eigenschaften* in her lucid study of the mystical tradition in twentieth-century German prose (1989). In contradistinction to previous scholars, who approached the issue of mysticism mainly from the perspective of a history of ideas by exploring Musil's reception of mystical sources, Wagner-Egelhaaf employs poststructuralist concepts that place mysticism in the overall context of Western culture as a culture based on writing. Medieval mystics, Wagner-Egelhaaf notes, attempt to describe the mystical experience that prompts them to write as a "dictation" from God. This phenomenon leads Wagner-Egelhaaf to suggest that modern mysticism encompasses a specific mode of writing that elicits a particular manner of reading. The relationship between Ulrich and Agathe displays just such a dynamic. Their conversations about the mystical experience circle around their readings in mystical sources; their utterances consist largely of quotations from or intertextual allusions to such sources; Ulrich is induced to write down his reflections in his diary, which Agathe secretly reads. Such aspects of the work, Wagner-Egelhaaf notes, indicate that the mystical communion between Ulrich and Agathe takes place in an interaction of the reading and writing process. God as source and telos of the mystical experience is thus replaced by writing as a medium of communion. Gerd-Theo Tewilt (1990) reaches ostensibly similar conclusions with regard to the *other condition* in *Der Mann ohne Eigenschaften* as a phenomenon constituted by and in language. Yet, whereas Tewilt draws on traditional aesthetics and language philosophy, Wagner-Egelhaaf emulates the poststructuralist theories of Jacques Derrida that challenge the primacy of oral language over writing. In their methodological differences, the two studies mark the epistemological divide characteristic of much of Germanistik in the 1980s and 1990s.

The great diversity of approaches derived from poststructuralist theories is indicated in Thomas Pekar's study on the "discourse of love" in Musil (1989), half of which is devoted to an examination of *Der Mann ohne Eigenschaften*. Pekar notes that in Musil's novel love is subject to division: the love relationships of all the major characters display a split between, on the one hand, the bodily aspects of love as a biologically determined drive and, on the other, its social manifestations, the codifications of desire in socially accepted modes of behavior. Pekar traces Musil's insight into the social organization of amorous emotions to the very beginning of his writing. Even the early "Varieté" sketches from around 1900, show Musil's awareness of what Pekar in contradistinction to *Liebestrieb* (love drive), calls *Liebesbetrieb* (love business). The motif of the *varieté* as a socially sanctioned marginal space where people seek, for a price, gratification of the sexual and scopic urges repressed by bourgeois society at large, survives in Musil's novel in Ulrich's relationship with Leona, the cabaret singer. Leona sells her body but displaces her emotional needs in her eating binges. In Bonadea the split between bodily needs and social dictates is evident in the contradiction between her nymphomania and her lofty ideal of bourgeois respectability. In Diotima, it centers around an idealization of spiritual purity that masks her sexual and spiritual frustration in her marriage to Tuzzi. Arnheim's excessively cerebral nature, Gerda Fischel's hysteria, and Clarisse's manic tendencies are similar indicators of the socially enforced division between body and soul. In part two of the novel, Pekar argues, the diagnosis of division is replaced by myths of unifying experience, all centering around Ulrich's relationship with Agathe. These take three different forms. The first variant is narcissistic, consisting of an endless process of mutual mirroring through communication; the second is hermaphroditic, encompassing the desire to become one bodily with the beloved in a mystical union; the third is dionysian, aiming toward a dissolution of the self in an intoxicated indulgence of animalistic urges. The three models of unification, Pekar notes, are contradictory and partly mutually exclusive, which may, at least in part, explain the aesthetic and intellectual problems Musil encountered with the continuation, respectively the conclusion of his novel. Pekar's study is richly textured and always attentive to the complexities of the issues involved. It is intellectually stimulating because of its eclectic combination of divergent methodologies and manages to avoid the kind of reductionism found only too often in Musil studies.

Two Swiss dissertations published in 1990 deal with psychological aspects of Musil's novel, to a certain extent reaching conclusions that are diametrically opposed to each other. Ruth Hassler-Rütti (1990) examines the tension between "madness" and "reality" by focusing on three of Musil's main characters: Ulrich, Clarisse, and Moosbrugger. Drawing on various anthropological, sociological, and psychological theories, Hassler-Rütti defines reality as the product of intersubjective communicative interactions in which a clear sense of personal identity, based on an inside-outside dichotomy, is formed. "Madness" in this context refers to a failed or distorted process of identity formation. Besides Agathe, Ulrich is the only character in the novel capable of recognizing that reality is not an external given but a product of the interplay of contingency and constant interpersonal negotiation. This enables him, Hassler-Rütti contends, to escape "madness," which is characterized in part by an effort to impose stasis upon phenomena subject to perpetual fluctuation.

While Hassler-Rütti is sensitive to Musil's text and attentive to detail, her approach skirts some of the more problematic aspects of Musil's novel, such as the connection between individual and collective "madness" (for example, the prospect of war looming over Musil's panorama of "Kakania"). Her largely positive assessment of Ulrich leads her to dismiss, somewhat vehemently, some of the more disturbing complexities of Ulrich's psychosexual disposition, evidenced in his generally destructive relationships with women and in particular in the possibly incestuous component of his relationship with Agathe. Hans-Rudolf Schärer (1990) focuses precisely on such matters and their psychosexual significance in his discussion of Musil's protagonist, employing a range of psychological theories of the self, including those of psychoanalyst Heinz Kohut. Starting with Ulrich's childhood reminiscences, Schärer observes a pattern of socialization that corresponds — almost too neatly — to the development of the narcissistic personality. With Ulrich, the early loss of the mother, in combination with the aloofness of the father, hinders the formation of a stable sense of self. Ulrich's love for Agathe, who as his sister is in a sense both identical to and different from him, thus becomes the emblem of his inability to overcome his narcissistic isolation. From this psychosexual perspective, Schärer views Ulrich's much heralded *Möglichkeitssinn* primarily as the product of the narcissistic phantasm of indeterminacy and omnipotence. Likewise, he all but debunks Ulrich's utopian schemes, traditionally the object of the highest praise in Musil criticism: favoring as they do theoretical speculation over active involvement in concrete, empirical reality, they emerge here as mechanisms that aid the narcissistic personality in maintaining its precarious balance in the face of contingency. Schärer offers a pragmatic elaboration of ideas introduced into Musil criticism by writers such as Klaus Laermann (1970) and outlined in two seminal essays on a more abstract theoretical level by Peter Dettmering (1981) and Hartmut Böhme (1982). Schärer, however, does not address the socio-political aspects of the problem. His objective is not to denounce, as it were, the character, but to offer a reading that puts Musil's protagonist in a critical perspective. He presents Ulrich as a model of modern socialization; the "man without qualities" emerges as the prototypical narcissistically disturbed personality. In his circumspect manner, Schärer manages to avoid a problem that has plagued a great deal of Musil criticism: he does not allow the power of Musil's language to dominate and contaminate his own critical discourse, as many of the affirmative critics do. At the same time, he remains respectful of Musil's artistic achievement.

Such a combination of sensitivity and respect on the one hand and a remarkable degree of freedom from contamination by Musil's language on the other distinguishes Gerhard Meisel's monograph of 1991 as one of the most significant contributions to Musil scholarship in recent years. It is difficult to do justice to Meisel's discussion of *Der Mann ohne Eigenschaften*, which combines a wide range of theoretical impulses in a fascinating exploration of the philosophical, intellectual, and psychosexual dimensions of Musil's novel. Meisel places Musil within the context of the new view of human nature that emerged around the turn of the century, as scientific thinking began to occupy and to absorb spheres of human experience traditionally excluded from the scientific paradigm. Musil's writing, like Freud's psychoanalysis and the emerging discipline of anthropology, constitutes a contribution to a *Wissenschaft vom Menschen*, an exploration of human experience guided by, and established partly in opposition to, natural science. In Meisel's view, Musil is the writer who most radically and consistently responded to the period's "*categorical paradigm shift* of the scientific world view" (217; Meisel's emphasis). Musil most clearly participated in the move away from teleological thinking in terms of linear notions of causality towards complex functional models of thought involving concepts of statistical likelihood and probability.

Meisel traces Musil's awareness of contemporary scientific theories by exploring a multitude of sources, establishing some surprising and insightful connections and parallels. In a brilliant reading of the opening section of Musil's novel, with its combination of meteorological discourse and traditional narrative, Meisel shows how the author draws on a wide range of contemporary scientific ideas. Musil's focus here, Meisel argues, does not lie in a parody of scientific language (as is often assumed); rather, the passage displays the extent to which Musil employs the most advanced epistemological theories of the time, in particular those concerning the nature of systems implied in the laws of thermodynamics. In Meisel's view, the opening of the novel establishes a "systemic equivalence of thermodynamic and narrative 'laboratory conditions'" (258). Scientific motifs reoccur throughout Musil's novel; for instance, combining psychoanalytic and semiotic perspectives, Meisel establishes parallels between the relationship of Ulrich and Agathe and the notion of entropy in modern physics. Both on the individual and on the general level, Musil's experiment ends in entropy: the Ulrich-Agathe relationship is subject to the irresolvable problem of incest; the sociopolitical question concerning the interconnection between *Parallelaktion* and impending war likewise becomes irresolvable. Meisel employs concepts derived from information theory to establish a correlation between the initial impulse of Musil's writing and its ultimate disintegration in a mass of manuscript drafts: in the terms developed by information theory, an ideal order — which Musil appears to be striving for — is identical with a maximum of disturbance (292). Viewed from this perspective, Meisel suggests, Musil's enterprise of collecting and analyzing a potentially infinite number of pieces of contingent minutiae in his analysis of the historical predicament of his era turned into an unwinnable race against time.

Over the decades, Musil criticism has shown signs of petrification and fatigue. It appears as though the ever-same issues and questions are repeatedly recycled in modified form. Yet works such as Meisel's revive the hope that it will become possible to address Musil's oeuvre in all its complexity, its grandeur, and its limitations without falling prey to the allure of the writer's extraordinarily powerful metaphorical language. In recent years, studies by younger Musil scholars have offered fresh perspectives and signs of intellectual independence from the pull exerted by Musil's conceptual apparatus. Good examples are a monograph by Gabriele Dreis (1992) on the impact of Jean-Jacques Rousseau's pedagogical ideas on Musil and a book by Frank Maier-Solgk (1992) on *Der Mann ohne Eigenschaften* as Musil's investigation into the nature and philosophy of history. Other recent contributions that provide innovative impulses to an elucidation of Musil's novel include an essay by Alexander Honold (1993) on the notion of leisure time and an analysis of the work in terms of chaos theory by Axel Krommer and Albert Kümmel (1993).

Musil's lifework, enthusiastically hailed by Claudio Magris as "the greatest book of our time" (1983, 60), is incomplete. Most interpretations of *Der Mann ohne Eigenschaften* explicitly or implicitly seek to address its significance and stature as a novel fragment. In one way or another, each critic quite literally constructs his or her own object of investigation, rewriting and "finishing" the book that Musil left uncompleted. The ceaseless efforts of the scholarly community to wrestle with the issues raised by Musil's monumental work may be an indication that perhaps the most food for thought is offered precisely by books that, like *Der Mann ohne Eigenschaften*, may have a beginning but no ending.

Concluding Unscientific Postscript

AFTER SOME FORTY YEARS of serious scholarship, it appears that Musil is firmly established as an author of major significance in twentieth-century literature. Even outside the field of literary criticism proper, his outstanding contribution to an analysis of modern European culture is recognized. For instance, Musil features prominently in several important studies on European modernism: Karl Heinz Bohrer's seminal investigation of "suddenness" (1981) culminates in a reading of *Der Mann ohne Eigenschaften*, as does Peter Bürger's study of modernist prose (1988). Bohrer argues that Musil's novel illustrates the disintegration in the modern mind of perceptions of time as a linear continuum. To Bürger, Musil's thinking and writing address in exemplary fashion the crucial "dilemma of modernity" (436), a predicament characterized by the simultaneous presence of an impulse to strive toward the resolution of pressing intellectual, ethical, and aesthetic questions and a realization that, ultimately, such issues can no longer be resolved. Judith Ryan, in *The Vanishing Subject* (1991), assigns Musil a crucial position in her exploration of the connection between empiricist (non-Freudian) psychology and literary modernism.

In the field of mainstream Germanistik, too, Musil turns up in a variety of different contexts. The link between aesthetic and psychosexual concerns in Musil's work is discussed by Peter von Matt in his far-ranging examination of the motif of betrayed love in Western literature (1989) and by Jacques Le Rider in his stimulating study of the crisis of male identity in the culture of fin-de-siècle Vienna (1990b). Most recently, Silvio Vietta (1992) has offered a highly sensitive reading of Musil's oeuvre in the context of an assessment of the multifaceted responses of German-speaking authors to the intellectual and psychological challenge of modernity. All of these works — from people not necessarily specializing in Musil — offer intellectual sophistication without losing sight of their readership, displaying a breadth of vision that contrasts markedly with the often myopic focus of much of Musil criticism.

The early 1990s mark a critical phase in the history of Musil scholarship. On a general level, all of Germanistik is undergoing changes, reflecting the momentous upheavals in central and eastern Europe in the wake of the demise of Communism and the unification of Germany. Such political changes render problematic the pursuit of German studies as a discipline focused primarily on literary criticism in the sense of textual explication; more and more,

Germanistik is being redefined to include cultural, political, and historical concerns. As a result, new and highly welcome influences are coming to Musil studies from neighboring disciplines such as feminist and gender theory, cultural semiotics, and communication studies.

Yet this cross-fertilization of contiguous fields of inquiry brings its own set of problems. Any transfer of critical vocabulary derived from a different discipline runs the risk of contributing to a proliferation of jargon. The absence of a consensus on a shared critical language has split the field of Musil studies into many diverse areas with little or no common ground. As a result, it is characterized by the acute sense of fragmentation that pervades Germanistik as a whole. The coexistence of divergent conceptual and methodological frames of reference is hailed by some critics as a sign of a healthy "pluralism" of modes of inquiry (Solms 1986), while others warn — not without some justification — of "conceptual anarchy" (Schröder-Werle 1991).

All the same, the academic machinery incessantly produces scholarly output. In his essay "Literat und Literatur" of 1931, Musil sardonically forecast the mechanisms to which this own writing would be subjected when he aptly characterized literary criticism as an endeavor to reduce literary works to a mere "pond of quotations" (*Zitatenteich, GW* II, 1206) in which critics fish for a set number of suitable citations to underscore a given point in their own argument. Much of Musil criticism displays just such reductive tendencies, a distressing phenomenon particularly when juxtaposed with Musil's outspoken emphasis upon the ethical dimension of the writing endeavor.

The intense interest in Musil on the part of a limited academic audience should not blind us to the crucial paradox inherent in his reputation: Musil may, in the words of Hans Heinz Hahnl, indeed have advanced to the status of a "favorite author of a European elite" (1981, 172), yet even in the academic sphere he has not achieved the kind of readership commensurate to his stature as a modern master. Perhaps it is the rather forbidding image of Musil as overly cerebral and demanding — created in part by the hectic activities of a specialized scholarly community — that seals him off, as it were, from the nonspecialist reading public. The quasi-obsessive focus of Musil criticism on his novel *Der Mann ohne Eigenschaften* contributes to such an image. Jean-François Peyret recognizes this link when he mockingly labels Musil's unfinished novel a "torture machine" (*Foltermaschine*, 1980, 31). Yet Peyret also emphasizes that Musil's reputation for difficulty results primarily from his intense commitment to exploring a given problem in a manner that does justice to the complexities of the issues involved. That Musil's main work remained unfinished, Peyret notes, has to do with his "love of perfection" (32). I would agree with Peyret's suggestion that Musil's writings pose problems mainly for those critics and readers who expect from a work of literature a confirmation of what they think they already know.

As early as 1953, Ernst von Salomon perhaps best described the proper attitude with which one should approach Musil's magnum opus, when he recommended reading the book in small but regular doses, a chapter or two a day. The effect, he promised, will each time be like that of an invigorating glass of champagne. The same holds true for all of Musil's writings: his short prose, his plays, his essays and journals offer stimulating reading of the rarest vintage. This book will have fulfilled its mission if it encourages and enables the reader, specialist and nonspecialist alike, to explore some of the most exquisite pleasures world literature has to offer — the pleasures of reading Robert Musil.

Bibliography

Musil's Works in German
Musil's Works in English
Bibliographies
Articles and Books

MUSIL'S WORKS IN GERMAN:

1906. *Die Verwirrungen des Zöglings Törleß.* Vienna, Leipzig: Wiener Verlag.
1908. *Beitrag zur Beurteilung der Lehren Machs.* Berlin-Wilmersdorf: Carl Arnold.
1911. *Vereinigungen.* Zwei Erzählungen. Munich, Leipzig: Georg Müller.
1921. *Die Schwärmer.* Schauspiel in drei Aufzügen. Dresden: Sibyllen.
1923a. *Grigia.* Novelle. Potsdam: Müller.
1923b. *Die Portugiesin.* Berlin: Rowohlt.
1924a. *Vinzenz und die Freundin bedeutender Männer.* Posse. Berlin: Rowohlt.
1924b. *Drei Frauen.* Novellen. Berlin: Rowohlt.
1927. *Rede zur Rilke-Feier in Berlin am 16. Januar 1927.* Berlin: Rowohlt.
1930. *Der Mann ohne Eigenschaften.* Roman. Erstes Buch. Berlin: Rowohlt.
1933. *Der Mann ohne Eigenschaften.* Roman. Zweites Buch. Berlin: Rowohlt.
1936. *Nachlaß zu Lebzeiten.* Zurich: Humanitas.
1937. *Über die Dummheit.* Vienna: Bermann-Fischer.
1943. *Der Mann ohne Eigenschaften.* Dritter Band. Aus dem Nachlaß. Edited by Martha Musil. Lausanne: Imprimerie Centrale.
1944. *Drei Frauen.* Zurich: Pegasus.
1952. *Der Mann ohne Eigenschaften. Gesammelte Werke in Einzelausgaben.* Vol. 1. Edited by Adolf Frisé. Hamburg: Rowohlt.
1955. *Tagebücher, Aphorismen, Essays und Reden. Gesammelte Werke in Einzelausgaben.* Vol. 2. Edited by Adolf Frisé. Hamburg: Rowohlt.
1957. *Prosa, Dramen, Späte Briefe. Gesammelte Werke in Einzelausgaben.* Vol. 3. Edited by Adolf Frisé. Hamburg: Rowohlt.
1961. *Das hilflose Europa: Drei Essays.* Munich: Piper.
1963. *Aus den Tagebüchern.* Berlin: Suhrkamp.
1965. *Theater: Kritisches und Theoretisches.* Edited by Marie-Louise Roth. Reinbek bei Hamburg: Rowohlt.
1966. *Vereinigungen.* Edited by Adolf Frisé. Munich: Piper.
1967a. *Die Amsel: Bilder.* Stuttgart: Reclam.
1967b. *Der deutsche Mensch als Symptom: aus dem Nachlaß.* Edited by Karl Corino, Elisabeth Albertsen, and Karl Dinklage. Reinbek bei Hamburg: Rowohlt.
1968. *Sämtliche Erzählungen.* Edited by Adolf Frisé. Reinbek bei Hamburg: Rowohlt.

1970. *Three Short Stories*. Edited by Hugh Sacker. London: Oxford University Press.
1971. *Robert Musil. Briefe nach Prag*. Edited by Barbara Köpplová and Kurt Krolop. Reinbek bei Hamburg: Rowohlt.
1976. *Tagebücher*. 2 vols. Edited by Adolf Frisé. Reinbek bei Hamburg: Rowohlt.
1978a. *Drei Frauen: Text, Materialien, Kommentar*. Edited by Karl Eibl. Munich, Vienna: Hanser.
1978b. *Gesammelte Werke*. 4 vols. Edited by Adolf Frisé. Identical with paperback edition *Gesammelte Werke in neun Bänden*. 9 vols. Reinbek bei Hamburg: Rowohlt.
1980. *Beitrag zur Beurteilung der Lehren Machs*. Edited by Adolf Frisé. Reinbek bei Hamburg: Rowohlt.
1981. *Briefe 1901–1942*. 2 vols. Edited by Adolf Frisé, with the collaboration of Murray G. Hall. Reinbek bei Hamburg: Rowohlt.
1988. *Frühe Prosa und aus dem Nachlaß zu Lebzeiten*. Reinbek bei Hamburg: Rowohlt.
1990. *Vereinigungen*. Edited by Hartmut Böhme. Frankfurt/Main: Suhrkamp.
1991. *Versuche, einen anderen Menschen zu finden. Robert Musil Lesebuch*. Reinbek bei Hamburg: Rowohlt.
1992. *Der literarische Nachlaß*. CD-ROM. Edited by Friedbert Aspetsberger, Karl Eibl, and Adolf Frisé. Reinbek bei Hamburg: Rowohlt.

MUSIL'S WORKS IN ENGLISH:

1953. *The Man without Qualities*. Vol. 1. Translated by Eithne Wilkins and Ernst Kaiser. London: Secker & Warburg; New York: Coward-McCann.
1955a. *The Man without Qualities*. Vol. 2. Translated by Eithne Wilkins and Ernst Kaiser. London: Secker & Warburg; New York: Coward-McCann.
1955b. *Young Törless*. Translated by Eithne Wilkins and Ernst Kaiser. London: Secker & Warburg; New York: Pantheon.
1960. *The Man without Qualities*. Vol. 3. Translated by Eithne Wilkins and Ernst Kaiser. London: Secker & Warburg; New York: Coward-McCann.
1965. *Tonka and other Stories*. Translated by Eithne Wilkins and Ernst Kaiser. London: Secker & Warburg. Republished as *Five Women*. New York: Delacorte, 1966.
1981. *The Blackbird*. Translated by Thomas Frick and Wilhelm Wiegand. Cambridge, Mass.: Simba Editions.
1982. *On Mach's Theories*. Translated by Kevin Mulligan. Washington, D.C.: Catholic University of America Press; Munich: Philosophia.
1983. *The Enthusiasts*. Translated by Andrea Simon. New York: Performing Arts Journal Publications.
1986. *Selected Writings*. Edited by Burton Pike. New York: Continuum.
1987. *Posthumous Papers of a Living Author*. Translated by Peter Wortsman. Hygiene, Colo.: Eridanos Press.

1990. *Precision and Soul. Essays and Addresses*. Edited and translated by Burton Pike and David S. Luft. Chicago, London: University of Chicago Press.

BIBLIOGRAPHIES (in chronological order):

Karthaus, Ulrich. 1965. "Musil-Forschung und Musil-Deutung. Ein Literaturbericht." *Deutsche Vierteljahrschrift für Literaturwissenschaft und Geistesgeschichte* 39 (3): 441–83.
Thöming, Jürgen C. 1968a. *Robert-Musil-Bibliographie*. Bad Homburg v. d. H., Berlin, Zurich: Gehlen. Bibliographien zum Studium der deutschen Sprache und Literatur 4.
———. 1968b. "Kommentierte Auswahlbibliographie zu Robert Musil." *Text + Kritik* 21/22: 61–67. Expanded in 1972 in *Text + Kritik* 21/22 (2nd edition): 73–87.
Roseberry, Robert L. 1974. *Robert Musil. Ein Forschungsbericht*. Frankfurt/Main: Fischer Athenäum.
Danner, Karl-Heinz. 1976. "Robert-Musil-Schrifttum 1970–1975." *Modern Austrian Literature* 9 (3/4): 210–39.
King, Lynda J. 1978. "Robert Musil Bibliography 1976/77." *Musil-Forum* 4: 104–16.
Arntzen, Helmut. 1980. *Musil-Kommentar sämtlicher zu Lebzeiten erschienener Schriften außer dem Roman "Der Mann ohne Eigenschaften."* Munich: Winkler. 279–310.
Freese, Wolfgang; Fourie, Regine. 1981. "Robert Musil: Ausgaben und neuere Forschung. Ein Bericht." *Acta Germanica* 14: 213–32.
Sihvo, Hannes. 1981/82. "Ein kleiner Streifzug durch die Musil-Forschung." *Jahrbuch für finnisch-deutsche Literaturbeziehungen. Mitteilungen aus der Deutschen Bibliothek*. Vol. 15/16. Helsinki: Deutsche Bibliothek. 35–44.
Arntzen, Helmut. 1982. *Musil-Kommentar zu dem Roman "Der Mann ohne Eigenschaften."* Munich: Winkler. 450–80.
Freese, Wolfgang. 1983. "Zur neueren Musil-Forschung. Ausgaben und Gesamtdarstellungen." *Text + Kritik* 21/22 (3rd edition): 86–148.
Mae, Michiko. 1983. "Robert-Musil-Bibliographie. Ergänzungsbibliographie 1980–1983." *Musil-Forum* 9 (1/2): 183–220.
Chevalier, Claude; Magnou, Jacqueline. 1987. "Bibliographie chronologique comentée des publications et critiques parues en français." *Musil-Forum. Wissenschaftliches Beiheft* 3.
Kümmerling, Bettina. 1987. "Robert-Musil-Forschung 1973–1987. Forschungsbericht." *Literatur in Wissenschaft und Unterricht* 20 (4): 540–70.
Fiala-Fürst, Ingeborg, ed. 1990. "Bibliographie der Rezeption Musils in Polen, Jugoslawien, der Sowjet-Union und der Tschechoslowakei." *Musil-Forum. Wissenschaftliches Beiheft* 4.
———, ed. 1991. "Robert Musil. Internationale Bibliographie der Sekundärliteratur 1984–1991." *Musil-Forum. Wissenschaftliches Beiheft* 5.
Iurlano, Fabrizio; Venturelli, Aldo. 1991/92. "Die Musil-Forschung in Italien 1965–1990." *Musil-Forum* 17/18: 171–205.

Markner, Reinhard. 1991/92. "Einige Ergänzungen zur jüngsten Musil-Bibliographie." *Musil-Forum* 17/18: 245–67.

ARTICLES AND BOOKS (in chronological order):

Kerr, Alfred. 1906. "Robert Musil." *Der Tag* (December 21). Reprinted 1911. *Die Aktion*, ed. Franz Pfemfert. Vol. 1. Berlin. 1229–33. Reprinted 1970 in Corino. 240–45.
Blei, Franz. 1907. "Robert Musil. *Die Verwirrungen des Zöglings Törleß*." *Die Opale* 1: 213.
Schaffner, Jakob. 1911. "*Verwirrungen des Zöglings Törleß* von Robert Musil." *Die neue Rundschau* 22: 1769–70.
Stoessl, Otto. 1912. "Erzählende Literatur. Romane." *Österreichische Rundschau* 8 (32): 71–76.
Wolfenstein, Alfred. 1913/14. "Robert Musils Novellen." *Die neue Kunst* 1: 217–19.
Müller, Robert. 1920/21. "Ein Beginner (Robert Musil)." *Der neue Merkur* 4: 860–62.
Diebold, Bernhard. 1921. *Anarchie im Drama: Kritik und Darstellung der modernen Dramatik*. Frankfurt/Main: Frankfurter Verlagsanstalt.
Balázs, Béla. 1923. "Grenzen." *Österreichische Rundschau* 19: 344–49.
Döblin, Alfred. 1924. "Über Robert Musil." *Berliner Tageblatt* (February 3). Reprinted 1963 in *Aufsätze zur Literatur*. Olten, Freiburg i. B.: Walter. 280–82.
Müller, Robert. 1924. "Der erotischste Schriftsteller." *Prager Presse* (August 31).
Blei, Franz. 1925. "Theatralische Krise." *Roland* 23 (21) (May 21): 33–34.
Bab, Julius. 1926. *Die Chronik des deutschen Dramas: Teil V: Deutschlands dramatische Produktion 1918–1926*. Berlin: Oesterfeld. 150–57.
Frisé, Adolf. 1931. "Robert Musil: *Mann ohne Eigenschaften*." *Germania* (December 17). Reprinted 1970 in Dinklage, Albertsen, and Corino. 298–300. Reprinted 1987 in Frisé. 9–12.
Prosper, Hans; Wagner, Marianne; Fischer, Max. 1931. "Aussprache über Robert Musil, *Der Mann ohne Eigenschaften*." *Der Vorstoß* 1: 1901–04.
Holländer, Felix. 1932. "Robert Musils *Vincenz oder die Freundin berühmter Männer* [sic] in der Truppe." *Lebendiges Theater. Eine Berliner Dramaturgie*. Berlin: S. Fischer. 9–13.
Jacob, Paul. 1932. "Robert Musil." *Revue d'Allemagne* 6: 503–17.
Frisé, Adolf. 1933. "Robert Musils *Der Mann ohne Eigenschaften*." *Der Gral. Monatsschrift für Dichtung und Leben* 27 (9): 697–99. Reprinted 1970 in Dinklage, Albertsen, and Corino. 300–302. Reprinted 1987 in Frisé. 13–16.
———. 1935. "Robert Musil oder vom Grenzschicksal der Kunst." *Die Tat. Unabhängige Monatsschrift* 27 (1): 53–64. Reprinted 1970 in Dinklage, Albertsen, and Corino. 303–16. Reprinted 1987 in Frisé. 17–32.
Ystade, Wolfgang. 1935. "Der Nobelpreisträger und warum wir bedauern." *Deutsche Zeitung* (November 20).
Blei, Franz. 1940. "Robert Musil." *Zeitgenössische Bildnisse*. Amsterdam: Allert de Lange. 222–28.

Kisch, Egon Erwin. 1942. "Auf den Tod Robert Musils." *Freies Deutschland/Alemania Libre* (Mexico) 1 (8): 29. Reprint 1975. Leipzig: Antiquariat der Deutschen Demokratischen Republik.

Lejeune, Robert. 1942. "Robert Musil." *Der Aufbau* 23 (34): 269–71; 23 (35): 276–79; 23 (36): 286–88. Republished 1942 as *Robert Musil. Eine Würdigung*. Zurich: Oprecht. Reprinted 1960 in Dinklage. 409–24.

Frisé, Adolf. 1948. "Die vergessenen Dichter. Nachdenklicher Rückblick auf eine kurze Epoche deutscher Literatur." *Die Zeit* 3 (42): 4. Reprinted 1987 in Frisé. 35–40.

Riskamm, Karl. 1948. "Robert Musils Leben und Werk." Diss. Vienna.

Anon. [Kaiser, Ernst; Wilkins, Eithne]. 1949. "Empire in Time and Space." *Times Literary Supplement* 48 (October 28): 689–90.

Maier, Anna. 1949. "Franz Kafka und Robert Musil als Vertreter der ethischen Richtung des modernen Romans." Diss. Vienna.

Csokor, Franz Theodor. 1950/51. "Robert Musil (1880–1942)." *Der Monat* 3 (26): 185–89. Reprinted 1960 under the title "Gedenkrede zu Robert Musils 80. Geburtstag." In Dinklage. 347–56.

Boeninger, Helmut R. 1952. "The Rediscovery of Robert Musil." *Modern Language Forum* 37: 109–19.

Baumann, Gerhart. 1953. "Robert Musil: Eine Vorstudie." *Germanisch-Romanische Monatsschrift* 34 (3): 292–316.

Kaiser, Ernst; Wilkins, Eithne. 1953. "Foreword." Robert Musil. *The Man without Qualities*. Vol. 1. London: Secker & Warburg; New York: Coward-McCann. III–XVIII.

Kesser, Armin. 1953. "Robert Musil." *Neue Zürcher Zeitung* (April 18): 4.

Mandel, Siegfried. 1953. "The Foibles Dissected." *New York Times Book Review* (June 7): 7.

von Salomon, Ernst. 1953. "Bitte an den Leser." *Die Zeit* (December 31).

Bachmann, Ingeborg. 1954. "Ins tausendjährige Reich." *Akzente* 1: 50–53.

Boehlich, Walter. 1954. "Untergang und Erlösung." *Akzente* 1: 35–50.

Braun, Wilhelm. 1954. "Musil's 'Erdensekretariat der Genauigkeit und Seele.' A clue to the philosophy of the hero in *Der Mann ohne Eigenschaften*." *Monatshefte* 46: 305–16.

Jens, Inge. 1954. "Studien zur Entwicklung der expressionistischen Novelle." Diss. Tübingen. 48–79.

Michel, Karl Markus. 1954. "Die Utopie der Sprache." *Akzente* 1: 23–35.

Requadt, Paul. 1954/55. "Zu Musils 'Portugiesin.'" *Wirkendes Wort* 5: 152–58. Reprinted 1982 in von Heydebrand. 321–32.

Fechter, Paul. 1955. "Zur Deutung der *Schwärmer*." *Das neue Forum* 4: 276–79.

Otten, Karl. 1955. "Robert Musil, Schwärmer und Rationalist." *Das neue Forum* 4: 273–75.

Rasch, Wolfdietrich. 1955. "Erinnerung an Robert Musil." *Merkur* 9, 148–58. Reprinted 1960 in Dinklage. 364–76.

Reiss, Hans. 1955. "Zum Stil und zur Komposition in der deutschen Prosaerzählung der Gegenwart." *Studium Generale* 8: 26–30.

Schneider, Rolf. 1955. "Tragik des Alleinseins: Der Dichter Robert Musil." *Neue deutsche Literatur* 10 (3): 106–12.
Zak, Eduard. 1955. "Gegen den Strom. Robert Musils *Mann ohne Eigenschaften*." *Neue deutsche Literatur* 10 (4): 118–36.
Tank, Lothar Kurt. 1955/56. "Robert Musils Tagebücher." *Eckart* 25: 346–48.
Allemann, Beda. 1956. "Musil." *Ironie und Dichtung*. Pfullingen: Neske. 177–220.
Berghahn, Wilfried. 1956. "Die essayistische Erzähltechnik Robert Musils. Eine morphologische Untersuchung zur Organisation und Integration des Romans *Der Mann ohne Eigenschaften*." Diss. Bonn.
Szondi, Peter. 1956. *Theorie des modernen Dramas (1880–1950)*. Frankfurt/Main: Suhrkamp.
Fischer, Ernst. 1957. "Das Werk Robert Musils: Versuch einer Würdigung." *Sinn und Form* 9 (5): 851–901.
Jens, Walter. 1957. "Der Mensch und die Dinge: Die Revolution der deutschen Prosa — Hofmannsthal, Rilke, Musil, Kafka, Heym." *Statt einer Literaturgeschichte*. Pfullingen: Neske. 59–85. Expanded edition 1978. 113–37.
Kaiser, Ernst. 1957. "*Der Mann ohne Eigenschaften*. Ein Problem der Wirklichkeit." *Merkur* 11 (2): 669–87.
Karsch, Walter. 1957. "Pilgerfahrt zu Musil. *Vinzenz und die Freundin bedeutender Männer* — Theaterbesuch in Köln." *Der Tagesspiegel* (December 15).
Schulze Vellinghausen, Albert. 1957. "Entdeckung nach dreiunddreißig Jahren. Robert Musils *Vinzenz und die Freundin bedeutender Männer* in Köln." *Frankfurter Allgemeine Zeitung* 234 (October 9).
Focke, Alfred. 1957/58. "Robert Musil. *Der Mann ohne Eigenschaften*. Zur Bewußtseinslage des modernen Menschen." *Der große Entschluß* 13: 28–34; 80–85.
Blanchot, Maurice. 1958. "Robert Musil." *La Nouvelle Revue Française* 6 (11): 301–09; 479–90. Reprinted 1959 in Maurice Blanchot. *Le livre à venir*. Paris: Gallimard. 165–84. 1962 in German in *Der Gesang der Sirenen. Essays zur modernen Literatur*. Transl. by Karl August Horst. Munich: Hanser. 184–206.
Fechter, Paul. 1958. *Das europäische Drama. Geist und Kultur im Spiegel des Theaters*. Vol. 3. *Vom Expressionismus zur Gegenwart*. Mannheim: Bibliographisches Institut. 209–12.
Lukács, Georg. 1958. *Wider den mißverstandenen Realismus*. Hamburg: Claassen.
Müller, Gerhard. 1958. "Die drei Utopien Ulrichs in Robert Musils *Mann ohne Eigenschaften*." Diss. Vienna.
Torberg, Friedrich. 1958. "Detektivspiel der Seele. Österreichische Erstaufführung der *Schwärmer* von Musil in der 'Tribüne.'" *Neuer Kurier* (May 31).
Kesting, Marianne. 1959. *Das epische Theater. Zur Struktur des modernen Dramas*. Stuttgart: Urban.
Strelka, Joseph. 1959. "Robert Musil. Der Utopist eines anderen Lebens." *Kafka, Musil, Broch und die Entwicklung des modernen Romans*. Vienna: Forum. 36–64.
Arntzen, Helmut. 1960. *Satirischer Stil in Robert Musils "Der Mann ohne Eigenschaften."* Bonn: Bouvier. Abhandlungen zur Kunst-, Musik- und Literaturwissenschaft 9. Second, expanded edition 1970. Third edition 1982.

Bachmann, Ingeborg. 1960. *Frankfurter Vorlesungen: Probleme zeitgenössischer Dichtung.* Reprinted 1980. Munich: Piper. Serie Piper 205.
Baumann, Gerhart. 1960. "Robert Musil. Die Struktur des Geistes und der Geist der Struktur." *Germanische-Romantische Monatsschrift* 41 (10): 420–42.
Csokor, Franz Theodor. 1960. "Gedenkrede zu Robert Musils 80. Geburtstag." In Dinklage. 347–56.
Dinklage, Karl, ed. 1960. *Robert Musil. Leben, Werk, Wirkung.* Reinbek bei Hamburg: Rowohlt.
———. 1960. "Musils Herkunft und Lebensgeschichte." In Dinklage. 187–264.
Fontana, Oskar Maurus. 1960. "Erinnerungen an Robert Musil." In Dinklage. 325–44.
Friedrich, Gerhard. 1960. "Robert Musil's 'Tonka.'" *Die Sammlung* 15: 652–59.
Fürst, Bruno. 1960. "Die Wiener Robert-Musil-Gesellschaft 1934–1938." In Dinklage. 237–81.
Kaiser, Ernst; Wilkins, Eithne. 1960. "Robert Musil und die Quadratwurzel aus minus Eins." In Dinklage. 157–74.
Lejeune, Robert. 1960. "Robert Musil. Eine Würdigung." In Dinklage. 409–424.
Loebenstein, Johannes. 1960. "Das Problem der Erkenntnis in Musils künstlerischem Werk." In Dinklage. 77–131.
Roth, Marie-Louise. 1960. "Robert Musil im Spiegel seines Werkes. Versuch einer inneren Biographie." In Dinklage. 12–48.
von Allesch, Johannes. 1960. "Robert Musil in der geistigen Bewegung seiner Zeit." In Dinklage. 133–42.
Wotruba, Fritz. 1960. "Erinnerung an Musil." In Dinklage. 400–404.
Zimmermann, Werner. 1960. "Robert Musil: 'Die Portugiesin.'" *Deutsche Prosadichtungen der Gegenwart. Interpretationen für Lehrende und Lernende.* 3. Düsseldorf: Schwann. 111–34.
Sokel, Walter H. 1960/61. "Robert Musils Narrenspiegel." *Neue deutsche Hefte* 7: 199–214. Reprinted 1963 in *Wort in der Zeit* 9 (8/9): 51–64.
Braun, Wilhelm. 1961. "An Interpretation of Musil's Novelle 'Tonka.'" *Monatshefte* 53: 73–85.
Dietrich, Margret. 1961. *Das moderne Drama. Strömungen, Gestalten, Motive.* Stuttgart: Kröner.
Pike, Burton. 1961. *Robert Musil: An Introduction to His Work.* Ithaca, N. Y.: Cornell University Press. 2nd edition 1972.
Schöne, Albrecht. 1961. "Zum Gebrauch des Konjunktivs bei Robert Musil." *Euphorion* 55: 196–220. Reprinted 1982 in von Heydebrand. 19–53.
Ziolkowski, Theodore. 1961. "James Joyces Epiphanie und die Überwindung der empirischen Welt in der modernen deutschen Prosa." *Deutsche Vierteljahrsschrift für Literaturwissenschaft und Geistesgeschichte* 35: 594–616.
Arntzen, Helmut. 1962. "Wirklichkeit als Kolportage. Zu drei Komödien von Georg Kaiser und Robert Musil." *Deutsche Vierteljahrsschrift für Literaturwissenschaft und Geistesgeschichte* 36: 544–61. Reprinted 1971 in Helmut Arntzen. *Literatur im Zeitalter der Information. Aufsätze, Essays, Glossen.* Frankfurt/Main: Athenäum. 305–22.

Braun, Wilhelm. 1962a. "An approach to Musil's *Die Schwärmer.*" *Monatshefte* 54: 156–70.
———.1962b. "Musil's *Vinzenz und die Freundin bedeutender Männer.*" *Germanic Review* 37: 121–34.
Frisé, Adolf. 1962. "Angriff auf eine Edition. Einige Hinweise." *Frankfurter Allgemeine Zeitung* 203 (September 3).
Hanke-Tjaden, Irma. 1962. "Der freie Geist und die Politik: zum Problem des Politischen bei Robert Musil." Diss. Freiburg i. Br.
Hermand, Jost. 1962. "Musils 'Grigia.'" *Monatshefte* 54: 171–82.
Kaiser, Ernst; Wilkins, Eithne. 1962. *Robert Musil: Eine Einführung in das Werk.* Stuttgart: Kohlhammer.
Karsch, Walter. 1962. *Wort und Spiel. Aus der Chronik eines Theaterkritikers 1945–1962.* Berlin: Argon.
Kermode, Frank. 1962. "A Short View of Musil." *Puzzles and Epiphanies.* London: Routledge & Kegan Paul. 91–107.
McCormick, E. Allen. 1962. "Ambivalence in Musil's *Drei Frauen*: Notes on Meaning and Method." *Monatshefte* 54: 183–96.
Minder, Robert. 1962. "Kadettenhaus, Gruppendynamik und Stilwandel von Wildenbruch bis Rilke und Musil." *Kultur und Literatur in Deutschland und Frankreich. Fünf Essays.* Frankfurt/Main: Insel. 73–93. Reprinted 1977. Frankfurt/Main: Suhrkamp. 76–95.
Rasch, Wolfdietrich. 1962. "Probleme der Musil-Edition I." *Frankfurter Allgemeine Zeitung* 233 (October 6). "Probleme der Musil-Edition II." *Frankfurter Allgemeine Zeitung* 239 (October 13).
von Wiese, Benno. 1962. "Robert Musil, 'Die Amsel.'" *Die deutsche Novelle von Goethe bis Kafka. Interpretationen.* Vol. 2. Düsseldorf: Bagel. 299–318.
Berghahn, Wilfried. 1963. *Robert Musil in Selbstzeugnissen und Bilddokumenten.* Reinbek bei Hamburg: Rowohlt. Rowohlts Monographien 81.
Kirchberger, Lida. 1963. "Musil's Trilogy. An Approach to *Drei Frauen.*" *Monatshefte* 55: 167–82.
Pongs, Hermann. 1963. *Romanschaffen im Umbruch der Zeit.* 4th edition. Tübingen: Verlag der deutschen Hochschullehrerzeitung. 319–78.
Rasch, Wolfdietrich. 1963. "*Der Mann ohne Eigenschaften.* Eine Interpretation." In *Der deutsche Roman Vom Barock bis zur Gegenwart.* Vol. 2. *Vom Realismus bis zur Gegenwart.* Ed. Benno von Wiese. Düsseldorf: Bagel, 1963. Reprinted 1967 in Rasch. 78–134.
Siegrist, Christoph. 1963. "Loecher im Denken. Zur Struktur von Robert Musils Roman *Toerless.*" *Bulletin of the Faculty of Arts.* Cairo. 25: 23–32.
Bausinger, Wilhelm. 1964. *Robert Musil. "Der Mann ohne Eigenschaften." Studien zu einer historisch-kritischen Ausgabe.* Reinbek bei Hamburg: Rowohlt.
Brosthaus, Heribert. 1964. "Robert Musils 'wahre Antithese.'" *Wirkendes Wort* 14: 120–40.
Hanke-Tjaden, Irma. 1964. "Politische Aspekte in Robert Musils Roman *Der Mann ohne Eigenschaften.*" *Die Pädagogische Provinz* 18: 597–616.

Jässl, Gerolf. 1964. "Mathematik und Mystik in Robert Musils Roman *Der Mann ohne Eigenschaften.*" Diss. Munich.
Rieth, Renate. 1964. "Robert Musils frühe Prosa. Versuch einer stilistischen Interpretation." Diss. Tübingen.
Scharang, Michael. 1964. "Musils Dramatik." *Wort in der Zeit* 10 (11): 36–45.
Baumann, Gerhart. 1965. *Robert Musil. Zur Erkenntnis der Dichtung.* Berne, Munich: Francke.
Bausinger, Wilhelm. 1965. "Robert Musil und die Ablehnung des Expressionismus." *Studi Germanici* N.S. 3: 383–89.
Braun, Wilhelm. 1965a. "The Confusions of Toerless." *Germanic Review* 40: 116–31.
———. 1965b. "Musil's *Die Schwärmer.*" *Publications of the Modern Language Association* 80: 292–98.
Brosthaus, Heribert. 1965. "Zur Struktur und Entwicklung des 'anderen Zustands' in Robert Musils Roman *Der Mann ohne Eigenschaften.*" *Deutsche Vierteljahrsschrift für Literaturwissenschaft und Geistesgeschichte* 39 (3): 388–440.
Geulen, Hans. 1965. "Robert Musils 'Die Versuchung der stillen Veronika.'" *Wirkendes Wort* 15: 173–87.
Goldgar, Harry. 1965. "The Square Root of Minus One: Freud and Robert Musil's *Törleß.*" *Comparative Literature* 17: 117–32.
Hoffmeister, Werner. 1965. "Die erlebte Rede im Werk Robert Musils." *Studien zur erlebten Rede bei Thomas Mann und Robert Musil.* The Hague: Mouton. 86–159. Studies in German Literature 2.
Irle, Gerhard. 1965. "Der psychiatrische Roman bei Robert Musil." *Der Psychiatrische Roman.* Stuttgart: Hippokrates. 124–48.
Karthaus, Ulrich. 1965a. *Der andere Zustand. Zeitstrukturen im Werke Robert Musils.* Berlin: Erich Schmidt. Philologische Studien und Quellen 25.
———. 1965b. "Musil-Forschung und Musil-Deutung. Ein Literaturbericht." *Deutsche Vierteljahrsschrift für Literaturwissenschaft und Geistesgeschichte* 39 (3): 441–83.
Kermode, Frank. 1965. "Preface." Robert Musil. *Tonka and Other Stories.* Transl. by Eithne Wilkins and Ernst Kaiser. London: Secker & Warburg. 7–13.
Kühn, Dieter. 1965. *Analogie und Variation. Zur Analyse von Robert Musils Roman "Der Mann ohne Eigenschaften."* Bonn: Bouvier. Bonner Arbeiten zur deutschen Literatur 13.
Melchinger, Siegfried. 1965. "Robert Musil: Die Brücke zum Imaginären." *Theater heute* 11 (6): 38–40.
Rasch, Wolfdietrich. 1965. "Zur Entstehung von Robert Musils Roman *Der Mann ohne Eigenschaften.*" *Deutsche Vierteljahrsschrift für Literaturwissenschaft und Geistesgeschichte* 39: 350–87. Reprinted 1967 in Rasch. 35–77.
Roth, Marie-Louise, ed. 1965. *Robert Musil: Theater, Kritisches und Theoretisches.* Reinbek bei Hamburg: Rowohlt.
Scharang, Michael. 1965a. "Robert Musil in Dramaturgie und Bühnengeschichte." Diss. Vienna.
———. 1965b. "Robert Musils theatralische Sendung." *Forum* 12 (137): 255–58.

Seidler, Ingo. 1965. "Das Nietzschebild Robert Musils." *Deutsche Vierteljahrsschrift für Literaturwissenschaft und Geistesgeschichte* 39 (3): 329–49.
Bauer, Sibylle. 1966. "Wahrhaftigkeitsproblematik (in den *Schwärmern*)." In Sibylle Bauer, Indrid Drevermann. *Ethik und Bewußtheit. Studien zu Robert Musil.* Cologne, Graz: Böhlau. 7–47. Reprinted 1982 in von Heydebrand. 333–79.
Kowal, Michael. 1966. "Robert Musil: Unread Master." *American German Review* 33 (1): 37–38.
Magris, Claudio. 1966. *Der habsburgische Mythos.* Salzburg: Otto Müller. 278–95.
Schröder, Jürgen. 1966. "Am Grenzwert der Sprache. Zu Robert Musils *Vereinigungen*." *Euphorion* 60: 311–34. Reprinted 1982 in von Heydebrand, 380–411.
Titche, Leon L. 1966. "Isis und Osiris: An interpretation of Robert Musil's poem." *Kentucky Foreign Language Quarterly* 13: 165–69.
Tober, Karl. 1966. "Robert Musils 'Grigia.'" *Sprachkunst als Weltgestaltung. Festschrift für Herbert Seidler.* Ed. Adolf Haslinger. Salzburg, Munich: Pustet. 334–48.
Trommler, Frank. 1966. *Roman und Wirklichkeit: Eine Ortsbestimmung am Beispiel von Musil, Broch, Roth, Doderer und Gütersloh.* Stuttgart: Kohlhammer.
von Heydebrand, Renate. 1966. *Die Reflexionen Ulrichs in Robert Musils Roman "Der Mann ohne Eigenschaften." Ihr Zusammenhang mit dem zeitgenössischen Denken.* Münster: Aschendorff.
White, John J. 1966/67. "Mathematical Imagery in Musil's *Young Törleß* and Zamyatin's *We.*" *Comparative Literature* 18: 71–78.
Bedwell, Carol. 1967. "Musil's 'Grigia': An analysis of cultural dissolution." *Seminar* 3: 117–26.
Braun, Wilhelm. 1967. "Musil's Anselm and 'the motivated life.'" *Wisconsin Studies in Contemporary Literature* 8: 517–27.
Gumtau, Helmut. 1967. *Robert Musil.* Berlin: Colloquium. Köpfe des XX. Jahrhunderts 45.
Nusser, Peter. 1967. *Musils Romantheorie.* The Hague, Paris: Mouton. De proprietatibus litterarum. Series practica 4.
Rasch, Wolfdietrich. 1967. *Über Robert Musils Roman "Der Mann ohne Eigenschaften."* Göttingen: Vandenhoeck & Ruprecht.
Reniers-Servranckx, Annie. 1967. "Robert Musil et le théâtre," *Études Germaniques* 22 (4): 587–91.
Schramm, Ulf. 1967. *Fiktion und Reflexion. Überlegungen zu Musil und Beckett.* Frankfurt/Main: Suhrkamp.
Sokel, Walter H. 1967. "Kleist's 'Marquise of O.,' Kierkegaard's 'Abraham,' and Musil's 'Tonka': Three Stages of the Absurd as the Touchstone of Faith." *Wisconsin Studies in Contemporary Literature* 8: 505–16. Reprinted 1967 in *Festschrift für Bernhard Blume. Aufsätze zur deutschen und europäischen Literatur.* Ed. Egon Schwarz. Göttingen: Vandenhoeck & Ruprecht. 323–32. Reprinted 1970 in Dinklage, Albertsen, and Corino. 57–70.
Albertsen, Elisabeth. 1968. *Ratio und "Mystik" im Werk Robert Musils.* Munich: Nymphenburger. Sammlung Dialog 22.

Arntzen, Helmut. 1968a. "Robert Musil und die Parallelaktionen." *Text + Kritik* 21/22: 3–11. Reprinted 1971 under the title "Robert Musil und die Parallelaktionen. (Zum 15. April 1967)." *Literatur im Zeitalter der Information. Aufsätze, Essays, Glossen.* Frankfurt/Main: Athenäum. 93–109. Reprinted 1972 in *Text + Kritik* 21/22, 2nd edition: 9–22.

———. 1968b. "'Die Reise ins Paradies.'" *Text + Kritik* 21/22: 42–47. Reprinted 1971 under the title "'Die Reise ins Paradies.' Zu dem gleichnamigen Kapitelentwurf in Musils Roman." *Literatur im Zeitalter der Information. Aufsätze, Essays, Glossen.* Frankfurt/Main: Athenäum. 134–47. Reprinted 1972 in *Text + Kritik* 21/22, 2nd edition: 23–34.

———. 1968c. "Seufzer zur Musilforschung." *Text + Kritik* 21/22: 68–75.

Boa, Elizabeth. 1968. "Austrian Ironies in Musil's *Drei Frauen.*" *Modern Language Review* 63: 119–31.

Corino, Karl. 1968. "Törleß ignotus: Zu den biographischen Hintergründen von Robert Musils Roman *Die Verwirrungen des Zöglings Törleß.*" *Text & Kritik* 21/22: 18–25. Reprinted 1972 in *Text + Kritik* 21/22, 2nd edition: 61–72.

Durzak, Manfred. 1968. "Geistesverwandschaft und Rivalität: Robert Musil." *Hermann Broch. Der Dichter und seine Zeit.* Stuttgart: Kohlhammer. 114–37.

Jesch, Jörg. 1968. "Robert Musil als Dramatiker." *Text + Kritik* 21/22: 26–33. Reprinted 1972 in *Text + Kritik* 21/22, 2nd edition: 49–60.

Kohlhase, Norbert. 1968. "From the Revolutionary Theatre to the Theatre without Qualities." *Agenor* 6: 36–45. In German 1968/69: "Von der Revolutionsbühne zum 'Theater ohne Eigenschaften.'" *Schweizer Monatshefte* 48: 717–31.

Kühne, Jörg. 1968. *Das Gleichnis. Studien zur inneren Form von Robert Musils Roman "Der Mann ohne Eigenschaften."* Tübingen: Niemeyer.

Rasch, Wolfdietrich. 1968. "Robert Musils 'Märchen vom Schneider.' Eine Satire auf die Situation des Schriftstellers." *Text + Kritik* 21/22: 39–42. Reprinted 1972 in *Text + Kritik* 21/22, 2nd edition: 35–39.

Reinhardt, Stephan. 1968. "Jahre ohne Synthese. Zu den Essays Robert Musils." *Text + Kritik* 21/22: 34–39. Reprinted 1972 in *Text + Kritik* 21/22, 2nd edition: 40–48.

Schelling, Ulrich. 1968. *Identität und Wirklichkeit bei Robert Musil.* Zurich, Freiburg i. Br.: Atlantis. Zürcher Beiträge zur deutschen Literatur- und Geistesgeschichte 30.

Stopp, Elisabeth. 1968. "Musil's *Törleß*: Content and Form." *Modern Language Review* 63: 94–118. Reprinted 1982 in German under the title "Musils *Törleß*: Inhalt und Form." In von Heydebrand. 207–49.

Wilkins, Eithne. 1968. "Gestalten und Namen im Werk Robert Musils." *Text + Kritik* 21/22: 48–58.

Bachmann, Dieter. 1969. "Robert Musil. 1880-1942." *Essay und Essayismus.* Stuttgart, Berlin, Cologne, Mainz: Kohlhammer. 157–92. Sprache und Literatur 55.

Bertschinger, Thomas. 1969. "Das Bild der Schule in der deutschen Literatur zwischen 1890 und 1914." Diss. Zurich: 152–71.

Brosthaus, Heribert. 1969. "Der Entwicklungsroman einer Idee: Untersuchungen zu Gehalt, Struktur und Stil in Robert Musils Roman *Die Verwirrungen des Zöglings Törleß*." Diss. Würzburg.

Freese, Wolfgang. 1969. *Mystischer Moment und reflektierte Dauer. Zur epischen Funktion der Liebe im modernen deutschen Roman*. Göppingen: Kümmerle. Göppinger Arbeiten zur Germanistik 14.

Graf, Günter. 1969. *Studien zur Funktion des ersten Kapitels von Robert Musils Roman "Der Mann ohne Eigenschaften." Ein Beitrag zur Unwahrhaftigkeitsthematik der Gestalten*. Göppingen: Kümmerle. Göppinger Arbeiten zur Germanistik 11.

Hagmann, Franz. 1969. *Aspekte der Wirklichkeit im Werke Robert Musils*. Frankfurt/Main, Berne: Peter Lang. Europäische Hochschulschriften 10.

Hatfield, Henry. 1969. "An Unsentimental Education: Robert Musil's *Young Törleß*." *Crisis and Continuity in Modern German Fiction. Ten Essays*. Ithaca, London: Cornell University Press. 35–48.

Oertel Sjögren, Christine. 1969. "Aberrations of the Narrator in Robert Musil's Erzählung 'Tonka.'" *Proceedings, Pacific Northwest Conference on Foreign Languages*. Vol. 20. Ed. Jerrold L. Mordaunt. 70–74.

Rasch, Wolfdietrich. 1969. "Robert Musils Komödie *Vinzenz und die Freundin bedeutender Männer*." *Das deutsche Lustspiel*. Ed. Hans Steffen. Vol. 2. Göttingen: Vandenhoeck & Ruprecht. 159–79.

Reinhardt, Stephan. 1969. *Studien zur Antinomie von Intellekt und Gefühl in Musils Roman "Der Mann ohne Eigenschaften."* Bonn: Bouvier. Abhandlungen zur Kunst-, Musik- und Literaturwissenschaft 80.

Sera, Manfred. 1969. "Utopie und Parodie in Robert Musils Roman *Der Mann ohne Eigenschaften*." *Utopie und Parodie bei Musil, Broch und Thomas Mann*. Bonn: Bouvier. 5–72. Bonner Arbeiten zur deutschen Literatur 19.

Berger, Albert. 1970. "Zur Satire in Robert Musils 'Unfreundlichen Betrachtungen.'" *Zeitschrift für deutsche Philologie* 89 (4): 560–76.

Corino, Karl. 1970. "Robert Musil und Alfred Kerr. Der Dichter und sein Kritiker." In Dinklage, Albertsen, and Corino. 236–83.

Dänzer, Hans. 1970. *Robert Musils Roman "Die Verwirrungen des Zöglings Törleß." Freilegung und Beschreibung*. Bamberg: aku-Fotodruck.

Dinklage, Karl; Albertsen, Elisabeth; Corino, Karl, eds. 1970. *Robert Musil. Studien zu seinem Werk*. Reinbek bei Hamburg: Rowohlt.

Düsing, Wolfgang. 1970. "Utopische Vergangenheit: Zur Erinnerungstechnik in Musils früher Prosa." *Zeitschrift für Deutsche Philologie* 89: 531–60.

Eibl, Karl. 1970. "Die dritte Geschichte. Hinweise zur Struktur von Robert Musils Erzählung 'Die Amsel.'" *Poetica* 2: 455–71. Reprinted 1982 in von Heydebrand. 412–33.

Krotz, Frederick W. 1970. "Robert Musils 'Die Amsel.' Novellistische Gestaltung einer Psychose." *Modern Austrian Literature* 3: 7–38.

Laermann, Klaus. 1970. *Eigenschaftslosigkeit. Reflexionen zu Musils Roman "Der Mann ohne Eigenschaften."* Stuttgart: Metzler.

Reniers(-Servranckx), Annie. 1970. "*Törleß*: Freudsche Verwirrungen?" in Dinklage, Albertsen, and Corino. 26–39.
Rothe, Wolfgang. 1970. "'Seinesgleichen geschieht.' Musil und die moderne Erzähltradition." in Dinklage, Albertsen, and Corino. 131–69.
Silone, Ignazio. 1970. "Begegnungen mit Musil." In Dinklage, Albertsen, and Corino. 82–85.
Thöming, Jürgen C. 1970. "Der optimistische Pessimismus eines passiven Aktivisten." In Dinklage, Albertsen, and Corino. 214–35.
von Büren, Erhard 1970. *Zur Bedeutung der Psychologie im Werk Robert Musils.* Zurich, Freiburg i. Br.: Atlantis. Zürcher Beiträge zur deutschen Literatur- und Geistesgeschichte 37.
Aler, Jan. 1971. "Als Zögling zwischen Maeterlinck und Mach. Robert Musils literarisch-philosophische Anfänge." *Probleme des Erzählens in der Weltliteratur. Festschrift für Käte Hamburger.* Ed. Fritz Martini. Stuttgart: Klett. 234–90.
Cohn, Dorrit. 1971. "Psycho-Analogies: A Means for Rendering Consciousness in Fiction." *Probleme des Erzählens in der Weltliteratur. Festschrift für Käte Hamburger.* Ed. Fritz Martini. Stuttgart: Klett. 291–302.
Corino, Karl. 1971. *Robert Musil - Thomas Mann. Ein Dialog.* Pfullingen: Neske.
Freese, Wolfgang. 1971. "Vergleichungen. Statt eines Forschungsberichts — über das Vergleichen Robert Musils mit Hermann Broch in der Literaturwissenschaft." *Literatur und Kritik* 6: 218–41.
Hüppauf, Bernd-Rüdiger. 1971. *Von sozialer Utopie zur Mystik. Zu Robert Musils "Der Mann ohne Eigenschaften."* Munich, Salzburg: Fink. *Musil-Studien* 1.
Müller, Gerd. 1971. *Dichtung und Wissenschaft. Studien zu Robert Musils Romanen "Die Verwirrungen des Zöglings Törleß" und "Der Mann ohne Eigenschaften."* Uppsala: Acta Universitatis Upsaliensia. 21–110. Studia Germanistica Upsaliensia 7.
Rose, Marilyn Gaddis. 1971. "Musil's Use of Simile in *Törleß*." *Studies in Short Fiction* 8: 295–300.
Schaffnit, Hans Wolfgang. 1971. *Mimesis als Problem. Studien zur einem ästhetischen Begriff der Dichtung aus Anlaß Robert Musils.* Berlin: de Gruyter. Quellen und Forschungen zur Sprach- und Kulturgeschichte der germanischen Völker N.F. 36.
Burgstaller, Erich. 1972. "Zu Robert Musils 'Amsel.'" *Sprachkunst* 3: 269–77.
Freese, Wolfgang. 1972. "Musil und Gottfried von Straßburg. Anmerkungen zur Methode und Sache eines literarischen Vergleichs." *Festschrift für Kurt Herbert Halbach zum 70. Geburtstag. Arbeiten aus seinem Schülerkreis.* Rose-Beate Schäfer-Maulbetsch, Manfred Günter Scholz, Günther Schweikle, eds. Göppingen: Kümmerle. 327–65. Göppinger Arbeiten zur Germanistik 70.
Freij, Lars. 1972. *'Türlosigkeit.' Robert Musils "Törleß" in Mikroanalysen mit Ausblicken auf andere Texte des Dichters.* Stockholm: Almquist & Wiksell. Stockholmer germanistische Forschungen 12.
Goltschnigg, Dietmar. 1972. "Kritische Anmerkungen zur Musil-Forschung." *Österreich in Geschichte und Literatur* 16 (3): 150–62.

Herwig, Dagmar. 1972. *Der Mensch in der Entfremdung. Studien zur Entremdungsproblematik anhand des Werkes von Robert Musil*. Munich: List.
Hochstätter, Dietrich. 1972. *Sprache des Möglichen. Stilistischer Perspektivismus in Robert Musils "Mann ohne Eigenschaften."* Frankfurt/Main: Athenäum.
Issler, Maria. 1972. *Robert Musil: "Die Verwirrungen des Zöglings Törleß." Versuch einer Interpretation*. Zurich: aku-Fotodruck.
Kaiser, Gerhard R. 1972. *Proust, Musil, Joyce. Zum Verhältnis von Literatur und Gesellschaft am Paradigma des Zitats*. Frankfurt/Main: Athenäum. 84–144.
Krotz, Frederick W. 1972. *"'Die Amsel,'" "Die Affeninsel," "Eine Kulturfrage." Interpretationen zu Robert Musil*. Munich: R. Oldenbourg. 7–61, 62–71, 72–84.
Müller, Götz. 1972. *Ideologiekritik und Metasprache in Robert Musils Roman "Der Mann ohne Eigenschaften."* Munich, Salzburg: Fink. Musil-Studien 2.
Naganowski, Egon. 1972. "Drei Versuche." *Literatur und Kritik* 7: 321–33.
Oczipka, Michael. 1972. "Die Verwirklichung des 'anderen Zustands' in den Stücken Robert Musils." Diss. Vienna.
Parry, Idris. 1972. "Wave-grain in the Wall." *Animals of Silence. Essays on Art, Nature and Folktale*. London: Oxford University Press. 76–84.
Reniers-Servranckx, Annie. 1972. *Robert Musil: Konstanz und Entwicklung von Themen, Motiven und Strukturen in den Dichtungen*. Bonn: Bouvier. Abhandlungen zur Kunst-, Musik- und Literaturwissenschaft 110.
Roth, Marie-Louise. 1972. *Robert Musil: Ethik und Ästhetik*. Munich: List.
Sanders, Hans. 1972. "Die Widerlegung der Vernunft aus dem Erlebnis oder Die Kapitulation der bürgerlichen Intelligenz vor dem Faschismus. Zu Musils 'Amsel.'" *Ideologiekritik im Deutschunterricht. Analysen und Modelle*. Ed. Heinz Ide et al. Frankfurt/Main, Berlin, Munich: Diesterweg. 86–95.
Appignanesi, Lisa. 1973a. "Femininity and Robert Musil's 'Die Vollendung der Liebe.'" *Monatshefte* 65 (1): 14–26.
———. 1973b. "Robert Musil: Femininity and Completeness." *Femininity and the Creative Imagination. A Study of Henry James, Robert Musil and Marcel Proust*. London: Vision; New York: Barnes & Noble. 81–156.
Baur, Uwe; Goltschnigg, Dietmar, eds. 1973. *Vom "Törleß" zum "Mann ohne Eigenschaften."* Munich, Salzburg: Fink. Musil-Studien 4.
Baur, Uwe. 1973a. "Musils Novelle 'Die Amsel.' Figurierung der Persönlichkeitsspaltung eines Rahmenerzählers." In Baur and Goltschnigg. 237–92.
———. 1973b. "Zeit und Gesellschaftskritik in Robert Musils Roman *Die Verwirrungen des Zöglings Törleß*." In Baur and Goltschnigg. 19–45.
Burckhardt, Judith. 1973. *"Der Mann ohne Eigenschaften" von Robert Musil. Oder das Wagnis der Selbstverwirklichung*. Berne: Francke. Basler Studien zur deutschen Sprache und Literatur 48.
Corino, Karl. 1973. "Ödipus oder Orest? Robert Musil und die Psychoanalyse." In Baur and Goltschnigg. 123–235.
Danner, Karl-Heinz, ed. 1973. *Materialien vom internationalen Kolloquium zu Fragen der Robert-Musil-Forschung*. Saarbrücken: Universität des Saarlandes.

Fischer, Nanda. 1973. "'Eine plötzliche und umgrenzt bleibende geistige Erregung...': Zum Novellenbegriff Robert Musils." *Monatshefte* 65: 224–40.
Heintel, Erich. 1973. "Glaube in Zweideutigkeit. Robert Musils 'Tonka.'" In Baur and Goltschnigg. 47–88.
Hönig, Christoph. 1973. "Musils Pläne für einen satirisch-utopischen Experimentalroman: *Land über dem Südpol* oder *Der Stern Ed.*" In Baur and Goltschnigg. 325–47.
Huber, Lothar. 1973. "Robert Musil's Törleß und die Krise der Sprache." *Sprachkunst* 4: 91–99.
Mattenklott, Gert. 1973. "Der 'subjektive Faktor' in Musils *Törleß*. Mit einer Vorbemerkung über die Historizität der sinnlichen Wahrnehmung." *Neue Hefte für Philosophie* 4: 47–73. Reprinted 1982 in von Heydebrand. 250–80.
Naganowski, Egon. 1973. "*Vinzenz* oder der Sinn des sinnvollen Unsinns." In Baur and Goltschnigg. 89–122.
Roth, Marie-Louise. 1973. "Robert Musil und das Theater." *Neue Zürcher Zeitung* 135: 51–52.
Röttger, Brigitte. 1973. *Erzählexperimente. Studien zu Robert Musils "Drei Frauen" und "Vereinigungen."* Bonn: Bouvier. Abhandlungen zu Kunst-, Musik- und Literaturwissenschaft 128.
Schneider, Günther. 1973. *Untersuchungen zum dramatischen Werk Robert Musils.* Berne, Frankfurt/Main: Peter Lang. Europäische Hochschulschriften 81.
Stefanek, Paul. 1973. "Theater zwischen Krise und Utopie. Zur Theaterkritik und –ästhetik Robert Musils." *Maske und Kothurn* 19: 304–20.
Böhme, Hartmut. 1974. *Anomie und Entfremdung. Literatursoziologische Untersuchungen zu den Essays Robert Musils und seinem Roman "Der Mann ohne Eigenschaften."* Kronberg/Taunus: Scriptor. Skripten Literaturwissenschaft 9.
Castex-Rieger, Elisabeth. 1974. "Musil in Frankreich: Verbreitung, kritische Aufnahme, Wirkung." *Literatur und Kritik* 9: 381–89.
Cohn, Dorrit. 1974. "Psyche and Space in Musil's 'Die Vollendung der Liebe.'" *Germanic Review* 49: 154–68.
Corino, Karl. 1974. *Robert Musils "Vereinigungen."* Munich, Salzburg: Fink. Musil-Studien 5.
Desportes, Yvon. 1974. "Étude comparative d'un style et d'une philosophie: une oeuvre de Musil à la lumière de Mach." *Revue d'Allemegne et de pays de langue allemande* VI: 79–90. Reprinted 1982 in German as "Vergleichende Untersuchung eines Stils und einer Philosophie: Ein Werk Musils aus der Sicht Machs." In von Heydebrand. 281–95.
Freese, Wolfgang. 1974a. "Anmerkungen zu neueren Arbeiten der Musil-Forschung." *German Quarterly* 47: 73–87.
———. 1974b. "Robert Musil als Realist. Ein Betrag zur Realismus-Diskussion." *Literatur und Kritik* 9: 514–44.
Goltschnigg, Dietmar. 1974. *Mystische Tradition im Roman Robert Musils. Martin Bubers "Ekstatische Konfessionen" im "Mann ohne Eigenschaften."* Heidelberg: Stiehm.

Magris, Claudio. 1974. "Musil und die 'Nähte der Zeichen.'" *Literaturwissenschaftliches Jahrbuch der Görres-Gesellschaft* 15: 189–219. Reprinted 1981 in Freese. 177–93.
Roseberry, Robert L. 1974. *Robert Musil. Ein Forschungsbericht.* Frankfurt/Main: Fischer Athenäum.
Rothe-Buddensieg, Margret. 1974. "Musil und der Triumph des Eros." *Spuk im Bürgerhaus. Der Dachboden in der deutschen Literatur als Negation der gesellschaftlichen Realität.* Kronberg/Taunus: Scriptor. 249–53.
Thöming, Jürgen C. 1974. *Zur Rezeption von Musil- und Goethe-Texten. Historizität der ästhetischen Vermittlung von sinnlicher Erkenntnis und Gefühlserlebnissen.* Munich, Salzburg: Fink. *Musil-Studien* 3.
Turner, David. 1974. "The evasions of the aesthete Törleß." *Forum for Modern Language Studies* 10 (1): 19–44.
Williams, Cedric Ellis 1974. "Robert Musil: Vanity Fair." *The Broken Eagle. The Politics of Austrian Literature from Empire to Anschluß.* London: Paul Elek. 148–86.
Corino, Karl. 1975. "Die ganz anderen Zustände. Krise der Robert-Musil-Gesellschaft hält an." *Frankfurter Rundschau* (July 4).
Doppler, Alfred. 1975. "Von der Wortbedeutung zum Textsinn. Zu Robert Musils Novelle 'Die Amsel.'" *Wirklichkeit im Spiegel der Sprache. Aufsätze zur Literatur des 20. Jahrhunderts in Österreich.* Wien: Europaverlag. 133–49.
Hall, Murray G. 1975a. "Tier und Tiermotivik im Prosawerk Robert Musils." Diss. Vienna.
———. 1975b. "Die religiöse Allegorie in Robert Musils 'Die Portugiesin.'" *Études Germaniques* 30: 76–79.
———. 1975c. "Der Schwärmerskandal 1929. Zur Rezeption von Robert Musils *Die Schwärmer*." *Maske und Kothurn* 21: 153–86. Reprinted 1975 in *Musil-Forum* 1: 37–60 and 201–24.
Halm, Heinz J. 1975. "Satirische Parabeln. Robert Musils Tiergeschichten im *Nachlaß zu Lebzeiten*." *Sprachkunst* 6: 75–86.
Schmidt, Jochen. 1975. *Ohne Eigenschaften. Eine Erläuterung zu Musils Grundbegriff.* Tübingen: Niemeyer. Untersuchungen zur deutschen Literaturgeschichte 13.
Schneider, Rolf. 1975. *Die problematisierte Wirklichkeit. Leben und Werk Robert Musils. Versuch einer Interpretation.* Berlin: Volk und Welt.
Schrader, Monika. 1975. *Mimesis und Poiesis. Poetologische Studien zum Bildungsroman.* Berlin, New York: de Gruyter.
Schröder-Werle, Renate. 1975. "Zur Vorgeschichte der Musil-Rezeption nach 1945. Hinweise zur Wiederentdeckung." *Musil-Forum* 1: 226–46.
Stelzmann, Rainulf A. 1975. "A Kantian faith in Musil's 'Tonka.'" *Germanic Review* 50: 294–304.
Althaus, Horst. 1976. *Zwischen Monarchie und Republik. Schnitzler, Kafka, Hofmannsthal, Musil.* Munich: Fink.
Aue, Maximilian. 1976. "Die Ablehnung romantischer Vorstellungen von Liebe, Natur und Tod in Robert Musils *Drei Frauen*." *Modern Austrian Literature* 9 (3/4): 240–56.

Baedecker, Karl. 1976. "Hinweise zur 'Amsel.'" *Musil-Forum* 2: 29–32.
Barnouw, Dagmar. 1976. "Literat und Literatur. Robert Musils Beziehung zu Franz Blei." *Modern Austrian Literature* 9 (3/4): 168–99.
Böhme, Hartmut. 1976. "Theoretische Probleme der Interpretation von Robert Musils Roman *Der Mann ohne Eigenschaften*." *Musil-Forum* 2 (1): 35–70. Reprinted 1982 in von Heydebrand. 120–159.
Braun, Wilhelm. 1976. "Neuere Interpretationen zu den *Verwirrungen des Zöglings Törleß*." *Modern Austrian Literature* 9 (3/4): 43–56.
Frier, Wolfgang. 1976. *Die Sprache der Emotionalität in den "Verwirrungen des Zöglings Törleß" von Robert Musil. Ein Beitrag zur angewandten Textlinguistik*. Bonn: Bouvier. Abhandlungen zur Kunst-, Musik- und Literaturwissenschaft 179.
Fuld, Werner. 1976. "Die Quellen zur Konzeption des 'anderen Zustands' in Robert Musils Roman *Der Mann ohne Eigenschaften*." *Deutsche Vierteljahrsschrift für Literaturwissenschaft und Geistesgeschichte* 50: 664–82.
Gradischnig, Hertwig. 1976. *Das Bild des Dichters bei Robert Musil*. Munich, Salzburg: Fink. *Musil-Studien* 6.
Hall, Murray G. 1976. "Ein perverser Dichter." *Musil-Forum* 2 (1): 137–38.
Henninger, Peter. 1976. "Schreiben und Sprechen. Robert Musils Verhältnis zur Erzählform am Beispiel von *Drei Frauen* und 'Die Amsel.'" *Modern Austrian Literature* 9 (3/4): 57–99.
Kisery, Pal. 1976. "Anmerkungen zu Robert Musils Modernität." *Musil-Forum* 2 (1): 71–80.
Krejic, Karel. 1976. "Franz Schamann und Robert Musil." *Musil-Forum* 2 (1): 85–94.
Marcovaldi, Gaetano; Zwettl, Walter. 1976. "Inventar des bei Prof. Gaetano Marcovaldi, Rom, befindlichen und von ihm verwalteten literarischen Nachlasses von Robert Musil." *Musil-Forum* 1 (2): 195–200.
Menges, Karl. 1976. "Robert Musil und Edmund Husserl. Über phänomenologische Strukturen im *Mann ohne Eigenschaften*." *Modern Austrian Literature* 9 (3/4): 131–54.
Morgenstern, Soma. 1976. "Dichten, denken, berichten. Gespräche zwischen [Joseph] Roth und Musil." *Musil-Forum* 2 (1): 12–18.
Oertel Sjögren, Christine. 1976. "The enigma of Musil's 'Tonka.'" *Modern Austrian Literature* 9 (3/4): 100–113. Reprinted 1982 under the title "Das Rätsel in Musils 'Tonka.'" In von Heydebrand. 434–49.
Schröder-Werle, Renate. 1976. "Von der Vermittlung zwischen Dichtung und Publikum in schwieriger Zeit. Notizen zum unbekannten *silberboot* (1935–37; 1946–52)." *Musil-Forum* 2 (2): 188–94.
Sokel, Walter H. 1976. "The Problem of Dualism in Hesse's *Demian* and Musil's *Törleß*." *Modern Austrian Literature* 9 (3/4): 35–42.
Strelka, Joseph. 1976. "'Seinesgleichen geschieht' oder Wie lange noch 'erfindet' man Musil-Kritik? Bemerkungen zum gegenwärtigen Stand der Nachlaßbearbeitung und der Editionsarbeiten am Werk Robert Musils." *Modern Austrian Literature* 9 (3/4): 200–209.

Thöming, Jürgen C. 1976. "Musil-Seminar zu Editionsfragen, 19. März 1976, Brüssel." *Musil-Forum* 2 (2): 292–300.
Braun, Wilhelm. 1976/77. "Die Wassermetapher in 'Die Vollendung der Liebe.'" *Colloquia Germanica* 10 (3): 237–46.
Castex, Elizabeth. 1976/77. "Probleme und Ziele der Forschung am Nachlaß Robert Musils." *Colloquia Germanica* 10 (3): 267–79.
Lange, Victor. 1976/77. "Musils 'Das Fliegenpapier.'" *Colloquia Germanica* 10 (3): 193–203. Reprinted 1982 in von Heydebrand. 450–61.
Roth, Marie-Louise. 1976/77 "Sinn und Ziel der internationalen Robert-Musil-Gesellschaft." *Colloquia Germanica* 10 (3): 280–89.
Schröder-Werle, Renate. 1976/77. "Zur Vorgeschichte der Musil-Rezeption nach 1945." *Colloquia Germanica* 10 (3): 247–66.
Barnouw, Dagmar. 1977. "Scepticism as a Literary Mode: David Hume and Robert Musil." *Musil-Forum* 3 (1): 34–56.
Hall, Murray G. 1977a. "Dokumente zur Musil-Rezeption." *Musil-Forum* 3 (1): 57–75.
———. 1977b. "Robert Musil und der Schutzverband deutscher Schriftsteller in Österreich." *Österreich in Geschichte und Literatur* 21: 202–21.
Heald, David. 1977. "Musil's Conception of 'Schauspielerei' as Novelist and Critic." *Maske und Kothurn* 23 (3): 244–55.
Magnou, Jacqueline. 1977. "*Törleß* — Eine Variation über den Ödipus-Komplex? Einige Bemerkungen zur Struktur des Romans." *Musil-Forum* 3: 134–58. Reprinted 1982 in von Heydebrand. 296–318.
Mauch, Gudrun. 1977. "Das Märchen in Musils Erzählung 'Die Amsel.'" *Literatur und Kritik* 12: 146–66.
Mulot, Sibylle. 1977. *Der junge Musil. Seine Beziehungen zu Literatur und Kunst der Jahrhundertwende*. Stuttgart: Heinz. Stuttgarter Arbeiten zur Germanistik 401.
Pfister, Manfred. 1977. *Das Drama. Theorie und Analyse*. Munich: Fink. Translated 1988 by John Halliday as *The Theory and Analysis of Drama*. Cambridge: Cambridge University Press.
Roth, Marie-Louise, ed. 1977. "Werk- und Nachlaßdokumentation. Robert Musil — *Nachlaß zu Lebzeiten.*" *Musil-Forum. Wissenschaftliches Beiheft* 1: 23–120.
Schier, Rudolf. 1977. "Robert Musils 'Tonka' als Vorläufer des 'Nouveau Roman.'" *Études Germaniques* 32: 40–45.
Cohn, Dorrit. 1978. *Transparent Minds. Modes of Representing Consciousness in Fiction*. Princeton, N.J.: Princeton University Press.
Dawlianidse, David. 1978. "Der Offene Romananfang. Am Beispiel von R. Musils Roman *Der Mann ohne Eigenschaften.*" *Musil-Forum* 4 (1): 35–59.
Eibl, Karl. 1978. *Robert Musil. "Drei Frauen." Text, Materialien, Kommentar*. Munich: Hanser. Hanser Literatur-Kommentare 13.
Freese, Wolfgang. 1978. "Brecht und historische Formen des Neinsagens." *Musil-Forum* 4: 221–43.
Grimm, Reinhold. 1978. "Neuer Humor? Die Komödienproduktion zwischen 1918 und 1932." *Nach dem Naturalismus. Essays zur modernen Dramatik*. Kronberg/Taunus: Athenäum. 75–100.

Holmes, Alan. 1978. *"Der Mann ohne Eigenschaften." An Examination of the Relationship between the Author, Narrator and Protagonist.* Bonn: Bouvier. Abhandlungen zur Kunst-, Musik-, und Literaturwissenschaft 259.

King, Lynda J. 1978. "The Relationship between Clarisse and Nietzsche in Musil's *Der Mann ohne Eigenschaften.*" *Musil-Forum* 4 (1): 21–34.

Krusche, Dietrich. 1978. "Selbstfindung und Partnerferne: Robert Musil: *Vereinigungen.*" *Orbis litterarum* 33: 310–29.

Mauser, Wolfram. 1978. "'Es hat sich alles so ereignet ...' Zu Robert Musils Erzählung 'Die Amsel.'" *Perspektiven psychoanalytischer Literaturkritik.* Ed. Sebastian Goeppert. Freiburg i. Br.: Rombach. 101–23.

Peters, Frederick G. 1978. *Robert Musil. Master of the Hovering Life. A Study of the Major Fiction.* New York: Columbia University Press.

Scholz, Ingeborg. 1978. *Studien zu Robert Musils "Nachlaß zu Lebzeiten."* Hollfeld: König. Königs Erläuterungen und Materialien 322.

Wiegmann, Hermann. 1978. "Musils Utopiebegriff und seine literaturtheoretischen Konsequenzen." *Literatur ist Utopie.* Ed. Gert Ueding. Vol. 1: Frankfurt/Main: Suhrkamp. 309–34.

Wucherpfennig, Wolf. 1978. "'Tonka' oder die Angst vor Erkenntnis." *Perspektiven psychoanalytischer Literaturkritik.* Ed. Sebastian Goeppert. Freiburg i. Br.: Rombach. 233–59.

Zehl-Romero, Christiane. 1978. "Musils 'letzte Liebesgeschichte.'" *Deutsche Vierteljahrsschrift für Literaturwissenschaft und Geistesgeschichte* 52: 619–34.

Albertsen, Elisabeth. 1979. "Ea oder die Freundin bedeutender Männer. Portrait einer Wiener Kaffeehaus-Muse." *Musil-Forum* 5: 21–37; 135–53.

Brasch, Thomas. 1979. "Robert Musil. *Die Verwirrungen des Zöglings Törless.*" *Die Zeit* (August 10). Reprinted 1987 in *Arbeitsbuch Thomas Brasch.* Ed. Margarete Häßel and Richard Weber. Frankfurt/Main: Suhrkamp. 255–57.

Cremerius, Johannes. 1979. "Robert Musil. Das Dilemma eines Schriftstellers vom Typus *poeta ductus* nach Freud." *Psyche* 33 (8): 733–72.

Fuder, Dieter. 1979. *Analogiedenken und anthropologische Differenz. Zu Form und Funktion der poetischen Logik in Robert Musils Roman "Der Mann ohne Eigenschaften."* Munich, Salzburg: Fink. Musil-Studien 10.

Gumtau, Helmut. 1979. "Musil, Berlin, und einiges mehr." *Musil-Forum* 5 (2): 232–37.

Henninger, Peter. 1979. "'Wissenschaft' und 'Dichtung' bei Musil und Freud." *Modern Language Notes* 94: 542–68.

Lyotard, Jean-François. 1979. *La condition post-moderne.* Paris: Minuit. Republished 1984 in English as *The Postmodern Condition.* Transl. Geoff Bennington and Brian Massumi. Minneapolis: University of Minnesota Press.

Mayer-König, Wolfgang. 1979. *Robert Musils Möglichkeitsstil.* Vienna: Gesellschaft der Kunstfreunde.

Meister, Monika. 1979. "Der Theaterbegriff Robert Musils. Ein Beitrag zur ästhetischen Theorie des Theaters." Diss. Vienna.

Monti, Claudia. 1979. "Funktion und Fiktion. Die Mach-Dissertation Robert Musils in den Jahren zwischen den *Verwirrungen des Zöglings Törleß* und den Essays." *Musil-Forum* 5 (1): 38–67; (2): 154–83.
Pike, Burton. 1979. "Musil and the City." *Musil-Forum* 5 (1): 68–87.
Rinderknecht, Siegfried. 1979. *Denkphantasie und Reflexionsleidenschaft. Musils Formsynthese im Roman "Der Mann ohne Eigenschaften."* Frankfurt/Main: R. G. Fischer.
Zeller, Rosmarie. 1979. "Karl Eibl. Robert Musil. Drei Frauen." *Musil-Forum* 5 (2): 244–48.
Arntzen, Helmut. 1980. *Musil-Kommentar sämtlicher zu Lebzeiten erschienener Schriften außer dem Roman "Der Mann ohne Eigenschaften."* Munich: Winkler.
Baur, Uwe; Castex, Elisabeth, eds. 1980. *Robert Musil: Untersuchungen.* Königstein/Taunus: Athenäum.
Castex, Elisabeth. 1980. "Auf der Suche nach der verlorenen Frau. Zur Problematik des Frauenbildes in Italo Svevos *La coscienza di Zeno* und Robert Musils *Der Mann ohne Eigenschaften*." *Robert Musil Nel Primo Centenario Della Nascita.* Innsbruck, Vienna: Istituto Italiano di Cultura. 51–62.
Frisé, Adolf. 1980. "Unvollendet — Unvollendbar? Überlegungen zum Torso des *Mann ohne Eigenschaften*." *Musil-Forum* 6 (1): 79–104.
Gumtau, Helmut. 1980. "Robert Musil und die 'Geschichtsbuch-Jahrzehnte.'" *Musil-Forum* 6 (2): 184–206.
Henninger. Peter. 1980. *Der Buchstabe und der Geist. Unbewußte Determinierung im Schreiben Robert Musils.* Frankfurt/Main, Berne, Cirencester: Peter Lang. Europäische Hochschulschriften 359; Literatur & Psychologie 4.
Heyd, Dieter. 1980. *Musil-Lektüre, der Text, das Unbewußte. Psychosemiologische Studien zu Robert Musils theoretischem Werk und zum Roman "Der Mann ohne Eigenschaften."* Frankfurt/Main, Berne, Cirencester: Peter Lang. Europäische Hochschulschriften 368.
Hickman, Hannah. 1980. "Der junge Musil und R. W. Emerson." *Musil-Forum* 6 (1): 3–13.
Kaizik, Jürgen. 1980. *Die Mathematik im Werke Robert Musils.* Vienna: Josef Steiner.
Karthaus, Ulrich. 1980. "War Musil Realist?" *Musil-Forum* 6 (1): 115–27.
Kreisky, Bruno. 1980. "Rede zur Eröffnung des Internationalen Musil-Symposions." *Literatur und Kritik* 149/150 (October/November): 515–17.
Luft, David S. 1980. *Robert Musil and the Crisis of European Culture 1880–1942.* Berkeley, Los Angeles, London: University of California Press.
Mae, Michiko. 1980a. "Robert Musils Novellentheorie." *Beiträge zur Germanistik* 1: 25–43.
———. 1980b. "Robert Musils Novellenband *Vereinigungen* in der Kritik seiner Zeit. Ein Beitrag zur historischen Rezeptionsanalyse." *Doitsu Bungaku* 65: 44–55.
Mauch, Gudrun B. 1980a. "Die Tradition des Grotesken in Robert Musils *Nachlaß zu Lebzeiten.*" *Musil-Forum* 6 (1): 43–62.
———. 1980b. "Robert Musils 'Bilder' im *Nachlaß zu Lebzeiten*." *Akten des VI. Internationalen Germanisten-Kongresses* 4: 507–11.

———. 1980c. "Robert Musils Erzählung 'Die Maus.'" *Colloquia Germanica* 13 (3): 253–57.
Meister, Monika. 1980a. "Robert Musil als früher Kritiker der 'Kulturindustrie.'" *Musil-Forum* 6: 157–70.
———. 1980b. "Robert Musils Zeitgenossen im Spiegel seiner Kritik." *Maske und Kothurn* 26: 271–85.
Moser, Walter. 1980. "Diskursexperimente im Romantext zu Musils *Der Mann ohne Eigenschaften*." In Baur and Castex. 170–97.
Mulot-Déri, Sibylle. 1980. "*Törleß* und der Dekadenz-Roman." *Studi Tedesci* 23 (2/3): 239–49.
Peyret, Jean-François. 1980. "Von jenen, die auszogen, den *Mann ohne Eigenschaften* zu verstehen." In Baur and Castex. 31–45.
Pila, Marie-Christine. 1980. "Commentaire à 'Das Doppel-Ich oder der Verlust der Persönlichkeit oder das Erlebnis eines Zigarrenhändlers.'" *Annali. Studi Tedeschi* 23 (2/3): 251–76.
Roth, Marie-Louise. 1980. *Robert Musil: "Les oeuvres pré-posthumes."* Vol 1: *Biographie et écriture*. Vol 2: *Genèse et commentaire*. Paris: Editions Recherches.
Ryan, Judith. 1980. "The Vanishing Subject: Empirical Psychology and the Modern Novel." *Publications of the Modern Language Association of America* 95: 857–69.
Schink, Helmut. 1980. "Das bodenlose Ich. Robert Musils *Verwirrungen des Zöglings Törleß*." *Jugend als Krankheit? Hermann Hesse, Robert Musil, Franz Kafka, Reinhold Schneider, Anne Frank, Franz Innerhofer*. Linz: Oberösterreichischer Landesverlag. 41–67.
Schmitz, Dietmar Bernhard. 1980. "Musils verlegter Weg zum Leser." *Musil-Forum* 6 (2): 213–22. Reprinted 1980 under the title "Musils erschwerter Weg zum Leser." In *Literatur und Kritik* 16 (160): 621–27.
Sera, Manfred. 1980. "'Werde, der du bist!' Die Darstellung der Selbsterfahrung in Robert Musils Novelle 'Die Portugiesin.'" *Musil-Forum* 6 (1): 145–56.
Stefanek, Paul. 1980a. "Musils Posse *Vinzenz* und das Theater der Zwischenkriegszeit." *Maske und Kothurn* 26: 249–70. Reprinted 1981 under the title "Musils Posse *Vinzenz* und das Theater." In Freese. 111–48.
———. 1980b. "Due Poeti in Cerca del Dramma. Überlegungen zur Dramaturgie Robert Musils und Luigi Pirandellos." *Musil Nel Primo Centario Della Nascita*. Innsbruck, Vienna: Istituto Italiano di Cultura. 63–70.
Strutz, Josef. 1980. "Musil und die italienische Philosophie." *Musil Nel Primo Centario Della Nascita* Innsbruck, Vienna: Istituto Italiano di Cultura. 113–19.
Tiebel, Ursula. 1980. *Theater von außen. Robert Musil als Kritiker*. Rheinfelden: Schäuble. Theater unserer Zeit 15.
Venturelli, Aldo. 1980. "Die Kunst als fröhliche Wissenschaft. Zum Verhältnis Musils zu Nietzsche." *Nietzsche-Studien* 9: 302–37.
von Becker, Peter. 1980. "'Ein Sinken ins Bodenlose, ohne unterzugehen.' Über Robert Musils *Schwärmer* und Erwin Axers Inszenierung am Burgtheater." *Theater heute* 8: 24–28.

Weissberg, Liliane. 1980. "Versuch einer Sprache des Möglichen. Zum Problem des Erzählens bei Robert Musil." *Deutsche Vierteljahrsschrift für Literaturwissenschaft und Geistesgeschichte* 54 (3): 464–84.
Winter, Ingrid. 1980. "Zeitperspektiven in Robert Musils *Die Verwirrungen des Zöglings Törleß*." *Modern Austrian Literature* 13 (3): 47–68.
Zeller, Rosmarie. 1980. "Musils Auseinandersetzung mit der realistischen Schreibweise." *Musil-Forum* 6 (1): 128–44.
Böhme, Hartmut. 1981. "Die Suche nach anderem Leben und die Kritik tradierter Ordnung: Robert Musil." *Sozialgeschichte der deutschen Literatur von 1918 bis zur Gegenwart*. Ed. Jan Berg et al. Frankfurt/Main: Fischer. 283–88.
Bohrer, Karl Heinz. 1981. *Plötzlichkeit. Zum Augenblick des ästhetischen Scheins*. Frankfurt/Main: Suhrkamp.
Castex, Elisabeth. 1981. "Zum neuesten Stand der Musil-Editions-Forschung und -Rezeption." *Musil-Forum* 7: 53–64.
Dettmering, Peter. 1981. "Narzißtische Konfiguration in Robert Musils *Der Mann ohne Eigenschaften*." *Psyche* 35 (12): 1122–35.
Frank, Manfred. 1981. "Erkenntniskritische, ästhetische und mythologische Aspekte der 'Eigenschaftslosigkeit' in Musils Roman." *Revue de Théologie et de Philosophie* 113: 241–57.
Freese, Wolfgang, ed. 1981. *Philologie und Kritik*. Munich, Salzburg: Fink. *Musil-Studien* 7.
Fritz, Axel. 1981. "Robert Musil als Dramatiker." *Schriften des Deutschen Instituts, Universität Stockholm* 11: 29–46.
Gargani, Aldo. 1981. "Wittgenstein's 'perspicuous representation' and Musil's 'illuminations.'" *Ethik. Grundlagen, Probleme und Anwendungen*. Ed. Edgar Morcher. Vienna: Hölder, Pichler, Tempsky. 508–14. Reprinted 1983 in Strutz. 110–19.
Goltschnigg, Dietmar. 1981. "Liebe, Moral und Psychotherapie in Robert Musils Erzählung 'Tonka' mit Rücksicht auf Jacques Lacan." *Psychoanalytische und psychopathische Literaturinterpretation*. Ed. Bernd Urban and Winfried Kudszus. Darmstadt: Wissenschaftliche Buchgesellschaft. 398–420.
Groeben, Norbert, ed. 1981. *Rezeption und Interpretation: Ein interdisziplinärer Versuch am Beispiel der "Hasenkatastrophe" von Robert Musil*. Tübingen: Narr. Empirische Literaturwissenschaft, Band 5.
Hahnl, Hans Heinz. 1981. "Zu Musils Aktualität." *Musil-Forum* 7 (1/2): 169–73.
Henninger, Peter. 1981. "Über Musils Stil und seine Wahrnehmung (aufgrund einer Textprobe aus dem *Mann ohne Eigenschaften*)." *Musil-Forum* 7 (1/2): 29–39.
Karthaus, Ulrich. 1981a. "*Der Mann ohne Eigenschaften* und die Phantasie. Überlegungen im Anschluß an Kant." *Musil-Forum* 7 (1/2): 111–17.
———. 1981b. "Robert Musil und der poetische Realismus." In Freese. 223–45.
Magnou, Jacqueline. 1981. "Zwischen Mach und Freud: Ich-Problematik in den Frühwerken Robert Musils." *Musil-Forum* 7: 131–41.
Mauser, Wolfram. 1981. "Robert Musil." *Handbuch der deutschen Erzählung*. Ed. Karl Konrad Polheim. Düsseldorf: Bagel. 483–90.
Meister, Monika. 1981. "Zur Theaterkritik Robert Musils." In Freese. 149–76.

Monti, Claudia. 1981. 'Musils 'Ratioid,' oder Wissenschaft als Analogie der Ratio." In Freese. 195–222. Reprinted 1982 in Farda and Karthaus. 175–96. Reprinted 1983 in Brokoph-Mauch. 205–35.
Olmi, Roberto. 1981. "Musil und Nietzsche." *Musil-Forum* 7: 119–29.
Paulson, Ronald M. 1981. "Myth and fairy tale in Robert Musil's 'Grigia.'" *The Turn of the Century. German Literature and Art, 1890–1915*. The McMaster Colloquium on German Literature, eds. Gerald Chapple and Hans H. Schulte. Vol. 2. Bonn: Bouvier. 135–48. Modern German Studies 5.
Petersen, Klaus. 1981. *Die "Gruppe 1925": Geschichte und Soziologie einer Schriftstellervereinigung*. Heidelberg: Carl Winter.
Pila, Marie-Christine. 1981. "Bühnenentwürfe im Nachlaß Robert Musils." *Nachlaß- und Editionsprobleme bei modernen Schriftstellern*. Ed. Marie-Louise Roth, Renate Schröder-Werle, Hans Zeller. Berne, Frankfurt/Main, Las Vegas: Peter Lang. Jahrbuch für Internationale Germanistik: Reihe A. Kongreßberichte 7: 73–76.
Rocek, Roman. 1981. "*Der Mann ohne Eigenschaften* — Roman ohne Ende?" *Musil-Forum* 7 (1/2): 143–53.
Röttger, Brigitte. 1981. "Robert Musil 'Das Fliegenpapier.' Eine strukturale Analyse anhand der Kategorien Ju. M. Lotmans." *Sub tua platano. Festgabe für Alexander Beinlich*. Emsdetten: Lechte. 509–15.
Schlüer, Klaus-Dieter. 1981. "Psychoanalytische Interpretation." In Groeben. 63–76.
Schönwiese, Ernst. 1981. "Musils Aktualität damals und heute." *Musil-Forum* 7 (1/2): 157–61.
Schröder-Werle, Renate. 1981. "Probleme einer künftigen Musil-Edition. Bestandsaufname und Lösungsvorschläge." In Freese. 13–52.
Stefanek, Paul. 1981. "Musils Posse *Vinzenz* und das Theater." In Freese. 111–48.
Strutz, Josef. 1981. *Politik und Literatur in Musils "Mann ohne Eignenschaften."* Königstein/Taunus: Hain. Literatur in der Geschichte, Geschichte in der Literatur 6.
Thöming, Jürgen C. 1981. "Zu einer Metapher in Musils *Schwärmern*." *Musil-Forum* 7: 85–97.
von Heydebrand, Renate. 1981a. "Versuch einer form-analytischen Interpretation." In Groeben. 31–52.
———. 1981b. "Geistesgeschichtliche Argumentation." In Groeben. 53–62.
Zeller, Rosmarie. 1981a. "'Die Versuchung der stillen Veronika.' Eine Untersuchung ihres Bedeutungsaufbaus." *Sprachkunst* 12: 364–81. Reprinted 1982 in Farda and Karthaus, 135–53.
———. 1981b. "Zur Modernität von Musils Erzählweise am Beispiel der Novellen *Vereinigungen* und *Drei Frauen*." *Musil-Forum* 7 (1/2): 75–84.
Arntzen, Helmut. 1982a. *Musil-Kommentar zu dem Roman "Der Mann ohne Eigenschaften."* Munich: Winkler.
———. 1982b. "Ulrich und Agathe — Heilige Gespräche." In Farda and Karthaus. 117–24.
Aspetsberger, Friedbert. 1982. "'Der andere Zustand' in its contemporary context." In Huber and White. 54–73.

Aue, Maximilian. 1982. "Musil und die Romantik. Einige grundsätzliche Überlegungen." In Farda and Karthaus. 125-134.
Beard, Philip H. 1982. "The 'End' of *The Man without Qualities*." *Musil-Forum* 8: 30–45.
Berg, Jan. 1982. "Theatrales Verstehen. Hans Neuenfels' Berliner *Schwärmer*-Inszenierung." *Musil-Forum* 8: 151–62.
Böhme, Hartmut. 1982. "Der Mangel des Narziß. Über Wunschstrukturen und Leiberfahrungen in Robert Musils *Der Mann ohne Eigenschaften*." In Farda and Karthaus. 45–85.
Braun, Wilhelm. 1982. "Musils 'Das Fliegenpapier.'" *Saarbrücker Hefte*: 63–67.
De Angelis, Enrico. 1982. *Robert Musil. Biografia e Profilo Critico*. Turin: Einaudi.
Düsing, Wolfgang. 1982. *Erinnerung und Identität. Untersuchungen zu einem Erzählproblem bei Musil, Döblin und Doderer*. Munich: Fink.
Eisele, Ulf. 1982. "Ulrichs Mutter ist *doch* ein Tintenfaß. Zur Literaturproblematik in Musils *Mann ohne Eigenschaften*." In von Heydebrand. 160–203. Reprinted 1984 in Ulf Eisele. *Die Struktur des modernen deutschen Romans*. Tübingen: Niemeyer. 114–50.
Esslin, Martin. 1982. "Musil's Plays." In Huber and White. 23–40.
Farda, Dieter P.; Karthaus, Ulrich, eds. 1982. *Sprachästhetische Sinnvermittlung*. Frankfurt/Main, Berne: Peter Lang. Europäische Hochschulschriften 493.
Farda, Dieter P. 1982. "Einige Bemerkungen zur aisthetischen Konstitutionsproblematik des Romans *Der Mann ohne Eigenschaften* von Robert Musil." In Farda and Karthaus. 19–44.
Frisé, Adolf. 1982. "Von einer 'Geschichte dreier Personen' zum *Mann ohne Eigenschaften*. Zur Entstehung von Robert Musils Romanwerk." *Jahrbuch der deutschen Schillergesellschaft* 26: 428–44.
Henninger, Peter. 1982. "Auge und Blick: Notationen zum Sehvorgang in Texten Robert Musils." In Farda and Karthaus. 86–96.
Huber, Lothar; White, John J., eds. 1982. *Musil in Focus. Papers from a Centenary Symposium*. London: Institute of Germanic Studies, University of London.
Huber, Lothar. 1982. "Satire and Irony in Musil's *Der Mann ohne Eigenschaften*." In Huber and White. 99–114.
Magnou, Jacqueline. 1982. "Grenzfall und Identitätsproblem oder die Rolle der Psychopathologie in der literarischen Praxis und Theorie Musils anhand der Novellen *Vereinigungen*." In Farda and Karthaus. 103–16.
Margwelaschwili, Giwi. 1982. "Die existential-ontologische Thematik in Musils *Der Mann ohne Eigenschaften*." *Musil-Forum* 8: 69–102.
Meister, Monika; Stefanek, Paul. 1982. "*Die Schwärmer* in Wien." *Musil-Forum* 8: 137–50.
Menges, Martin. 1982. *Abstrakte Welt und Eigenschaftslosigkeit. Eine Interpretation von Robert Musils "Der Mann ohne Eigenschaften" unter dem Leitbegriff der Abstraktion*. Frankfurt/Main, Berne: Peter Lang.
Militzer, Gerti. 1982. "Die Arbeitsstelle für Robert-Musil-Forschung an der Universität des Saarlandes." *Saarbrücker Hefte*: 33–37.

Paulson, Ronald M. 1982. *Robert Musil and the Ineffable: Hieroglyph, Myth, Fairy Tale and Sign.* Stuttgart: Heinz. Stuttgarter Arbeiten zur Germanistik 112.
Sokel, Walter H. 1982. "Musils *Mann ohne Eigenschaften* und die Existenzphilosophie." In Farda and Karthaus. 97–102.
Swales, Martin. 1982. "Narrator and hero: observations on Robert Musil's *Törleß*." In Huber and White. 1–11.
Tiefenbacher, Herbert. 1982. "Robert Musil: *Die Verwirrungen des Zöglings Törleß*." *Textstrukturen des Entwicklungs- und Bildungsromans.* Königstein/Taunus: Hain. 141–63. Hochschulschriften Literaturwissenschaft 54.
von Heydebrand, Renate, ed. 1982. *Robert Musil.* Darmstadt: Wissenschaftliche Buchgesellschaft. Wege der Forschung 588.
Zaunschirm, Thomas. 1982. *Robert Musil und Marcel Duchamp.* Klagenfurt: Ritter.
Zeller, Hans. 1982. "Vitium aut virtus? Philologisches zu Adolf Frisés Musil-Ausgaben, mit prinzipiellen Überlegungen zur Frage des Texteingriffs." *Zeitschrift für deutsche Philologie. Sonderheft: Probleme neugermanistischer Edition* 101: 210–44.
Allemann, Beda. 1983. "Robert Musil und die Zeitgeschichte." *Literatur und Germanistik nach der Machtübernahme. Colloquium zur 50. Wiederkehr des 30. Januar 1933.* Ed. Beda Allemann. Bonn: Bouvier. 90–117.
Arntzen, Helmut. 1983. "Symptomen-Theater. Robert Musil und das Theater seiner Zeit." *Zur Sprache Kommen. Studien zur Literatur- und Sprachreflexion, zur deutschen Literatur und zum öffentlichen Sprachgebrauch.* Münster: Aschendorff. 257–65.
Berger, Peter L. 1983. "Das Problem der mannigfaltigen Wirklichkeiten: Alfred Schütz und Robert Musil." *Sozialität und Intersubjektivität.* Ed. Richard Grathoff, Bernhard Waldenfels. Munich: Fink. 229–51.
Böschenstein, Bernard. 1983. "Historischer Übergang und System der Ambivalenz: zum *Mann ohne Eigenschaften*." In Brokoph-Mauch. 181–89.
Braun, Wilhelm. 1983. "Musils *Vinzenz und die Freundin bedeutender Männer*." *Musil-Forum* 9 (1/2): 173–78.
Brokoph-Mauch, Gudrun, ed. 1983. *Beiträge zur Musil-Kritik.* Berne, Frankfurt/Main: Peter Lang. New Yorker Studien zur neueren deutschen Literaturgeschichte 2. Identical edition in series Europäische Hochschulschriften 596.
Cejpek, Lucas. 1983. *Wahn und Methode. Robert Musils "Der Mann ohne Eigenschaften. Roman."* Graz: dbv-Verlag.
Erickson, Susan J. 1983. "Essay/body/fiction: the repression of an interpretive context in an essay of Robert Musil." *German Quarterly* 56: 580–93.
Frank, Manfred. 1983. "Auf der Suche nach einem Grund. Über den Umschlag von Erkenntniskritik in Mythologie bei Musil." *Mythos und Moderne. Begriff und Bild einer Rekonstruktion.* Ed. Karl Heinz Bohrer. Frankfurt/Main: Suhrkamp. 318–62.
Freese, Wolfgang. 1983. "Zur neueren Musil-Forschung. Ausgaben und Gesamtdarstellungen." *Text + Kritik* 21/22: 86–148.
Fuld, Werner. 1983. "Der Schwierige. Zu Verlagsproblemen Robert Musils." *Text + Kritik* 21/22: 44–62.

Goltschnigg, Dietmar. 1983 "Robert Musil: *Der Mann ohne Eigenschaften* (1930ff.)." *Deutsche Romane des 20. Jahrhunderts*. Ed. Paul Michael Lützeler. Königstein/Taunus: Athenäum. 218–35.

Karthaus, Ulrich. 1983. "War Musil Realist?" In Brokoph-Mauch. 13–24.

King, Lynda J. 1983. "The New Woman in Robert Musil's Comedy *Vinzenz und die Freundin bedeutender Männer*." *Modern Austrian Literature* 16 (1): 23–36.

Magris, Claudio. 1983. "Hinter dieser Unendlichkeit: die Odyssee des Robert Musil." In Brokoph-Mauch. 49–62.

Meister, Monika. 1983. "Der 'andere Zustand' in der Kunstwirkung." In Brokoph-Mauch. 237–55.

Monti, Claudia. 1983. *Musil: La Metafora Della Scienza*. Naples: Tullio Pironti.

Morgenstern, Soma. 1983. "Robert Musil — György Lukács: eine Begegnung." *Studi Tedeschi. Annali. Sezione Germanica*. 23 (2/3): 315–21.

Naganowski, Egon. 1983. "Robert Musils *Vinzenz*, der Dadaismus und das Theater des Absurden." In Brokoph-Mauch. 63–74.

Olmi, Roberto. 1983. "Die Gegenwart Nietzsches." In Brokoph-Mauch. 87–109.

Perronnet, Jacques. 1983. "'Isis und Osiris.'" In Brokoph-Mauch. 278–88.

Reis, Gilbert. 1983. *Musils Frage nach der Wirklichkeit*. Königstein/Taunus: Hain.

Roth, Marie-Louise. 1983a. "Essay und Essayismus bei Robert Musil." *Probleme der Moderne. Studien zur deutschen Literatur von Nietzsche bis Brecht. Festschrift für Walter Sokel*. Ed. Benjamin Bennett, Anton Kaes, William J. Lillyman. Tübingen: Niemeyer. 117–31.

———. 1983b. "Robert Musil als Aphoristiker." In Brokoph-Mauch. 289–320.

Stern, Joseph Peter. 1983. "History in Robert Musil's *Törless*." *Teaching the Text*. Ed. Susanne Kappeler, Norman Bryson. London: Routledge & Kegan Paul. 35–55.

Strelka, Joseph. 1983a. "Claudine und Veronika. Zur weiblichen Doppelfigur von Robert Musils *Vereinigungen*." *Probleme der Moderne. Studien zur deutschen Literatur von Nietzsche bis Brecht. Festschrift für Walter Sokel*. Ed. Benjamin Bennett, Anton Kaes, William J. Lillyman. Tübingen: Niemeyer. 133–42.

Strelka, Joseph. 1983b. "Robert Musils 'Geschichte aus drei Jahrhunderten.'" In Brokoph-Mauch. 257–62.

Strutz, Josef, ed. 1983a. *Robert Musil und die kulturellen Tendenzen seiner Zeit*. Munich: Fink. *Musil-Studien* 11.

———. 1983b. "Robert Musil und die Politik. *Der Mann ohne Eigenschaften* als 'Morallaboratorium.'" In Strutz. 160–71.

Wallner, Friedrich. 1983. "Musil als Philosoph." In Strutz. 93–109.

West Nutting, Peter. 1983. "Uncaging Musil's 'Amsel.'" *Publications of the Modern Language Association of America* 98: 47–59.

Willemsen, Roger. 1983. "Claudine und Gilles — Die Latenz des Verbrechens in Robert Musils Novelle 'Die Vollendung der Liebe.'" In Strutz. 29–58.

Zeller, Rosmarie. 1983. "Zur Komposition von Musils *Drei Frauen*." In Brokoph-Mauch. 25–48.

Beckers, Gustave. 1984. "Strategien dialektischen Humors in Robert Musils Roman *Mann ohne Eigenschaften*." *Musil-Forum* 10: 86–91.

Blasberg, Cornelia. 1984. *Krise und Utopie der Intellektuellen. Kulturkritische Aspekte in Robert Musils Roman "Der Mann ohne Eigenschaften."* Stuttgart: Heinz. Stuttgarter Arbeiten zur Germanistik 140

Cejpek, Lucas. 1984. "Von der Abwesenheit des Krieges. Friede im *Mann ohne Eigenschaften*." In Strutz and Strutz. 203–19.

Charrière-Jacquin, Marianne. 1984. "*Der Mann ohne Eigenschaften* als Suche nach einer hermaphroditischen Sprache. Wechselspiel des Konvexen und Konkaven." In Strutz and Strutz. 73–90.

Gargani, Aldo. 1984. "*Die Verwirrungen des Zöglings Törleß* von Robert Musil." *Wien 1870-1930. Traum und Wirklichkeit.* Ed. Tino Erben. Salzburg: Residenz. 246–50.

Hartinger, Ingram. 1984. "Der Besuch im Irrenhaus oder lang ersehnte Annäherung an Latein-Amerika. Zu einem Tagebuchtext Robert Musils." In Strutz and Strutz. 220–39.

Henninger, Peter. 1984. "Verhaltene Phantasien. Robert Musils narrative Gedankenprosa." *Musil-Forum* 10: 120–31.

Hickman, Hannah. 1984. *Robert Musil and the Culture of Vienna.* Beckenham, London & Sydney: Croom Helm. La Salle, Ill.: Open Court.

Hoppler, Rudolf. 1984. "Musils 'Amsel.' Paradiesvogel des Narziß." In Strutz and Strutz. 187–202.

Howald, Stephan. 1984. *Ästhetizismus und ästhetische Literaturkritik.* Munich: Fink. *Musil-Studien* 9.

Jennings, Michael W. 1984. "Mystical Selfhood, Self-Delusion, Self-Dissolution. Ethical and Narrative Experimentation in Robert Musil's 'Grigia.'" *Modern Austrian Literature* 17 (1): 59–77.

Kieser, Rolf. 1984. "Das ontologische Kunststück: Robert Musil." *Erzwungene Symbiose: Thomas Mann, Robert Musil, Georg Kaiser und Bertolt Brecht im Schweizer Exil.* Berne, Stuttgart: Haupt. 81–190.

Mae, Michiko. 1984. "Die Verschränkung des Prinzips der Motivation und des Strukturprinzips der Vereinigung in den Bildern von Musils Novelle 'Die Vollendung der Liebe.'" *Musil-Forum* 10: 57–68.

Magnou, Jacqueline. 1984. "Schicksale sind vom Zentralen aus gestaltet. 'Die Vollendung der Liebe.'" *Musil-Forum* 10: 69–74.

Moser, Walter. 1984. "The Factual in Fiction. The Case of Robert Musil." *Poetics Today* 5: 411–28.

Pott, Hans-Georg. 1984. *Robert Musil.* Munich: Fink.

Reis, Gilbert. 1984. "Eine Brücke ins Imaginäre. Gleichnis und Reflexion in Robert Musils *Mann ohne Eigenschaften*." *Euphorion* 78: 143–59.

Roth, Marie-Louise. 1984. "'Die Amsel.' Ein Interpretationsversuch." In Strutz and Strutz. 173–86.

Sokel, Walter H. 1984. "Robert Musils Kampf um die Mimesis. Zur Poetologie seiner Anfänge." *Musil-Forum* 10: 238–41.

Strutz, Josef; Strutz, Johann, eds. 1984. *Robert Musil — Literatur, Philosophie, Psychologie.* Munich, Salzburg: Fink. *Musil-Studien* 12.

Strutz, Josef. 1984. "Von der 'biegsamen Dialektik.' Notiz zur Bedeutung Kants, Hegels und Nietzsches für das Werk Musils." In Strutz and Strutz. 11–21.
Vogt, Guntram. 1984. "Robert Musils ambivalentes Verhältnis zur Demokratie." *Exilforschung* 2: 310–38.
Wallner, Friedrich. 1984. "Sehnsucht nach Verweigerung. Musil und Nietzsche." In Strutz and Strutz. 91–109.
Wicht, Gérard. 1984. *'Gott meint die Welt keineswegs wörtlich.' Zum Gleichnisbegriff in Robert Musils Roman "Mann ohne Eigenschaften."* Frankfurt/Main, Berne, New York: Peter Lang. Europäische Hochschulschriften 792.
Willemsen, Roger. 1984a. *Das Existenzrecht der Dichtung: Zur Rekonstruktion einer systematischen Literaturtheorie im Werk Robert Musils*. Munich: Fink.
———. 1984b. "Die sentimentale Gesellschaft. Zur Begründung einer aktivistischen Literaturtheorie im Werk Robert Musils und Robert Müllers." *Deutsche Vierteljahrsschrift für Literaturwissenschaft und Geistesgeschichte* 58 (2): 289–316.
———. 1984c. "Über die Möglichkeit eines Musil-Kommentars." *Göttingische Gelehrte Anzeigen* 236 (3/4): 231–49.
Wilson, Catherine. 1984. "Morality and the Self in Robert Musil's 'The Perfecting of a Love.'" *Philosophy and Literature* 8 (2): 222–35.
Alt, Peter-André. 1985. *Ironie und Krise, Erzählen als Form ästhetischer Wahrnehmung in Thomas Manns "Zauberberg" und Robert Musils "Mann ohne Eigenschaften."* Frankfurt/Main, Berne, New York: Peter Lang. Europäische Hochschulschriften 722.
Ambros, Gerda. 1985. "Robert Musils *Schwärmer*. Entfernte Biographien." In Strutz and Strutz. 78-94.
Arntzen, Helmut. 1985. *Roger Willemsen. Eine Fallstudie*. Münster: Sonderdruck im Selbstverlag.
Baltz-Balzberg, Regina. 1985. "Antidekadenzmoral bei Musil und Nietzsche." In Strutz and Strutz. 204–26.
Brokoph-Mauch, Gudrun. 1985. *Robert Musils "Nachlaß zu Lebzeiten."* New York, Berne, Frankfurt/Main: Peter Lang. New Yorker Studien zur neueren deutschen Literaturgeschichte 4.
Charrière-Jacquin, Marianne. 1985. "Musils *Schwärmer*, Lebenskampf? Kartenspiel? Kammermusik?" In Strutz and Strutz. 24–43.
Cometti, Jean-Pierre. 1985. "Psychoanalyse und Erzählung." In Strutz and Strutz. 153–65.
Corino, Karl. 1985. "'Alpha' — Modell Nr. 2. Bemerkungen zum biographischen Hintergrund von Robert Musils Posse *Vinzenz und die Freundin bedeutender Männer*." In Strutz and Strutz. 95–109.
Dinklage, Karl. 1985. "Ende der *Schwärmer* — Ende des *Mann ohne Eigenschaften*." In Strutz and Strutz. 227–43.
Erickson, Susan J. 1985. "Musils 'Der Vorstadtgasthof.' A narrative analysis." *Neophilologus* 69: 101–14.

Homann, Renate. 1985. "Literatur und Erkenntnis. Robert Musils Erzählung 'Tonka.'" *Deutsche Vierteljahrsschrift für Literaturwissenschaft und Geistesgeschichte* 59 (4): 497–518.

Howes, Geoffrey C. 1985. "Robert Musil and the Legacy of Ralph Waldo Emerson." Diss. University of Michigan.

Karthaus, Ulrich. 1985. "Musils Theaterbegriff." In Strutz and Strutz. 143–52.

Köhler, Andrea; Adam, Christine; Hamm, Horst; Pfeiffer, Joachim. 1985. "Bekenntnis und Abwehr. Eine Analyse von Robert Musils Schreibprozeß am Beispiel seiner Novelle 'Die Versuchung der stillen Veronika.'" *Freiburger literaturpsychologische Gespräche* 4: 101–22.

Meuthen, Erich. 1985. "Törleß im Labyrinth." *Deutsche Vierteljahrsschrift für Literaturwissenschaft und Geistesgeschichte* 59 (1): 125–44.

Moore, Gene M. 1985. *Proust and Musil: The Novel as Research Instrument*. New York: Garland.

Moser, Manfred. 1985. "Erinnerung, blitzartiger Einfall und — natürlich — die Ironie." In Strutz and Strutz. 110–42.

Naganowski, Egon. 1985. "*Die Schwärmer* als Bühnenstück." In Strutz and Strutz. 62–77.

Neuenfels, Hans. 1985. "Die Biographie der Unruhe" *Robert Musil. Die Schwärmer. Ein Film*. Reinbek bei Hamburg: Rowohlt. 7–54.

Schmidt, Jochen. 1985. "Robert Musil: die Genie-Moral eines Mannes ohne Eigenschaften; der 'potentielle Mensch' als der schöpferische Mensch." *Die Geschichte des Genie-Gedankens in der deutschen Literatur, Philosophie und Politik*. Vol. 2: Darmstadt: Wissenschaftliche Buchgesellschaft. 278–98.

Stefanek, Paul. 1985a. "Musil und das Theater, 60 Jahre nach dem Essay 'Der Untergang des Theaters.'" In Strutz and Strutz. 44–61.

———. 1985b. "Lesedrama? — Überlegungen zur szenischen Transformation 'bühnenfremder' Dramaturgie." *Das Drama und seine Inszenierung. Vorträge des Internationalen literatur- und theatersemiotischen Kolloquiums in Frankfurt/Main, 1983*. Ed. Erika Fischer-Lichte. Tübingen: Niemeyer. 133–45.

Strelka, Joseph P. 1985. "Musils Novelle 'Grigia' als Gegenstück der 'Vollendung der Liebe.'" *Litterature et culture allemandes. Hommages à Henri Plard*. Ed. by Roger Goffin, Michael Vanhelleputte and Monique Weyembergh-Boussart. Brussels: Editions de l' Université de Bruxelles. 335–43.

Strutz, Johann; Strutz, Josef, eds. 1985. *Robert Musil. Theater, Bildung, Kritik*. Munich, Salzburg: Fink. Musil-Studien 13.

Willemsen, Roger. 1985. *Robert Musil: Vom intellektuellen Eros*. Munich, Zurich: Piper.

Zima, Peter V. 1985. "Robert Musils Sprachkritik. Ambivalenz, Polyphonie und Dekonstruktion." In Strutz and Strutz. 185–203.

Zobel, Klaus. 1985. "Robert Musil: 'Fischer an der Ostsee,'" "Robert Musil: 'Der Riese Agoag.'" *Textanalysen*. Paderborn, Munich, Vienna, Zurich: Schöningh: 225–32; 286–95.

Berthoff, Warner. 1986. "'Why Does One Thing Happen and Not Another?': *The Man without Qualities.*" *Literature and the Continuances of Virtue.* Princeton, N.J.: Princeton University Press. 158–222.

Böhme, Hartmut. 1986. "Die 'Zeit ohne Eigenschaften' und die 'Neue Unübersichtlichkeit.' Robert Musil und die *posthistorie.*" In Strutz and Strutz. 9–33.

Cetti Marinoni, Bianca. 1986. "Verfremdungseffekte bei Robert Musil als Stücke-Schreiber." In Strutz and Strutz. 104–32.

Chiarini, Paolo, ed. 1986. *Musil, Nostro Contemporaneo.* Rome: Istituto Italiano di Studi Germanici.

Dowden, Stephen. 1986. "The Cloud of Polonius: Rewriting Reality in Robert Musil's *Mann ohne Eigenschaften.*" *Sympathy for the Abyss. A Study in the Novel of German Modernism: Kafka, Broch, Musil and Thomas Mann.* Tübingen: Niemeyer. 57–93. Studien zur deutschen Literatur 90.

Erickson, Susan J. 1986. "The psychopoetics of Narrative in Robert Musils 'Die Portugiesin.'" *Monatshefte* 78 (2): 167–81.

Goltschnigg, Dietmar. 1986. "Die Rolle des geisteskranken Verbrechers in Robert Musils Erzählung 'Die Vollendung der Liebe' und im *Mann ohne Eigenschaften.*" In Chiarini. 103–16.

Hafner, Heinz. 1986. "Figurenkonstellation und Vermittlungsstruktur. Zu Musils *Die Verwirrungen des Zöglings Törleß.*" *Zeitschrift für Semiotik* 8 (1/2): 35–40.

Heftrich, Eckhard. 1986. *Musil. Eine Einführung.* Munich, Zurich: Artemis.

Henninger, Peter. 1986. "La résistance du texte: à propos des *Exaltés.*" *Robert Musil, Colloque de Royaumont.* Ed. Jean-Pierre Cometti. Royaumont: Editions de Royaumont. 83–105.

Kim, Rae-Hyeon. 1986. *Robert Musil. Poetologische Reflexionen zur Geschichtlichkeit der Literatur.* Bonn: Bouvier. Literatur und Reflexion 4.

Knüfermann, Volker. 1986. "Die Gefährdung des Narziß oder: Zur Begründung und Problematik der Form in Thomas Manns *Der Tod in Venedig* und Robert Musils *Die Verwirrungen des Zöglings Törleß.*" *Dialog mit der Moderne, Jacob Steiner zum 60. Geburtstag.* Roland Jost, Hansgeorg Schmidt-Bergmann, eds. Frankfurt/Main: Athenäum. 84–95.

Longuet-Marx, Anne. 1986. *Proust, Musil. Partages d'Ecritures.* Paris: Presses Universitaires de France.

Raddatz, Fritz J. 1986. "Monsieur le vivisecteur. Die Tagebücher Robert Musils." *Die Zeit* (May 16).

Solms, Wilhelm. 1986. "Ein Ausweg aus dem Interpretationspluralismus? Kontroverse anläßlich einer Meinungserhebung zu Robert Musils 'Hasenkatastrophe.'" *Kontroversen alte und neue.* Ed. Albrecht Schöne. Vol. 11. Tübingen: Niemeyer. 148–61.

Strutz, Johann; Strutz, Josef, eds. 1986. *Kunst, Wissenschaft und Politik von Robert Musil bis Ingeborg Bachmann.* Munich, Salzburg: Fink. *Musil-Studien* 14.

Vogt, Guntram. 1986. "Robert Musil. Politik als Methode. Zum Kontext von Kunst, Wissenschaft, Politik." In Strutz and Strutz. 146–64.

Willemsen, Roger. 1986a. "Devotionalien. Über Musils 'Tonka' und Godards *Je vous salue Marie.*" In Strutz and Strutz. 81–103.

———. 1986b. "Dionysisches Sprechen. Zur Theorie einer Sprache der Erregung bei Musil und Nietzsche." *Deutsche Vierteljahrsschrift für Literaturwissenschaft und Geistesgeschichte* 60 (1): 104–35.

Zahlmann, Christel. 1986. "Die Dynamik der Leere. Zu Robert Musils Drama *Die Schwärmer*." *Phantasie und Deutung. Psychologisches Verstehen von Literatur und Film. Frederick Wyatt zum 75. Geburtstag.* Wolfram Mauser, Ursula Renner, Walter Schönau, eds. Würzburg: Königshausen & Neumann. 169–79.

Allais, Kai. 1987. "Geräusche — Textlichkeit und Serialität. Musils Novelle 'Die Versuchung der stillen Veronika.'" In Strutz. 77–94.

Schaunig-Baltz-Balzberg, Regina. 1987. "Musils 'Rezept: Organisation.' Zur Klagenfurter Nachlaß-Forschung unter Karl Dinklage." In Strutz. 16–26.

Classen, Albrecht. 1987. "Robert Musil: *Mann ohne Eigenschaften*: Der antizipatorische Charakter des ersten Buches." *Carleton Germanic Papers.* Otawa: Carleton University. Vol. 15. 1–16.

Corino, Karl. 1987. "Robert Musil." *Genie und Geld. Vom Auskommen deutscher Schriftsteller.* Nördlingen: Geno. Reprinted 1991. Reinbek bei Hamburg: Rowohlt. 424–47.

Dresler-Brumme, Charlotte. 1987. *Nietzsches Philosophie in Musils Roman "Mann ohne Eigenschaften."* Frankfurt/Main: Athenäum. Literatur in der Geschichte, Geschichte in der Literatur 13.

Frisé, Adolf. 1987. *Plädoyer für Robert Musil.* Reinbek bei Hamburg: Rowohlt.

Horn, Peter. 1987. "'Wenn ich den Sinn wüßte, so brauchte ich dir wohl nicht erst zu erzählen.'" *Euphorion* 81 (4): 391–413.

Jakob, Michael. 1987. "Von der 'Frau ohne Eigenschaften' zum *Mann ohne Eigenschaften*. Anmerkungen zu Clarisse." In Strutz. 116–33.

Kontje, Todd. 1987. "Motivating Silence: The Recreation of the 'Eternal Feminine' in Robert Musils 'Tonka.'" *Monatshefte* 79 (2): 161–71.

Lethen, Helmut. 1987. "Eckfenster der Moderne. Wahrnehmungsexperimente bei Musil und E. T. A. Hoffmann." In Strutz. 195–229.

Luserke, Matthias. 1987. *Wirklichkeit und Möglichkeit. Modaltheoretische Untersuchungen zum Werk Robert Musils.* Frankfurt/Main, Berne, New York: Peter Lang. Europäische Hochschulschriften 1000.

Martens, Lorna. 1987. "Musil and Freud. The 'Foreign Body' in 'Die Versuchung der stillen Veronika.'" *Euphorion* 81 (2): 100–18.

Middell, Elke. 1987. "Robert Musils *Mann ohne Eigenschaften*. Annäherungen." *Weimarer Beiträge* 33: 981–1003.

Moser, Walter. 1987. "Zwischen Wissenschaft und Literatur. Zu Robert Musils Essayismus." *Verabschiedung der (Post-)Moderne? Eine interdisziplinäre Debatte.* Gérard Raulet and Jacques Le Rider, eds. Tübingen: Narr. 167–96.

Payne, Philip. 1987. *Robert Musil's Works, 1906–1924. A Critical Introduction.* Frankfurt/Main, Berne, New York: Peter Lang. Europäische Hochschulschriften 961.

Pfeiffer, Peter C. 1987. "Nicht Fisch und nicht Fleisch. Robert Musils Reaktion auf den Nationalsozialismus." In Strutz. 145–63.

Pott, Hans-Georg. 1987. "Musil und das Problem einer Ethik nach Freud." In Strutz. 44–59.
Reis, Gilbert. 1987. "Perspektivische Verkürzungen des Verstandes. Wirklichkeitsdarstellung unter dem Gesichtspunkt der Subjektivität." *Euphorion* 81 (2): 119–30.
Roth, Marie-Louise. 1987a. *Robert Musil: L'homme au double regard.* Paris: Editions Balland.
———. 1987b. "Vincent et l'amie des personnalités. Essai d'interpretation." *Sinn und Symbol. Festschrift für Joseph P. Strelka zum 60. Geburtstag.* Ed. Karl Konrad Polheim. Frankfurt/Main, Berne, New York: Peter Lang. 433–41.
Strutz, Josef, ed. 1987. *Robert Musils "Kakanien" — Subjekt und Geschichte. Festschrift für Karl Dinklage zum 80. Geburtstag.* Munich, Salzburg: Fink. *Musil-Studien* 15.
Thurnhofer, Hubert. 1987. *Musil als Philosoph oder die Vivikation des PduG.* Vienna: Thurnhofer.
Vogl, Joseph. 1987. "Grenze und Übertretung. Der anthropologische Faktor in Robert Musils *Die Verwirrungen des Zöglings Törleß*." In Strutz. 60–76.
Wallner, Friedrich. 1987. "Das Konzept einer Philosophie als Dichtung und einer Dichtung als Philosophie." In Strutz. 134–44.
Wallraff, Günter. 1987. "Die Bob-Hansen-Story. Ein literarischer Test (1968)." *Reportagen 1963–1974.* Ed. Dorlies Pollmann. Cologne: Kiepenheuer & Witsch. 147–159.
Aue, Maximilian. 1987/88. "Das Prinzip der kleinsten Schritte. Musil und das 'ungelöste Problem des Naturalismus' am Beispiel der 'Vollendung der Liebe.'" *Musil-Forum* 13/14: 34–45.
Cejpek, Lucas. 1987/88. "Geschichte als Literatur. Zu einer Philosophie der Geschichten. Robert Musils *Mann ohne Eigenschaften*." *Musil-Forum* 13/14: 113–24.
Neumer, Katalin. 1987/88. "Die Verwirrungen im Labyrinth der Sprache. Ein Interpretationsversuch zu Musils *Törleß*." *Musil-Forum* 13/14: 5–21.
Webber, Andrew. 1987/88. "Sense and Sensuality in Musils *Törleß*." *German Life and Letters* 41: 106–30.
Alt, Peter-André. 1988. "Allegorische Formen in Robert Musils Erzählungen." *Jahrbuch der deutschen Schillergesellschaft* 32: 314–43.
Balme, Christopher. 1988. "Grotesque Farce in the Weimar Republic." *Farce.* Ed. James R. Redmond. Cambridge: Cambridge University Press. 173–84. Themes in Drama 10.
Barnouw, Dagmar. 1988. "Ulrich, a Life: Robert Musil and the Experiment of the Real." *Weimar Intellectuals and the Threat of Modernity.* Bloomington, Indianapolis: Indiana University Press. 78–120.
Bohn, Ralf. 1988. *Transversale Inversion. Symptomatologie und Genealogie des Denkens in der Philosophie Robert Musils.* Würzburg: Königshausen & Neumann. Epistemata: Reihe Literaturwissenschaft 33.
Braun, Wilhelm. 1988. "Bemerkungen zur englischen *Schwärmer*-Übersetzung." In Daigger and Militzer. 203–8.

Bürger, Peter. 1988. "Literarische Form als Denkform. Musils *Mann ohne Eigenschaften*." *Prosa der Moderne*. Frankfurt/Main: Suhrkamp. 422–37.

Cellbrot, Hartmut. 1988. *Die Bewegung des Sinnes. Zur Phänomenologie Robert Musils im Hinblick auf Edmund Husserl*. Munich: Fink. *Musil-Studien* 17.

Cetti Marinoni, Bianca. 1988. *"Come si fa con un saggio"* — Robert Musil e la genesi degli *"Schwärmer."* Milan: Franco Angeli. German version see 1992.

Classen, Albrecht. 1988. "Musils Novelle 'Tonka' im Licht des Neuen Testaments." *Colloquia Germanica* 21: 169–84.

Corino, Karl. 1988. *Robert Musil — Leben und Werk in Bildern und Texten*. Reinbek bei Hamburg: Rowohlt.

Daigger, Annette; Militzer, Gerti, eds. 1988. *Die Übersetzung literarischer Texte am Beispiel Robert Musil: Beiträge des internationalen Übersetzer-Kolloquiums in Straelen vom 8.–10. Juni 1987*. Stuttgart: Heinz. Stuttgarter Arbeiten zur Germanistik 207.

Farda, Dieter P. 1988. *mundus pluralis. Robert Musils Roman "Mann ohne Eigenschaften" im Wechselspiel von Reflexion und Phantasie*. Heidelberg: Carl Winter.

Frank, Manfred. 1988. "Remythisierte Erkenntniskritik (Robert Musil)." *Gott im Exil. Vorlesungen über die Neue Mythologie*. Part II. Frankfurt/Main: Suhrkamp. 315–32.

Fuchs, Annette. 1988. "'Augen-Blicke.' Zur Kommunikationsstruktur der 'Bilder' in Robert Musils *Nachlaß zu Lebzeiten*." *Der Deutschunterricht* 40 (1): 66–79.

Heering-Düllo, Cornelia. 1988. "'Stumme Taten aus den Stirnen.' Zum Problem von Identität und Kommunikation in Robert Musils Novelle 'Die Portugiesin.'" *Literatur für Leser* 1: 35–51.

Hüppauf, Bernd-Rüdiger. 1988. "Über das Mästen von Begriffen und die Furcht vor der Erfahrung. Bemerkungen zur Sprache in Robert Musils *Nachlaß zu Lebzeiten*." *Die Fremdheit der Sprache. Studien zur Literatur der Moderne*. Jochen C. Schulze, Hans-Ulrich Treichel, Dietmar Voss, eds. Hamburg: Argument. 26–47.

Jennings, Michael W. 1988. "Robert Musil." *Major Figures of modern Austrian Literature*. Donald G. Daviau, ed. Riverside: Ariadne Press. 315–39.

Kontje, Todd. 1988. "Organized Violence/Violating Order. Robert Musil's *Die Verwirrungen des Zöglings Törleß*." *Seminar* 24 (3): 239–54.

Mae, Michiko. 1988. *Motivation und Liebe. Zum Strukturprinzip der Vereinigung bei Robert Musil*. Munich: Fink, 1988. *Musil-Studien* 16.

Payne, Philip. 1988. *Robert Musil's "The Man without Qualities": A Critical Study*. Cambridge, New York, Melbourne: Cambridge University Press.

Pietsch, Reinhard. 1988. *Fragment und Schrift. Selbstimplikative Strukturen bei Robert Musil*. Frankfurt/Main, Berne, New York: Peter Lang. Europäische Hochschulschriften 1082.

Renner, Rolf Günter. 1988. "Postmoderne Perspektiven im Text der klassischen Moderne: Robert Musil." *Die Postmoderne Konstellation. Theorie, Text und Kunst im Ausgang der Moderne*. Freiburg: Rombach. 124–44.

Rußegger, Arno. 1988. "'Isis und Osiris.' Zur Metafiktionalität in Musils Ästhetik-Theorie." *Sprachkunst* 19 (1): 1–20.
Ryan, Judith. 1988. "Validating the Possible: Thoughts and Things in James, Rilke and Musil." *Comparative Literature* 40 (4): 305–17.
Schiller, Dieter. 1988. "Die Grenze der Kultur gegen die Politik. Zu Robert Musils Rede auf dem Pariser Kongreß 1935." *Zeitschrift für Germanistik* 2: 274–90.
Söder, Thomas. 1988. *Untersuchungen zu Robert Musils "Verwirrungen des Zöglings Törleß."* Rheinfelden: Schäuble. Deutsche und vergleichende Literaturwissenschaft 11.
Sokel, Walter H. 1988. "*Der Mann ohne Eigenschaften* und das achtzehnte Jahrhundert." *Das neuzeitliche Ich in der Literatur des 18. und 20. Jahrhunderts.* Ed. Ulrich Fülleborn, Manfred Engel. Munich: Fink. 293–305.
Strutz, Josef. 1988. "Unzutreffend." *Kleine Zeitung* (Klagenfurt) (August 28): 41.
Venturelli, Aldo. 1988. *Robert Musil und das Projekt der Moderne.* Frankfurt/Main, Berne, New York: Peter Lang. Europäische Hochschulschriften 1039.
Wilkins, Sophie. 1988. "Einige Notizen zum Fall der Übersetzerin der Knopf-Auflage des *Mann ohne Eigenschaften.*" In Daigger and Militzer. 75–90.
Bangerter, Lowell A. 1989. *Robert Musil.* New York: Continuum.
Bey, Gesine. 1989. "'Bei mir laudabile.' Zu Robert Musils Berliner Studienjahren." *Wissenschaftliche Zeitschrift der Humboldt-Universität, Berlin* 38: 659–66.
Blasberg, Cornelia. 1989. "Verwirrungen eines Ingenieurs. Robert Musil in Stuttgart oder: Literatur aus Langeweile." *Spuren* 7. Marbach a. N.: Deutsche Schillergesellschaft.
Bogosavljevic, Srdan. 1989a. "'Die knäbisch nackten ersten sonnenharten Tage.' Zum Bildsystem von Robert Musils Novelle 'Die Portugiesin.'" *Musil-Forum* 15: 76–93.
———. 1989b. "Zwei Erzählungen von Robert Musil: 'Kleine Lebensreise' und 'Kindergeschichte.'" *Modern Austrian Literature* 22 (2): 15–31.
Brooks, Daniel Josef. 1989. "Aesthetic Nietzscheanism in *Mann ohne Eigenschaften.*" *Musil-Forum* 15: 94–112.
Cetti Marinoni, Bianca. 1989. "'Liebe ist gar nie Liebe.' Zum Verhältnis von Liebesthematik und dramatischer Struktur in Musils Theater." *Studi Tedeschi* 30: 143–78.
De Tullio, Chiara. 1989. "Die *Schwärmer* in der Musil-Literatur. Forschungsbericht." *Musil-Forum* 15: 18–38.
Dimter, Walter. 1989. "'Österreichs ernstester Dichter.' Zu Robert Musils Briefen." *Die österreichische Literatur. Ihr Profil von der Jahrhundertwende bis zur Gegenwart (1880-1980).* Herbert Zeman, ed. Vol. 2. Graz: Akademische Druck- und Verlagsanstalt. 959–88.
Hall, Murray G. 1989. "Der Preis der Stadt Wien." *Musil-Forum* 15: 166–70.
Hoffmann, Lynda. 1989. "Hinter verschlossenen Türen: ist Törleß wirklich 'türlos'?" *Musil-Forum* 15: 5–17.
Kayser, Martina. 1989. *Marcel Proust, Robert Musil: Versuche einer Glücksfindung.* Frankfurt/Main, Berne, New York, Paris: Peter Lang. Europäische Hochschulschriften 1026.

Magris, Claudio. 1989. "Die Odyssee des Robert Musil." *Merkur* 33: 139-55.
Moser, Manfred. 1989. "Ing. Dr. phil. Robert Musil: Ein Soldat erzählt." *Arsenale der Seele. Literatur- und Medienanalyse seit 1870.* Ed. Friedrich A. Kittler, Georg Christoph Tholen. Munich: Fink. 97–115.
Pekar, Thomas. 1989. *Die Sprache der Liebe bei Robert Musil.* Munich: Fink. Musil-Studien 19.
Pennisi, Francesca. 1989. *Auf der Suche nach Ordnung. Die Entstehungsgeschichte des Ordnungsgedanken bei Robert Musil von den ersten Romanentwürfen bis zum ersten Band von "Mann ohne Eigenschaften."* St. Ingbert: Röhrig.
Pestalozzi, Karl. 1989. "Metaphysische Klaustrophobie: Maeterlinck als Schlüssel zu Musils *Törleß*." *Krisis der Metaphysik.* Ed. Günter Abel, Jörg Salaquarda. Berlin, New York: de Gruyter. 498–520.
Radbruch, Knut. 1989. "Mathematik als Lebensform." *Mathematik in den Geisteswissenschaften.* Göttingen: Vandenhoeck & Ruprecht. 56–61.
Rogowski, Christian. 1989. "'Das muß ein Ende haben!' Reflections on the Ending of Musil's *Vinzenz und die Freundin bedeuter Männer*." *Musil-Forum* 15: 39–59.
Ryan, Judith. 1989. "Each One as She May: Melanctha, Tonka, Nadja." *Modernity and the Text. Revisions of German Modernism.* Andreas Huyssen, David Bathrick, eds. New York, Oxford: Columbia University Press. 95–109.
Thöming, Jürgen C. 1989. "Die *Schwärmer* alternativ." *Musil-Forum* 15: 60–75.
Venturelli, Aldo. 1989. "Die Erfindung der Geschichte. Musils Auffassung der Geschichte in *Mann ohne Eigenschaften*." *Die österreichische Literatur. Ihr Profil von der Jahrhundertwende bis zur Gegenwart (1880–1980).* Ed. Herbert Zeman. Vol. 2. Graz: Akademische Druck- und Verlagsanstalt. 1037–50.
von Matt, Peter. 1989. *Liebesverrat: die Treulosen in der Literatur.* Munich: Hanser.
Wagner-Egelhaaf, Martina. 1989. *Mystik der Moderne. Die visionäre Ästhetik der deutschen Literatur im 20. Jahrhundert.* Stuttgart: Metzler.
Whitinger, Raleigh. 1989. "*Törleß'* moral Development. Reflections on a Problem of Musil Criticism." *Modern Austrian Literature* 22 (1): 19–34.
Akashi, Eichiro. 1990. "Über die Grenze der Begriffe und die Funktion der Bilder in Musils 'Tonka.'" In Strutz and Kiss. 97–114.
Böhme, Hartmut. 1990. "Erinnerungszeichen an unverständliche Gefühle." Afterword to Robert Musil. *Vereinigungen. Zwei Erzählungen.* Frankfurt/Main: Suhrkamp. 185–221.
Cetti Marinoni, Bianca. 1990. "Zum Werdegang der *Schwärmer* in Frisés Ausgabe der Schriften von Musil." *Musil-Forum* 16: 38–44.
Diersch, Manfred. 1990. "Draußen, Drinnen und Ich. Ernst Machs 'Spiegel der Erkenntnis' als Anregung für österreichische Erzählkunst des 20. Jahrhunderts." In Strutz and Kiss. 29–42.
Finlay, Marike. 1990. *The Potential of Modern Discourse. Musil, Peirce, and Perturbation.* Bloomington, Indianapolis: Indiana University Press.
Giampieri Deutsch, Patrizia. 1990. "Mach, Freud, Musil: Die Frage nach dem Subjekt." *Sigmund Freud House Bulletin* 14 (2): 47–56.

Hassler-Rütti, Ruth. 1990. *Wirklichkeit und Wahn in Robert Musils Roman "Mann ohne Eigenschaften."* Frankfurt/Main, Berne, New York: Peter Lang. Europäische Hochschulschriften 1189.

Horn, Peter. 1990. "Man verkriecht sich hinter seine Haut. Zu Robert Musils *Die Schwärmer*." *Acta Germanica* 20: 79–105.

Le Rider, Jacques. 1990a. "Between Modernism and Postmodernism: The Viennese Identity Crises." *Austrian Studies*. Edward Timms and Ritchie Robertson, eds. Vol. 1. New York: Columbia University Press.

———. 1990b. *Das Ende der Illusion. Die Wiener Moderne und die Krisen der Identität*. Vienna: Österreichischer Bundesverlag.

Lobner, Hans. 1990. "Sigmund Freud und Robert Musil — Ein Sprachvergleich." *Sigmund Freud House Bulletin* 14 (2): 30–45.

Longuet-Marx, Anne. 1990. "Proust, Musil — Ethiken des Schreibens." In Strutz and Kiss. 53–66.

Nadermann, Peter. 1990. *Schreiben als anderes Leben. Eine Untersuchung zu Robert Musils "Mann ohne Eigenschaften."* Frankfurt/Main, Berne, New York, Paris: Peter Lang. Bochumer Schriften zur deutschen Literatur 17.

Pfeiffer, Peter C. 1990. *Aphorismus und Romanstruktur. Zu Robert Musils "Der Mann ohne Eigenschaften."* Bonn: Bouvier. Bonner Arbeiten zur deutschen Literatur 46.

Rogowski, Christian. 1990a. "'Lauter unbestimmte Größen.' Zu Ingeborg Bachmanns Hörspielbearbeitung der *Schwärmer* von Robert Musil." In Strutz and Kiss. 191–210.

———. 1990b. "Seduced Seducers: Strindberg as Intertext in Robert Musil's Comedy *Vinzenz und die Freundin bedeutender Männer*." *Deutsche Vierteljahrsschrift für Literaturwissenschaft und Geistesgeschichte* 64 (3): 549–59.

Schärer, Hans-Rudolf. 1990. *Narzißmus und Utopismus. Eine literaturpsychologische Untersuchung zu Musils "Der Mann ohne Eigenschaften."* Munich: Fink. *Musil-Studien* 20.

Strutz, Josef; Kiss, Endre, eds. 1990. *Genauigkeit und Seele. Zur österreichischen Literatur seit dem Fin de siécle*. Munich, Salzburg: Fink. *Musil-Studien* 18.

Tewilt, Gerd-Theo. 1990. *Zustand der Dichtung. Interpretationen zur Sprachlichkeit des "anderen Zustands" in Robert Musils "Der Mann ohne Eigenschaften."* Münster: Aschendorff. Literatur als Sprache. Literaturtheorie — Interpretation — Sprachkritik 7.

Völse, Hans-Joachim. 1990. *Im Labyrinth des Wissens. Zu Robert Musils Roman "Der Mann ohne Eigenschaften."* Wiesbaden: Deutscher Universitätsverlag.

von Dassanowsky-Harris, Robert. 1990. "The 'Nicht-Ich' and Collaboration: The Socio-Political Implications of Self in Musil's *Die Verwirrungen des Zöglings Törleß*." *Germanic Notes* 21: 22–25.

Bogosavljevic, Srdan. 1991. "Zur Poetik der Bilder in den *Vereinigungen*." *Rapial* 1 (1): 1–3.

Brooks, Daniel Josef. 1991. "Ataraxy vs. Anxiety: Robert Musil and the Post-Nietzschean Skeptical Mode." *Rapial* 1 (2): 5–8.

Cetti Marinoni, Bianca. 1991. "Denken im Drama. Zu Robert Musils Stück *Die Schwärmer.*" *Rapial* 1 (1): 4-7.
Düsing, Wolfgang. 1991. "Goethe in ironischer Beleuchtung. Zur Klassik-Rezeption in Musils *Mann ohne Eigenschaften.*" *Jahrbuch der deutschen Schillergesellschaft* 35: 257-74.
Eibl, Karl. 1991. "Es müssen nicht immer Bücher sein." *Jahrbuch der deutschen Schillergesellschaft* 35: 349-51.
Erhart, Claus. 1991. *Der ästhetische Mensch bei Robert Musil. Vom Ästhetizmus zur schöpferischen Moral.* Innsbruck: Germanistisches Institut, Universität. Innsbrucker Beiträge zur Kulturwissenschaft, Germanistische Reihe 43.
Frisé, Adolf. 1991. "Mißdeutungen und Fehlschlüsse. Wie Robert Musil bisweilen von der Kritik gesehen wird." *"Die in dem alten Haus der Sprache wohnen." Festschrift für Helmut Arntzen.* Ed. Eckehard Czucka, Thomas Althaus, Burkhard Spinnen. Münster: Aschendorff. 365-75.
Goltschnigg, Dietmar. 1991. "Theoretische und historische Aspekte der Komödie *Vinzenz und die Freundin bedeutender Männer.*" In Hickman. 151-71.
Grotzer, Peter. 1991. "Das Erschrecken vor dem Doppelsinn. Zu Musils *Törleß.*" *Die zweite Geburt. Figuren des Jugendlichen in der Literatur des 20. Jahrhunderts.* Vol. 1. Zurich: Amman. 61-73.
Hickman, Hannah, ed. 1991. *Robert Musil and the Literary Landscape of His Time.* Salford, England: Department of Modern Languages, University of Salford.
Honnef-Becker, Irmgard. 1991. *"Ulrich lächelte." Techniken der Relativierung in Robert Musils Roman "Der Mann ohne Eigenschaften."* Frankfurt/Main, Berne, New York, Paris: Peter Lang. Trierer Studien zur Literatur 20.
Huber, Lothar. 1991. "Nietzsches 'freier Geist' und das Repertoire der deutschen Literatur um 1910: Zu Ideologie und Struktur von Musils Novelle 'Die Vollendung der Liebe.'" In Hickman. 35-52.
Hüppauf, Bernd. 1991. "Musil in Paris. Robert Musils Rede auf dem Kongreß zur Verteidigung der Kultur (1935) im Zusammenhang seines Werkes." *Zeitschrift für Germanistik. Neue Folge* 1 (1): 55-69.
Kamata, Michio. 1991. "Erzählender Geist oder reflektierte Subjektivität? Zu Thomas Manns *Zauberberg* und Robert Musils *Mann ohne Eigenschaften.*" *"Die in dem alten Haus der Sprache wohnen." Festschrift für Helmut Arntzen.* Ed. Eckehard Czucka. Münster: Aschendorff. 323-34.
Kümmerling-Meibauer, Bettina. 1991. *Die Kunstmärchen von Hofmannsthal, Musil und Döblin.* Cologne, Weimar, Vienna: Böhlau. Kölner Germanistische Studien 32.
Lahme-Gronostaj, Hildegard. 1991. *Einbildung und Erkenntnis bei Robert Musil und im Verständnis der "Nachbarmacht" Psychoanalyse.* Würzburg: Königshausen & Neumann. Epistemata: Reihe Literaturwissenschaft 65.
Lavin, Carmen. 1991. "Patterns of Expectation in Musil's *Der Mann ohne Eigenschaften.*" In Hickman. 172-89.
Lungstrum, Janet. 1991. "Conceiving the Text: Nietzschean Inspiration in Musil's 'Tonka.'" *German Quarterly* 64 (4): 488-500.

Meisel, Gerhard. 1991. *Liebe im Zeitalter der Wissenschaft vom Menschen. Das Prosawerk Robert Musils.* Opladen: Westdeutscher Verlag.
Petersen, Jürgen H. 1991. *Der deutsche Roman der Moderne. Grundlegung — Typologie — Entwicklung.* Stuttgart: Metzler. 114–31.
Renner, Rolf Günter. 1991. "Transformatives Erzählen. Musils Grenzgang im *Mann ohne Eigenschaften.*" *Germanic Review* 66 (2): 70–80.
Ryan, Judith. 1991. *The Vanishing Subject. Early Psychology and Literary Modernism.* Chicago: University of Chicago Press.
Schröder-Werle, Renate. 1991. "*Die Verwirrungen des Zöglings Törleß* oder was sonst ist Literatur? Versuch einer deskriptiven Standortbestimmung." In Hickman. 190–227.
Schwartz, Agata. 1991. "Robert Musil als Dramatiker, Theaterkritiker und –theoretiker." *Fidibus. Zeitschrift für Literatur und Literaturwissenschaft* 19 (1): 1–65.
Tewilt, Gerd-Theo. 1991. "Bewegung und Geschichte in Robert Musils *Nachlaß zu Lebzeiten.*" *"Die in dem alten Haus der Sprache wohnen." Festschrift für Helmut Arntzen.* Eckehard Czucka, ed. Münster: Aschendorff. 353–64.
Wagner-Egelhaaf, Martina. 1991a. "'Anders ich' oder: Vom Leben im Text. Robert Musils Tagebuch-Heft 33." *Deutsche Vierteljahrsschrift für Literaturwissenschaft und Geistesgeschichte* 64 (1): 152–73.
———. 1991b. "'Wirklichkeitserinnerungen.' Photographie und Text bei Robert Musil." *Poetica* 23 (1/2): 217–56.
Webber, Andrew J. 1991. "The beholding eye: visual compulsion in Musil's works." In Hickman. 94–111.
Zeller, Rosmarie. 1991. "Robert Musil und das Theater seiner Zeit." In Hickman. 134–50.
Burmann, Anna. 1991/92. "Vom 'Ekel am Erzählen'; und von dem, was nicht aufhören kann zu sprechen. Über das ästhetische Begehren von Musils *Vereinigungen.*" *Rapial* 1 (3): 13–16 [I]; 1 (4): 12–14 [II]; 2 (1): 8–11 [III].
Altmann, Volker. 1992. *Totalität und Perspektive. Zum Wirklichkeitsbegriff Robert Musils im "Mann ohne Eigenschaften."* Frankfurt/Main, Berlin, Berne, New York, Paris, Vienna: Peter Lang. Literaturhistorische Untersuchungen 19.
Bonacchi, Silvia. 1992. "Robert Musils Studienjahre in Berlin 1903–1908." *Musil-Forum. Beilage* 1: 1–58.
Braun, Wilhelm. 1992. "Ferdinand Stader, *Die Schwärmer* und die konstruktive Ironie." In Brokoph-Mauch. 115–22.
Brokoph-Mauch, Gudrun, ed. 1992. *Robert Musil: Essayismus und Ironie.* Tübingen: Francke. Edition Orpheus 6.
Cejpek, Lucas, ed. 1992. *Nach Musil. Denkformen.* Vienna, Berlin: Turia & Kant.
Cetti Marinoni, Bianca. 1992. *Essayistisches Drama. Die Entstehung von Robert Musils Stück "Die Schwärmer."* Munich, Salzburg: Fink. Musil-Studien 21.
Corngold, Stanley. 1992. "Patterns of Justification in *Young Törleß.*" *Neverending Stories. Toward a Critical Narratology.* Ann Fehn, Ingeborg Hoesterey, Maria Tatar, eds. Princeton, N.J.: Princeton University Press. 138–49.

Dreis, Gabriele. 1992. *"Ruhelose Gestaltlosigkeit des Daseins." Pädagogische Studien zum "Rousseauismus" im Werk Robert Musils.* Munich: Fink. *Musil-Studien* 23.
Griesheimer, Frank; Prinz, Alois, eds. 1992. *Wozu Literaturwissenschaft?* Tübingen: Francke.
Harrison, Thomas. 1992. *Essayism: Conrad, Musil, and Pirandello.* Baltimore, London: Johns Hopkins University Press.
Jungk, Peter Stephan. 1992. "Die Vergessene. Robert Musil und Herma Dietz. Ein Beitrag zur Musil-Forschung." *Die neue Rundschau* 103 (2): 151–61.
Kampits, Peter. 1992. "Musil und Wittgenstein." In Brokoph-Mauch. 153–60.
Kyora, Sabine. 1992. *Psychoanalyse und Prosa im 20. Jahrhundert.* Stuttgart: Metzler. 162–238.
Maier-Solgk, Frank. 1992. *Sinn für Geschichte. Ästhetische Subjektivität und historiologische Reflexion bei Robert Musil.* Munich: Fink. *Musil-Studien* 22.
Meier Ruf, Ursula. 1992. *Prozesse der Auflösung. Subjektstruktur und Erzählform in Robert Musils "Drei Frauen."* Berne, Berlin, Frankfurt/Main, New York, Paris, Vienna: Peter Lang. Europäische Hochschulstudien 1319.
O'Connor, Kathleen. 1992. *Robert Musil and the Tradition of the German Novelle.* Riverside, Calif.: Ariadne.
Rogowski, Christian. 1992. "'Ein andres Verhalten zur Welt.' Robert Musil und der Film." *Sprachkunst* 23 (1): 105–18.
Roth, Marie-Louise. 1992. "'Kann ein Pferd lachen?' Musils Ironie, eine perspektivische Verschiebung?" In Brokoph-Mauch. 123–35.
Rußegger, Arno. 1992. "Der literarische Nachlaß Robert Musils als CD-ROM-Edition." *Rapial* 2 (1): 2–4.
Vietta, Silvio. 1992. "Musils *Der Mann ohne Eigenschaften.*" *Die literarische Moderne. Eine problemgeschichtliche Darstellung der deutschsprachigen Literatur von Hölderlin bis Thomas Bernhard.* Stuttgart: Metzler. 89–103.
Honold, Alexander. 1993. "Die verwahrte und die entsprungene Zeit. Paul Kellers *Ferien vom Ich* und die Zeitdarstellung im Werk Robert Musils." *Deutsche Vierteljahrsschrift für Literaturwissenschaft und Geistesgeschichte* 67 (3): 302–21.
Krommer, Axel; Kümmel, Albert. 1993. "Pendelbewegungen des Sinns. Vorschlag einer informations- und chaostheoretischen Bewertung des *Mann ohne Eigenschaften.*" *Rapial* 3 (3): 2–11.
Kuzniar, Alice A. 1993. "Inside/Out: Robert Musil's 'Die Portugiesin.'" *Modern Austrian Literature* 26 (2): 91–106.
Pott, Hans-Georg, ed. 1993. *Robert Musil: Dichter — Essayist — Wissenschaftler.* Munich: Fink. *Musil-Studien* 8.
Rogowski, Christian. 1993. *Implied Dramaturgy. Robert Musil and the Crisis of Modern Drama.* Riverside, Calif.: Ariadne.
Vogt, Guntram, 1993. "Die offenen Grenzen des Ich bei Robert Musil." *Rapial* 3 (1): 9–14.

Index

Adam, Christine 78, 207
Adenauer, Konrad 148
Adorno, Theodor W. 37, 48, 66, 106, 122
"Die Affeninsel" 135
Akashi, Eichiro 125, 126, 213
Albertsen, Elisabeth 32, 35, 49, 105, 153, 154, 156, 189, 197
Aler, Jan 61, 63, 70, 191
Allais, Kai 50, 81, 82, 86, 209
Allemann, Beda 16, 47, 123, 147, 148, 149, 150, 156, 184, 203
Allesch, Ea von
  see von Allesch, Ea
Allesch, Johannes von
  see von Allesch, Johannes
Alt, Peter-André 160, 206, 210
Althaus, Horst 194
Altmann, Volker 216
Ambros, Gerda 95, 96, 206
"Die Amsel" 8, 19, 121, 130–145
Anderer Zustand 2, 3, 31, 86, 106, 108, 118, 139, 151, 164, 169
Andrian, Leopold von
  see von Andrian, Leopold
Appia, Adolphe 105
Appignanesi, Lisa 75, 76, 84, 92, 116, 192
Arbeitsstelle für Robert-Musil-Forschung, Saarbrücken 5, 35, 38, 56
Aristotle 108
Arntzen, Helmut 2, 31, 33, 47, 48, 49, 52, 101, 102, 103, 106, 107, 111, 122, 149, 150, 156, 181, 185, 189, 198, 202, 203, 206
Artaud, Antonin 99
Aspetsberger, Friedbert 38, 202

Aue, Maximilian 47, 83, 117, 195, 202, 210
Axer, Erwin 93, 101

Bab, Julius 182
Bachmann, Dieter 189
Bachmann, Ingeborg 18, 22, 23, 24, 25, 56, 90, 183, 185
Bachofen, Johann Jakob 75, 76, 114, 126, 127
Baedecker, Karl 137, 195
Bakhtin, Mikhail 50, 54, 140, 162
Balázs, Béla 12, 49, 78, 142, 182
Balme, Christopher 110, 211
Baltz-Balzberg, Regina 206, 209
Bangerter, Lowell A. 6, 97, 212
Barnouw, Dagmar 195, 196, 211
Barthes, Roland 50, 162
Bateson, Gregory 53, 76
Battaille, Georges 167
Baudrillard, Jean 166
Bauer, Sibylle 92, 188
Baumann, Gerhart 22, 24, 73, 113, 183, 185, 187
Baur, Uwe 62, 133, 134, 135, 136, 192, 198
Bausinger, Wilhelm 29, 30, 37, 186, 187
Beard, Philip H. 202
Becher, Johannes R. 12
Becker, Peter von
  see von Becker, Peter
Beckers, Gustave 205
Beckett, Samuel 104
Bedwell, Carol 188
Beißner, Friedrich 30, 37
Beitrag zur Beurteilung der Lehren Machs 9, 44, 56, 61, 63

Belobratow, Alexander W. 6
Benjamin, Walter 15, 48, 87
Benn, Gottfried 132
Berg, Jan 202
Berger, Albert 132, 141, 190
Berger, Peter L. 169, 203
Berghahn, Wilfried 30, 31, 34, 59, 100, 102, 111, 150, 153, 160, 184, 186
Berthoff, Warner 53, 208
Bertschinger, Thomas 189
Bey, Gesine 52, 212
"Bilder" 143
Binet, A. 79
"The Blackbird"
    see "Die Amsel"
Blanchot, Maurice 6, 184
Blasberg, Cornelia 52, 155, 205, 212
Blass, Ernst 10
Blei, Franz 8, 10, 12, 16, 79, 80, 105, 140, 182, 183
Bloch, Ernst 12
Boa, Elizabeth 115, 116, 189
"Die Bob-Hansen-Story" 32
Boehlich, Walter 22, 183
Boeninger, Helmut R. 23, 183
Bogosavljevic, Srdan 6, 143, 144, 212, 215
Böhme, Hartmut 37, 47, 84, 85, 86, 155, 156, 157, 164, 166, 167, 173, 193, 195, 200, 202, 208, 214
Bohn, Ralf 168, 169, 211
Bohrer, Karl Heinz 176, 200
Bonacchi, Silvia 52, 53, 217
Böschenstein, Bernard 203
Brasch, Thomas 59, 197
Braun, Wilhelm 59, 60, 62, 65, 76, 91, 100, 103, 114, 131, 183, 185, 186, 187, 188, 195, 196, 202, 203, 211, 217
Brecht, Bertolt 11, 12, 31, 99, 102, 104, 106, 109, 110, 111, 159
Breton, André 124
Breuer, Josef 77, 82, 83, 86
Briefe 3, 11, 44, 55

Broch, Hermann 14, 105, 132, 164
Brokoph-Mauch, Gudrun 141, 142, 196, 199, 203, 206, 217
Brooks, Daniel Josef 212, 214
Brosthaus, Heribert 30, 131, 141, 186, 187, 190
Buber, Martin 38, 152, 158, 160
Büchner, Georg 94, 105
Burckhardt, Judith 160, 192
Büren, Erhard von
    see von Büren, Erhard
Bürger, Peter 124, 176, 211
Burgstaller, Erich 131, 191
Burmann, Anna 86, 216

"Can a Horse Laugh?"
    see "Kann ein Pferd lachen?"
Cassirer, Paul 8
Castex, Elizabeth
    see Castex-Rieger, Elisabeth
Castex-Rieger, Elisabeth 5, 35, 193, 196, 198, 200
Cejpek, Lucas 50, 165, 166, 203, 205, 210, 217
Cellbrot, Hartmut 155, 170, 211
Cervantes, Miguel de 167
Cetti Marinoni, Bianca 90, 98, 99, 104, 109, 111, 208, 211, 212, 214, 217
Cézanne, Paul 125
Charrière-Jacquin, Marianne 95, 96, 205, 207
Chevalier, Claude 5, 181
Chiarini, Paolo 6, 208
"Children's Story"
    see "Kindergeschichte"
Chomsky, Noam 64
Church, Barbara Hall 17, 18
Church, Henry Hall 17
Classen, Albrecht 124, 209, 211
Claudel, Paul 105
Cohn, Dorrit 72, 75, 120, 121, 150, 191, 193, 196
"Collateral Campaign"
    see *Parallelaktion*
Columbus, Christopher 44

Cometti, Jean-Pierre 207
Cooperman, Stanley 23
Corino, Karl 9, 13, 14, 15, 25, 31, 35, 37, 38, 44, 45, 52, 60, 74, 76, 77, 78, 79, 82, 87, 105, 122, 128, 189, 190, 191, 192, 193, 194, 207, 210, 211
Corngold, Stanley 71, 217
Coseriu, Eugen 135
Craig, Edward Gordon 105
Cremerius, Johannes 44, 45, 46, 197
Csokor, Franz Theodor 14, 19, 20, 25, 183, 185

Daigger, Annette 5, 211
Danner, Karl-Heinz 35, 181, 192
Dänzer, Hans 190
Dassanowsky-Harris, Robert von
  see von Dassanowsky-Harris, Robert
Dawlianidse, David 155, 196
De Angelis, Enrico 6, 202
Deleuze, Gilles 50, 85, 143
"Denkmale" 55
De Rais, Gilles 80, 81
Derrida, Jacques 50, 95, 161, 170, 171
Descartes, René 59, 81
Desportes, Yvon 63, 70, 193
Dettmering, Peter 173, 200
De Tullio, Chiara 99, 213
"Der Dichter in dieser Zeit" 15
Diebold, Bernhard 182
Diersch, Manfred 169, 214
Dietrich, Margret 91, 185
Dietz, Herma 124, 128
Dimter, Walter 15, 213
Dinklage, Karl 17, 25, 26, 29, 30, 31, 35, 56, 95, 185, 190, 207
Döblin, Alfred 10, 11, 12, 19, 167, 182
"Das Doppel-Ich" 107
Doppler, Alfred 135, 194
Dos Passos, John 167
Dostoyevsky, Fjodor M. 126
Dowden, Stephen 208

Drei Frauen 12, 13, 18, 34, 113–129, 136
Dreis, Gabriele 175, 217
Dresler-Brumme, Charlotte 209
"The Dual I"
  see "Das Doppel-Ich"
Duchamp, Marcel 50
Duerr, Hans Peter 121, 122
Dürrenmatt, Friedrich 100, 102
Durzak, Manfred 14, 189
Düsing, Wolfgang 59, 65, 119, 135, 136, 190, 202

Eibl, Karl 42, 118, 119, 121, 131, 133, 190, 196, 215
Eigenschaftslosigkeit 33, 116, 154, 158, 159
Eisele, Ulf 50, 162, 163, 166, 170, 202
Emerson, Ralph Waldo 6, 152
"The Enchanted House"
  see "Das verzauberte Haus"
The Enthusiasts
  see *Die Schwärmer*
Erhart, Claus 97, 215
Erickson, Susan J. 120, 121, 127, 128, 204, 207, 208
Essayism 2, 56, 153
Esslin, Martin 94, 202

Farda, Dieter P. 46, 169, 202, 211
Faulkner, William 32, 147
Faulstich, Werner 40, 139, 140
Fechter, Paul 89, 91, 183, 184
Fernliebe 2
Fiala-Fürst, Ingeborg 2, 6, 181
Fielding, Henry 167
Finlay, Marike 53, 54, 214
"Fischer an der Ostsee" 141
Fischer, Ernst 14, 24, 114, 184
Fischer, Max 182
Fischer, Nanda 193
Fischer, Samuel 10
"Fishermen on the Baltic"
  see "Fischer an der Ostsee"
Flaubert, Gustave 87

"Das Fliegenpapier" 130, 131, 135, 136, 138, 142, 143
"The Flypaper"
see "Das Fliegenpapier"
Focke, Alfred 147, 184
Fontana, Oskar Maurus 12, 14, 19, 25, 185
Fontane, Theodor 148
Forschungsstelle Robert-Musil-Nachlaß, Vienna 35
Foucault, Michel 50, 53, 66, 68, 79, 143, 165, 167
Fourie, Regine 181
Frankfurt school 33, 37, 66, 106, 154
Frank, Leonhard 163
Frank, Manfred 170, 200, 204, 211
Frazer, James G. 120
Freese, Wolfgang 2, 23, 152, 160, 181, 190, 191, 193, 197, 200, 204
Freij, Lars 60, 61, 64, 191
Freytag, Gustav 108
Freud, Sigmund 10, 12, 44, 45, 46, 54, 60, 66, 71, 74, 75, 77, 78, 82, 83, 86, 87, 88, 114, 115, 119, 122, 146, 154, 161, 174
Friedrich, Gerhard 113, 185
Frier, Wolfgang 39, 64, 65, 195
Frisch, Efraim 14
Frisé, Adolf 3, 15, 16, 19, 20, 21, 22, 25, 26, 27, 29, 30, 31, 34, 38, 41, 42, 43, 47, 48, 57, 91, 146, 151, 160, 182, 183, 186, 198, 202, 209, 215
Fritz, Axel 107, 200
Frye, Northrop 67
Fuchs, Annette 143, 211
Fuder, Dieter 155, 161, 197
Fuld, Werner 13, 47, 195, 204
Fürst, Bruno 4, 25, 185

Gadamer, Hans-Georg 170
Gargani, Aldo 66, 67, 169, 200, 205
Genette, Gérard 98, 120
Gesammelte Werke 3, 13, 42, 177

"Geschichte aus drei Jahrhunderten" 141
Geulen, Hans 72, 187
Giampieri Deutsch, Patrizia 45, 214
Girgensohn, Karl 158
Goethe, Johann Wolfgang 41, 53, 63, 130, 136
Goldgar, Harry 44, 60, 187
Goltschnigg, Dietmar 38, 59, 79, 80, 111, 157, 158, 191, 192, 193, 200, 203, 208, 215
Gombrowicz, Witold 104
Gradischnig, Hertwig 64, 195
Graf, Günter 190
Greimas, A. J. 64
Greisinger, Hermann 139
Griesheimer, Frank 52, 217
"Grigia" 12, 113–129, 158
Grimm, Reinhold 110, 197
Groeben, Norbert 40, 138, 139, 200
Grosz, George 12
Grotzer, Peter 59, 215
Guattari, Félix 143
Gumtau, Helmut 188, 197, 198

Habermas, Jürgen 30, 37, 53
Hafner, Heinz 208
Hagmann, Franz 131, 136, 190
Hahnl, Hans Heinz 177, 200
Hall, Murray G. 9, 11, 12, 13, 16, 93, 130, 194, 195, 196, 213
Halm, Heinz J. 135, 139, 194
Hamm, Horst 78, 207
Handke, Peter 94, 120
Hanke-Tjaden, Irma 33, 186, 187
"Hare Catastrophe"
see "Hasenkatastrophe"
Harrison, Thomas 6, 217
Hartinger, Ingram 50, 205
"Hasenkatastrophe" 40, 135, 138, 139
Hassler-Rütti, Ruth 173, 214
Hatfield, Henry 60, 190
Hauptmann, Gerhart 13, 99
Heald, David 11, 196
Heering-Düllo, Cornelia 124, 211

Index

Heftrich, Eckhard 96, 208
Hegel, G. W. F. 90, 91, 98, 109
Heidegger, Martin 67, 69, 123, 124, 148, 151, 155, 169
Heintel, Erich 116, 122, 193
Heisenberg, Werner 53
Henninger, Peter 32, 45, 46, 47, 50, 54, 71, 77, 78, 82, 84, 96, 118, 121, 122, 126, 129, 136, 137, 161, 195, 197, 198, 200, 202, 205, 208
Henze, Hans Werner 90
Hermand, Jost 114, 186
Herwig, Dagmar 192
Hesse, Hermann 14, 23, 64
Heyd, Dieter 45, 50, 77, 161, 165, 198
Heydebrand, Renate von
 see von Heydebrand, Renate
Heym, Georg 58, 132
Hickman, Hannah 6, 198, 205, 215
Hitler, Adolf 15, 164
Hochstätter, Dietrich 155, 156, 157, 192
Hoffmann, E. T. A. 142
Hoffmann, Lynda 60, 213
Hoffmeister, Werner 26, 31, 150, 187
Hofmannsthal, Hugo von
 see von Hofmannsthal, Hugo
Holländer, Felix 100, 182
Holmes, Alan 159, 160, 197
Homann, Renate 122, 123, 207
Hönig, Christoph 4, 193
Honnef-Becker, Irmgard 215
Honold, Alexander 175, 217
Hoppler, Rudolf 137, 145, 205
Horkheimer, Max 37, 66, 106, 122, 155
Hornbostel, Erich Moritz von
 see von Hornbostel, Erich Moritz
Horn, Peter 97, 143, 209, 214
Horváth, Ödön von
 see von Horváth, Ödön
Howald, Stephan 155, 157, 205
Howes, Geoffrey C. 6, 207
Huber, Lothar 62, 149, 193, 202, 215

Hüppauf, Bernd-Rüdiger 16, 155, 191, 211, 215
Husserl, Edmund 61, 158, 170
Huysmans, Joris-Karl 80

Ibsen, Henrik 13, 93, 99
Ingarden, Roman 41, 155
Internationale Robert-Musil-Gesellschaft, Vienna 38
Ionesco, Eugène 104
Irle, Gerhard 147, 187
Iser, Wolfgang 40, 41
Issler, Maria 192
Iurlano, Fabrizio 6, 181

Jacob, Paul 14, 182
Jacottet, Philippe 19
Jakob, Michael 209
Jässl, Gerolf 187
Jauss, Hans-Robert 40, 41
Jennings, Michael W. 121, 205, 211
Jens, Inge 24, 72, 183
Jens, Walter 58, 59, 61, 184
Jesch, Jörg 102, 189
Jessner, Leopold 105
Joyce, James 14, 32, 53, 59, 75, 167
Jung, Carl Gustav 28, 44, 101, 120, 135
Jungk, Peter Stephan 128, 217

Kafka, Franz 10, 19, 20, 23, 58, 130, 132, 135, 147, 158, 164
Kaiser, Ernst 20, 21, 23, 26, 27, 28, 29, 30, 38, 44, 56, 58, 60, 89, 91, 100, 113, 121, 151, 160, 183, 184, 185, 186
Kaiser, Gerhard R. 53, 192
Kaiser, Georg 11, 101
Kaizik, Jürgen 93, 106, 198
Kakanien 3, 55, 173
Kamata, Michio 215
Kampits, Peter 169, 217
Kandinsky, Vassily 158
"Kann ein Pferd lachen?" 144

Kant, Immanuel 69, 126, 127, 151, 161, 168
Karsch, Walter 89, 90, 92, 100, 109, 184, 186
Karthaus, Ulrich 1, 31, 47, 108, 109, 149, 151, 168, 181, 187, 198, 201, 202, 204, 207
"Katakombe" 105
Kaus, Gina 105
Kayser, Martina 213
Kermode, Frank 4, 186, 187
Kerr, Alfred 8, 9, 12, 182
Kesser, Armin 19, 183
Kesting, Marianne 91, 102, 184
Key, Ellen 61, 152
Kierkegaard, Sören 115, 176
Kieser, Rolf 17, 47, 205
Kim, Rae-Hyeon 123, 124, 142, 208
"Kindergeschichte" 144
King, Lynda J. 107, 181, 197, 204
Kirchberger, Lida 114, 115, 127, 186
Kisch, Egon Erwin 12, 16, 17, 183
Kisery, Pal 195
Kiss, Endre 214
Klages, Ludwig 75, 139, 152, 164
"Kleine Lebensreise" 144
Klein, Melanie 126
Kleist, Heinrich von
    see von Kleist, Heinrich
Klotz, Volker 90
Knüfermann, Volker 67, 68, 208
Köhler, Andrea 78, 207
Kohlhase, Norbert 31, 102, 104, 189
Kohut, Heinz 67, 96, 137, 173
Kolle, Oswald 32
Kontje, Todd 116, 209, 211
Kowal, Michael 55, 188
Kreisky, Bruno 4, 38, 198
Krejic, Karel 195
Kretschmer, Ernst 142, 152
Kristeva, Julia 45, 50
Kritische Theorie
    see Frankfurt school
Krommer, Axel 175, 218
Krotz, Frederick W. 131, 133, 190, 192

Krusche, Dietrich 76, 77, 197
Kühn, Dieter 151, 187
Kühne, Jörg 31, 153, 164, 189
Kümmel, Albert 175, 218
Kümmerling, Bettina 2, 181, 216
Kümmerling-Meibauer, Bettina
    see Kümmerling, Bettina
Kuzniar, Alice A. 128, 129, 218
Kyora, Sabine 86, 87, 217

Lacan, Jacques 45, 46, 50, 54, 66, 71, 77, 86, 96, 97, 122, 137, 161, 166
"The Lady from Portugal"
    see "Die Portugiesin"
Laermann, Klaus 33, 42, 154, 155, 156, 164, 173, 190
Lahme-Gronostaj, Hildegard 126, 216
Laing, R. D. 79
Lämmert, Eberhard 128
"Land above the South Pole or Planet Ed" see "Land über dem Südpol oder Der Stern Ed"
Landauer, Gustav 164
"Land über dem Südpol oder Der Stern Ed" 4
Lange, Victor 136, 196
Lao-Tsu 53
Lavin, Carmen 216
Lejeune, Robert 17, 25, 183, 185
Leonhard, Rudolf 12
Le Rider, Jacques 176, 214
Lessing, Gotthold Ephraim 167
Lethen, Helmut 52, 142, 143, 209
Lévy-Bruhl, Lucien 152
"Little Life Sojourn"
    see "Kleine Lebensreise"
Lobner, Hans 45, 214
Lochner, Elmar 139
Loebenstein, Johannes 185
Longuet-Marx, Anne 5, 53, 208, 214
Lotman, J. M. 138
Luft, David S. 6, 15, 29, 48, 56, 93, 102, 198
Luhmann, Niklas 125
Lukács, Georg 37, 47, 132, 159, 184

Index

Lungstrum, Janet 216
Luserke, Matthias 168, 209
Lützeler, Paul Michael 158
Lyotard, Jean-François 50, 167, 197

Mach, Ernst 9, 44, 48, 61, 63, 70, 98, 119, 125, 151, 152, 169
Mae, Michiko 10, 78, 79, 80, 81, 83, 85, 181, 198, 199, 205, 212
Maeterlinck, Maurice 58, 61, 69, 105, 152, 155
Magnou, Jacqueline 5, 79, 181, 196, 201, 202, 205
Magris, Claudio 6, 175, 188, 194, 204, 213
Maier, Anna 20, 22, 183
Maier-Solgk, Frank 175, 217
Malraux, André 16
Mandel, Siegfried 23, 183
Der Mann ohne Eigenschaften 1, 3, 5, 6, 13, 14, 15, 17–32, 34, 35, 37, 39, 43, 45, 48, 50, 51, 53, 54, 56, 72, 77, 80, 87, 89, 91, 92, 95, 96, 97, 99, 100, 101, 102, 104, 113, 114, 116, 119, 125, 133, 134, 136, 141, 142, 144, 146–175, 176, 177
Mann, Thomas 14, 19, 23, 26, 67, 68, 114, 150
The Man without Qualities
   see *Der Mann ohne Eigenschaften*
"Das Märchen vom Schneider" 55
Marcovaldi, Gaetano 19, 27, 34, 195
Marcuse, Ludwig 14
Margwelaschwili, Giwi 203
Markner, Reinhard 2, 182
Martens, Lorna 82, 83, 86, 209
Marx, Karl 33, 37, 64, 132, 133, 157, 159
Matt, Peter von
   see von Matt, Peter
Mattenklott, Gert 37, 52, 62, 65, 193
Mauch, Gudrun B.
   see Brokoph-Mauch, Gudrun
Mauser, Wolfram 137, 197, 201
Mauthner, Fritz 118, 164

Mayer-König, Wolfgang 38, 198
McCormick, E. Allen 186
Meier Ruf, Ursula 127, 128, 217
Meisel, Gerhard 50, 51, 54, 85, 86, 126, 129, 174, 175, 216
Meister Eckhart 158
Meister, Monika 105, 106, 107, 109, 198, 199, 201, 203, 204
Melchinger, Siegfried 102, 187
Menges, Karl 195
Menges, Martin 164, 203
Meuthen, Erich 67, 68, 69, 207
Michel, Karl Markus 22, 153, 183
Middell, Elke 210
Militzer, Gerti 203, 211
Minder, Robert 59, 186
Möglichkeitssinn 2, 101, 112, 153, 159, 169, 173
"The Monkey Island"
   see "Die Affeninsel"
Monti, Claudia 47, 169, 198, 201, 204
"Monuments"
   see "Denkmale"
Moore, Gene M. 53, 207
Morgenstern, Soma 195, 204
Moser, Manfred 50, 141, 207, 213
Moser, Walter 162, 199, 206, 210
Müller, Gerd 61, 70, 191
Müller, Gerhard 147, 184
Müller, Götz 155, 192
Müller, Gregor 18
Müller, Robert 10, 12, 105, 182
Mulligan, Kevin 56
Mulot-Déri, Sibylle
   see Mulot, Sibylle
Mulot, Sibylle 42, 196, 199
Musil, Alfred 13, 78, 120
Musil, Hermine 66, 78, 120, 137
Musil, Martha 15, 17, 18, 19, 20, 21, 78, 84, 118
Musil Research Unit, Reading 35

Nachlaß 3, 27, 28, 30, 34, 35, 37, 42, 43, 55, 57, 103, 153, 160
   on CD-ROM 3, 42, 57, 160

Nachlaß zu Lebzeiten 3, 5, 16, 18, 40, 130–145
Nadermann, Peter 50, 214
Naganowski, Egon 6, 93, 95, 100, 103, 104, 109, 192, 193, 204, 207
Neuenfels, Hans 93, 94, 95, 207
Neumer, Katalin 210
Nietzsche, Friedrich 16, 30, 48, 68, 80, 117, 120, 133, 151, 152, 155, 164, 165, 169
Novalis 61, 117, 128, 148
Nusser, Peter 152, 153, 160, 188

O'Connor, Kathleen 83, 87, 127, 128, 144, 145, 217
Oczipka, Michael 92, 103, 107, 192
Oertel Sjögren, Christine 116, 117, 126, 190, 195
Oldenbürger, Hartmut A. 139
Olmi, Roberto 169, 201, 204
On Mach's Theories
  see *Beitrag zur Beurteilung der Lehren Machs*
Other Condition
  see *anderer Zustand*
Otten, Karl 89, 183

"Panama" 103, 105, 107
Parallelaktion 27, 29, 56, 159
Parry, Idris 192
Paulson, Ronald M. 119, 120, 201, 203
Payne, Philip 6, 96, 210, 212
Peirce, Charles S. 53
Pekar, Thomas 50, 81, 97, 116, 125, 172, 213
Pekny, Romuald 100
Pennisi, Francesca 213
"The Perfection of Love"
  see "Die Vollendung der Liebe"
Perronnet, Jacques 204
Pestalozzi, Karl 69, 70, 213
Peters, Frederick G. 6, 39, 197
Petersen, Jürgen H. 216
Petersen, Klaus 12, 201
Peyret, Jean-François 177, 199

Pfeiffer, Joachim 78, 207
Pfeiffer, Peter C. 48, 210, 214
Pfister, Manfred 110, 196
Pflegerl, Dietmar 101
Picasso, Pablo 67
Pietsch, Reinhard 50, 170, 171, 212
Pike, Burton 6, 26, 56, 72, 91, 130, 185, 198
Pila, Marie-Christine 107, 199, 201
Pinthus, Kurt 10
Pirandello, Luigi 15, 99, 105
Piscator, Erwin 12
Pissaro, Camille 125
Pitoëff, Sacha 90
Plato 84
Plotinus 49
Pongs, Hermann 146, 147, 186
"Die Portugiesin" 12, 113–129
Posthumous Papers of a Living Author
  see *Nachlaß zu Lebzeiten*
Pott, Hans-Georg 50, 51, 65, 66, 70, 116, 121, 122, 129, 142, 166, 206, 210, 218
Prinz, Alois 52, 217
"Prologue to the Melodrama *The Zodiac*" see "Vorspiel zu dem Melodrama *Der Tierkreis*"
Prosper, Hans 182
Proust, Marcel 5, 32, 53

Radbruch, Knut 213
Raddatz, Fritz J. 47, 208
Rasch, Wolfdietrich 29, 30, 100, 103, 150, 183, 186, 187, 188, 189, 190
Rathenau, Walter 10, 155, 164
Ratioïd/nicht-ratioïd 2, 127, 131
Reader-Response Criticism 39, 40, 155
Rede zur Rilke-Feier 12
Reich, Willi 19
Reinhardt, Max 11, 105
Reinhardt, Stephan 33, 189, 190
Reis, Gilbert 65, 108, 130, 204, 206, 210
Reiss, Hans 113, 184
Reiter, Heinrich 66, 78, 120, 137

Reniers, Annie
  see Reniers-Servranckx, Annie
Reniers-Servranckx, Annie 34, 60, 92, 102, 116, 117, 121, 130, 188, 191, 192
Renner, Rolf Günter 52, 167, 212, 216
Requadt, Paul 113, 183
Rieth, Renate 78, 187
Rilke, Rainer Maria 10, 12, 58, 59, 143, 164
Rinderknecht, Siegfried 198
Riskamm, Karl 20, 22, 183
Robert Musil Archiv, Klagenfurt 29, 35, 38, 56
Rocek, Roman 201
Rogowski, Christian 52, 90, 92, 93, 98, 99, 103, 110, 111, 213, 214, 217, 218
Rose, Marilyn Gaddis 191
Roseberry, Robert L. 2, 181, 194
Rosenberg, Alfred 158
Rosenthal, Annina 19, 20
Roth, Joseph 195
Roth, Marie-Louise 5, 25, 31, 34, 36, 38, 41, 56, 102, 105, 109, 110, 137, 138, 140, 141, 144, 156, 158, 185, 187, 192, 193, 196, 199, 204, 206, 210, 217
Rothe-Buddensieg, Margret 63, 66, 194
Rothe, Wolfgang 131, 133, 191
Röttger, Brigitte 74, 121, 126, 130, 137, 193, 201
Rousseau, Jean-Jacques 175
Rousset, Jean 19
Rowohlt, Ernst 14, 19, 20, 21, 30, 31, 32
Rußegger, Arno 52, 57, 212, 217
Ryan, Judith 124, 125, 176, 199, 212, 213, 216

Sanders, Hans 132, 133, 134, 135, 192
Sartre, Jean-Paul 92
"Satyrspiel" 103
Schaffner, Jakob 182

Schaffnit, Hans Wolfgang 155, 161, 191
Schamann, Franz 42
Scharang, Michael 90, 91, 92, 98, 109, 187
Schärer, Hans-Rudolf 173, 214
Schaukal, Richard 42
Schaunig-Baltz-Balzberg, Regina
  see Baltz-Baltzberg, Regina
Scheler, Max 22, 139, 152
Schelling, Friedrich Wilhelm 168
Schelling, Ulrich 189
Schier, Rudolf 120, 126, 196
"Die Schildkröte" 103, 105, 111
Schiller, Dieter 16, 212
Schiller, Friedrich 108, 110, 123
Schink, Helmut 199
Schlegel, Friedrich 148
Schlöndorff, Volker 31, 59, 90
Schlüer, Klaus-Dieter 139, 201
Schmidt, Jochen 116, 117, 158, 159, 164, 194, 207
Schmitz, Dietmar Bernhard 43, 199
Schneider, Günther 12, 89, 92, 93, 100, 103, 184, 193
Schneider, Rolf 24, 64, 114, 159, 194
Schnitzler, Arthur 75, 93
Schoeck, Otmar 141
Scholz, Ingeborg 130, 197
Schöne, Albrecht 26, 31, 149, 150, 185
Schönwiese, Ernst 1, 18, 19, 201
Schrader, Monika 167, 194
Schramm, Ulf 33, 188
Schröder, Jürgen 73, 74, 188
Schröder-Werle, Renate 15, 20, 70, 71, 177, 194, 195, 196, 201, 216
Schulze Vellinghausen, Albert 100, 184
Schütz, Alfred 169
Die Schwärmer 10, 11, 12, 13, 26, 56, 89–99, 102, 107, 108, 109, 111, 114
Schwartz, Agata 111, 112, 216
Seidler, Ingo 30, 188
Sellner, Gustav Rudolf 89

Sera, Manfred 120, 142, 190, 199
Siegrist, Christoph 186
Siems, Friedrich 100
Sihvo, Hannes 181
Silone, Ignazio 14, 191
Simmel, Georg 152
Simon, Andrea 56
"Slovenian Village Funeral"
    see "Slowenisches Dorfbegräbnis"
"Slowenisches Dorfbegräbnis" 143
Söder, Thomas 69, 168, 212
Sokel, Walter H. 47, 64, 83, 115, 116, 148, 149, 167, 168, 185, 188, 195, 203, 206, 212
"Ein Soldat erzählt" 141
"A Soldier's Tale"
    see "Ein Soldat erzählt"
Solms, Wilhelm 140, 177, 209
Sprachkrise 58, 62, 65, 164
Staiger, Emil 155
Stanislavsky, Constantin 105
Stanzel, Franz 128
Stefanek, Paul 11, 94, 103, 109, 111, 193, 199, 201, 203, 207
Stein, Gertrude 124
Stelzmann, Rainulf A. 127, 194
Sterne, Laurence 167
Sternheim, Carl 11
Stern, Joseph Peter 52, 204
Stoessl, Otto 9, 182
Stopp, Elisabeth 60, 61, 189
"Story from Three Centuries"
    see "Geschichte aus drei Jahrhunderten"
Strassburg, Gottfried von
    see von Strassburg, Gottfried
Strauß, Botho 94
Strelka, Joseph P. 29, 78, 122, 140, 184, 195, 204, 207
Strindberg, August 99, 110
Strobl, Karl Hans 42
Strutz, Johann 206, 208, 209
Strutz, Josef 6, 47, 48, 56, 163, 164, 199, 201, 204, 205, 206, 208, 209, 210, 212, 214

Swales, Martin 203
Swedenborg, Emanuel 22
Swift, Jonathan 167
Szondi, Peter 91, 92, 98, 184

Tagebücher 3, 16, 25, 41, 56, 58, 59, 92, 160
Tank, Lothar Kurt 184
"Tempora Meier" 103, 111
"The Tailor's Tale"
    see "Das Märchen vom Schneider"
Tewilt, Gerd-Theo 144, 171, 215, 216
"The Temptation of Quiet Veronika"
    see "Die Versuchung der stillen Veronika"
Theweleit, Klaus 66
Thöming, Jürgen C. 1, 31, 40, 41, 47, 60, 76, 94, 98, 131, 133, 134, 135, 155, 181, 191, 194, 195, 201, 213
Three Women
    see *Drei Frauen*
Thurnhofer, Hubert 50, 210
Tiebel, Ursula 102, 105, 106, 107, 200
Tiefenbacher, Herbert 203
Titche, Leon L. 188
Tober, Karl 121, 188
Toller, Ernst 12
"Tonka" 24, 50, 113–129
Torberg, Friedrich 89, 184
"Triëdere" 131, 141, 142, 143
Trommler, Frank 33, 59, 188
Turner, David 63, 64, 70, 194
"The Turtle"
    see "Die Schildkröte"

Über die Dummheit 16
Uhse, Bernd 16
"Unfriendly Meditations"
    see "Unfreundliche Betrachtungen"
"Unfreundliche Betrachtungen" 132
Unions
    see *Vereinigungen*
Utopianism 2

Václavek, Ludvík E. 6

Valéry, Paul 73
Venturelli, Aldo 6, 169, 181, 200, 212, 213
Vereinigungen 9, 12, 13, 24, 34, 37, 71, 72–88, 114, 125, 136, 161
"Die Versuchung der stillen Veronika" 9, 72–88
Die Verwirrungen des Zöglings Törleß 8, 12, 13, 24, 31, 34, 37, 39, 44, 54, 58–71, 90, 136
"Das verzauberte Haus" 79, 136
Vietta, Silvio 176, 217
Viertel, Berthold 11
Vinzenz and the Lady-friend of Important Men
  see *Vinzenz und die Freundin bedeutender Männer*
Vinzenz und die Freundin bedeutender Männer 11, 13, 99, 100–112
Vogt, Guntram 47, 48, 206, 209, 218
Vogl, Joseph 68, 210
"Die Vollendung der Liebe" 9, 41, 72–88, 122
Völse, Hans-Joachim 50, 215
Voltaire 23, 167
von Andrian, Leopold 7
von Allesch, Ea 105
von Allesch, Johannes 15, 25, 105, 185
von Becker, Peter 94, 200
von Büren, Erhard 44, 60, 191
von Dassanowsky-Harris, Robert 69, 70, 215
von Heydebrand, Renate 31, 38, 40, 48, 74, 138, 139, 152, 158, 162, 188, 201, 203
von Hofmannsthal, Hugo 11, 12, 48, 58, 59, 111, 164
von Hornbostel, Erich Moritz 74
von Horváth, Ödön 110
von Kleist, Heinrich 115
von Matt, Peter 52, 176, 213
von Salomon, Ernst 178, 183
von Strassburg, Gottfried 152, 160
von Wiese, Benno 130, 131, 140, 186

"Vorspiel zu dem Melodrama *Der Tierkreis*" 103, 105, 111

Wagner, Marianne 182
Wagner-Egelhaaf, Martina 50, 52, 171, 213, 216
Wallner, Friedrich 169, 205, 206, 210
Wallraff, Günter 32, 210
Watzlawick, Paul 76
Webber, Andrew 71, 210, 216
Wedekind, Frank 11, 104
Weininger, Otto 75
Weismann, Willi 18
Weissberg, Liliane 48, 200
Weiss, Peter 67
Werfel, Franz 163
West, Anthony 23
West Nutting, Peter 140, 205
White, John J. 188, 202
Whitinger, Raleigh 213
Wicht, Gérard 153, 164, 165, 206
Wiegmann, Hermann 197
Wieland, Christoph Martin 168
Wiese, Benno von
  see von Wiese, Benno
Wildgans, Anton 99, 163
Wilkins, Eithne 20, 21, 23, 26, 27, 28, 29, 30, 35, 38, 44, 56, 58, 89, 91, 100, 113, 121, 151, 160, 183, 185, 186, 189
Wilkins, Sophie 56, 212
Willemsen, Roger 47, 49, 50, 51, 52, 80, 81, 84, 97, 108, 109, 130, 204, 206, 208, 209
Williams, Cedric Ellis 47, 194
Wilson, Catherine 81, 206
Winter, Ingrid 200
Wirklichkeitssinn 2
Wittgenstein, Ludwig 115, 118, 165, 169
Wolfenstein, Alfred 10, 182
Woolf, Virginia 147
Wortsman, Peter 56
Wotruba, Fritz 16, 185
Wucherpfennig, Wolf 119, 122, 197

Young Törless
    see *Die Verwirrungen des Zöglings Törleß*
Ystade, Wolfgang 15, 182

Zahlmann, Christel 96, 209
Zak, Eduard 24, 184
Zaunschirm, Thomas 50, 203
Zehl-Romero, Christiane 160, 197
Zeller, Hans 43, 203
Zeller, Rosmarie 5, 12, 47, 75, 111, 120, 129, 198, 200, 201, 202, 205, 216
Zima, Peter V. 208
Zimmermann, Werner 185
Ziolkowski, Theodore 59, 185
Zobel, Klaus 130, 208
Zuckmayer, Carl 11
Zwettl, Walter 195